MOTION PICTURES

MOTION PICTURES

The Development of an Art

by A.R. Fulton

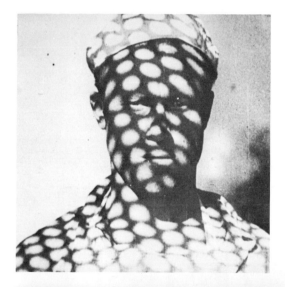

REVISED EDITION

UNIVERSITY OF OKLAHOMA PRESS
NORMAN

By A. R. Fulton

Motion Pictures: The Development of an Art (Norman, 1960; revised, 1980)
Drama and Theatre Illustrated by Seven Modern Plays (New York, 1946)

Library of Congress Cataloging in Publication Data

Fulton, Albert Rondthaler, 1902–
  Motion pictures.

  Bibliography: p.
  Includes index.
  1. Moving-pictures.   I. Title.
PN1994.F83 1980   791.43'09   79–6711

To Ila

Contents

Illustrations

Preface to the Revised Edition

A revised edition of *Motion Pictures* has enabled me not only to emend biographical and historical data but to include discussions of additional films, some of them produced since the publication of the first edition. In revising I have adhered to the original purpose of the book, namely, to explain what makes motion pictures unique as an art of narration.

If there is a key word for this purpose, it is *cinematic*. All motion pictures are, in a sense, cinematic. *Cinema* ("motion") is the international word for them. Moving pictures they were called at first—the motion-picture machine, adapted to a peculiarity of the human eye, making the images in the pictures seem to move. This kind of motion is represented by the machine, that is, the use of the machine as distinct from the art that the machine makes possible. But by *cinematic* I mean something more than this kind of motion.

What makes a film cinematic is the way it narrates. "I am less interested in telling stories," Alfred Hitchcock declares, "than in the manner of telling them." It is the manner of telling that makes the memorable film memorable. Because the cinematic manner bears certain resemblances to the dramatic and the epic, comparisons are helpful. Accordingly, as in the first edition, some of the films chosen for illustration are adaptations of plays, novels, and short stories, the purpose being not so much to point out likenesses and differences as by so doing to explain what makes a film a film, that is, what makes it cinematic. To enjoy motion pictures we need not understand how they narrate. But understanding not only adds a dimension to our enjoyment but also increases our appreciation of their province, their accomplishments, and their possibilities.

For assistance of various kinds in the preparation of this edition, I am grateful to Marvin Felheim, Stuart McDougal, Frank Beaver, Hugh Cohen, Yon Barna, Karen Higgins, John and Susan Harvith, Margareta Akermark, James Limbacher, Tino Ballio, Russell Merritt, Pare Lorentz, Miles Kreuger, Albert Kalson, John Hand, Mary Corliss, Eileen Browser, Howard Burton, and James Fulton.

I am particularly indebted to Arthur Lennig for his scholarly criticism of not only the first edition of *Motion Pictures* but much of the manuscript for this one.

A. R. Fulton

Acknowledgments

Permissions have been granted to quote from the following copyrighted material: W. H. Auden, "Night Mail"—poem reprinted by permission of Her Britannic Majesty's Postmaster General and John Grierson, producer of the film *Night Mail;* J. M. Barrie, "Alice Sit-by-the-Fire," *The Plays of J. M. Barrie* (New York: Charles Scribner's Sons, 1945); Stephen Vincent Benét, "The Devil and Daniel Webster," *The Selected Works of Stephen Vincent Benét* (New York: Rinehart and Co., 1937)—quotations reprinted by permission of the publishers and Brandt and Brandt, agents for the estate of Stephen Vincent Benét; Maurice Bessy and Lo Duca, *Georges Méliès, Mage; et "Mes Mémoires" par Méliès* (Paris: Editions Prisma, 1945); Willa Cather, *Not Under Forty* (New York: Alfred A. Knopf, 1936); Sergei Eisenstein, *Film Form,* ed. and trans. Jay Leyda (New York: Harcourt, Brace and Co., 1949); A. R. Fulton, "It's Exactly Like the Play," *Theatre Arts,* vol. 37 (March, 1953)—quotations reprinted by permission of *Theatre Arts* magazine; A. R. Fulton, "Stroheim's 'Greed,'" *Films in Review,* vol. 6 (June–July, 1955)—quotations reprinted by permission of *Films in Review;* Lillian Gish, "The Birth of an Era," *Stage,* vol. 14 (January, 1937)—quotations reprinted by permission of Lillian Gish; St. John Hankin, "A Note on Happy Endings," *The Dramatic Works of St. John Hankin,* 3 vols. (New York: Richards Press, 1912); Theodore Huff, script for *The Birth of a Nation*—quotations reprinted by permission of the Museum of Modern Art Film Library; David Lean, "Brief Encounter," *Penguin Film Review,* no. 4 (London and New York, 1947)—quotations reprinted by permission of Penguin Books, publishers; David Lean, "Extract from the Post-Production Script of *Great Expectations:* Pip Steals the Food," *The Cinema 1952*—quotations reprinted by permission of Penguin Books, publishers; Pare Lorentz, *The River* (New York, 1938)—quotations reprinted by permission of Pare Lorentz, author and director of the motion picture; W. Somerset Maugham and R. C. Sherriff, "The Facts of Life," *Quartet* (Garden City: Doubleday and Co., 1950); Liam O'Flaherty, *The Informer* (New York: Harcourt, Brace and Co., 1925); Karel Reisz, *The Technique of Film Editing,* 3d ed. (London and New York: Focal Press, in cooperation with the British Film Academy, 1955); Marie Seton, *Sergei M. Eisenstein* (New York: A. A. Wyn, 1952)—quotations reprinted by permission of the publisher (all rights reserved in the U.S.A.); Robert Emmet Sherwood, *Abe Lincoln in Illinois* (New York: Charles Scribner's Sons, 1939); Seymour Stern, "An Index to the Creative Work of David Wark Griffith," Special Supplement to *Sight and Sound,* Index Series no. 8, part 2 (September, 1946)—quotations reprinted by permission of the British Film Institute; Seymour Stern, "The Birth of a Nation," Special Supplement to *Sight and Sound,* Index Series no. 4 (July, 1945)—quotations reprinted by permission of the British Film Institute; Robert Lewis Taylor, "Moviemaker," *The New Yorker,* June 11, June 18, and June 25, 1949; Ingmar Bergman. *Wild Strawberries* (New York: Simon and Schuster, 1960); Deena Boyer, *The Two Hundred Days of 8½,* (New York: Macmillan Co., 1964); Frank Capra, *The Name Above the Title* (New York: Macmillan Co., 1971)—copyright 1971 by Frank Capra; Joel W. Finler, ed., *Greed: A Film by Erich von Stroheim* (New York: Simon and Schuster, 1972)—by permission of Lorimer Publishers, London; "Free," *The New Yorker,* July 6, 1963; Eadweard Muybridge, *Animals in Motion* (New York: Dover Publications, 1957); Alain Robbe-Grillet, *For a New Novel* (New York: Grove Press, 1965)—reprinted by permission of the publisher; Virgil Thomson, *Virgil Thomson* (New York: Alfred A. Knopf, 1966).

The illustrations are reproduced by courtesy of the Museum of Modern Art Film Stills Archives; Photo Collection of John & Susan Edwards Harvith, the Mary Pickford Company; Pare Lorentz; International Film Seminars (*Louisiana Story* rented by Films Inc.); the J. Arthur Rank Organization; Pinewood Studios; Janus Films; Vauban Productions; and Rizzoli Film.

MOTION
PICTURES

1.
The Machine

Although the attempt to represent the illusion of motion by pictures is older than civilization, the art of motion pictures was not created until the twentieth century. From that prehistoric day when an artist drew a many-legged boar on the wall of a cave in Altamira, Spain, down through the ages, during which time various other devices were originated to depict motion, man had to wait until modern times before motion pictures could be born. This waiting was necessary because motion pictures depend, to a greater extent than any other art, upon machinery. Motion pictures, the newest of the arts, the only art to originate in the twentieth century, are a product of the Machine Age.

Motion pictures did not originate as an art but as a machine. They were invented. That is, the machinery that makes the pictures, and that makes them motion pictures, was invented. Thus the term *motion pictures* means the machine as well as the art.

If you were to hold a piece of sixteen-millimeter motion-picture film up to the light, you would see that it is a series of little pictures arranged crosswise to the length of the film. Each picture, or frame, is approximately four-fifths of an inch wide and three-fifths of an inch high. Examining the frames in relation to one another, you notice that, although each frame may be

a picture of the same scene, the position of the objects in each frame is slightly different. When the film, which contains sixteen frames to each foot of film, is run through the motion-picture projector at the rate of twenty-four frames a second, enlarged images of the frames are cast in corresponding succession onto the screen.

The projector operates on the principle of that old toy the magic lantern (and of its modern counterpart, the slide projector). When a glass slide was inserted in the lantern, an image of the slide was cast upon the screen by means of a light directed through the slide and, to enlarge the image, through a magnifying lens. The frames in the film are comparable to the slides in the magic lantern. The images of the frames as they are cast upon the screen do not move any more than the images of the magic-lantern slides moved. The term *motion pictures* is therefore misleading. The pictures do not move but only seem to.

The illusion of motion is caused partly by persistence of vision, the optical fact—said to have been discovered by the astronomer Ptolemy in the second century—that it takes the eye a fraction of a second to record the impression of an image and transmit it to the brain and that, having received the impression, the eye retains it one-twentieth to one-tenth of one second after the image itself has disappeared. Accordingly, the motion-picture projector includes a mechanism which draws the film between the light and the lens in a stop-and-go motion, the film pausing long enough at each frame to allow the eye to take in the picture; then, as a shutter closes and the eye retains the image, the mechanism propels the film ahead to the next frame. The perforations along the edge of the film enable the teeth of the driving mechanism to engage the film and not only to move it along from one frame to the next but also to hold it steady. The stop-and-go motion gives the illusion of a continuous picture. If the film did not pause at each frame, the impression that the eye receives would be blurred.

The illusion that motion pictures move depends also on the imagination of the spectator. Watching a succession of pictures, each one representing a change in the position of the image from that of the preceding one, the spectator imagines that the image is moving because he associates it with a corresponding object that he has seen actually moving. Furthermore, he imagines that he sees more than the camera has photographed. The film moves through the camera at the rate of twenty-four frames a second. Every second, then, the camera takes twenty-four individual snapshots, each of which, in a standard motion-picture camera, is exposed in 1/60 second. Like the projector, the camera operates with a stop-and-go motion, the shutter opening for 1/60 second to allow the exposure and then closing for the film to move ahead to the next frame. Because the shutter is closed more than half the time, the camera photographs less than half of what happens. But when the film is projected onto the screen, persistence of vision compensates for the missing action. Accordingly, the spectator has the illusion not only that the pictures are moving but that he is seeing more than twice as much as he actually sees. What he would see, for example, in a two-hour film would be only forty-eight minutes of pictures.

Some of the principles of motion-picture machinery were understood long before the motion-picture machine was invented and rudimentary variations of it were devised. Apart from such early devices as Leonardo da Vinci's *camera obscura,* its origin is the magic lantern, the first known version of which was invented by the Dutch scientist Christian Huygens about 1655.[1] Samuel Pepys records in his diary for August 19, 1666, that a Mr. Reeves, a London perspective-glass maker, brought him "a lanthorn with pictures in glasse, to make strange things appear on a wall, very pretty." In 1828 Joseph Plateau, a Belgian physicist, devised a machine he called a phenakistiscope ("deceitful view"), whereby the illusion of motion was effected by pictures on a revolving disc viewed through notches on a second revolving disc. Six years later Simon Ritter von Stampfer, a professor of geometry at the Vienna Polytechnical Institute, constructed a similar device, the stroboscope ("whirling view"). One of the popular early versions of the motion-picture projector was the zoetrope, or wheel of life. Devised in 1833 by the British mathematician William George Horner as the daedaleum (after Daedalus), it consisted of a shallow cylinder about a foot in diameter with vertical slots in the edge and, on the inside, a series of pictures that, seen through the slots, seemed to move when the cylinder was turned. By 1853 Franz von Uchatius, an Austrian artillery officer, had constructed a projector incorporating the principle of the phenakistiscope with that of the magic lantern. By means of a revolving light passing through a series of twelve pictures arranged in a circle on glass, his machine projected images of the drawings onto a wall so that they appeared to move. Another kind of wheel machine, patented in 1861 by Coleman Sellers, a Philadelphia machinist, was an arrangement whereby photographs were mounted on paddles. Sellers called it the kinematoscope. Of such were the gropings toward the motion-picture machine. They were, however, gropings in the direction of motion-picture projection. The motion-picture camera had to wait for the invention not only of photography but of photographic film.

Photography originated in 1837 when the Frenchman Louis Daguerre invented a process whereby a photograph could be exposed on a chemically coated plate. Although the sitter for a daguerreotype had to remain motionless for the several minutes required to expose the plate, refinements in the process decreased the time. The next step consisted of negatives on glass, after which came the wet-plate process.

Thus it was that in 1872 Eadweard Muybridge, a San Francisco photographer, in order to determine whether a trotting horse simultaneously lifts all four feet off the ground, was able to take some photographs at Sacramento, California. In May of that year, according to his own account, he "made several negatives of a celebrated horse named Occident, while trotting, laterally, in front of his camera . . . ," and the resulting photographs "were sufficiently sharp to give a recognizable silhouette portrait of the driver, and some of them exhibited the horse with all four of his feet clearly lifted, at the same time, above the surface of the ground."[2] With the cooperation of Leland Stanford, a former governor of California and the owner of race horses, Muybridge continued his investigation at Stanford's stock farm at Palo Alto. (The story is that Stanford was trying to win a bet of $25,000 that a trotting horse takes all his feet off the ground simultaneously.) By means of a row of electrically controlled cameras set up parallel to a track and triggered by the wheels of the sulky, Muybridge obtained a series of photographs representing a trotting horse. He experimented further by photographing with two-lensed cameras, thereby producing stereoscopic pictures. By placing the appropriate halves of the pictures in a pair of zoetropes, which were revolved at the same speed, the halves being made simultaneously visible by means of mirrors, he obtained "a very satisfactory reproduction of an apparently solid miniature horse trotting, and of another galloping."[3] Improving on his use of the zoetropes, he devised an instrument he called a zoopraxiscope, which he demonstrated in a lecture in San Francisco in 1880 and in the Paris laboratory of the French physiologist Etienne Marey in 1881.

Like Muybridge, Marey studied the movement of animals and, to facilitate his study, invented some photographic devices. In 1882 he constructed what he called a photographic gun. An instrument for photographing birds in flight, the gun operated on the principle of the revolver, the chambers containing photographic plates which recorded pictures when the trigger was released. In 1888 Marey explained to the French Academy of Science an apparatus that he had devised for recording a series of impressions at the rate of twenty a second. "If by means of a special device, based on the employment of an electro-magnet," he told the Academy, "the paper is arrested during the period of exposure, 1/5000 second, the impression will possess all the clearness that is desirable."[4] The arresting of the paper would make provision, of course, for persistence of vision.

In 1887, if not before, Ottomar Anschutz, in Germany, invented his electrical tachyscope. This was a viewing machine on which photographs, which Anschutz had taken with twenty-four cameras, were mounted on the periphery of an iron wheel. As the wheel turned, the photographs, lighted by an intermittent electrical flash, were viewed directly, that is, not projected. In 1894, however, Anschutz obtained a French patent for "a process of projection of images in stroboscopic movement."

Meantime Emile Reynaud, a French inventor by improving on the zoetrope, developed a viewing machine called the praxinoscope, which in 1882 he combined with a projector for showing animated drawings. At first he put the drawings on paper rolls, but in 1888 he put them on celluloid ribbon perforated between the frames. Then in 1892 he opened his performances of "living pictures" at the Musée Given in Paris, inaugurating the enterprise with a presentation of some of Muybridge's animal photographs, and successfully continued the performances for several years after cinematography had become a reality.

Thomas Edison has been given credit for inventing motion pictures. It would be more nearly accurate to say that Edison, coordinating the ideas of other inventors, promoted in his laboratory the building of both a motion-picture camera and a motion-picture projector. Edison was an inventor aware of the importance of patents on devices that could be manufactured for profit. Since he saw no commercial value in motion pictures, it is remarkable that he concerned himself with them at all. But he was trying to perfect his phonograph, and he said that in 1887 the idea occurred to him that "it was possible to devise an instrument which should do for the eye what the phonograph does for the ear, and that by a combination of the two, all motion and sound could be recorded and reproduced simultaneously."[5] He investigated the idea so desultorily, however, that nine years elapsed before the projection of motion pictures onto a screen became a practical reality. He assigned one of his assistants, twenty-eight-year-old William Kennedy Laurie Dickson, to the project.

Edison said years later that he had only one fact to guide him, "the principle of optics technically called the persistence of vision."[6] But he and Dickson were also familiar with the zoetrope, and they knew about Muybridge's horse pictures and Marey's photographic gun. In fact, Edison said that the germ of his idea came from the zoetrope and the work of Muybridge, Marey, and others. Dickson started with the zoetrope. Since Edison had already invented a phonograph record and since the purpose was to give eyes to the phonograph, Dickson built a device that seemed to incorporate both zoetrope and record. It was a cylinder somewhat larger than the phonograph cylinder and containing microscopic photographs. Dickson placed it and a phonograph cylinder side by side on a shaft and recorded sound on the phonograph cylinder as synchronously as possible with the photographs. But the pictures were less satisfactory than the sound, and Dickson tried something different.

Incorporating in his camera a stop-motion device, he took pictures on sheets of sensitized celluloid—pictures so small that he recorded about two hundred of them in a spiral arrangement around a single cylinder. After developing and fixing the celluloid, he placed it on a transparent drum. When the drum was turned, a device lighted up each image from the inside. Here, gropingly but unerringly, he had established an important principle—that motion pictures depend on light passing through the frame, whether the frame is projected onto a screen or viewed directly. But the curvature of the cylinder brought only the center of each picture into focus. Dickson took another step.

Abandoning the idea of a cylinder, he obtained some celluloid-based film recently developed by John Carbutt of Philadelphia.[7] Perforations along the edge enabled the teeth of a locking device to hold the film steady as a mechanism moved it, in a stop-and-go motion, through the camera. The year was 1891. Dickson had discovered motion-picture film and recorded a motion picture on it.

From the negative he made a positive print. So that the pictures could be viewed, he placed the printed film in a boxlike structure about four feet high and two feet square. Propelled by a battery-powered motor, the film ran on a loop between an electric lamp and a shutter. The pictures were viewed by flashes under a magnifying lens as the viewer looked through a slit in the top of the box. The little viewing machine was called a kinetoscope, the name representing a combination of the Greek *kinetos* (movable) and *scope* (viewing). The camera was called the kinetograph (*graphein*, to write).

Like the original phonograph—an apparatus equipped with earphones—the kinetoscope was a device for an individual viewer, not for a group, although there is evidence that in 1889, while experimenting with the kinetoscope, Dickson succeeded in projecting a moving picture onto a screen by means of a converted tachyscope. The evidence has been controverted, but it has been established that the next year, at the Edison Paris Exposition in New York, a moving picture was indeed projected. Quoting a report in

the *Western Electrician* of April 12, 1890—
"A magic lantern of almost unimaginable
power casts upon the ceiling from the top
of the tower such pictures as seem to be
the actual performances of living persons"
—Gordon Hendricks declares, "Here we
have what was surely a tachyscope projection by Dickson."[8]

In 1891, Edison applied for patents on
his camera and on "an apparatus for exhibiting photographs of moving objects." The
patents were granted in the spring of 1893,
and Edison contracted to manufacture kinetoscopes for Raff & Gammon, a firm
organized expressly to sell them. Raff &
Gammon would pay Edison $200 apiece for
the kinetoscopes and retail them for $300
to $350.[9] Thus on April 14, 1894, Andrew
M. Holland, a Canadian, opened a kinetoscope parlor at 1155 Broadway in New York
City. The scene was a shoe store which
Holland had converted for his purpose and
in which he had set up ten kinetoscopes.
Each of the machines contained a fifty-
foot film made with the kinetograph at the
Edison plant at West Orange, New Jersey.

The year before, a building for the taking
of motion pictures had been put up at the
Edison plant. Designed by Dickson, it was
forty-eight feet long by fourteen feet wide
—narrowing to ten feet in width for the
twenty feet at the end where the camera
was housed—and so constructed that a
fifteen-by-fourteen-foot section of the roof,
about midway, could be opened to admit
light. Any desired angle of the rays of the
sun could be obtained, for the whole building
was swung on a graphited center in the
manner of a swinging bridge and turned on
a circular track. Dickson called it the kinetograph theatre. Because it was covered
with tar paper on the outside and painted
black on the inside—to bring the actors
into sharp relief—it was familiarly known
as the Black Maria. In it Dickson filmed
bits of current variety-show acts—dancers,
acrobats, contortionists, trained animals—
each act abridged to be pohotgraphed on
not more than fifty feet of film. Sandow the
Strong Man appeared before the kineto-

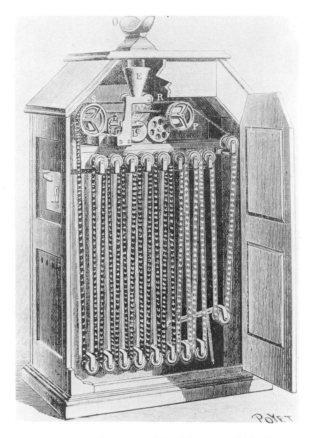

A kinetoscope. *Courtesy of the Museum of Modern Art, New York*

graph, as did Annie Oakley, Buffalo Bill,
and Ruth St. Denis. One film represented
part of a scene from a popular farce of the
day, Charles Hoyt's *A Milk White Flag.* The
repertoire included reenacted scenes such
as *The Execution of Mary Queen of Scots,*
which, however, was not filmed in the Black
Maria but outdoors. This little film was one
of the first to incorporate trick photography;
in it the beheading of the unfortunate lady
leaves nothing to the imagination.

The Black Maria. *Courtesy of the Museum of Modern Art*

Keeping in mind Edison's declaration that it was possible to record and reproduce sound and motion simultaneously, Dickson had experimented accordingly, but the experiments were not successful. The nearest he seems to have come to synchronization was to record pictures and music separately and then to accompany the pictures with the sound. In the spring of 1895 some of the kinetoscopes were equipped with phonographs so that, by means of earphones, the viewer could hear music while looking at the pictures. Kinetoscopes so equipped were called kinetophones.

Not long after the kinetoscope parlor opened, it attracted the attention of Otway and Gray Latham, two young southerners visiting in New York. It occurred to the Latham brothers that this new toy might be a means of making money if it were used to present pictures of prizefights. Accordingly, with Samuel J. Tilden, Jr. and Enoch Rector they formed the Kinetoscope Exhibition Company, and in August of 1894, they opened a parlor at 83 Nassau Street, in New York. The films they offered the public for the occasion were of a six-round fight between Michael Leonard and Jack Cushing, photographed in a ten-foot ring in the Black Maria. The capacity of the kinetoscope had been increased for the occasion from 50 to 150 feet of film, and each of the six enlarged kinetoscopes presented a short round of the fight. About 950 feet in length, this was the longest motion picture that had yet been made. Shortly thereafter, when Colonel

Woodville Latham, the father of Otway and Gray, visited the parlor, Otway asked him whether the films they were showing in the kinetoscopes could be projected onto a screen. The answer was yes.

The Lathams set about devising a projection machine as well as a motion-picture camera. Because their projector—for which, incidentally, they received suggestions from William Kennedy Dickson—only copied the principle of the kinetoscope, it was of less significance than their camera. In the kinetograph, the film was wound and unwound directly from one reel to another. Since the resulting strain of more than forty or fifty feet of film would break the film, the kinetograph could not take a continuous picture of more than about fifteen seconds in length. Enoch Rector devised a sprocket which slackened off enough film in a loop to prevent the stop-and-go motion from tugging at the unwinding reel. Allowing the camera to take as long a film as a reel would hold, this little device—called the Latham Loop—was an important contribution to the motion-picture machine.[10]

At the time Edison applied for a United States patent on the kinetoscope, he was asked whether he wished to take out foreign patents on it as well. When told that foreign patents would cost $150 more, Edison is said to have replied, "It isn't worth it." Thus when Robert W. Paul, a London manufacturer of scientific instruments, was asked, in 1894, to duplicate the kinetoscope, he not only did so but—finding to his amazement that it was not patented in England—manufactured and sold, within the next two years, about sixty of the machines. Then, to supply his customers with films, he built a camera which not only incorporated a stop-motion device similar to that originated by Edison and Dickson but was portable. He also built a projector—the bioscope—which took into account the all-important principle of persistence of vision and thus effected the necessary intermittent motion. As the film passed through the projector, it was made to pause longer at each frame than between frames and thereby allowed the eye time to "take in" each picture. He demonstrated this machine, for the first time, at Finsbury Technical College, in February of 1896.

Meanwhile, in Germany, Max Skladanowski had built and patented a motion-picture machine which he modeled, like Paul's, after the kinetoscope and which he also called the bioscope. In November of 1895, Skladanowski demonstrated it as the concluding entertainment on a variety bill at the Wintergarten in Berlin. The showing consisted of two films of about forty-eight frames each.

In France the Lumière brothers—Auguste and Louis—manufacturers of photographic equipment, had also been experimenting with motion pictures. Beginning, as Paul did, with the kinetoscope, which was shown in France for the first time in 1894—only a few months after it had been introduced in the United States—they found that the continuous motion in the kinetoscope would not do for a projection machine. Accordingly they built a stop-motion device. They also built a camera which differed from Edison's kinetograph in the speed at which the film was fed through it; that is, in the number of pictures, or frames, it recorded each second. Whereas the kinetograph took forty-eight frames a second, the Lumières decided on sixteen as the proper rate. (The standard rate has since been established as twenty-four.) By early 1895, they had completed both projector and camera and had taken some pictures, and on March 22, at their factory in Lyons, they demonstrated their accomplishment. They called their projector the *cinématographe,* a name reminiscent of Sellers' paddle-wheel machine, as well as of the kinetoscope and the kinetograph, and anticipating the universal word for motion pictures—*cinema* (Gr. *kinema,* motion).

After several other demonstrations, including one at the Sorbonne, the Lumières opened an establishment in Paris to show their machine to the public and charge admission. They rented the Salon Indien in the basement of the Grand Café on the

Boulevard des Capucines, putting the enterprise under the direction of their father, Antoine Lumière, and there on the afternoon of December 28, 1895, the premiere took place. Each film, like Edison's, was fifty feet long, and there were about ten films. Included were *Lunch Hour at the Lumière Factory,* which shows workers leavin the plant at Lyons; *Arrival of a Train at a Station,* in which the oncoming locomotive is said to have terrified the spectators; *A Game of Cards,* in which the players are Antoine Lumière, the conjurer Trewey, who sits opposite him and is the dealer, and Louis Lumière's father-in-law, Winckler, the Lyons brewer, who pours out some beer; *Baby's Lunch,* a picture that Louis Lumière had taken of Auguste and Mme Lumière with their infant daughter on the walk beside the Lumière house; *Blacksmiths, The Rue de la République,* a Lyons traffic scene; and *Bathing Beach,* in which the waves break on the shore. Admission was one franc, and the receipts on that opening day were thirty-five francs. The essential principles of motion-picture photography and projection having at last been applied in a commercial enterprise, motion pictures were born.

The idea that Edison had begun investigating eight years before had thus become a reality. Edison originated the idea which, by the ingenious work of Dickson, took the form of the kinetoscope; but the kinetoscope became the motion picture independently of Edison, in a way that he had not originally intended and over a course that he could not have foreseen. Even the kinetoscope was not Edison's invention. First, there was Dickson; and besides Dickson, other inventors contributed to the process which led deviously from the laboratory in West Orange, New Jersey, to the Grand Café in Paris, from the peep-show box to motion pictures.

Then there were those who, although they were off the path of this progress, were experimenting with motion pictures at the time. There was, for example, William Friese-Greene, a photographer of Bath, England. Friese-Greene's epitaph describes

him as "The Inventor of Cinematography," and attempts have been made to support this claim. Together with John Rudge, an optician, and Mortimer Evans, a civil engineer, Friese-Greene built a motion-picture camera and applied for a patent on it in 1889; but it has not been established that he effected the successful projection of motion pictures onto a screen. Although Friese-Greene apparently wrote to Edison suggesting that moving pictures might be made a part of the phonograph—after Edison already had this idea—he neither completed a machine for this purpose nor directly contributed to the course leading from the kinetoscope to motion pictures as perfected by the Lumières.

The tendency to simplify has given Edison credit as the inventor of motion pictures. To point out that he was not, that in fact no one individual may be said to have been the sole inventor, is not to minimize the importance of his idea or even of the kinetoscope. That it was the Lumières who first built a machine incorporating the progress made by other inventors, who improved the rate of speed at which a film should pass through a camera, and who first demonstrated the completed machine as a commercial reality is a fact that those who would simplify cannot disregard. Ironically, however, if the premiere at the Grand Café late in 1895 had been delayed only four months, Edison would have had the distinction not only of originating the idea that led to motion pictures but also of introducing the motion-picture machine to the world. As it was, on April 23, 1896, he introduced it to the United States.

Even though, at the time he was working on the kinetoscope, Dickson had effected the projection of a motion picture onto a screen, Edison had refused to put projection machines on the market. When Norman Raff proposed that they do so, Edison is reported to have replied that the company was selling kinetoscopes for $300 to $350 apiece and making money and that if they sold machines which would enable a large group of people to see the films simultaneously, there would be use for only about ten of them in all the United States. But now the Lathams had a projector, which, as the pantopticon, they demonstrated publicly on May 20, 1895, in New York City. The pantopticon operated on the principle of the kinetoscope—that is, in its continuous motion—but it projected a four-minute film of a boxing match which Otway Latham had directed on the roof of Madison Square Garden. Here was competition. Edison assigned one of his assistants, Charles H. Kayser, to the project of building a machine that would be better than the Lathams'. Meanwhile, however, Thomas Armat, of Washington, one of those inventors who were also experimenting with motion pictures, had constructed a stop-motion mechanism for a projector, which he demonstrated at the Cotton States Exposition in Atlanta, Georgia, in September of 1895. Edison was informed of Armat's invention, and, early in 1896, an agreement was reached whereby Edison would manufacture a projection machine incorporating Armat's device. The machine would be marketed under the Edison name but would be labeled "Armat designed." The name chosen for the new machine was vitascope.

On April 14, 1896, under the ambiguous headline "Edison's Latest Triumph," the *New York Times* reported:

Thomas A. Edison and Albert Bial have perfected arrangements by which Edison's latest invention, the vitascope, will be exhibited for the first time anywhere at Koster & Bial's Music Hall. Edison has been at work on the vitascope for several years.

The vitascope projects upon a large area of canvas groups that appear to stand forth from the canvas, and move with great facility and agility, as though actuated by separate impulses. In this way the bare canvas before the audience becomes instantly a stage upon which living beings move about.

Mr. Bial said yesterday: "I propose to reproduce in this way at Koster & Bial's scenes from various successful plays and operas of the season, and well-known statesmen and celebrities will be represented as, for instance, making a speech or performing some important act or series of acts

with which their names are identified. No other manager in this city will have the right to exhibit the vitascope."

Five days later, the first newspaper advertisement of a moving picture appeared in the *Times.* At the foot of Koster & Bial's theatre announcement of their current attraction—the monologuist Albert Chevalier "together with all the other Great Foreign Stars"—could be read: "Extra—Due notice will be given of the first public exhibition of Edison's latest marvel, THE VITASCOPE." The "due notice," appearing two days later, gave the date of the premiere—April 23—and on that morning the Koster & Bial advertisement gave the vitascope top billing, Chevalier and the "Great Foreign Stars" being summarily relegated to second place.

The premiere of the vitascope was more auspicious than that of the *cinématographe* on that winter afternoon four months before in the basement room on the Boulevard des Capucines. Koster & Bial's, in Herald Square, was one of New York City's popular music halls. Edison himself came over from New Jersey for the occasion and occupied a box seat. Armat was there, too, taking charge in the projection booth set up in the second balcony.

The next morning the *Times* reported as follows:

The new thing at Koster & Bial's last night was Edison's vitascope, exhibited for the first time. The ingenious inventor's latest toy is a projection of his kinetoscope figures in stereopticon fashion, upon a white screen in a darkened hall. In the center of the balcony of the big music hall is a curious object, which looks from below like the double turret of a big monitor. In the front of each half of it are two oblong holes. The turret is neatly covered with the blue velvet brocade which is the favorite decorative material in this house. The white screen used on the stage is framed like a picture. The moving figures are about half life size.

When the hall was darkened last night a buzzing and roaring were heard in the turret, and an unusually bright light fell upon the screen. Then came into view two precious blonde young persons of the variety stage, in pink and blue dresses, doing the umbrella dance with commendable celerity. Their motions were all clearly defined. When they vanished, a view of an angry surf breaking on a sandy beach near a stone pier amazed the spectators. The waves tumbled in furiously and the foam of the breakers flew high in the air. A burlesque boxing match between a tall, thin comedian and a short, fat one, a comic allegory called "The Monroe Doctrine," an instant of motion in Hoyt's farce, "A Milk White Flag," repeated over and over again, and a skirt dance by a tall blonde completed the views, which were all wonderfully real and singularly exhilarating. For the spectator's imagination filled the atmosphere with electricity, as sparks crackled around the moving lifelike figures.

So enthusiastic was the appreciation of the crowd long before the extraordinary exhibition was finished that vociferous cheering was heard. There were loud calls for Mr. Edison, but he made no response.

Of the films included in that first showing of the vitascope, it was, the *Times* reported in its Sunday edition two days later,

the waves tumbling in on a beach and about a stone pier that caused the spectators to cheer and marvel most of all. Big rollers broke on the beach, foam flew high, and weakened waters poured far up on the beach. Then great combers arose and pushed each other shoreward, one mounting above the other, and they seemed to fall with mighty force and all together on the shifty sand, whose yellow receding motion could be plainly seen.

Edison apparently realized, however, that the use of motion pictures to provide entertainment by the sheer novelty of the device itself could not be exploited for long. The *Times* announced:

Mr. Edison is working hard for the absolute perfection of his machine, and at the same time is arranging for the securing of pictures the like of which, in other than inertness, the public has never seen.

He has bought, for about $5000, two ancient, but still serviceable locomotives and several dozen flat cars. He has built about a quarter of a mile of railroad track in a secluded spot, not far from his laboratory. In a few weeks he will start a train

from each end of the track, and will run them to a crash. The engines and cars will be manned, just as trains are in active service, and all the incidents of a train wreck will be caught by machines stationed at short intervals near the track.

Machines have been sent to Rome, and in a short while the entire stage at Koster & Bial's will be occupied by a realistic representation of Pope Leo XIII, saying mass in the Sistine Chapel.[11]

This kind of use of motion pictures had, in fact, been predicted a year before. After the Lathams had publicly projected their boxing match picture, Howard B. Hackett wrote in the *New York World:*

You will sit comfortably and see fighters hammering each other, circuses, suicides, hangings, electrocutions, shipwrecks, scenes on the exchanges, street scenes, horse races, football games —almost anything in fact in which there is action, as if you were on the spot during the actual event.[12]

Hackett's prediction was coming true. In 1896, when motion pictures had become a practical reality, when they had evolved into the device essentially as it was to remain, their future lay, it seemed, in providing entertainment by presenting scenes of actuality.

Charles Frohman, the theatrical producer, saw how this use might be extended to the theatre. After attending that first showing of the vitascope, he declared:

That settles scenery. Painted trees that do not move, waves that get up a few feet and stay there, everything in scenery we simulate on our stages will have to go. When art can make us believe that we see actual living nature, the dead things of the stage must go.

And think what can be done with this invention? For instance, Chevalier comes on the screen. The audience would get all the pantomime of his coster songs. The singing, words fitted to gestures and movements, could be done from the wings or behind the curtain. And so we could have on the stage at any time any artist, dead or alive, who ever faced Mr. Edison's invention.[13]

Whether the invention may be called "Mr. Edison's" is—as the records show—open to question. But there is no question about motion pictures' having originated, not as an art, but as a machine. The ingenuity and effort, not of artists, but of inventors, mechanics, photographers, engineers, and manufacturers made the machine possible. The purpose of these men—from Muybridge with his pictures of Leland Stanford's horses to Edison with his vitascope—was not artistic, but utilitarian: to perfect a machine that would have a use. The machine is still being perfected, but in Edison's Armat-designed vitascope, or in the Lumières' *cinématographe,* the invention culminated. Appropriately, the first motion-picture shows were billed as machines: at the Grand Café, "LE CINÉMATOGRAPHE" (*"Cet appareil,"* the announcement began) and at Koster & Bial's, "Edison's latest marvel, the VITASCOPE."

2.
"Arranged Scenes"

Among the spectators at the first public showing of the Lumière films was the proprietor and director of the Théâtre Robert-Houdin, on the Boulevard des Italiens in Paris. He was Georges Méliès, and his theatre specialized in shows of magic and transformations. His introduction to the *cinématographe* was to result in a transformation far greater than any he had ever effected on the stage.

Méliès was a man of amazing versatility. He was not only proprietor and director of the Robert-Houdin but also its stage manager, scene designer, and principal actor. He understood machinery, was himself a mechanic, and constructed machines for his trick effects. He was a cartoonist and satirist. Somehow his background, inclination, and experience had prepared him better than anyone else—including the Lumières—to appropriate the motion-picture machine and start motion pictures on their way to becoming art.

Méliès was born in Paris on December 8, 1861, the son of a well-to-do shoe manufacturer. Early in his school life he became possessed, as he said, by the demon of drawing. He drew portraits and caricatures of his teachers and his fellow students and sketches of landscapes that had the appearance of theatrelike decor. By the time he was ten years old, he was constructing puppet shows and theatre scenery of cardboard. After a year of military service, he returned to Paris, intending to enter the Ecole des Beaux-Arts and become a painter. But his father wanted him to become an industrialist. How could anyone, he asked his son, enter such a profession as painting and keep from starving? So Méliès entered his father's factory. Here he occupied himself with machinery and thus acquired a dexterity in mechanics. A year in London, where he went to learn English, also contributed to the preparation for the time when the motion-picture machine would be ready for him. Not understanding the language well enough to appreciate plays in the London theatres, he used to go to Egyptian Hall, where the famous conjurer Maskelyne presented scenic illusions and other shows of magic. After returning to Paris, he was a frequent spectator at the "theatre of illusions," the Robert-Houdin, presided over by the magician Houdin himself. Merely by watching Houdin's automatons from a seat in the audience, Méliès reconstructed them and actually made them work. Soon he was giving performances of magic himself, at first in *salons* and then in public theatres. His sense of humor gave his performances a comic slant that was later to be evidenced in his films. He became an illustrator for the satirical journal *La Griffe,* in which his caricatures of General Boulanger were said to have contributed largely to the failure of the general's attempt to overthrow the Republic and establish a dictatorship. In 1888, having come into considerable means, Méliès bought the Théâtre Robert-Houdin. Now he was in his element. He renovated the establishment and began there a proprietorship that was to last for thirty-six consecutive years.

A man of the theatre, and of his kind of theatre in particular, Méliès was fascinated on that December afternoon in 1895 as he watched the Lumière films projected onto the screen in the basement room of the Grand Café. He realized at once that here was a way of extending the unsophisticated entertainment he was providing at the Robert-Houdin. He had, in fact, already introduced there a sort of screen entertainment by concluding each performance with the projection of a series of pictures on colored glass in a machine similar to the magic lantern—travel scenes, hand-painted cartoons, snowfalls, day-and-night effects, lightning, and decorated rosettes which revolved. By a special lighting device, scenes were made to dissolve one into another. Méliès saw in the motion-picture machine an apparatus even more magical than the magic lantern. He offered at once to buy or rent the *cinématographe.* He said, years later, that Antoine Lumière, who refused not only his offer to 10,000 francs but also 50,000 francs offered by the director of the Folies-Bergère, gave as the reason for his refusal his wish to exploit the machine himself.

Méliès learned, however, that Robert Paul had come to the continent from London to sell his bioscope, which would project Edison kinetoscope films. He bought one of Paul's machines, procured some Edison films, and, early in 1896, opened at the Robert-Houdin the first cinema theatre in the world. He even improved on the bioscope by designing a loop device, similar to the Lathams', to prevent the film's breaking.

Now came the great step. Dissatisfied with the films he could buy, Méliès decided to make motion pictures himself. He was aware that the *cinématographe* was reversible, and,

understanding the mechanism, he made a camera out of the bioscope. Then he was faced with another obstacle: no film stock was available to him in France.

Méliès has been called a film pioneer. He had the temperament of the pioneer in being undaunted by obstacles and ingenious in surmounting them. The difficulty about film stock was minor compared to obstacles that Méliès was to face throughout his career. Having heard that Paul had some film in London, Méliès went there, but Paul would sell him no less than a case of Eastman film, and a case cost 45,000 francs. Not knowing whether he could ever recoup 45,000 francs invested in blank film but having faith that he could, Méliès bought a case. The case being hermetically sealed, he did not discover until he got back to Paris that the film was not perforated. However, he had an instrument for perforating film made, and although the instrument was crude, Méliès patiently perforated some film with it and set out to take his first pictures. Then he encountered still another obstacle: equipment he had used for developing film, as an amateur photographer, could not be employed for films as long as Eastman's. At first he tried cutting the films into strips short enough to develop in his photographic trays, fusing them after they were dry. Then he devised a developing machine consisting of a drum around which he wound the film and which, operated by a crank, revolved in a semicircular tub of developing solution.

The first motion pictures that Méliès made were like others of the time—brief depictions of the passing scene. His very first film, which he called *A Game of Cards* and which he made in the spring of 1896 on the grounds of his house at Montreuil sous Bois, a Paris suburb, is similar to the Lumière film of the same subject. With his portable camera, he was not restricted to Montreuil and was soon photographing uncomplicated incidents in and about Paris—street scenes, a train arriving at a station, boats on the Seine, and so forth. He went to Le Havre and took pictures of the seashore. Inasmuch as the film could not be removed from the camera in daylight and the camera held only sixty-five feet of film, Méliès had to make many tiring trips between the shore and a Le Havre photographer's. One of Méliès's early films is a primitive newsreel: the Czar of Russia and his cortege going to Versailles.

Méliès's career was inevitably leading him to an attempt to bring stage and motion pictures together. Even in 1896 he made some films more suggestive of the kind of entertainment he was providing at the Théâtre Robert-Houdin than of actuality; *Conjuring, Conjurer Making Ten Hats in Sixty Seconds, The Vanishing Lady,* and *The Haunted Castle.* These were, essentially, pictures Méliès made of acts on the bills at the Robert-Houdin, except that he had not photographed them in the theatre but outdoors. They represented the first steps away from films of actuality toward scenes arranged especially for the camera. In *The Haunted Castle,* even the scenery was arranged, the background representing the first *mise en scène* Méliès ever filmed, if not the first in the history of motion pictures.

Of the films Méliès made that first year, the most interesting cinematically is *The Vanishing Lady.* Although it is ostensibly a motion picture of a magician's trick, Méliès made the lady vanish, not by a stage device, but by manipulation of the camera. He had discovered this kind of manipulation by accident. One day in the fall of 1896, as he was prosaically photographing traffic in la Place de l'Opéra, the mechanism in his camera jammed. In the minute that it took him to reengage the film, the scene changed, and when he projected the resulting picture he was startled to notice that an omnibus suddenly changed into a hearse, and men into women. Méliès the magician realized that he had inadvertently performed with his camera a trick as amazing as any he had ever performed in the theatre. As a result, in *The Vanishing Lady* the lady vanishes, not through a trap door, but by a stopping of the camera, as Dickson had stopped the camera in *The Execution of Mary Queen*

of Scots three years earlier. Méliès had discovered that the arrangement which characterizes motion pictures is more than the arrangement of the objects photographed. He had discovered that he could not only photograph the magic he made on his stage but also make magic with the motion-picture machine itself. He exploited this possibility only slightly because he was a man of the theatre. He incorporated the trick in his films because he was a magician.

He made *The Vanishing Lady* and other films for exhibition at his theatre, but he was soon selling films to other exhibitors, too. He associated himself with a man named Reulos, and in October, 1896, their advertisements appeared in the newspapers: "Animated photographs for sale every day at the Théâtre Robert-Houdin." They called their organization Star Film. Its trademark, a star, which appeared on all its film titles, was the precursor of the Pathé rooster, the Metro-Goldwyn-Mayer lion, etc. With Reulos and Korsten, a mechanic at the Robert-Houdin, Méliès built a projector, patented it as the *Kinetographe,* and put it on the market. He opened a sales shop in the autumn of 1896 at 14, Passage de l'Opéra. The venture with the *Kinetographe,* however, did not last a year. Méliès even gave up using the *Kinetographe,* which could be converted into a camera, in making his own pictures, in favor of a Demeny-Gaumont machine and, later, of a Lumière *cinématographe.*

One day early in 1897 the singer Paulus came to Méliès with an interesting request. It will be remembered that Charles Frohman, after seeing Edison's vitascope, had suggested that Chevalier be photographed singing and that the film be projected while Chevalier sang from the wings. Whether Paulus had gotten the idea from Frohman or thought of it himself, he presumably asked Méliès to make motion pictures of him singing some of the songs that had made him famous so that the pictures might be shown to the accompaniment of his offstage singing. The plan was for Paulus to appear before the camera as he sang in the music halls, that is, in costume and makeup, and in front of scenery appropriate to the songs. Realizing that taking the pictures outdoors at Montreuil would be unsatisfactory, not only because the scenery would be crude, but also because the limited time during which the sun's rays would be favorable might oblige Paulus to make several trips from Paris before the project could be completed, Méliès decided to take the pictures at the Théâtre Robert-Houdin. He arranged on the stage there the appropriate scenery and rigged up electric arc lights, which he had used for trick effects. The arc light was not yet perfected, but by careful attention to the mechanism which brought the carbon to combustion, Méliès maintained a light constant enough to take a picture of about one minute's duration. Thus he filmed Paulus singing five of his songs. These were the first films made under electric light.

Those five little films represent Méliès last groping step toward bringing the camera into the theatre. Now he was to proceed directly. Making the films of Paulus had demonstrated that what was needed was an arrangement whereby stage equipment could be utilized without dependence on the impractical arc lights—in other words, the need for a theatre illuminated by sunlight. It would be a photographer's studio equipped with stage properties and stage scenery.

That spring Méliès built such a studio on the grounds of his house at Montreuil. It was a rectangular structure (about 56 feet by 18 feet) with glass sides and a gable roof. The camera was set up at one end and scenery at the other.

Transformation had been in Méliès's repertoire at the Robert-Houdin. Having effected a transformation by accident when he projected his film of the traffic scene, he subsequently made the trick film *The Vanishing Lady* by photographing the subject outdoors. Now, having a studio for theatre-like staging, he effected transformations even more theatrical and more astonishing. He expanded on the trick of transformation in a variety of ways. In the sixty-five-foot film *The Magical Box,* Méliès used this trick at least five times. First, a magician makes a box suddenly appear on a table. A boy jumps out of the box and is cut in half at a touch of the magician's wand. The two halves are transformed into two boys, who begin wrestling. At another touch of the wand, one of the boys disappears; the other, whom the magician picks up, is transformed into two flags. In his film *The Adventures of William Tell* (1898), a suit of armor comes to life, and *The Devil in a Convent* (1899) involves transformations of scenery as well as of actors. It is no wonder that Walt Disney has been called Méliès's heir.

Méliès discovered, also by accident, the fade, the device by which a scene is gradually disclosed on the screen as the intensity of light increases—a fade-in—or is made to disappear gradually as the intensity of light decreases—a fade-out. It had been Méliès's practice to decrease the aperture of the lens toward the end of each scene to prevent the film from being fogged. When the film was edited, this part was discarded. But one day, by mistake, an uncut film was projected. Méliès noticed that the fading of the scene made a more effective transition—like the slow closing of a theatre curtain at the end of a scene—than an abrupt cut. It was a fade-out, which gave him the idea of introducing the scene with a fade-in.

Méliès's knowledge of still photography and his experience with the motion-picture camera led him to the discovery of other ways in which the camera could effect tricks. One of these ways was the dissolve. By applying the principle of double exposure to motion pictures, Méliès discovered the dissolve, a linking device whereby, as one scene fades out, another fades in—in other other words, a simultaneous fade-out and fade-in. He also adapted to motion pictures the photographic techniques of the vignette and photography upon a black ground. These techniques illustrated what Méliès meant when he declared that in motion pictures it is possible to do the impossible.

He reconstructed and filmed in his studio actual events such as *The Dreyfus Affair*

(1899) and *The Coronation of Edward VII* (1902).

The reconstruction of actuality led Méliès to employ two other devices: the small model and the taking of pictures through an aquarium. The first of these was not Méliès's invention. The second was an adaptation of a theatre trick. To effect the trick for motion pictures, Méliès merely placed a large aquarium, containing seaweed and fish, in front of the subject of the camera.

The films that Méliès was making in his studio at that time continued to represent a transference to the screen of the tricks he had performed on the stage at the Robert-Houdin. Most of them were short films, like *Conjuring,* in which Méliès acted the magician. A few comprised two or more 65-foot films in one—such as *The Laboratory of Mephistopheles* (1897) and *The Devil in a Convent,* each a 195-foot film.

It occurred to Méliès that motion pictures would permit the joining of strips of film to make up not only the same scene but also a number of scenes relating to one subject. Accordingly, *The Dreyfus Affair* comprises twelve scenes, each representing an episode in the case of the falsely accused officer. Méliès had already made some short films of reconstructed actuality—such as *Sea Fighting in Greece* (1897) and *The Blowing up of the Maine in Havana Harbor* (1898), each 130 feet in length—but *The Dreyfus Affair,* composed of thirteen 65-foot films, took fifteen minutes to screen.

Cinderella (1899), produced just after *The Dreyfus Affair,* was the kind of film with which Méliès was most successful. It was one of those films of "artificially arranged scenes" which represent his attempt to produce and film in his studio the kind of entertainment he staged at his theatre. Méliès was unequaled in reproducing the magic effected by combining theatrical tricks with cinematic ones. No print of *Cinderella* has been preserved, but from the Star Film catalogue one learns that it was "a production in grand spectacle illustrating each of the scenes of the fairy tale" and that it was "augmented by marvelous tricks, scenic effects, dissolving views, ballets, marches, etc., in which more than thirty-five persons participate." The titles of the twenty scenes, totaling 410 feet of film, are also suggestive of what the film was like, including trick devices that Méliès had incorporated in earlier films:

1. Cinderella in Her Kitchen.
2. The Fairy, Mice, and Lackeys.
3. The Transformation of the Rat.
4. The Pumpkin Changed to a Carriage.
5. The Ball at the King's Palace.
6. The Hour of Midnight.
7. The Bedroom of Cinderella.
8. The Dance of the Clocks.
9. The Prince and the Slipper.
10. The Godmother of Cinderella.
11. The Prince and Cinderella.
12. Arrival at the Church.
13. The Wedding.
14. Cinderella's Sisters.
15. The King, Queen, and Lords.
16. The Nuptial Cortege.
17. The Bride's Ballet.
18. The Celestial Spheres.
19. The Transformation.
20. The Triumph of Cinderella.

Some of Méliès's other arranged scenes are also "adaptations": *Little Red Riding Hood* (1901), *Robinson Crusoe* (1902), *The Damnation of Faust* (1903), *Faust and Marguerite* (1904), *The Palace of the Arabian Nights* (1905), *Rip's Dream* (1905), and so forth.

Méliès found his studio too small and decided to enlarge it. Over the playing space he built a stagehouse high enough to accommodate a grid, on which stagehands could manipulate scenery and special effects. He flanked the playing space with wings, each extending about ten feet, thereby widening this part of the studio to about thirty-eight feet. Behind the wings and the playing space, the addition provided for scene docks and dressing rooms. A pit ten feet deep under the playing space allowed for the use of trap doors. To soften the hard shadows cast by the iron framework as the sun beat through the glass, Méliès arranged cloth shades. A shedlike wing at the opposite end

The studio at Montreuil. *Courtesy of the Museum of Modern Art*

The playing space (Méliès leaning over railing). *Courtesy of the Museum of Modern Art*

Curtain conceals camera (Méliès at left). *Courtesy of the Museum of Modern Art*

of the studio from the playing space housed the camera. It is not known whether Méliès ever moved the camera during the filming of the scene. In *The Man with the Rubber Head* (1901), a trick involves the apparent inflation of a man's head until it bursts, and it has been suggested that Méliès effected the trick by moving the camera toward the head. But among Méliès's drawings a plan for this particular trick indicates a man seated on a dolly and concealed except for his head, and the dolly is on an inclined plane leading up to the camera.

Adjoining the studio Méliès built a replica of the main wing, except that it had a concrete floor and, instead of roof and sides,

a framework over which awnings were stretched for protection against rain. Here he built scenery and filmed some of his scenes.

All of the scenery, properties, set pieces, and trick machinery that Méliès had employed at the Théâtre Robert-Houdin he reconstructed in his studio. He designed the models of the scenery, which was then built and painted by his decorator and assistants. Méliès found that for motion-picture scenery he had to modify the use of paint. Whereas in the theatre he obtained innumerable color effects, his camera recorded only various shades of gray, from black to white. Blue, he discovered, would become

One of Méliès's drawings for *A Trip to the Moon. Courtesy of the Museum of Modern Art*

white in the film, and red, green, and yellow, black. His films were colored by hand, on the prints themselves, but all of the photographed objects—scenery, furniture, properties, and even carpets—were painted in grisaille. Ready for filming, they looked, Méliès said, like funeral decorations.

Mme Thuillier supervised all of the coloring of Méliès's films from 1897 to 1912. Each of her twenty assistants was a specialist in one color. A change from one frame to the next was another means of effecting a trick. An actor would thus in a flash be made to change costumes. Color for films was not, however, an invention of Méliès's, since it had been used in still photography

and in 1894 by Edison in the film *The Dance of Annabelle.*

Costumes had to be of a particular fabric, not only to photograph well, but to take the proper colors. The studio contained an enormous store of costumes of all kinds, of various periods and countries, together with accessories such as hats, wigs, armor, and ornaments.

The complex establishment at Montreuil epitomized what motion-picture studios were to become: the main studio, with its elaborately equipped playing space; the costume room, with its many workers, presided over by Mme Méliès; the studio for building of scenery, machinery, and properties; a printing laboratory in Paris and, later, another one on the grounds at Montreuil; an auxiliary laboratory where films were colored; and Méliès's offices in le Passage de l'Opéra.

The success of *The Dreyfus Affair* and *Cinderella* encouraged Méliès to make other long films. In 1900 he produced *Joan of Arc* (813 feet) and *A Christmas Dream* (520 feet) and, the next year, *Little Red Riding Hood* (520 feet) and *Bluebeard* (690 feet). During this time, however, he continued to make short films.

To Méliès motion pictures were a means of presenting on a screen the kind of entertainment he presented on the stage of the Robert-Houdin. In the films in which he plays the magician, he makes an entrance and bows as to the audience and bows again before making an exit. In the long films, the scenes are presented in sequence, as in a theatre. The dissolves which link them are a trick device used in place of scene shifting. The position of the camera never changes. One sees all the scenes as from a centrally located theatre seat.

Because Méliès thought of motion pictures in terms of the stage, he brought to them the organization of the theatre and consequently the conception of the director as the unifying artist. But as he worked with this new medium he discovered that there are differences as well as likenesses between the method of the stage and that of motion pictures. The *mise en scène* for a film, he said, is quite like that for the stage, except that the artist ought to know how to combine everything on paper and consequently to be author, stage manager, designer, and, often, actor.[1] Differentiating between acting for the stage and acting for the screen, he observed that a good cinema actor is one who knows how to be understood without speaking and whose gestures, although necessarily exaggerated, must be precise. Although Méliès thought of the camera primarily as a machine to record his arrangements on the stage, he realized that what the spectator sees in the theatre and what the camera records are significantly different. He cautioned that, since figures in

photographs hide one another, the greatest care should be taken to show off the principal characters in front and moderate the activity of secondary characters, always guarding against gesticulating at the wrong time, that otherwise the picture would give the impression of a jumble of people who keep moving and that the audience, not knowing which to watch, would not understand the action. Only the machine is the spectator, he said, and nothing is worse than looking into it and being concerned with it when one is playing, as invariably happens, the first time, to actors used to the stage and not to the *cinématographe*.

At first Méliès had difficulty in obtaining actors for films because the actors felt that motion pictures were beneath their dignity. In his early films he employed workers at the Robert-Houdin, his neighbors, members of his family, and even his domestic servants. But the poorly paid dancers at the Châtelet accepted Méliès's offer to appear in films. Then opera dancers followed suit, and finally actors of the Comédie Française. Méliès built up a classification of performers according to their capacities. But in the trick scenes he played the principal roles himself because, with the exception of an acrobat named André Deed, he could never make his comedians understand the one thousand and one fine points that meant the good execution of a complicated trick.

Méliès worked meticulously. Although D. W. Griffith was later to be credited with being the first motion-picture director to rehearse scenes—the "once-again method," it came to be called—it was not unusual for Méliès to spend eight or nine hours on a tableau which would last only two minutes in screening.

Not only was Méliès author, stage manager, designer, and actor—as he said the motion-picture artist should be—but he was also choreographer, creator of special effects, costumer, and property man. He was, in addition, producer and distributor. No worker in motion pictures ever encompassed more.

After he built his studio Méliès decided

to make a cinema theatre of the Robert-Houdin. His advertisements in September of 1897 read:

Henceforth the shows of prestidigitation will not take place except at matinees, on Sundays and holidays, at half past two. Evenings will be reserved for cinematography. The single price of admission in the evening is fixed at 0 fr., 50.[2]

Before the end of the year, however, he resumed his stage performances. For a while in 1898 he devoted Sunday evenings to cinema at the Robert-Houdin, but after that he presented films only as part of his shows of magic.

In 1900, Méliès founded the Trade Committee of Motion Picture Producers, the headquarters of which were the foyer of the Robert-Houdin. Elected president, he served in that capacity until 1912.

In 1908 and 1909 he presided at the first two International Congresses of the Cinema. At the first of these he proved—against the resistance of other producers—the necessity of establishing an international standard of perforation of film. It was also at this congress that Méliès balked at an attempt to impose a single price for the sale of films, contending that a uniform price would result in mediocre motion pictures. To the charge of a representative of one of the large companies that, being only an artist, Méliès did not understand that to build up a business one must have the largest possible market, he replied, as he says in his memoirs:

I am only an artist, so be it. That is something. But it is for just that reason that I cannot agree with you. I say the cinema is an art, for it is the product of all the arts. Now either the cinema will progress and perfect itself to become more and more an art, or if it remains stationary and without possible progress, if the price of sale is fixed, it will go down in ruin at short notice. That is what concerns me. Do not think that I consider myself lowered in being scornfully called an artist. For if you, a businessman, do not have artists to make films for you, I ask, what can you sell?

After the extensive counterfeiting of his film *A Trip to the Moon* (1902) in the United States, Méliès opened a branch office in New York under the direction of his brother Gaston. On taking charge, Gaston Méliès published as a preface to the Star Film catalogue a warning to infringers. The preface constitutes a succinct appraisal of Méliès's importance in the history of motion pictures:

George Méliès, proprietor and director of the Théâtre Robert-Houdin in Paris, is the originator of this genre of films composed of artificially arranged scenes. The creation of this kind of film has given a new life to commercial films at a time when they were dying out. He conceived the idea of representing comic, magic, and mystery views, and his creations have since often been imitated without success.

A great number of American, French, and English film manufacturers, looking for novelty but lacking the necessary talent to create it, have deemed it easier and more economical to counterfeit the Star films and to advertise their shameless counterfeits. That explains the simultaneous appearance in a well-known New York newspaper of advertisements of four or five different firms for the celebrated *Trip to the Moon.* Each of these firms pretended to be the real creator. All of these pretensions were uniformly false.

Gulliver's Travels, The Dream of an Astronomer, Cinderella, Little Red Riding Hood, Bluebeard, A Christmas Dream are some of the personal creations of M. Georges Méliès, who himself originated the ideas, painted the scenery, conceived the accessories, and played the scenes.

In opening a branch in New York we are ready and energetically resolved to engage suits against all infringers and other pirates. We will not repeat it; we will act.

After founding the New York branch, Méliès built a printing laboratory on his property at Montreuil so that a film could be processed immediately after the photographing of a scene. Previously films had to be taken into Paris for development, with the result that when a film turned out to be unsatisfactory, Méliès was put to the additional expense of calling the cast together again for a retake.

Méliès had taken his first pictures himself. Then he trained a professional operator. Méliès made his negatives in duplicate so that that one of them could be shipped to

New York where positive prints were made for distribution in the United States. He obtained two negatives by having two cameras functioning side by side simultaneously. His daughter Georgette became the operator of the second camera.

Méliès continued to make films until 1914. Then disaster struck him. That was the year the war began, and its immediate and first effect on Méliès was the closing of the Théâtre Robert-Houdin. Méliès established a theatre of "Artistic Varieties" at Montreuil and with his son, his daughter, and a troupe of Parisian performers played there until 1923, as he says in his memoirs, "all the chief masterpieces in the repertory of opera, comic opera, and operetta, and a number of dramas, vaudeville acts, and comedies." Méliès himself played more than ninety-eight of the most varied roles.

Meantime, all was not going well with the merchandising of his films. Other producers were now renting instead of selling films. But Méliès, who had put his profits into buildings and equipment and who had no business partners, was not able to finance a rental plan. Furthermore, Gaston Méliès had decided, without consulting his brother, to make motion pictures himself and inaugurated his plan by going west with a large troupe of cowboys and Indians. In a year he lost so much of his brother's money that the New York branch had to close.

By 1923 Méliès was bankrupt. The receipts from the Theatre of Varieties had not even met his general expenses, and all of his property had to be sold. His poignant account in his memoirs documents a part of motion-picture history:

One can imagine his chagrin when he had to quit his family property, where he had lived for sixty-one years and in which he had passed his prime with all the members of his family. What heartbreak when he was forced to abandon the cinematography which he loved, and what pain when for more than a month he saw carried away by the secondhand dealers, dealers in old furniture and scrap, all the valuable material which had cost him twenty years of hard labor and

which, naturally, was bought for nothing. It was the same with the laboratories, the shops, and installations at the Passage de l'Opéra and with those at Montreuil. These last included a number of buildings, stores of costumes, and sheds where the most cumbersome and baroque objects, of which only the stores of the Châtelet could give an idea, were accumulated: aeroplanes, balloons, dirigibles, helicopters, tramways, automobiles, railroads, locomotives, staircases, and practicable props, carpentry work of all kinds, weapons, accessories of all sorts, in brief, more than one can imagine. The pity was that his lyric theatre, his last means of sustenance, situated on the grounds of his property, was razed as a result of the conveyance of the land, thus taking away his last resources. This voluminous mass of material proved above all the fact that Méliès was the first to institute, in his films, gigantic constructions, elegantly built in flats and in staff and decorated to represent rocks, glaciers, grottoes, infernal and celestial regions, in which locomotives, automobiles, or other vehicles were, in his films, victims of the most burlesque and fantastic accidents.

In 1923 Méliès, his daughter, his son, his son-in-law, and their two little girls, the last hardly four months old, finally quitted the family home, without hope of ever seeing it again. For this vast property, containing a magnificent park, was broken up into parts and sold by lots. At the same time, his theatre in Paris, the Théâtre Robert-Houdin, was being demolished for the building of the Boulevard Haussmann, and Méliès was suddenly obliged to remove the furnishings of that theatre as well as all the equipment at the Passage de l'Opéra, also included in the demolitions. The misfortune overwhelmed him. What to do with all the cases containing the hundreds of negatives on which he had so painstakingly worked, inasmuch as he had not the least place in which to put them, and because for lack of funds he could not longer continue his profession of the cinema? In a moment of anger and exasperation he ordered the destruction of all of that precious material.

Although destitute, Méliès did not give up. He organized concerts at seaside resorts, sometimes playing in light opera, sometimes giving interludes of magic. Then, when the season was over, he toured the provinces. In 1924 he was employed for five months reequipping the stage of a Sarrebruck Theatre, which was being restored after its destruction during the war. The next year he returned to Paris and obtained a little stand for the sale of candy and toys in the Gare Montparnasse. It was here, in 1929, that he was discovered, long after those who had known him in his motion-picture days had supposed him dead. Léon Druhot, the editor of the *Ciné Journal,* was passing through the station one day and heard Méliès called by name. He walked over to the man spoken to and said, "Pardon, Monsieur, I just heard your name. Could you by chance be a relative of Georges Méliès, who worked in the motion pictures before the war?"

"Why certainly, Monsieur," Méliès replied. "I am even his nearest relative, for I am Georges Méliès!"

After questions and explanations, Druhot said, "But you cannot stay here at your age. You are an illustrious Frenchman and world renowned in motion pictures. Listen. I am going to undertake at once a campaign that I hope will have results."

In his paper the next day, Druhot announced his discovery. Reporters and photographers descended upon the stand in the railway station, and Méliès was famous again. Some of his films were found and shown at a series of gala soirees. Méliès was made a Chevalier of the Legion of Honor, having chosen Louis Lumiére as his sponsor. At the annual banquet of the French Motion-Picture Syndicate, the president declared that the motion-picture industry owed Méliès a place. This, incidentally, he never received. In fact it was two years before a pension was obtained for him, whereby he could quit the stand and, with his wife and his granddaughter, take up residence in a château maintained by the Mutual Organization of the Cinema at Orly, near Paris. Here Méliès spent his last years classifying cinematic documents and writing his memoirs. He died on January 21, 1938.

During his career in motion pictures, Méliès made about five hundred films, and of the barely fifty which have been preserved, the best is *A Trip to the Moon.*

The title is exact. *A Trip to the Moon* tells, in thirty scenes, the story of a trip the members of the Scientific Congress take to the moon and back. The film opens with the astronomers' meeting at which the trip is planned, then shows the building of the shell in which the astronomers are to travel and of the monster gun that is to project the shell, the takeoff from the earth, the arrival on the moon, the adventures with the hostile lunar inhabitants, the escape to the shell and return to earth, and concludes with a reception in the astronomers' honor.

The scenes are said to be based on Jules Verne's *From the Earth to the Moon* and H. G. Wells's *The First Men in the Moon,* but Méliès's treatment is so original that any connection is superficial. The plot is similar to that on which Méliès based at least two other films — *The Impossible Voyage* (1904) and *The Conquest of the Pole* (1912) — each presenting a professional group planning a fantastic trip, the construction of the means of travel, the departure, the arrival, bizarre adventures, the return, and the reception.

The scenes of *A Trip to the Moon* are described in the Star Film catalogue as follows:

1. The Scientific Congress at the Astronomic Club.
2. Planning the Trip. Appointing the Explorers and Servants. Farewell.
3. The Workshops; Constructing the Projectile.
4. The Foundries. The Chimney-stack. The Casting of the Monster Gun.
5. The Astronomers Enter the Shell.
6. Loading the Gun.
7. The Monster Gun. March Past the Gunners. Fire!!! Saluting the Flag.
8. The Flight Through Space. Approaching the Moon.
9. Landed Right in the Eye!!!
10. Flight of the Shell into the Moon. Appearance of the Earth from the Moon.
11. The Plain of Craters. Volcanic Eruption.
12. The Dream (the Bolies, the Great Bear, Phoebus, the Twin Stars, Saturn).

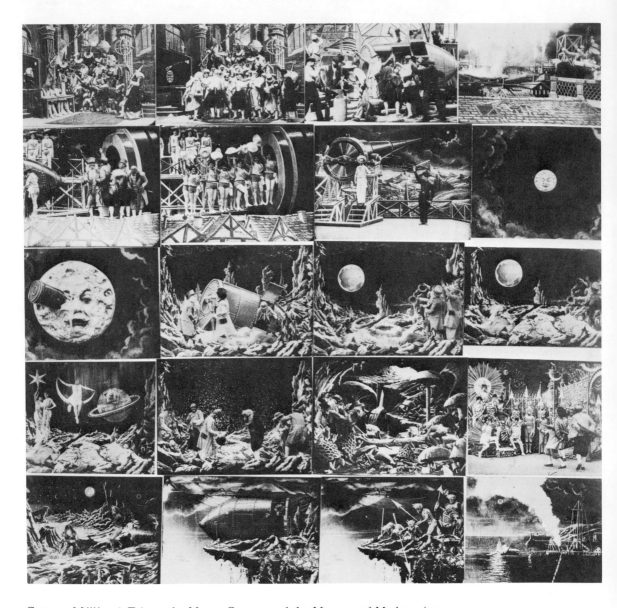

Georges Méliès, *A Trip to the Moon. Courtesy of the Museum of Modern Art*

13. The Snowstorm.
14. 40 Degrees below Zero. Descending a Lunar Crater.
15. In the Interior of the Moon. The Giant Mushroom Grotto.
16. Encounter with the Sélénites. Homeric Fight.
17. Prisoners!!
18. The Kingdom of the Moon. The Sélénite Army.
19. The Flight.
20. Wild Pursuit.
21. The Astronomers find the Shell again. Departure from the Moon.
22. Vertical Drop into Space.
23. Splashing into the Open Sea.
24. At the Bottom of the Ocean.
25. The Rescue. Return to Port.
26. Great Fete. Triumphal March Past.
27. Crowning and Decorating the Heroes of the Trip.
28. Procession of Marines and Fire Brigade.
29. Inauguration of the Commemorative Statue by the Mayor and Council.
30. Public Rejoicings.

The style of *A Trip to the Moon* is typical of Méliès. Its phantasmagoria represents his particular blend of theatre and cinema, and its satire of the scientists and their ideas of the universe manifests his humor. The first film about interplanetary travel, it has a freshness and wit lacking in its later solemn counterparts about rockets and spaceships. The meeting of the bearded astronomers, got up in medieval robes and tall pointed caps, turns into a lively squabble. As the voyagers go aborad the shell, it is pushed into the gun by a line of buxom chorus girls who take off their hats and wave them as though at the audience. The astronomers' dream could have been dreamed only by Méliès, and only he could have staged it for the camera. The film contains no subtitles—and needs none. In its dependence only on pictures to tell the story, *A Trip to the Moon* is cinematic.

The film is characteristic of the way Méliès's experiments seemed inevitably to lead. It is a series of arranged scenes incorporating elaborate theatre decor and trick devices. In the Museum of Modern Art

print of the film, the last five "views" are missing. The other twenty involve fifteen different sets, most of them elaborately represented on back cloths and cutouts. The astronomers meet in a castlelike hall with fluted columns and leaded windows. The factory scene has a glass-windowed background somewhat like the roof and sides of the Montreuil studio. The scene for the foundries is represented as being viewed from rooftops, which form the lower part of the set. In the following scene, the shell is resting on rooftops too, but not on the same rooftops. There is even a different set for the scene in which the gun is fired, the backing for this scene being a perspective of rough terrain and sky. For the scenes on the moon, the sets are particularly original in their representation of giant mushrooms and other strange flora, bizarre peaks, and lunar craters.

The sets represented something new in motion pictures, and Méliès's magic touch made them original and startling. Smoke pours from the chimneys of the gun factories. When the shell strikes the moon in the eye, the moon winces and drops tears. The scenery on the moon's horizon descends like a Henri Rousseau forest scene in sudden animation, and beyond it the earth rises. In the astronomers' dream a comet crosses the sky, faces appear in the stars of the Great Bear, a figure leans out the window of a planet, and snow falls. An umbrella that has been turned into a mushroom grows tall in a few seconds. And when the shell falls into the ocean, there is an underwater scene which adapts Méliès's trick of photographing through an aquarium.

Although the acting in *A Trip to the Moon* seems by modern standards crude, it must be remembered that the film was made not only a quarter of a century before motion pictures talked but also at a time when, except for Méliès, motion-picture directors were little concerned with a distinction between acting for the screen and for the stage. But even *A Trip to the Moon,* which Méliès made early in his career, evidences the hand of the director who formulated rules for motion-picture acting.

Since *A Trip to the Moon,* like all of Méliès's films, was printed without credit titles, actors were not identified with particular roles. Méliès, however, is recognizable as the leader of the expedition. Years later Méliès recalled, in a letter to Jean LeRoy, that the woman on the crescent was played by Bluette Bernon, a music-hall singer; the Sélénites were acrobats from the Folies-Bergère; the stars, ballet girls of the Théâtre du Châtelet; and the principal men, Victor André of the Cluny Theatre and Delpierre and Farjaux-Kelm-Brunnet, music-hall singers. Méliès designed the costumes as well as the sets. Particularly original are costumes for the Sélénites—part bird, part man, and part lobster.

All of the shots in *A Trip to the Moon* are, of course, long. The scenes represent, as nearly as Méliès could contrive them, what they would have looked like on a stage, observed from a center seat in the orchestra. Even the scene in which the shell approaches the moon, in the manner of a zoom shot, was effected more likely by a plaster-of-paris moon being moved up to the camera —as in Méliès's plan for *The Man with the Rubber Head*—than by the camera being moved. The limited playing space in the Montreuil studio and the unvarying distance of the camera from this area tended to keep the acting in profile—particularly noticeable in entrances and exits and in groupings of crowd scenes.

Although *A Trip to the Moon* is primarily a series of arranged scenes, it incorporates cinematic elements. The scene in which the shell approaches the moon puts us, as it were, in place of the astronomers—the kind of effect obtained by what has come to be called the "subjective camera." Méliès makes the Sélénites vanish suddenly, changes an umbrella into a mushroom, and links the scenes by dissolves. But cinematic though these devices may be, Méliès regarded them only as part of the abracadabra of his show. To him they were one with the smoke-belching chimneys, the descending horizon, and the moving planets. He had happened on stop-motion photography and the dissolve, and he used these and other techniques because they were effective tricks.

A Trip to the Moon was one of the first films, if not the first, for which a musical score was especially composed. The music written for it by the orchestra leader of the Olympia Theatre is said to have pleased the public so much that the style became *à la lune.*

When the film was completed Méliès invited exhibitors to a special screening. Here he met with another obstacle. Shortly before his death he recorded what happened, and his account not only explains how he got his film before the public but is a commentary on the little world of the Paris boulevards at the turn of the century, and particularly on the perseverance and ingenuity of a remarkable entrepreneur:

A score of spectators were present (those who at the time were established in the suburbs or in Paris itself). I sat down at the piano and improvised an accompaniment, and the film was projected. I expected an immediate success, for seeing it that morning myself, I had found it amusing.

To my great surprise the screening terminated in a glacial silence. Needless to say, I was distressed at the result after the long, difficult, and expensive work. I said to myself, there's no doubt about it, it's a beautiful failure. One of them finally made up his mind and shot at me, "How much do you sell that for?"

I replied, "Why at the same price as other films, 1 franc, 50 centimes per metre in black, 3 francs in color. There are 280 metres. That makes 420 francs in black and 840 francs colored."

I can say that never in my life have I had such exclamations of reprobation concerning a screening. Consider, films up to that time had been between 20 and 60 metres at the most, and I had made a film 280 metres long, the first of that consequence.[3]

I must certainly have given my spectators the impression that I was a candidate for an insane asylum. Exclamations rained from everywhere: "It's ridiculous, a film at that price!" "It's never happened before!" "You won't sell a single one!" "Anybody would be ruined with pictures at that price!" etc.

And the procession toward the exit commenced and grew. I detained one of them by the arm and said to him, "Listen, will you make a deal?" He was nonplussed, and I asked, "Where are you located now?"

"At the Foire du Trône," he replied.

"Good. Now I am hastily going to make you a large sign, painted in distemper like the scenery, with an enormous moon receiving the shell in the eye, accompanied by the title of the film and the inscription *Unpublished and sensational.* I will bring it to you at six o'clock. You will post it. I will let you have the film for the evening. You will project it at each show. I will not ask a cent of you, but I wish to see the effect on the public. At midnight, if it is a failure I will take the film back and that is that. If the film pleases, I will sell it to you, if you wish it of course. I will take it back if you do not want it. There. Does that suit you?"

"Well, all right."

That was his reply, curt and poetic.

That evening all was ready. The crowd started to arrive, the promenading got under way, the public congregated in front of the large moon, but the sign, which made them all laugh, was received by the most jesting remarks: "It's a joke." "It's a hoax." "Do they take us for fools in this establishment?" "Do you think anybody could go to the moon to take photographs?"

(The public at that time, not yet initiated into the faking of the cinema, imagined that only real things could be photographed.)

The result was that, in spite of the depreciatory remarks of the critical, there were at the first screening about fifteen slightly sympathetic spectators ready to see the presentation, as if something had mystified them.

After a series of films of twenty or thirty metres in length, the famous *Trip,* announced outside, finally came on.

During the first scene the audience kept silent. During the second they began to be interested. At the third, there were some laughs; at the fourth, the fifth, and the sixth they became louder and louder, not stopping until the end. At the last scenes it was frantic. No one had ever seen a film like it, for it was the first of its kind, which explains the effect produced.

On going out, the spectators made an enthusiastic verbal advertisement for the newcomers who, at the sound of the applause, had gathered outside the little establishment. From that moment there was an incredible stampede of crowded houses until midnight. They even had to curtail the series of little films to increase the number of showings. In short, the receipts were more impressive than any of my exhibitors had ever received.

I have never learned how, in the world of exhibitors, the news spread with such incredible rapidity. It is certain that the next day all the exhibitors in France were informed of the triumphant success of *A Trip to the Moon,* and orders flowed in from all sides.[4]

No film had ever been so successful. It was soon being shown throughout Europe and the United States. In 1902, when Thomas L. Tally opened his Electric Theatre in Los Angeles, California, his program included *A Trip to the Moon.* Tally's print, incidentally, had not been licensed by Méliès's office. Three prints of the film had been bought from Méliès and sent to the United States, where unauthorized copies were made and exploited by the hundreds, film copyrights not yet having been established. As a result Méliès's own sale of the film stopped before he had recouped its cost of about 10,000 francs. But, as he good-naturedly observed later, thanks to infringers like Thomas Edison the name of Méliès became known throughout the world, even though the publicity was a little costly.

A Trip to the Moon and other films which Méliès made in the same manner demonstrated that the scope of motion pictures was not limited to actuality. These films implied more than a camera recording the passing scene. Arranged scenes implied an arranger, a director—the artist. Working in the medium of the theatre, the artist was confined only by his imagination and capacity to create. Méliès created theatrelike subjects and recorded them by the device of motion pictures. In this way he brought to the screen the organization of the theatre, the involved organization that unites the arts and crafts of many workers—the author, the director, the stage manager, the scene designer, the actor, and the producer. Being all of these specialists himself, Méliès anticipated not only the complexity of the motion-picture industry but also its specialization. That is enough to justify his epithet, "motion-picture pioneer." In addition, Méliès the magician discovered that tricks can be performed with the camera, that the artist can manipulate not only the scene but also the medium of motion pictures. He discovered that motion pictures are more than a device. Of Méliès, D. W. Griffith said, "I owe him everything."[5]

3.
Arranged
Shots

Up to the time that Méliès produced *A Trip to the Moon,* no comparable films had been made. In the United States, motion pictures had been exploited primarily as a novelty. To maintain the novelty the Edison Company and rival producers varied the subjects of their cameras, but the variety of the subjects was limited for the most part to the passing scene. The camera was only a device.

There was, however, variety in the way the device was exploited. After the introduction of the vitascope, Raff & Gammon took pictures on the roof of their office building on Twenty-eighth Street so that their actors would not have to make the trip over to the Black Maria in West Orange. On this rooftop studio, which was just a platform set up in front of the camera, they filmed an incident from a current stage hit *The Widow Jones.* A fifty-foot film, it was a close-up of the two principal players, May Irwin and John C. Rice, and its title, *The Kiss,* is completely descriptive. It was the motion-picture sensation of 1896. In March of 1897, Enoch Rector exposed 11,000 feet of film in recording the Corbett-Fitzsimmons prizefight at Carson City, Nevada—the longest film that had ever been made of a single event. A play produced in New York that summer—*The Good Mr. Best* by John M. McNally—included motion-picture scenes to show what was taking place in various rooms of a house.

This film had been made by J. Stuart Blackton, a newspaper reporter and illustrator, and Albert E. Smith, an entertainer. They had bought a projecting kinetoscope from Edison—calling it the "American vitagraph" —and had gone into the motion-picture business together. In the fall Blackton and Smith produced, on the roof of the Morse Building on Nassau Street in New York, a forty-five-foot film, *The Burglar on the Roof,* with Blackton in the title role. The following winter, in competition with a motion picture of the Passion Play enacted in Horitz, Bohemia, and exhibited in Philadelphia, Pennsylvania, a Passion Play was filmed on the roof of the Grand Central Palace. The American version, 2,100 feet long, was exhibited in January of 1898 at the Eden Musée to the accompaniment of a "lecturer" who recited the text. The following April, war with Spain having been declared, Blackton and Smith made a motion picture which they called *Tearing Down the Spanish Flag.* This little film, in which two eighteen-inch flags were interchanged on a pole, represented a groping toward the creative use of motion pictures: although the film was purported to be a presentation of reality, the subject was expressly composed for the camera. A year later Blackton and Smith filmed the Windsor Hotel fire in New York and thereby produced a newsreel. In 1902,

Thomas L. Tally opened his Electric Theatre in Los Angeles, presenting an hour's program of films for ten cents—"up to date high class moving picture entertainment, especially for ladies and children." This was the first theatre in the United States devoted exclusively to motion pictures. At the St. Louis Exposition in 1903, George C. Hale, a former chief of the Kansas City Fire Department, presented a novel exhibit of travel films which had been photographed from moving trains—novel because to obtain the illusion of travel Hale screened his *Tours and Scenes of the World* in a theatre built to resemble a railway coach, seating arrangements and all. The ticket taker was costumed as a conductor. After the patrons had gone aboard, a locomotive bell rang, a whistle blew, the car rocked, and the pictures appeared on a screen at the end of the car. When the Exposition closed, Hale took his *Tours and Scenes of the World* about the country for two years to his immense profit.

Such is the extent to which the production of motion pictures in the United States had progressed almost a decade after the appearance of the kinetoscope. Then in the fall of 1903 Edwin S. Porter (1870–1941) made *The Great Train Robbery.*

There is nothing in Porter's background and early life to distinguish him from other motion-picture pioneers who—with the exception of Méliès—were not artists but mechanics, manufacturers, inventors, and entrepreneurs. Porter was born in Connellsville, Pennsylvania, the son of a merchant. He had a public-school education, but by the time he was eighteen he had been a plumber, an exhibition skater, a sign painter, a custom tailor, and a telegrapher. In the spring of 1898, after three years in the navy, where he is said to have impressed his superiors by inventing electrical devices for the improvement of communications, he came to New York and began his career in motion pictures. In the spring of 1896, motion pictures, in the form of the vitascope, were beginning too. Porter obtained a job operating the vitascope for Raff & Gammon. But before the year was out, having his doubts that the

vitascope would succeed as a monopoly, he was persuaded by Harry Daniels to form a partnership for the exhibition of motion pictures in the British West Indies and Central America with a rival machine, Kuhn and Webster's projectorscope. The following spring, in New York again, Porter showed films with a projectorscope to advertise Scotch whisky and other commodities. Projected from behind a screen on a roof overlooking Herald Square, the film attracted such crowds that, according to Terry Ramsaye, Porter was arrested for blocking traffic.[1] After another tour with the projectorscope, this time to Canada, Porter became the operator of the projector at the Eden Musée. Then he returned to the Edison Company. As Edison's cameraman, Porter photographed the yacht races for the America's Cup and obtained some startlingly effective backlighted pictures because he had been jockeyed into a position on the referee's boat, from which he had had to photograph against the sun.

Porter made pictures typical of those of the time—vaudeville turns, uncomplicated incidents contrived for approximately fifty feet of film, travel scenes, and newsreellike films such as those of yacht races and prizefights. Méliès's films were, of course, being shown in the United States; were, in fact, being duplicated by the Edison Company and sold at a profit. Impressed with Méliès's arrangement of scenes to tell stories, Porter decided to make a narrative film himself. The result, in late 1902 or early 1903, was *The Life of an American Fireman,* a story about a fireman rescuing a mother and child from a burning house. Porter constructed his film out of some fire-department scenes he found among the stock of the Edison Company together with scenes he shot expressly for his purpose and, like Méliès, linked the scenes with dissolves.

A description of *The Life of an American Fireman* appeared in the Edison Company catalogue of 1903. Whereas the Star catalogue only lists titles for the scenes in Méliès's films, the Edison catalogue provides a scenario of Porter's film.

SCENE 1: The Fireman's Vision of an Imperiled Woman and Child

The fire chief is seated at his office desk. He has just finished reading his evening paper and has fallen asleep. The rays of an incandescent light rest upon his features with a subdued light, yet leaving his figure strongly silhouetted against the walls of his office. The fire chief is dreaming, and the vision of his dream appears in a circular portrait on the wall. It is a mother putting her baby to bed, and the impression is that he dreams of his own wife and child. He suddenly awakens and paces the floor in a nervous state of mind, doubtless thinking of the various people who may be in danger from fire at the moment.

Here we dissolve to a picture of the second scene.

SCENE 2: Close View of a New York Fire-Alarm Box

Shows lettering and every detail in the door and apparatus for turning in an alarm. A figure then steps in front of the box, hastily opens the door, and pulls the hook, thus sending the electric current which alarms hundreds of firemen and brings to the scene of the fire the wonderful apparatus of a great city's Fire Department.

Again dissolving the picture, we show the third scene.

SCENE 3: Sleeping Quarters

A row of beds, each containing a fireman peacefully sleeping, is shown. Instantly upon the ringing of the alarm the firemen leap from their beds and, putting on their clothes in the record time of five seconds, a grand rush is made for a large circular opening in the floor through the center of which runs a brass pole. The first fireman to reach the pole seizes it and, like a flash, disappears through the opening. He is instantly followed by the remainder of the force. This in itself makes a most stirring scene.

We again dissolve the scene to the interior of the apparatus house.

SCENE 4: Interior of Engine House

Shows horses dashing from their stalls and being hitched to the apparatus. This is perhaps the most thrilling and in all the most wonderful of the seven scenes of the series, it being absolutely the first moving picture ever made of a genuine interior hitch. As the men come down the pole and land upon the floor in lightning-like rapidity, six doors in the rear of the engine house, each heading a horse-stall, burst open simultaneously, and a huge fire horse, with head erect and eager

for the dash to the scene of the conflagration, rushes from each opening. Going immediately to their respective harness, they are hitched in the almost unbelievable time of five seconds and are ready for their dash to the fire. The men hastily scamper upon the trucks and hose carts, and one by one the fire machines leave the house, drawn by eager, prancing horses.

Here we again dissolve to the fifth scene.

SCENE 5: Apparatus Leaving Engine House

We show a fine exterior view of the engine house, the great door swinging open and the apparatus coming out. This is the most imposing scene. The great horses leap to their work, the men adjust their fire hats and coats, and smoke begins pouring from the engines as they pass our camera.

Here we dissolve and show the sixth scene.

SCENE 6: Off to the Fire

In this scene we present the best fire run ever shown. Almost the entire fire department of the large city of Newark, New Jersey, was placed at our disposal, and we show countless pieces of apparatus, engines, hook-and-ladders, hose towers, hose carriages, etc., rushing down a broad street at top speed, the horses straining every nerve and evidently eager to make a record run. Great clouds of smoke pour from the stacks of the engines, thus giving an impression of genuineness to the entire series.

Dissolving again, we show the seventh scene.

SCENE 7: Arrival at the Fire

In this wonderful scene we show the entire fire department as described above, arriving at the scene of action. An actual burning building is in the center foreground. On the right back-ground the fire department is seen coming at great speed. Upon the arrival of the different apparatus, the engines are ordered to their places, hose is quickly run out from the carriages, ladders are adjusted to the windows, and streams of water are poured into the burning structure. At this crucial moment comes the great climax of the series. We dissolve to the interior of the building and show a bed chamber with a woman and child enveloped in flame and suffocating smoke. The woman rushes back and forth in the room, endeavoring to escape, and, in her desperation throws open the window and appeals to the crowd below. She is finally overcome by the smoke and falls upon the bed. At this moment the door is smashed in by an ax in the hands of a powerful fire hero. Rushing into the room, he

Edwin S. Porter, *The Life of an American Fireman.*

Courtesy of the Museum of Modern Art

tears the burning draperies from the window and smashes out the entire window frame, ordering his comrades to run up a ladder. Immediately the ladder appears, he seizes the prostrate form of the woman and throws it over his shoulder as if it were an infant and quickly descends to the ground. We now dissolve to the exterior of the burning building. The frantic mother having returned to consciousness, and clad only in her night clothes, is kneeling on the ground imploring the firemen to return for her child. Volunteers are called for, and the same fireman who rescued the mother quickly steps out and offers to return for the babe. He is given permission at once to once more enter the doomed building and without hesitation rushes up the ladder, enters the window, and after a breathless wait, in which it appears he must have been overcome by smoke, he appears with the child in his arms and returns safely to the ground. The child, being released and upon seeing its mother, rushes to her and is clasped in her arms, thus making a most realistic and touching ending of the series.

The uncomplicated story that the film tells is germane to the medium. Rescue from peril has become the stock-in-trade of motion pictures, and the technique by which excitement and suspense are increased in the presentation of such situations is familiar. It is easy to imagine how the incident that comprises *The Life of an American Fireman* would be presented in a film today. The film would crosscut (cut back and forth between scenes to represent simultaneous action in separate locales) between the wife and child in the burning house and the fire department coming to the rescue. Each shot of the interior of the house would present the danger as increasingly intense, and each shot of the firemen would bring them nearer. The shots would vary in other ways, too. There would be close-ups of the principal characters and close shots of sections of the speeding fire engine. Porter's film does in part anticipate this type of treatment. There is even a close shot—of a fire-alarm box as a hand reaches up to turn in the alarm. The vision of the fire chief's dream "appears in a circular portrait on the wall." This is the dream balloon, a device borrowed from the cartoonist who represents a character's

thoughts by picturing them in a circle above the character's head. In *The Life of an American Fireman* the dream balloon serves the purpose of crosscutting. And Porter gropes toward crosscutting in the scene of the rescue. According to the description in the catalogue, the scene consists of three shots: (1) the arrival of the fire department, (2) the rescue of the woman in the room, and (3) an exterior shot in which the fireman goes back to rescue the child, the camera remaining on the scene during "a breathless wait."

Furthermore, there is evidence that Porter comes even closer to crosscutting than the catalogue description implies. In one existing print the rescue scene is broken down into five shots: (1) the arrival of the fire department, (2) the fireman entering the room and carrying the woman to the window, (3) the fireman carrying the woman down the ladder and then going back to rescue the child, (4) the fireman rescuing the child in the room, and (5) the fireman carrying the child down the ladder. Kenneth Macgowan suggests that the description in the catalogue is based on a paper print of the film as it was entered for copyright, and that the print may have been made from a negative only partly edited.[2]

Meanwhile Porter was occupied in turning out other films for the Edison Company, including *Uncle Tom's Cabin* and *The Road of Anthracite*. The advertisement for *Uncle Tom's Cabin* announced that "every scene has been posed in accordance with the famous author's version." The film was 1,100 feet long, longer than any other that had been made previously in the United States. Influenced by the method of the play *Uncle Tom's Cabin,* rather than by that of Harriet Beecher Stowe's novel, from which the play had been adapted, Porter built up the film to a series of fourteen scenes, together with a prologue. His film was accordingly no more cinematic than Méliès's arranged scenes. *The Road of Anthracite,* made to advertise the cinder-free travel on the Delaware, Lackawanna & Western Railroad, is composed of three shots of the mythical

Phoebe Snow, "all in white who rode on the road of anthracite": Phoebe Snow getting onto the train; Phoebe—in a medium-close shot—seated in what appears to be the interior of a Pullman; and Phoebe—still immaculately white—getting off the train. Marie Murray, a photographer's model, played Phoebe Snow, and Porter made the film on the Lackawanna railroad.

It has been contended that Porter's inspiration for *The Great Train Robbery* was not the films of Méliès but certain British films —in particular, James Williamson's *Attack on a China Mission* (1900)—and that several episodes in *The Great Train Robbery* plagiarize another British film, Frank Mottershaw's *Robbery of the Mail Coach,* which was produced earlier in 1903 than Porter's film. This assertion of Porter's indebtedness is based, however, only on catalogue descriptions of these films, which have been lost. But catalogue descriptions, which tend to represent films as more exciting and complicated than they are, may imply editing that is not in them. Whether Porter ever saw *Attack on a China Mission* or *Robbery of the Mail Coach* and whether these films were actually as the catalogue represents them have not been established. But of films still in existence, *The Great Train Robbery* is the first that is essentially cinematic.

Train robberies were familiar occurrences in the West in the early 1900s and were prominently written up in newspapers and magazines. There had even been a play called *The Great Train Robbery,* from which Porter borrowed the title, but not the plot, for his film. Porter's plot, according to the 1904 Edison catalgoue, is as follows:

SCENE 1: Interior of a Railroad Telegraph Office
Two masked robbers enter and compel the operator to get the "signal block" to stop the approaching train, and make him write a fictitious order to the engineer to take water at this station, instead of "Red Lodge," the regular watering stop. The train comes to a standstill (seen through window of office), the conductor comes to the window, and the frightened operator delivers the order while the bandits crouch out of sight, at the same time keeping him covered with their revolvers.

As soon as the conductor leaves, they fall upon the operator, bind and gag him, and hastily depart to catch the moving train.

SCENE 2: Railroad Water Tower
The bandits are hiding behind the tank as the train, under the false order, stops to take water. Just before she pulls out they stealthily board the train between the express car and the tender.

SCENE 3: Interior of Express Car
Messenger is busily engaged. An unusual sound alarms him. He goes to the door, peeps through the keyhole, and discovers two men trying to break in. He starts back bewildered, but, quickly recovering, he hastily locks the strong box containing the valuables and throws the key through the open side door. Drawing his revolver, he crouches behind a desk. In the meantime the two robbers have succeeded in breaking in the door and enter cautiously. The messenger opens fire, and a desperate pistol duel takes place in which the messenger is killed. One of the robbers stands watch while the other tries to open the treasure box. Finding it locked, he vainly searches the messenger for the key and blows the safe open with dynamite. Securing the valuables and mail bags they leave the car.

SCENE 4: This Thrilling Scene Shows the Tender and Interior of the Locomotive Cab, While the Train is Running Forty Miles an Hour
While two of the bandits have been robbing the mail car, two others climb over the tender. One of them holds up the engineer while the other covers the fireman, who seizes a coal shovel and climbs up on the tender, where a desperate fight takes place. They struggle fiercely all over the tank and narrowly escape being hurled over the side of the tender. Finally they fall, with the robber on top. He seizes a lump of coal and strikes the fireman on the head until he becomes senseless. He then hurls the body from the swiftly moving train. The bandits then compel the engineer to bring the train to a stop.

SCENE 5: Shows the Train Coming to a Stop
The engineer leaves the locomotive, uncouples it from the train, and pulls ahead about 100 feet while the robbers hold their pistols to his face.

SCENE 6: Exterior Scene Showing Train
The bandits compel the passengers to leave the coaches, "hands up," and line up along the tracks.

One of the robbers covers them with a revolver in each hand, while the others relieve the passengers of their valuables. A passenger attempts to escape and is instantly shot down. Securing everything of value, the band terrorize the passengers by firing their revolvers in the air, while they make their escape to the locomotive.

SCENE 7:
The desperadoes board the locomotive with this booty, compel the engineer to start, and disappear in the distance.

SCENE 8:
The robbers bring the engine to a stop several miles from the scene of the "hold up" and take to the mountains.

SCENE 9: A Beautiful Scene in a Valley
The bandits come down the side of a hill, across a narrow stream, mounting their horses, and make for the wilderness.

SCENE 10: Interior of Telegraph Office
The operator lies bound and gagged on the floor. After struggling to his feet, he leans on the table and telegraphs for assistance by manipulating the key with his chin and then faints from exhaustion. His little daughter enters with his dinner pail. She cuts the rope, throws a glass of water in his face, and restores him to consciousness, and, recalling his thrilling experience, he rushes out to give the alarm.

SCENE 11: Interior of a Typical Western Dance Hall
Shows a number of men and women in a lively quadrille. A "tenderfoot" is quickly spotted and pushed to the center of the hall and compelled to do a jig, while bystanders amuse themselves by shooting dangerously close to his feet. Suddenly the door opens, and the half-dead telegraph operator staggers in. The dance breaks up in confusion. The men secure their rifles and hastily leave the room.

SCENE 12: Shows the Mounted Robbers Dashing Down a Rugged Hill
at a terrific pace, followed closely by a large posse, both parties firing as they ride. One of the desperadoes is shot and plunges headlong from his horse. Staggering to his feet, he fires at the nearest pursuer, only to be shot dead a moment later.

SCENE 13
The three remaining bandits, thinking they have eluded the pursuers, have dismounted from their horses, and after carefully surveying their surroundings, they start to examine the contents of the mail pouches. They are so grossly engaged in their work that they do not realize the approaching danger until too late. The pursuers, having left their horses, steal noiselessly down upon them until they are completely surrounded. A desperate battle then takes place, and after a brave stand all the robbers and some of the posse bite the dust.

SCENE 14: A Life-Size Picture of Barnes,
leader of the outlaw band, taking aim and firing point-blank at the audience. The resulting excitement is great. This scene can be used to begin or end the picture.

In making *The Great Train Robbery,* Porter hit on elements which directors who came after him were to refine and elaborate as peculiar to motion-picture art. There is, for example, the story itself. Being 800 feet long and taking almost twelve minutes to screen, *The Great Train Robbery* tells a story that was—and still is—a popular one: a conflict involving law and order, in particular, a conflict presented in vigorous physical action—holdups at gunpoint, the frenzied alarm, flight and pursuit on horseback, and a gun battle in which "after a brave stand all the robbers and some of the posse bite the dust." Later, when the camera was to become more flexible, tilting and panning were to give meaning to scenes in a way that the stage could not. In the scene in which the robbers climb down from the locomotive and take to the mountains, the camera pans with them as they cross the roadbed and tilts to follow them down the embankment. The next scene opens as they come running through the woods from the background toward the camera. Then, as they turn left, the camera pans with them again, this time revealing what they are running toward—their horses. Whether it was Porter's intention to move the camera for this purpose or, as in the preceding shot, to move it merely to include as much action as possible, the effect is cinematically obtained. The scene which "shows the tender and interior of the locomotive cab while the train is running forty miles an hour" represents another kind of camera movement, namely, tracking: Porter shot the scene from the top of the baggage car.

But the reason that *The Great Train Robbery* is considered the first really cinematic film is because of the way in which the scenes, that is, the shots, are arranged. For example, the situation at the beginning of scene 10 is identical with that at the end of scene 1—the operator lying bound and gagged on the floor of the telegraph office. In fact, Porter may well have filmed the action as a single scene. But the point is that, in putting the film together, he divided the scene into two parts and between the parts placed scenes 2 through 9, the arrangement thereby implying that, while the operator lies bound and gagged, the action of the intervening scenes is occurring. There is also the implication that the quadrille in the dance hall, in scene 11, is in progress, not only while the operator "rushes out to give the alarm" at the end of scene 10, but while the robbers "make for the wilderness" in scene 9. The main lines of action are united in scene 12, the pursuers and the pursued together in the same scene. The last scene, in which the leader of the outlaws fires point-blank at the audience, forces the spectator, John Howard Lawson observes, "to identify himself more closely with what has taken place."[3] Whether Porter intended the shot to serve this purpose or whether, as the catalogue description implies, the purpose is only to create excitement and the shot therefore has no significant relationship to any other shot—"This scene can be used to begin or end the picture"—the cut from the shot concluding with the "desperate battle" to that of the outlaw firing at the audience represents a groping toward a subjective point of view: we are the posse being fired upon. The effect may be likened to that of the zoom shot in *A Trip to the Moon*.

Although *The Great Train Robbery* is

"This scene can be used to begin or end the picture." (Porter, *The Great Train Robbery*). *Courtesy of the Museum of Modern Art*

called the first western, none of its scenes was filmed farther west than New Jersey. Porter's association with the officials of the Lackawanna railroad when he was making *The Road of Anthracite* stood him in good stead. When he began work on *The Great Train Robbery,* the Lackawanna loaned him a train. He shot the train scenes on the Lackawanna track in the vicinity of Paterson, New Jersey, and the scenes of the chase and pursuit on horseback in Essex County Park, near West Orange.

Porter's actors included Frank Hunaway, a former United States cavalryman; Max Aronson, who had already appeared in Edison films; and George Barnes, a performer at Huber's Museum, a New York variety house. Barnes is the robber who fires point-blank at the audience; Aronson played several parts, including a bandit, a

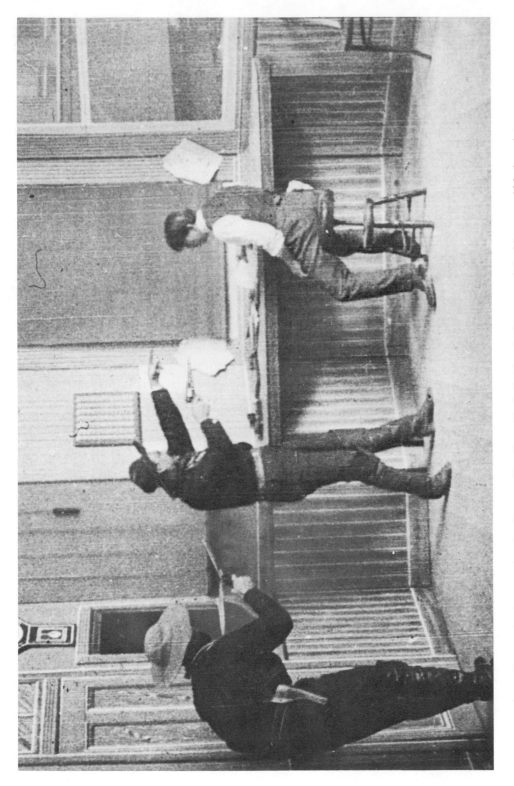

Contrasting images of reality (Porter, *The Great Train Robbery*). *Courtesy of the Museum of Modern Art*

Contrasting images of reality (Porter, *The Great Train Robbery*). *Courtesy of the Museum of Modern Art*

passenger on the train, and the fireman. Aronson, who later became famous as the screen cowboy Bronco Billy Anderson, is said to have missed the first day of shooting of *The Great Train Robbery* because, riding out to location from a West Orange livery stable, he was thrown from his horse. Employees of the Edison plant at West Orange were supers in the scene in which the passengers are held up. Marie Murray, the Phoebe Snow of *The Road of Anthracite,* appears in the dance-hall scene.

Evaluated by modern standards of motion-picture production, *The Great Train Robbery* is obviously crude. With the exception of the close-up of Barnes, all of the shots are long. The interior scenes are theatrelike not only in the spatial lenght of the shots but in the unvarying angle of the camera. The realism of the outdoor scenes contrasts strangely with the staginess of the interior ones—the unconvincing backgrounds for the telegrapher's office and the mail car and the lamp and stove painted on the set for the dance-hall scene. In the interior scenes, the actors play in profile, and some of their gestures are so broad that they are ludicrous. In the acting there is a general lack of what is called the illusion of the first time. The dance-hall scene, in which the telegrapher's entrance is lost in the confusion of the crowd, violates Méliès's admonition that "the greatest care must be taken to show off the principal characters in front and moderate the ardor of secondary characters, always guarding against gesticulating at the wrong time, which in photographing gives the effect of a jumble of people who keep moving." Finally the substitution of a dummy to represent the fireman thrown off the speeding train is hardly deceptive.

The arranged scenes of *A Trip to the Moon* are more artistic than the staging in *The Great Train Robbery.* But the importance of *The Great Train Robbery* to the history of motion pictures is not in the arrangement within each scene but in the arrangement of shots in relation to one another. In becoming art, motion pictures came to depend—as art does—on arrangement, and the arrangement on which the motion pictures primarily depend is that of the pictures themselves. Although Méliès's films show a trace of this kind of arrangement, the emphasis in them is on the photographed objects—the actors and the scenery. Porter discovered that the cinematic method is based not so much on the shots as on the way the shots are arranged. Thus he discovered editing.

4.
"Famous Players in Famous Plays"

The Great Train Robbery was popular. Heretofore, with the exception of Méliès, producers had exploited motion pictures primarily as a novelty. By 1903 their films, depicting scenes from real life, vaudeville skits, and reenacted bits from plays, were less amazing than they had been on that April evening at Koster & Bial's seven years earlier. But *The Great Train Robbery* was different. Here was a motion picture that created interest by something more than the illusion of motion. In it, the device and the pictures were fused as they had not been before, even in the films of Méliès's arranged scenes. Porter's arrangement was of a different kind. Although in 1903 no one—not even Porter—appreciated the significance of editing, audiences liked *The Great Train Robbery* because it told a story in an exciting way. Other films were rushed into production to capitalize on its success—*An Attack on the Agent, The Car Man's Danger, The Little Train Robbery, A Desperate Encounter.* Porter directed some of these films himself; the Edison Company told him to.

Although Porter directed several hundred other films, he did little toward perfecting the kind of arrangement he had happened on in *The Great Train Robbery.* However, as Lewis Jacobs has pointed out, in *The Ex-Convict* (1904), Porter arranged the scenes to show a contrast between the impoverished home of the hero and the mansion of a manufacturer, and in *The Kleptomaniac* (1905), he not only contrasted the legal treatment accorded a poor woman caught shoplifting with that accorded a wealthy and equally guilty woman but also paralleled the stories of the two women. In *The Dream of a Rarebit Fiend* (1906), he effected trickery through stop-motion photography, double exposure, and other devices in the manner of Méliès, but arranged the scenes more in the manner of *The Great Train Robbery* than of *A Trip to the Moon.* But for the most part Porter adhered closely to a formula that had resulted in profitable films. Before editing was to be established as the basis of the art, motion pictures would have to wait for D. W. Griffith.

If *The Great Train Robbery* did not establish editing, it established the story film. Motion pictures at that time depended less on the novelty of the device than on the use to which the device was put, and the one-act stories were popular. Motion pictures, as a business, picked up.

No other art is as dependent on business exploitation as motion pictures. The very origin of motion pictures is commercial—a patented mechanical device—and the development of the art has been advanced and retarded by business expediency. Edison freed his pictures from the little peep-show box, not because he recognized the artistic advantage of a screen, but because he recognized Latham as a competitor. Seven years later one of Edison's mechanics discovered editing. The resulting popularity of *The Great Train Robbery* and of films patterned after it was an impetus to further business exploitation.

A few months before *The Great Train Robbery* was produced, Harry and Herbert Miles, Cincinnati photographers who had taken some motion pictures in Alaska, established a film exchange in San Francisco. Before that time producers had sold their films outright to exhibitors. Why not, Harry Miles had reasoned, buy a film for $100.00, rent it to an exhibitor for a week for $50.00 and to another for a second week for $50.00 more, and keep the profits on the rental thereafter? It was about as simple as that. The idea, which was put into practice by Miles and his brother, appealed to certain smalltime businessmen, and film exchanges sprang up throughout the country. By 1907 there were more than one hundred of these establishments. The increasing popularity of films was an impetus to the new business, and the new business was an incentive to the production of films.

In the fall of 1905, John Harris and Harry Davis, who had been engaged in various theatre enterprises, converted a store in Pittsburgh into a place for showing motion pictures. They equipped it with ninety-six chairs discarded from an opera house, a secondhand projector, and, adopting an innovation of Méliès's, a piano. Having decided on an admission price of five cents, they called their little house the Nickelodeon (*odeon* being Greek for "small theatre"). The Nickelodeon opened with *The Great Train Robbery*. The receipts on the first day are reported to have been $22.50 and on the second, $76.00. Within two weeks the theatre became so popular that showings started at eight o'clock in the morning and continued until midnight. The Nickelodeon was soon taking in more than $1000.00 a week. Within a year almost a hundred nick-

elodeons were opened in Pittsburgh alone. *Nickelodeon* became a common noun. The nickelodeons, like the film exchanges, increased the demand for films, and the demand was further increased as operators began changing their bills more frequently than once a week. Some houses were soon presenting a new bill daily.

If there was money in renting and exhibiting films, there was also money in making them. Only a small amount of capital was needed to make a film. Although Edison's machines were patented, the principle of the motion-picture camera was known, and various types of cameras were constructed. Some of these, Edison thought, infringed on his patents, and the history of motion pictures in the first decade of the twentieth century is marked by lawsuits over patent rights. Cameras, however, were somehow obtained, and small one-reel films were turned out. A film, even though it contained half a dozen scenes, could be completed in a day. Rooftops of office buildings served as studios, for makeshift scenery could be arranged in the sunlight—as yet the only source of light for making motion pictures in the United States. Sometimes cameras were set up in city streets and parks and in the country, and scenes were filmed against these realistic backgrounds. Actors received five dollars a day. Producer, director, and cameraman were the same person. In 1906, ten years after the appearance of the vitascope, motion pictures were being made in various parts of the United States. Although there was no motion-picture center, such as Hollywood, more pictures were produced in New York City and the surrounding area than in any other locality.

It was about this time that the mercury-vapor lamp became a means of filming by artificial light. The Biograph, the Edison, and the Vitagraph companies accordingly moved indoors. Biograph took over a house on Fourteenth Street, Vitagraph established quarters in Brooklyn, and Edison built a motion-picture factory in the Bronx.

In 1908 competition in the motion-picture business resulted in the formation of the

Motion Picture Patents Company, a trust comprising the American producers Biograph, Edison, Essanay, Kalem, Lubin, Selig, and Vitagraph, the distributor George Kleine, and the French firms Méliès and Pathé. Patents were pooled, the members of the trust agreed to pay royalties to Edison for the use of his machines, and an agreement was made with the Eastman Kodak Company whereby Eastman would supply film stock only to the members. The formation of the Patents Company was announced on January 1, 1909. Motion pictures had become big business.

The growth of motion pictures as a business was greater than their growth as art. The film companies were still turning out short one-reel pictures hardly more indicative of what the art was to become than *The Great Train Robbery.* Even though short stories, epic poems, plays, and operas were now being adapted to the screen, the scope of the adaptations was limited to the length of a reel of film, that is, to about one thousand feet, or twelve minutes' running time. (Twelve minutes—as Terry Ramsaye points out—became the standard length for a film because, during the early history of the motion pictures, films were booked into vaudeville theatres as turns, and the length of a vaudeville turn was twelve minutes.) Furthermore, the producers were making money with one-reel films, and they saw no reason to change an established and profitable practice. In 1909, J. Stuart Blackton directed a five-reel film, *The Life of Moses,* for Vitagraph, but the company released it a reel at a time, one reel a week, beginning in January, 1910. Later in 1910, Vitagraph produced a three-reel version of *Uncle Tom's Cabin,* but it too was released in single reels. The next year, however, when Griffith made a two-reel adaptation of Tennyson's *Enoch Arden* and the film was released in separate reels, popular demand of the nickelodeon patrons resulted in the two reels' being screened in one showing.

The telling impetus toward the so-called feature-length film, however, was to come from Europe. Up to this time, European films had not advanced the art of motion pictures any further than had those made in the United States. But in France and Italy producers had at least begun to make films longer than 1,000 feet, first in two reels and then in three and four. In 1912, Louis Mercanton, a Paris theatre director, made a three-reel film that was to have far-reaching consequences.[1]

That spring Sarah Bernhardt, recognized internationally as the greatest actress of her time, had appeared in Paris in the historical play *Queen Elizabeth* by Emile Moreau. Although *Queen Elizabeth* failed and was withdrawn after a few performances, Mercanton asked Mme Bernhardt to let him film it. Bernhardt had already appeared in motion pictures as early as 1900, when she was filmed in the dueling scene from *Hamlet,* and later she had starred in a film version of *La Tosca.* In 1912 actors far less renowned than the divine Sarah disdained motion pictures, but her attitude was different. In the first place, Mercanton's offer gave her an opportunity to recoup some of the thousands of francs lost through the failure of *Queen Elizabeth* on the stage. Besides, appreciating the transience of the actor's art, Bernhardt used to say that motion pictures were her one chance for immortality. She not only consented to appear before Mercanton's camera but also, it is said, made the screen adaptation of the play. *Queen Elizabeth* was consequently produced as a film.

Queen Elizabeth tells of the legendary affair between Elizabeth I, Queen of England, and Robert Devereux, Earl of Essex. According to the story, the interception of a ring which Elizabeth had given Essex, with instructions to return it when he needed her help, resulted in the carrying out of his death sentence for treason. The melodrama in the legend appealed to Moreau, and he fashioned the action of his play upon it. To complicate the situation and to motivate the interception of the ring, Moreau has Essex in love, not with Elizabeth, but with the Countess of Nottingham, and he has the Earl of Nottingham discover the Countess in the arms of Essex and thereupon not only instigate the charge of treason but intercept the ring to prevent the revocation of the death sentence. Abetted by Lord Bacon, Nottingham is successful and Elizabeth, who learns the truth too late, dies of grief.

In presenting the play on the screen, Bernhardt had to reckon with the fact that, whereas a play tells its story primarily by dialogue, a motion picture relies primarily on pictures. The solution to this problem was to present as much of the film action as possible in pantomime and augment the pantomime with explanatory titles. Obviously all of the dialogue could not be represented unless the titles were inordinately long and numerous, in fact, unless all of the dialogue in the script of Moreau's play were printed on the film. Consequently, details had to be deleted or at least compressed. In the play, for example, there is a lengthy scene in which the Countess of Nottingham confesses to Elizabeth the truth about the interception of the ring, Elizabeth prompting the story from her bit by bit. In the film the confession scene is summarized in a title and pantomimed in less than two minutes. In the play the Countess seems to be dying at the time she confesses, and she dies the same hour as the Queen does; in the film the deletion of minor incidents spares not only her life but her health.

While recognizing the limitations of the screen, Bernhardt must have been impressed with an advantage that the screen has over the stage. As an actress she was naturally familiar with the problem of scenery in the theatre. Even if she had not written plays, as in fact she had, she knew that it is incumbent on the playwright to tell his story with as few changes of scenery as are consistent with dramatic effectiveness. On the screen, however, scene shifting is no problem at all.

Taking advantage of this difference in scenery, Bernhardt arranged the playing of the film in twenty-three scenes and, reckoning with the difference in dialogue, depended on about as many subtitles. The continuity which evolved may be indicated as follows:

Subtitle: The Queen, anxiously awaiting news of the Spanish Armada, is struck by the enthusiasm and noble bearing of Earl Essex, who alone is confident of success. Drake arrives and announces the total defeat of the Spaniards.
SCENE 1: A pavilion.

Subtitle: Essex, who has become the Queen's favorite, is present at a performance of *The Merry Wives of Windsor* and presents Shakespeare to the Queen.
SCENE 2: A room in the palace, a stage at left.

Subtitle: The fortuneteller.
SCENE 3: A courtyard. The fortuneteller is conducted into the palace.

Subtitle: The fortuneteller predicts an unhappy future for the Queen and tells Essex that he will die on the scaffold.
SCENE 4: Same as Scene 2.

Subtitle: The Queen, greatly upset by the forecast, places her ring on Essex' finger and tells him should he ever be in trouble, on his returning it she will save him however great his fault may be.
(SCENE 4 resumes.)

Subtitle: The Countess of Nottingham, who loves Essex, cannot conceal her grief on hearing the prophecy.
SCENE 5: A throne room.

Subtitle: Departure of Essex for Ireland as Lieutenant General.
(SCENE 5 resumes.)

Subtitle: Essex bids the Countess farewell.
SCENE 6: A hall. Essex enters upstage, comes forward, and goes through a curtained doorway at the right.

SCENE 7: The Countess' apartment.

Subtitle: The Earl of Nottingham discovers his wife in the arms of Essex.

SCENE 8: The hall again. Nottingham enters upstage, comes down to the doorway, pushes the curtain aside, draws back startled, and walks in.

SCENE 9: The Countess' apartment. Nottingham enters in the background but is unnoticed by the Countess and Essex.

Subtitle: Nottingham swears vengeance on Essex and confides his plans to Lord Bacon, the bitter enemy of Essex.

SCENE 10: The hall again. Nottingham watches Essex leave the Countess' apartment. Bacon enters, and he and Nottingham converse.

Subtitle: Nottingham and Bacon write the Queen an anonymous letter accusing Essex of treason.
SCENE 11: A room.

SCENE 12: Another room. Bacon enters, puts the letter on the table, and goes out. The Queen enters with attendants, sees the letter, and reads it. Essex is announced and enters. The others leave him alone with the Queen. The Countess enters with a lady in waiting. The lady and the Queen go out, leaving Essex with the Countess.

Subtitle: The Queen discovers Lord Essex is unfaithful. She believes the anonymous letter and orders his arrest.
(SCENE 12 resumes.)
The Queen reenters as Essex is embracing the Countess. A guard of soldiers is summoned and Essex is conducted out.

Subtitle: Essex is taken to Westminster to be tried. The Queen, desiring to save Essex, sends for the Countess of Nottingham to persuade him to return her ring as a sign of submission.
SCENE 13: Another room. Through a large opening upstage Essex, the executioner, guards, and others are seen passing in procession, the Queen watching from the room. The Queen speaks to a lady in waiting, and the lady goes out.

SCENE 14: The Countess' apartment. The lady enters and speaks to the Countess. The lady and the Countess go out.

SCENE 15: The room of Scene 13 again. The lady announces the Countess and withdraws. As the Queen and the Countess converse, Bacon enters downstage and eavesdrops.

Subtitle: Bacon informs Nottingham of the Queen's intentions.
SCENE 16: A room, archways separating downstage area from a hallway upstage.

Subtitle: Yielding to the entreaties of the Countess, Essex gives her the ring.
SCENE 17: The room of Scene 16, but the camera

has been moved to the left. The procession again. Essex leaves the procession and comes forward to the Countess.

Subtitle: Nottingham prevents his wife from returning the ring to the Queen and throws it in the Thames.
SCENE 18: A hall. Nottingham meets the Countess, takes the ring from her, and throws it out the window.

Subtitle: Elizabeth signs Essex' death warrant, believing him to be too proud to ask for clemency.
SCENE 19: The room of Scene 13.

Subtitle: The execution.
SCENE 20: A courtyard, scaffold in the center. Essex mounts the scaffold. As the executioner raises his axe, the scene ends.

Subtitle: The Queen visits the body of Essex and discovers that the ring is missing.
SCENE 21: A pillared vault, Essex' body on bier in foreground.

Subtitle: Queen Elizabeth forces the horrible truth from the Countess. "May God forgive you. I never will!"
SCENE 22: A room

Subtitle: After the death of her lover, Queen Elizabeth never had another happy moment and gradually faded away. The death of Queen Elizabeth.
SCENE 23: The throne room. The Queen, in the presence of the court, dies standing up and falls forward in front of the throne.

Subtitle: *Sic transit gloria mundi.*

Since the purpose of *Queen Elizabeth* was to present a world-renowned actress on the stage, the film is highly suggestive of the theatre—as though Mercanton had set up the camera in the orchestra of the Théâtre Sarah Bernhardt and the play had been enacted behind the proscenium. Except for a slight pan shot in scene 2 and again in scene 18, the camera remains stationary. All of the shots are long shots, and the acting is directed toward the camera. The sets and the furniture are arranged as they would be on the stage, and the audience seems to view the scenes across the footlights. This illusion is created even before the first scene, for accompanying the credit titles are individual shots of the four leading players in stagelike poses—Mme Bernhardt and Mme Romaine actually bowing to the camera. The spectator is reminded of the theatre even after the last scene, for a shot is appended to present Bernhardt taking a curtain call.

No previous film had been more carefully staged. The scenery is theatrical; even the outdoor scenes are more suggestive of the theatre than of reality. The film takes advantage, however, of the possibility of more frequent changes of scene and greater variety and elaborateness of sets than would be practicable in a theatre. The sets make concessions to the period represented, as exemplified in the parquetry floors, the flagstone paving, the mullioned windows, the pillars, the arches, and other architectural details.

In comparing *Queen Elizabeth* with modern films, one must take into account not only the difference between acting for the stage and acting for the screen but also the stage conventions of the theatre in which Bernhardt had been brought up. Although from the beginning of her career she had revolted against acting in the manner of the theatre of the grand style, this style is evidenced in the plays in which she appeared. One of the characteristics of the style is the star system, whereby the star is not only more important than the play but also more important than the rest of the cast. Playwrights wrote plays as vehicles for particular stars. In this kind of play the star is given built-up entrances, big scenes, and the center of attention throughout. Scenes are written so that the star makes an entrance after the scene has begun and leaves the stage before the scene is over. In the production of the play the manner is accentuated by stage groupings, timing, and so forth. In *Queen Elizabeth,* Bernhardt makes her first entrance after the courtiers have grouped themselves to receive her, and the scene does not end until she is trium-

phantly borne out by her attendants. Her entrance in the scene in which Elizabeth views the body of Essex is particularly theatrical. At the beginning of the scene attention is drawn from Essex lying on the bier, in the foreground, to a door surmounted by an arched grille, in the background. Attention is drawn to the door by a light from behind, silhouetting the grille. Then the door opens, revealing a lighted passage, and a guard enters. The guard stations himself to one side. The attention of the spectator having been thus directed, Bernhardt makes her entrance. This is not the method of motion pictures but of the theatre—the theatre of the grand style.

This kind of theatre was also characterized by spectacle. Shakespeare's plays, for example, as they were produced in the nineteenth century, were expanded to include elaborate processions and scenic effects for their own sake. In *Queen Elizabeth* there is a suggestion of this type of spectacle in the procession in which Essex is taken to Westminster. In scene 13 the procession passes slowly across the background as Elizabeth watches. In scene 17 it appears again, halting as Essex leaves it to speak to the Countess and then, as he joins it, moving on. The play within the play is spectacle almost for its own sake. If it has any other reason for being included, it is that since a scene is needed to represent Essex as the Queen's favorite, and since Shakespeare is said to have written *The Merry Wives of Windsor* because Elizabeth wanted to see Falstaff in love, it would be appropriate to have Elizabeth and Essex watching a performance of the play.

It is pathetically ironic that Bernhardt considered motion pictures her one chance for immortality, for her fame as an actress depended more than anything else on her voice. According to May Agate, the French poet Théodore de Banville called Bernhardt "The Muse of Poetry itself. A secret instinct moves her. She recited verse as the nightingale sings, as the wind sighs, as water murmurs."[2] In her later years, after she had suffered the amputation of her leg and as a

Theatre of the Grand Style (Mercanton, *Queen Elizabeth*). *Courtesy of the Museum of Modern Art*

result played only while sitting or, as in *Camille*, lying down, she held audiences by virtue of her voice alone. Thus the silence of the screen was no small barrier for her to reckon with in *Queen Elizabeth*. It is as though she had been struck dumb or as though she knew that she was playing to a stone-deaf audience. She compensates for our deafness by exaggerating facial expression and gesture and by inserting a few subtitles. The compensation is generally successful, although here and there the pantomime is unfortunately overdone. It is infelicitous, for example, in the scene in which Elizabeth caresses the dead Essex, particularly since we are all too conscious of what, as the preceding scene ended, was about to

happen to Essex's head on the scaffold. Bernhardt plays the death scene standing up, as she did in the play. May Agate, who appeared in the play with her, says:

Even in her last throes of suffering she made no appeal to pity. There was no truck with the pedants; she died standing up, falling forward onto a mass of cushions, not writhing, senile, amongst them as is recorded historically. It was a great piece of acting, and if the play had been called *La Reine X* the French would have lapped it up as they did her Lucrece.[3]

Whereas, in the manner of the theatre of the grand style, this bit of acting was effective on the stage, it seems less so on the silent screen, at least today. On the other hand we have become so accustomed to talking pictures that we do not take into account the great handicap under which Bernhardt was working. And so we laugh at some of the scenes in *Queen Elizabeth.*

But Bernhardt was a great actress and, if we would appreciate the difference in time and technique, we would be less condescending toward her performance in this film. We would recognize, for example, that her gestures, although necessarily broad, are purposeful and complete. They are exaggerated, but they are never awkward. We would notice the way she uses her hands. May Agate recalls Bernhardt telling her, "Never, under any circumstances, allow both your hands to drop to your sides, unless you want deliberately to convey despondency." Miss Agate adds, "I never remember seeing Madame Sarah even once adopt the attitude she condemned. Usually one hand would be fingering a necklace or holding a flower, the other would be half-spread, palm downwards away from the body, never flaccid but tensed and ready for action, as befits a mind which is working."[4]

We should also remember that in 1912, when *Queen Elizabeth* was filmed, Bernhardt could hardly walk, and then only by leaning on someone's arm. Seven years earlier, in an accident in a Rio de Janeiro theatre, she had seriously injured her knee. She never recovered from the injury, and in 1915 her leg was amputated. By 1912 it was necessary that stage sets and positions of other actors be arranged so that she would not have to take more than two steps alone. As she makes her first entrance in *Queen Elizabeth,* she grasps the back of a conveniently placed chair, but inconspicuously; in fact, her step seems almost vigorous. At the conclusion of the scene she is carried off on a portable bench. At the beginning of scene 2 she is already seated, and she makes her exit on the arm of Lou Tellegen, as Essex. In only four other scenes does she walk, and in these she relies for support on members of the cast. If it is ironic that she of the golden voice depended on the silent screen for immortality, so it is pathetic that, having made her debut in the motion

pictures in the dueling scene from *Hamlet,* she was now forced by lameness to resort to these subterfuges in *Queen Elizabeth.* But subterfuge is part of the actress's art, and Bernhardt was an actress.

All, however, is not subterfuge. In the first place she had chosen a part in which agility of movement would not have been necessary anyway. At the time Essex was beheaded, Elizabeth was sixty-seven years old. In 1912 that was Bernhardt's age—not apparent, however, in the film. She seems younger, for her vivacity of expression, vigor of gesture, and erectness of posture more than compensate for her not moving about on the stage. In fact, playing opposite the twenty-nine-year-old Tellegen, she makes their age difference seem even less than that between the aging queen and her young favorite, who was thirty-four when he died. In the scene in which Elizabeth discovers the anonymous letter, Bernhardt makes a complete turn in sitting down. If the turn seems artificial it is because it accords with the conventions of acting at the time, not because the actress who skillfully executes it is crippled. It is significant that Bernhardt plays the death scene standing up. Whenever her acting in *Queen Elizabeth* seems exaggerated, it should be remembered that she is compensating not only for her infirmity but also for our deafness.

Today *Queen Elizabeth* is condescendingly referred to as a photographed play—which is what Mercanton intended it to be. Few of the subtitles, however, stand for dialogue; most of them forecast action. On the other hand, five of the twenty-three scenes constituting the film are not prefaced by subtitles at all—an economy effected by the arrangement of the scenes. For example, since the subtitle prefacing scene 6 indicates that Essex is going to bid the Countess farewell, no title prefaces scene 7, in which the farewell takes place. Even the dramatic significance of Bacon's eavesdropping in scene 15 is obvious—no title is necessary to point it out, and there is none.

Now that sound is an adjunct of motion pictures and the camera has become comparatively flexible, plays adapted to the screen are thought to be less theatrelike than *Queen Elizabeth*. The sound track permits the adaptation of as much dialogue as the play contains. The camera, moving about freely, gives the spectator the impression that he is not confined to his seat in the theatre but can come closer to the scene, up onto the stage itself, and watch the scene from all sides, even from above and below. Movement of the camera, however, does not make an adapted play essentially less like a play than *Queen Elizabeth*—nor does dialogue spoken on a sound track. On the contrary, a play adapted in only these ways is even more like a play than *Queen Elizabeth* because it talks.

Queen Elizabeth was filmed in Paris in May of 1912. Meanwhile, in the United States, Edwin S. Porter, who had left Edison three years earlier, was now the head of Rex, a motion-picture company he had formed with the film distributor William Swanson. (The Rex trademark, which Porter designed, was a ring of stars and was later to be the trademark of Paramount.) Together with Joseph Engel and Adolph Zukor, Porter formed the Engadine Company and bought the American rights to *Queen Elizabeth* for the reputed sum of $35,000. Engel was also a member of Rex, and Zukor, a former Chicago furrier who in 1903 had acquired an interest in a penny arcade and had risen in the motion-picture business through managing nickelodeons, was now treasurer of the Marcus Loew Enterprises. These men planned, however, not merely to exploit Mercanton's film but to produce films of their own to present, as Zukor phrased it, "famous players in famous plays." Porter was to direct these films.

The star system had already become an institution in motion-picture production. At first producers had discouraged the identification of their players, fearing that popularity would result in demands for increase in salary, and for a while the public identified screen favorites only epithetically: "The Man with the Sad Eyes," "the Biograph Girl," "Little Mary," and so on. In 1910, Carl Laemmle, head of the Independent Motion-Picture Company, reversed this policy and deliberately publicized by a ruse the company's leading actress—previously identified as "the IMP Girl"—as Florence Lawrence. Miss Lawrence thus became the first movie star. When the patent companies refused to follow suit their players began to go over to the independents. In 1913, Biograph gave in by posting names and pictures of its players. The star system was established.

Even before the prints of *Queen Elizabeth* reached the United States, the Engadine Company gave way to the Famous Players Film Company. Daniel Frohman, the theatrical producer, brought his prestige to the enterprise by joining the new company and by lending the Lyceum Theatre in New York for the first showing of the film. The premiere of *Queen Elizabeth,* a private matinee on July 12, 1912, was reminiscent of that evening sixteen years before when Edison unveiled his vitascope at Koster & Bial's. Because of Bernhardt's renown as an actress and Frohman's prestige as a play producer, the event at the Lyceum was even more impressive. The audience at the premiere of *Queen Elizabeth* was made up of literary, theatre, and other artistic folk, and they had come to see a motion picture, not in a nickelodeon or a music hall but in a staid Broadway theatre. Motion pictures had become respectable.

Queen Elizabeth was popular, and Zukor and his partners were encouraged to go ahead with their own productions of "famous players in famous plays." They had persuaded James O'Neill, Eugene O'Neill's father, to be filmed in *The Count of Monte Cristo*—a romantic play in which he had been touring the United States for years—and production, under Porter's direction, had already begun. Meantime, however, word reached the Famous Players Film Company that Selig, a motion-picture company in Chicago, was about to release a three-reel version of *The Count of Monte Cristo* based directly on Dumas's novel. Even though the filmed play would have been different, Zukor and his partners felt that it would be inauspicious to inaugurate their enterprise with a film on a similar subject with a similar title. Accordingly, they substituted *The Prisoner of Zenda,* which Porter had also begun directing. Thus *The Prisoner of Zenda* (1912), starring James K. Hackett, a former Broadway matinee idol, became the first of the company's own productions of "famous players in famous plays." Then the incomparable Minnie Maddern Fiske consented to be filmed in *Tess of the D'Urbervilles,* in which she had appeared on the stage. Other famous players followed suit, and the trend strengthened the respectability that *Queen Elizabeth* had brought to motion pictures.

By the same token the importance of the motion-picture actor was strengthened. Mary Pickford, who had become known, because of her parts in the Biograph films, as Little Mary and the Girl with the Curls and who had just completed a season on Broadway in a play called *A Good Little Devil,* not only was filmed in *A Good Little Devil,* for Famous Players in 1913 but also signed a contract with Zukor to become a Famous Players actress. It was then only a step to Charles Chaplin, the prime example of the domination of the actor in motion pictures.

Queen Elizabeth indeed had far-reaching consequences. But except for encouraging the making of multiple-reel films, it did little to advance motion pictures as art. The advance was to come in another way and from other quarters, and in those quarters it had already begun.

5.
D.W. Griffith:
Early Films

If any film produced by the Edison Company rivals the fame of *The Great Train Robbery,* it is *Rescued from an Eagle's Nest,* for with this one-reeler David Wark Griffith inaugurated his career in motion pictures. Early in 1908 Griffith, an out-of-work actor, appeared at the Edison studio with a motion-picture synopsis he had adapted from *La Tosca.* The synopsis was refused, but Griffith was offered a part in a film that Edwin S. Porter was about to make. This was *Rescued from an Eagle's Nest,* in which a child is carried away by an eagle and rescued from the eagle's nest on a cliff, and Griffith was hired to play the part of the mountaineer who climbs the cliff and rescues the child. The film was shot in the studio and on the Palisades of the Hudson River. Suspended on a wire, an imitation eagle carries off the child in one of the studio-shot scenes in which the painted backdrops are reminiscent of those in *The Great Train Robbery.* If the rescue, shot in natural surroundings, is more credible, it is because of the surroundings. Nor does *Rescued from an Eagle's Nest* represent an advance over *The Great Train Robbery* as cinema.

Griffith wanted to be a writer, He used to say that he would rather have written one page of *Leaves of Grass* than to have made all the motion pictures ever conceived. Although some of his stories and poems were published in magazines, he was unable to make a living from writing and so he had gone on the stage. He had, however, received a thousand dollars from James K. Hackett for a play called *A Fool and a Girl.* Hackett produced the play in Washington in 1907 but it closed after a week's run. It is said that Griffith made the adaptation of *La Tosca* because he had seen some films in a nickelodeon and thought them stupid, and that his *Tosca* synopsis was rejected because it contained too many scenes. If true, the reason for its rejection is as ironic as Griffith's having begun his career in motion pictures by enacting the part of a hero who makes a rescue, for a rescue was to climax many a Griffith film.

Griffith had been acting, on and off, since he was twenty years old when he joined a group organized in his hometown of Louisville, Kentucky, to play in nearby towns. Two years later, after an unsuccessful tour in Michigan with another acting troupe, he was playing minor roles in the Meffert Stock Company. When he was not acting he supported himself in other ways—working for a construction company, shoveling ore in Tonawanda, New York (where he had been stranded when a play failed there), picking hops, and working aboard a lumber ship plying the West Coast. He was a member of Ada Gray's troupe, with which he played in *Trilby* and *East Lynne*. He appeared as Abraham Lincoln in *The Ensign,* produced by the Neill Alhambra Stock Company in Chicago. He played in *Fedora* with the Melbourne MacDowell Company and as Sir Francis Drake in Nance O'Neill's production of *Elizabeth, Queen of England.* In 1906, while in Boston acting in *Rosmersholm* and *Magda,* he married the actress Linda Arvidson. Then came the failure of his play and his turn to motion pictures.

It would not have been surprising if Griffith, whose training had been in the theatre, had used motion pictures as a device to photograph plays in the manner of Sarah Bernhardt's *Queen Elizabeth.* That, on the contrary, he should have exploited the device in the direction that Porter had indicated in *The Great Train Robbery*—but far beyond anything that Porter had attempted—is not easily explained. It may be observed, however, that the theatre and the motion pictures are akin in one respect—they are representational—and that in creating the art of the motion pictures Griffith expanded the representational possibilities of the theatre.

Whether his theatre background explains his creation of this art, his social background explains much of the content of his films. The seventh of eight children, he was born on a farm in Oldham County, Kentucky, on January 22, 1875. His father, Jacob Wark Griffith, had served in the First Kentucky Cavalry in the Mexican War, had joined one of the wagon trains to California in 1850, and had been elected to the Kentucky legislature. After the outbreak of the Civil War, he reenlisted in his old regiment and emerged from the war a colonel. Brought up in a southern home in those years not long after the war, David Wark learned of the Lost Cause and of a way of life that no longer existed. (In *The Birth of a Nation* the first of the Piedmont scenes is introduced by the title: "In the Southland. Piedmont, South Carolina, the home of the Camerons, where life runs in a quaintly way that is to be no more.") Lewis Jacobs contends that "the sentimental bias implanted in Grif-

fith by his father was reinforced by the boy's love of poetry in the Victorian manner,"[1] and he ascribes to Griffith's literary taste Griffith's choice of romantic subjects for his films, as well as his choice of actresses—Mae Marsh, Mary Pickford, Lillian Gish, Blanche Sweet—all counterparts of the girlish, delicate, pretty heroines of the Victorian era. It might be observed, however, that here and there, particularly in Griffith's early films, there are exceptions to Jacobs's observation about Victorian heroines.

At the death of the colonel, when David was ten years old, the Griffiths were nearly impoverished. Mrs. Griffith and the children moved into a small house occupied by the oldest son and his wife and then to Louisville. David, whose formal education ended before he had been in high school a year, obtained a variety of jobs: selling magazine subscriptions and the *Encyclopaedia Britannica,* running an elevator in a department store, and clerking in a bookstore. Occasionally he ushered at the Macauley Theatre, where he saw plays performed by the great touring companies headed by famous actors and actresses of the time. Having become fascinated with the stage, he began his career as an actor. When in 1897 he joined the Meffert Stock Company, he took for his stage name Lawrence Griffith.

His experience in *Rescued from an Eagle's Nest,* however, did not diminish his ambition to be a writer. Failing to sell his stories to the Edison people, he took them down to the Biograph studio on East Fourteenth Street. Biograph bought from him *Old Isaacs the Pawnbroker, Ostler Joe* (an adaptation of a poem by George P. Sims), and *At the Crossroads of Life* and produced them as motion pictures in 1908. Griffith acted in *Ostler Joe* and *At the Crossroads of Life* as well as in three other films that Biograph produced that year—*The Music Master, When Knights Were Bold,* and *The Stage Rustler.* Then Biograph's general manager, H. N. Marvin, asked him to direct a picture. According to Linda Arvidson, Griffith demurred at first and then accepted Marvin's offer conditionally:

"Now if I take this picture-directing job and fall down, then you see I'll be out of my acting job, and you know I wouldn't like that; I don't want to lose my job as an actor down here."

"Otherwise you'd be willing to direct a picture for us?"

"Oh, yes, indeed I would."

"Then if I promise that if you fall down as a director, you can have your acting job back, you will put on a moving picture for us?"

"Yes, then I'd be willing."[2]

The film was called *The Adventures of Dollie.* It is a sentimental and improbable story about a little girl kidnapped by gypsies out of revenge and returned to her parents after a cask in which the gypsies have placed her falls off a wagon into a stream and is found floating in a cove. The cameraman assigned to this one-reel production was Arthur Marvin, H. N. Marvin's brother. Before shooting began, Griffith asked for and received advice from G. W. Bitzer, a Biograph cameraman who had joined the company in 1896 as an electrician. Later, Bitzer—Billy Bitzer—became Griffith's cameraman in a partnership that lasted for sixteen years. Griffith's stage experience resulted in more care in the selection of the cast than had been the practice in the production of previous films. For the mother of the child Griffith chose Linda Arvidson —not, he told her, because she was his wife, but because she was a good actress. For the father he selected a young actor he had happened to see coming out of a booking agency, and thus Arthur Johnson, who had never before acted in a film, began a career that made him a screen star. Griffith had told Bitzer that he wanted as a location for the film a swift stream close to a house. The place chosen was Sound Beach, Connecticut, now known as Old Greenwich. Filming was completed on June 18 and 19, 1908, and Griffith's first picture had its premiere on July 14 at Keith and Proctor's Theatre in Union Square, New York.

The Biograph Company was so pleased with *The Adventures of Dollie* that Griffith became the company's director. His second picture, an Indian melodrama called *The*

Red Man and the Child, filmed on the Passaic River in New Jersey, was released just two weeks after the premiere of *The Adventures of Dollie.* Before the end of the year, the Biograph Company had released forty-four films, the product of Griffith's first six months as a director. In one of these—*After Many Years,* an adaptation of Tennyson's *Enoch Arden*—Griffith cuts from a shot of Annie to a close-up of her and then to Enoch on the desert island. It is said that Griffith invented the close-up. It would be more accurate to say that he established its cinematic value. The close-up is as old as motion pictures. *Fred Ott's Sneeze,* entered for copyright in 1894, is a close-up. So is the two-shot of May Irwin and John C. Rice in 1896. These and other pre-Griffith close-ups that are unrelated to preceding or following shots are, however, no more cinematic than studio portraits. The cut to the close-up of Annie, however, not only draws attention to her but, followed by the shot of Enoch, links the characters in the crosscutting. Here is clear evidence of the application of the principle that Porter groped toward: that the arrangement of shots is the basis of cinematic construction. But Griffith's innovation was so bold that the studio became concerned. Linda Arvidson records this colloquy:

"How can you tell a story jumping about like that? The people won't know what it's about."

"Well," said Mr. Griffith, "doesn't Dickens write that way?"

"Yes, but that's Dickens; that's novel writing: that's different."

"Oh, not so much, these are picture stories: not so different."[3]

Griffith was soon becoming innovative with lighting. On a January day in 1909 he was directing a film in Central Park. The branches of the trees were encrusted with ice, and he had Arthur Marvin shoot some of the scenes against the sun, as Porter had been forced to do in photographing the yacht race. In the resulting film, entitled *The Politician's Love Story,* the trees are outlined in light—an effect called back-

Establishing shot (Griffith, *The Lonely Villa*)

lighting. A few days later, in filming *Edgar Allan Poe,* Griffith inaugurated Rembrandt lighting, whereby a profile is lighted as in a portrait. Heretofore lighting in motion pictures had been "arbitrary," that is, light cast flatly merely to make an image clearly visible. In *A Drunkard's Reformation* and *Pippa Passes* (both in 1909), the lighting is "natural" in that it originates, or seems to originate, in a natural source. A scene in *The Drunkard's Reformation* is illuminated by light from a fireplace, and in *Pippa Passes* the sun seems to be the source of light in Pippa's room, the light varying according to the time of day.

In the spring of 1909 Griffith made a film in which the arrangement of shots consists, for the most part, of crosscutting. The story is about a husband leaving his wife and children alone in a house in the country, about robbers breaking in, and about the husband returning in time to rescue his family. Based on a synopsis credited to Mack Sennett, it was entitled *The Lonely Villa.* Griffith had crosscut previously, the first time, in *The Fatal Hour,* the preceding year, and directors at Pathé and Vitagraph had incorporated crosscuts in two films before *The Fatal Hour* was released, but no film produced before *The Lonely Villa* depends so much on this kind of editing.

Griffith puts the film together in 53 shots. There are no subtitles. The first shot sets the scene: an exterior view of the lonely villa. It is the kind of shot called an establishing shot, that is, a shot that establishes the whereabouts of a scene or the relationship of details to be shown subsequently in a closer shot or shots. In *The Lonely Villa* it sets not only the scene but the tone: the lonely villa in the background and three figures, who prove to be robbers, lurking in the shrubbery in the left foreground. Then follow shots of the butler and the maid being given the day off and leaving the house, of the delivery of a false message to lure the husband away, of the husband placing a pistol on the table for his wife's protection, of the messenger removing the bullets from the pistol while the wife is helping her husband on with his coat, of an affectionate leave-taking, and of the husband driving off in his chauffeured touring car. Now begins the crosscutting between the robbers breaking in and the wife and children barricading themselves in a room by piling furniture against the door. Then Griffith intercuts shots of the husband: the automobile breaks down in front of an inn, from which the husband telephones and thereby learns of the peril at home. The wife at the telephone waves the pistol as though she is telling her husband that it is empty. Then one of the robbers cuts the telephone wire. Delayed because the chauffeur cannot start the automobile, the husband crosses the road (the camera panning accordingly) to a gypsy camp, where he obtains a horse-drawn wagon and in it, together with assistants, drives away. Intercut now with brief shots of the robbers breaking down a door and of the wife and children retreating to an adjoining room are even briefer shots of the speeding wagon. All of the chief characters converge in the final shot: seconds after the robbers have forced their way into the room, the rescuers enter.

The race against time in *The Lonely Villa* is in the genre of the chase, which Alfred Hitchcock has called "the final expression of the motion-picture medium."[4] In *The Great Train Robbery,* also a chase film, Porter groped toward a manipulation of time by cutting back from scene 9 to scene 1, the implication being that the intermediate action had been happening "meanwhile." Otherwise the scenes are arranged chronologically, as in *A Trip to the Moon.* But Griffith takes advantage of the possibility of motion pictures not only for instant transference from one scene to another but for control of tempo by varying the temporal length of shots. As the chase nears its end, the lengths decrease and the excitement thereby increases. The term "Griffith last-minute rescue," which came to refer to such an ending, implies not so much the rescue as the exciting way leading up to it. Whereas in *The Great Train Robbery* the principal motion is within each shot, in *The Lonely Villa* the principal motion comes from the editing. The husband in the wagon, the wife and children in the room, the robbers at the door—these shots contain motion, but what brings the sequence alive is the way in which the shots are arranged.

In *A Corner in Wheat,* made later the same year, Griffith edits for a different purpose. Parts of the story are adapted from Frank Norris's *The Octopus* and "A Deal in Wheat"—the farmer setting out to market to sell his wheat but coming home empty-handed, the cornering of the market, the breadline at the bakery, the contrast between rich and poor, the ironic climax, and so forth. The opening shots are of slow-paced rural scenes, the first of which is of farmers sowing wheat. Then follow shots of feverish activity in the office of the wheat king and on the wheat exchange. The wheat king corners the market and, to celebrate, gives a lavish banquet, oblivious of the poor turned away from the bakery because they cannot afford the increased price of bread. The wheat king suffocates in a bin of his own wheat, and the film ends with another scene in the wheat field.

Whereas the exterior scenes are suggestive of paintings—the Biograph Company pointed out that the scene of the farmers sowing wheat is an animated reproduction of Millet's "The Sowers"—the interiors are suggestive of the stage. The interior scenes are in full shots. Panic on the wheat exchange is represented by a crowd jumping about excitedly on a curving flight of steps whereby most of the actors are made equally visible. (The staging here, however, accords with Norris's description, in *The Pit,* of the corn and wheat pits in the Chicago Board of Trade Building, including not only the steps but the dial indicating the current price of wheat and the bulletin blackboards.) In the banquet scene the wheat king's friends stand on either side of an unrealistically narrow dining table extending upstage, the wheat king, downstage, facing them. At the conclusion of the death scene, played against a painted drop, the friends form a tableau, one of them holding the dead man's head so that it all but faces the camera.

Stagelike as these scenes are, Griffith does not construct the film like a play. His contrasts are cinematic as he interpolates in the banquet scene a still from a preceding shot—a flashback of the poor turned away from the bakery. He edits in five shots the scene in which the wheat king falls to his death, and he intercuts the scene with shots of simultaneous action elsewhere. In the first shot of the film the farmers approach from across the field, turn in the foreground, and start back, one of them driving a horse-drawn cultivator. In the last shot the same motion is repeated by a single sower.

In January of 1910, attracted by the mild climate and sunlight, Griffith took most of the Biograph players to California, together with his cameramen Arthur Marvin and Billy Bitzer. Thus began a practice he was to continue during the rest of his tenure with Biograph, that is, to make films in California during the first half of the year and in the East the latter half. Accordingly it happened that he filmed *The Lonedale Operator* at Inglewood early in 1911.

SHOT 20

SHOT 36

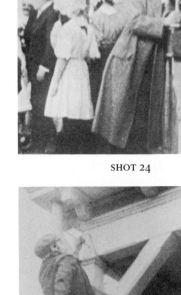

SHOT 24

Above and facing page:
Some shots in the crosscutting (Griffith, *The Lonely Villa*)

SHOT 38

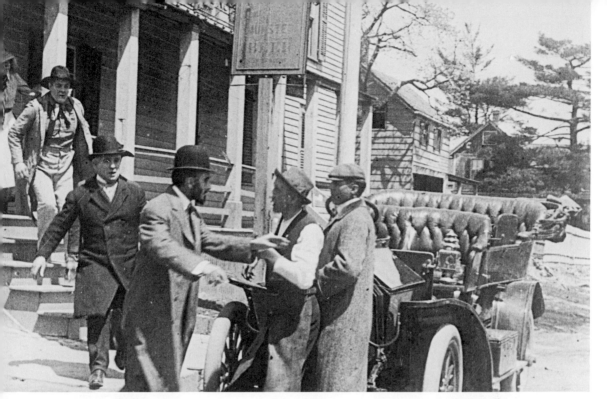

SHOT 42

SHOT 49

SHOT 51

SHOT 52

SHOT 53

Panic on the exchange (Griffith, *A Corner in Wheat*)

Flashback for contrast (Griffith, *A Corner in Wheat*)

D. W. Griffith, *A Corner in Wheat*

The Lonedale Operator is *The Lonely Villa* made into a railroad film. A husband, on account of an emergency, leaving his wife in sole charge of their children in a lonely villa that is then besieged by robbers becomes a telegraph operator who on account of an emergency leaves his daughter in sole charge of a railroad station—called Lonedale—which is then besieged by robbers. Such similarities continue throughout—the father offers his daughter a pistol for her protection, an affectionate scene takes place between the daughter and the engineer who is to be her rescuer, the girl makes known her plight by telegraph, an incident delays the rescue and prolongs the suspense, and so on, until the engineer arrives at the railroad station only seconds after the robbers have broken down the door to the telegraph room.

The plot, however, embellishes that of the earlier film. *The Lonely Villa* begins abruptly with the appearance of the robbers, but *The Lonedale Operator* first establishes the relationships between the other main characters. When the robbers appear they are intent on a payroll being shipped by train. Accordingly there is a scene in an office from which the payroll pouch is dispatched, another as the pouch is put aboard

Flashback for contrast (Griffith, *A Corner in Wheat*)

the train, and still another as the train arrives at Lonedale. The plot of *The Lonely Villa* depends as much on the telephone as that of *The Lonedale Operator* on the telegraph, but, whereas dependence on the telephone overworks coincidence in the former, the telegraph is indigenous to the latter. The *scène à faire* in which the wife discovers that the pistol is empty become farce in *The Lonedale Operator.* When the rescuers enter they find the operator holding the robbers at bay with what the robbers take to be a pistol —a monkey wrench. The villains are then made to doff their hats and bow low to the girl who has so ingeniously foiled them.

Embellished though the plot is, Griffith tells the story, as in *The Lonely Villa,* without subtitles.

But what is chiefly interesting about *The Lonedale Operator* is its difference from *The Lonely Villa* as cinema. Although only about a quarter again as long as the earlier film, it is edited in almost twice as many shots (97 to *The Lonely Villa*'s 53). The significant difference, however, is not so much the number of shots as their apportionment and their variety in spatial and temporal length. For example, whereas in *The Lonely Villa* 18 shots, or over a third the total number in the film, are devoted to

Crosscutting (Griffith, *The Lonedale Operator*)

Crosscutting (Griffith, *The Lonedale Operator*)

the comparatively static telephone conversation and only 7 to the crosscutting as the husband comes to the rescue, in *The Lonedale Operator* the rescue sequence comprises 38 shots. Griffith gets the story under way at a leisurely pace. The shots in which he introduces the characters average half a minute. But after the operator carries the pouch into the station, Griffith intercuts 33 shots, averaging three or four seconds—of the robbers approaching the station; of the operator becoming aware of them, locking the door, and telegraphing for help; of the other operator asleep at his desk; of the robbers attempting to break into the waiting room; of the sleeping operator waking up, taking down the message, and rushing out with it to the engineer, and so forth. Griffith slows the tempo as the operator brings the engineer a second message and as the engineer and the fireman climb aboard the locomotive, which then moves away from the station. With increasing rapidity Griffith intercuts shots of the engineer and the fireman in the cab of the locomotive, of the besieged operator, of the robbers breaking in, of the locomotive coming down the track, and so on. Just before the arrival at Lonedale, he slows the cutting by holding for nearly half a minute a shot of the engineer and the fireman moving excitedly about in the cab. But he does not thereby change the tempo, only the source of the motion —from motion effected by editing to motion within the shot. The 28 shots in the rescue sequence, as contrasted to the 7 in *The Lonely Villa,* admit of greater flexibility in tempo and accordingly of more effective building up of suspense.

In *The Lonely Villa* Griffith cuts only between scenes; in *The Lonedale Operator* he cuts *within* scenes. The scene in which the payroll pouch and the robbers arrive on the same train comprises three shots. In the first, as the operator waits at the door of the baggage car, the robbers emerge from under the car and, unnoticed by the operator, start across the platform. In the second they cross the platform and go down an embankment. And in the third the operator

receives the pouch and carries it into the station. Here again is evidence of Griffith's appreciation of the possibilities of editing that seem to have eluded Porter. There being no editing within scenes in *The Great Train Robbery,* the contents of each scene are presented as unselectively as in *Queen Elizabeth.* But Griffith realized that by editing he could control our attention. Compare, for example, the scene of the holdup of the passengers in *The Great Train Robbery* with that of the arrival of the train at Lonedale. In the former there is only acting to identify the passenger who attempts to escape. Before he breaks away from the group lined up along the track and is shot, he sways, but the motion is inconspicuous because he is not singled out from the other passengers. Nor, except by acting, is attention drawn to the bandit who shoots him. But by presenting the robbers and the operator together in the first shot and by concentrating on the robbers in the second and on the operator in the third, Griffith not only effects motion by editing but introduces the villains. Concurrently he inaugurates suspense: the operator is now in danger but unaware of it. In a scene in the telegraph room he cuts from a medium-close shot of the operator at her desk to a longer shot that, taking in the room from side to side, enables us to see her get up, cross to the door, and go out. To make the transition inconspicuous, he makes the cut as the girl gets up. Later he reverses the pattern: a medium shot as the operator enters and crosses to the desk; then a closer one as she sits down.

Griffith interpolates in the rescue scene a close shot of the wrench, on which the farcical ending depends. In *The Lonely Villa* the robber removing the bullets from the pistol is as important to the plot as the wrench but is comparatively inconspicuous, as though Griffith were limited by the method of the stage. The story of *The Lonedale Operator* as outlined in the Biograph bulletin implies that not only the robbers but we are to be deceived by the wrench. If the outcome is thus to be a surprise, Griffith deliberately does not let us see the wrench

Editing within a scene (Griffith, *The Lonedale Operator*)

Editing within a scene (Griffith, *The Lonedale Operator*)

Editing within a scene (Griffith, *The Lonedale Operator*)

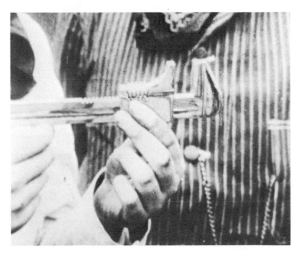

Cinematic Interpolation (Griffith, *The Lonedale Operator*)

in a close shot until the last scene. Whatever his intention, the shot of the wrench occurring at the proper moment is cinematic.

Increasing the number of shots enables Griffith to bridge the gap between the rescuers on their way and the rescuers at the scene of the rescue. In *The Lonely Villa* we see the wagon coming down a road and,

in the next shot, the husband entering the room; in *The Lonedale Operator* Griffith makes the transition in six shots.

The film also represents a development in the content of shots—an extension of Griffith's concern for composition and staging, for example, in *A Corner in Wheat*. The

Top left—SHOT 90: *Exterior. Long shot.* Locomotive approaches around a curve—railroad-station platform at right.

Top right—SHOT 91: *Interior. Medium-close shot.* Locomotive cab. Locomotive comes to a stop. Engineer and fireman climb out.

Middle left—SHOT 92: *Exterior. Long shot.* Locomotive at left of platform. Engineer and fireman climb down and cross platform.

Middle right—SHOT 93: *Exterior. Long shot.* Railroad station. Engineer and fireman go into station.

Bottom left—SHOT 94: *Interior. Medium-long shot.* Waiting room. Engineer and fireman enter and cross to door of telegraph room.

SHOT 95: *Interior. Medium shot.* Telegraph room. Operator holds off robbers. Engineer and fireman enter.

longest shot in *The Lonedale Operator*— nearly a minute—is played in a rural setting, farm buildings visible over the crest of a hill in the right background and a leafy branch bending over the scene in the left foreground. The girl and the engineer approach through the foliage and play the rest of the scene in front of it. The locomotive, an 1878 Baldwin 4-4-0 that Griffith obtained from the Santa Fe, helps to compose some of the shots. We see it passing the Lonedale station and then, as it goes into a curve, spurting white steam from its cylinders. We view the interior of the cab from the tender—in effect a moving camera —reminiscent of the shot of the cab in *The Great Train Robbery*. We see the locomotive approaching around a curve, coming straight down the track, rounding another curve, and so on. In a practice anticipated at least as early as *The Lonely Villa*, in which the lobby of the inn where the hus-

Continuity title (Griffith, *The New York Hat*)

band telephones seems crowded with extras, Griffith here and there stages activity in the background of a scene to reinforce realism in the main action in the foreground. While a man in the payroll office is filling the pouch, locking it, and handing it over to the expressman, people come and go. Sitting at her desk, a stenographer converses with a visitor. When the visitor leaves, she starts to type, stops, raises the cover of the typewriter, makes an erasure, closes the cover, and resumes typing. In the scene in which the pouch is put aboard the baggage car the train comes into the station from around a curve, a string of boxcars framing the scene on one side, the edge of the station on the other, and stops so that the forward door of the baggage car is near the camera. The only essential action in the scene is the handing up of the pouch to the baggageman, but in the background the conductor and the brakeman swing down from the day coach as the train comes to a stop, some passengers get off, a passenger gets on, a baggage truck is wheeled up to the far door of the baggage car, a trunk is unloaded, and so forth.

The New York Hat (1912) is not about a rescue but about the clearing up of a misunderstanding. Because the village gossips and Mary's father do not know why the young minister has bought Mary a stylish hat—the reason is made clear to us by an insert in the first scene—the situation is one of dramatic irony. Based on a scenario by sixteen-year-old Anita Loos, *The New York Hat* is a story of character, however stereotyped the characters may be—the innocent heroine, the suspicious father, the kindly minister, the self-righteous gossips.

In *The Lonedale Operator* and *The Lonely Villa* the main relationships are between characters in separate scenes: the operator in the telegraph room, the robbers at the door, the engineer in the locomotive; but in *The New York Hat* the main relationships are between characters *within* scenes: Mary and her father, Mary and the minister, Mary and the church board. There is, for example, the after-church scene, in which Mary is snubbed by the gossips. Not only does Griffith present the scene in a single shot but, as in the payroll-office scene in *The Lonedale Operator,* he stages activity in the background. Behind Mary and the gossips are other people coming out of church while in the background of the scene, at the top of the steps, the minister is conversing with three young women. On the other hand, Griffith edits the scene at the hat shop in eleven shots, intercut with a shot of the minister leaving the parsonage. Three of these shots in particular are exemplary of motion effected primarily by editing within the scene: Shot 11 concentrates on the hat and, together with shot 12, is visual evidence of the hat's being, according to a preceding title, "The village sensation." Shot 12 reinforces the effect of shot 11. And shot 13 singles out the two main characters and makes the point not only that Mary admires the hat but that the minister notices that she admires it. These shots lead to the title "The minister remembers his trust." The editing of the scene in which Mary is confronted by the church board provides the primary motion and contrasts the innocent girl with her stern-faced investigators.

Like *A Corner in Wheat, The New York Hat* depends here and there on subtitles

D. W. Griffith, *The New York Hat*

SHOT 11: *Close shot.* The hat being placed in the window.

SHOT 12: *Medium shot.* Group on sidewalk looking at hat. Mary enters along sidewalk and joins the group. Minister enters.

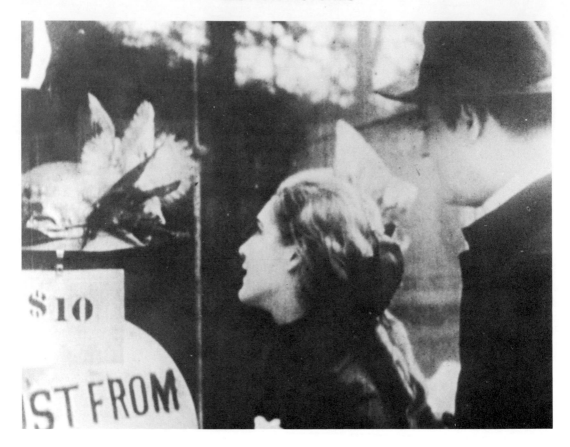

SHOT 13: *Medium-close shot.* Mary and minister.

to interpret the pictures or emphasize a point. *The Lonely Villa* and *The Lonedale Operator,* on the other hand, tell their stories by pictures alone—that is, by pictures edited. Even the telephone conversation in the former and the telegrams in the latter are not duplicated in words. But in *A Corner in Wheat,* for example, the scene of men rushing in and out of an office would not be clear without the subtitle "In the city the wheat king engineers the great corner in wheat," nor that of a crowd jumping up and down without the subtitle "Cornering the market." Some of the pantomime in *The*

New York Hat is self-explanatory. Of Mary Pickford's acting in this film, Iris Barry comments: "Mary gives herself a self-disparaging look in the mirror, arranges one glove to look like a pair, and trips hopefully outdoors. This is neither literature nor theatre: it is pure film."[5] Whether one agrees that it is not theatre, the point is that a subtitle here would be redundant. On the other hand, Griffith explains by subtitle the scene in which Mary is confronted by the church board. He also depends on subtitles to indicate a shift in time ("Sunday morning"), to create dialogue ("Daddy, can't I have a new

A subtitle would be redundant (Griffith, *The New York Hat*).
Courtesy of the Museum of Modern Art

hat?"), and to express a subjective point of view ("The minister recalls his trust.").

In attempting to see Griffith's early films as they appeared to their first audiences we are at a disadvantage, so accustomed have we become to a way of storytelling that to those audiences was unprecedented. But we can return after we have seen his later films. If we do, then the fascination for us is a recognition of how unerringly in the early ones he moves toward his masterpieces. There is hardly the composition of a scene, an arrangement of a shot, or the pattern of a sequence, for example, in *The Birth of a Nation* or *Intolerance* that does not have its prototype in the more than four hundred films that he made before 1914.

The success of the two-reel *Enoch Arden* and several subsequent two-reel films that the Biograph Company permitted Griffith to make was an impetus to longer films. So was the success of *Queen Elizabeth* and other, even longer, foreign films. The Italian *Quo Vadis?* (1912), in eight reels, opened in April, 1913, at the Astor Theatre in New York, at an admission price of a dollar, and after a run of twenty-two weeks appeared in other cities. That summer Griffith made his four-reel *Judith of Bethulia* (released in 1914). The story, originating in the book of Judith in the Apocrypha, had been the source of a play, *Judith of Bethulia,* by Thomas Baily Aldrich. Griffith would have been familiar with the play because Nance O'Neill had intended to revive it during the Boston engagement and had begun rehearsals while Griffith was still with the company. Although Biograph had not ob-tained the rights to the play, a copy of it is said to have been at Griffith's side while he was directing the film. In its subject, its spectacle, and its scope, *Judith of Bethulia* anticipates *Intolerance.*

Griffith had left Biograph in the fall of 1913 and joined the Majestic Film Company, which had recently been organized by Harry and Roy Aitkin, and for which he directed and supervised the making of films until late the next spring. Then he persuaded the Aitkins to allow him to make a longer film than had ever been made. The result was *The Birth of a Nation.*

6.
D.W. Griffith: The Birth of a Nation and Intolerance

In looking about for a subject for the film that was to become *The Birth of a Nation,* Griffith was attracted to a novel by Thomas Dixon, a southerner who had been a lawyer, legislator, and popular Baptist minister before turning to writing. This was *The Clansman,* published in 1905, a remarkably undistinguished, biased, and socially objectionable novel about the Reconstruction period after the Civil War. Dixon had adapted *The Clansman* to the stage, including in his adaptation some material from his first novel, *The Leopard's Spots. The Clansman* opened in 1906 and ran for five years. Griffith and the Aitkins obtained the film rights. In adapting *The Clansman,* play and novel, to the screen, Griffith extended the subject to include the Civil War as well as the Reconstruction.

Griffith not only directed the film but took entire charge of production, even to raising some of the money. (The cost was $110,000, many times the amount ever spent on a film before.) The exterior scenes were shot in southern California and the interior scenes in the Fine Arts Studio, on the edge of Hollywood. Sherman's March to the Sea was shot in the San Fernando Valley. Griffith rented large areas of Whittier County for the ride-of-the-clan sequence. He secured horses, artillery pieces, and various other military equipment together with a vast amount of other properties and costumes. He saw to it, for example, that uniforms for officers and men of the Confederate and Union armies were correct for the period. Extra players included Civil War veterans.

After six weeks of rehearsing, shooting began on July 4, 1914. Lillian Gish's account of Griffith's method implies that rehearsing continued even after the shooting began: "We were rarely assigned parts," Miss Gish wrote, "and the younger members of the company always rehearsed for the older members when the story was being developed, as all the 'writing' was done by Griffith as he moved groups of characters around. . . . When the story was ready to go before the camera, the older players . . . came forward and acted the parts they had been watching us rehearse for them. . . . Very often we would play episodes without knowing the complete story. . . . Only Griffith knew the continuity of *The Birth of a Nation* in its final form."[1] The actual shooting took nine consecutive weeks, and additional scenes were shot later. Then Griffith spent more than three months in editing.

By the end of the year the film was completed in twelve reels—the longest American film that had ever been made. Under the title *The Clansman,* it had previews at the Loring Opera House, Riverside, Cal-

In the trenches (Griffith, *The Birth of a Nation*)

ifornia, on January 1 and 2, 1915, and on February 8 entered upon a seven-month engagement at Clune's Auditorium in Los Angeles. On February 20 it was shown in New York City for the censors and a selected audience. It is said that Dixon suggested to Griffith that the title *The Clansman* was too tame, that it ought to be *The Birth of a Nation,* the title by which the film was announced in the trade press before the New York preview. The "world premiere," took place March 3 at the Liberty Theatre in New York; it was billed as *The Birth of a Nation.* It remained at the Liberty Theatre for forty-four consecutive weeks, a record not to be broken until 1925 by *The Covered Wagon.* It played twice daily, with all the effects later to be associated with so-called colossals—reserved seats, tickets sold in advance, souvenir programs, costumed ushers, full-orchestra accompaniment, and so on. *The Birth of a Nation* went on tour throughout the United States like a play, accompanied by an orchestra and shown at leading theatres; it appeared at La Scala and at Drury Lane in London; it toured the Continent; and it was shown in China, and

in India. By 1930, according to Seymour Stern, *The Birth of a Nation* had been seen by more than one hundred million people and had grossed far in excess of twenty million dollars.[2]

In a curtain speech at the premiere in New York, Dixon declared that "no one save the son of a soldier and a Southerner could have made such a picture."[3] Because of his upbringing Griffith would not have perceived the bias in Dixon's novel. Consequently *The Birth of a Nation,* which presents the view that the Civil War was the result of only a disagreement about slavery, makes the issue an emotional one and distorts the social implications. Negroes, the film implies, are inferior. The good Negroes are good because they are the faithful servants of their masters. The others are a threat to the white man and must be suppressed. Thus the Ku Klux Klan is justified—and glorified. It is made the salvation of the South. In its salvation of individual characters, the Klan is a *deus ex machina* effected in a Griffith last-minute rescue.

The theme of *The Birth of a Nation* is expressed in one of the titles—"the agony which the South endured that a nation might be born." It is the tragedy of the Civil War. To illustrate the theme, Griffith treats his subject in two main parts—the Civil War and the Reconstruction period—together with a prologue and an epilogue. The prologue pictures the introduction of slavery into America during the seventeenth century and the rise of the Abolitionist movement in the North during the nineteenth. Part 1 presents the Civil War from its beginning to the surrender of Lee to Grant at Appomattox and the assassination of Lincoln in Ford's Theatre five days later. Part 2, the Reconstruction, shows the exploitation of the southern Negroes by the carpetbaggers —who, according to one of the titles, would "crush the White South under the heel of the Black South"—and the resulting rise of the Ku Klux Klan.

Against this epic background Griffith presents a double love story—that of Ben Cameron (the Little Colonel), a southerner, and Elsie Stoneman, a northerner, and that of

In the Cameron kitchen (Griffith, *The Birth of a Nation*)

Margaret Cameron, Ben's sister, and Phil Stoneman, Elsie's brother. The misfortunes of the two pairs of lovers are made to parallel the Civil War and the troubles of the Reconstruction, and their fortunes the resulting new birth of freedom promised in the epilogue. The chief characters and incidents thus not only parallel but also symbolize the main action of the war.

Griffith's style is characterized by symbolism. There is symbolism in the relation of the love stories to the main story and in more specific ways. "Hostilities," reads a subtitle as the kitten pounces on the puppies at the feet of Dr. Cameron, "the kindly master of Cameron Hall." The close shot of a cotton blossom in Ben Cameron's hand

may be taken as symbolic of the staple on which southern economy depends, but in the context in which we see it—a context to be pointed out later—it also implies another kind of dependence. A shot of Silas Lynch mistreating a dog is followed by a scene in which Ben and Elsie fondle a bird. In one of the war scenes there is a close shot of parched corn, the meager food of the southern soldiers. Later, after the war is over, there is another close shot of parched corn—in the Cameron kitchen.

Griffith's romantic strain accounts in part for a lack of shading in characterization. The characters in *The Birth of a Nation* are no more subtle than their counterparts in *The Clansman*. The characters, however,

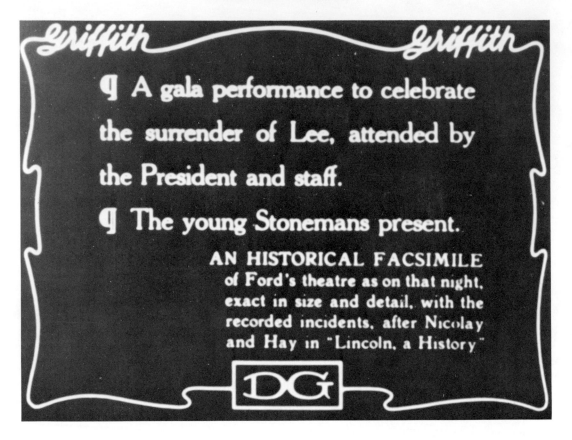

¶ A gala performance to celebrate the surrender of Lee, attended by the President and staff.

¶ The young Stonemans present.

AN HISTORICAL FACSIMILE of Ford's theatre as on that night, exact in size and detail, with the recorded incidents, after Nicolay and Hay in "Lincoln, a History"

Documentation (Griffith, *The Birth of a Nation*)

are less important than their relationship to the epic background or even the background itself.

Griffith turned historian to get his sets as nearly like their originals as possible. This painstaking effort is evidenced in the titles preceding scenes that represent specific historical events, as, for example, Lincoln signing the proclamation for the first call for volunteers. A footnote to the title prefacing this scene reads: "An Historical Facsimile of the President's Executive Office on that occasion, after Nicolay and Hay in 'Lincoln, a History.'" Scenes similarly documented include those of Lee's surrender at Appomattox, the assassination of Lincoln in Ford's Theatre, and the riot in the Master's Hall. ("The Riot in the Master's Hall" is verbatim the title of a chapter in *The Clansman*. The hall is that of the South Carolina House of Representatives, and the Master is Dr. Cameron, who in the old days had been a member.)

Griffith was meticulous in enacting details of these scenes in accordance with his research. In the Ford's Theatre sequence, for example, the president's box combines the two upper boxes to the right of the stage —in keeping with the record. That morning the theatre manager had removed the partition separating the boxes, in accordance with the custom of thus forming a state box on the occasion of the president's attendance at the theatre. The president's party consists of the president, Mrs. Lincoln, a young lady, and a young man in military uniform—in accordance with the fact that the Lincolns took an army officer and his fiancee to the theatre with them that evening—and they arrive, also in accordance with fact, at 8.30, after the performance has begun. It is said that John Wilkes Booth, who was familiar with Laura Keene's production of *Our American Cousin,* knew that a line in Asa Trenchard's soliloquy after Mrs. Mountchessington's exit, in act 3, scene 2, always got a laugh; that Harry Hawk, who played Trenchard, would be alone on the stage at that time, which would be about quarter past ten; and that he planned to enter the president's box during the laughter. Griffith prefaces the appearance of Booth with the subtitle "Time, 10.13. Act III, Scene 2," and he has Booth fire as Trenchard chases Mrs. Mountchessington off—substituting visual action for the line in the soliloquy. Watching the play, Lincoln takes his wife's hand in his and, a few seconds before Booth fires, reaches back and draws a shawl over his shoulders—details that not only accord with the record but, in the film, constitute dramatic irony.

Griffith gives Belascolike attention to detail, some of it likely to go unnoticed on a first viewing. In the Ford's Theatre sequence the opened door in the hallway leading to the president's box gives a glimpse of the audience in the gallery. After making her entrance in the play, Laura Keene comes down to the footlights and receives flowers. A spotlight follows two of the actors as they come forward. Here and there in the film Griffith stages a scene against a background of realistic activity reminiscent of the pay-roll office in *The Lonedale Operator* and the after-church scene in *The New York Hat.* Arriving at the military hospital, Mrs. Cameron is stopped by the sentry outside the ward while at the back of the anteroom soldiers converse at a desk. In the ward the essential action concerns Ben Cameron, in the foreground. Meanwhile, however, the wounded lie behind him on their cots or sit up, the doctors and nurses go about their duties, and—in accordance with Dixon's allusion to checkers in the corresponding scene in *The Clansman*—a checker game is in progress. When the army surgeon tells Mrs. Cameron that her son is to be hanged as a guerilla, our attention is on the grief-stricken mother, but meanwhile, as though to universalize the situation, a weeping woman in the background is being helped out of the ward.

Watching *The Birth of a Nation* nowadays, we take for granted many effects that have become commonplace in films. Griffith's talent as a director is evidenced no less in the handling of crowd scenes than in attention to detail: the dance in Piedmont, the battles, the audience in Ford's Theatre, the South Carolina legislature in session, the ride of the clan, and so forth. Griffith stages scenes or parts of scenes in shadows. The bonfire celebrations at night in the streets of Piedmont seem to be illuminated by the fires, and the night battles by flashes from exploding shells. Scenes of nocturnal activities of the clan appear to be moonlit. Actually, however, at least according to Billy Bitzer,[4] there was no night photography in *The Birth of a Nation;* the miniature model of the burning of Atlanta was the only scene he could recall that was not shot in sunlight.

Some of the acting in *The Birth of a Nation* seems stilted not only because of its contrast to the realism in the film but also because of its dependence on pantomime. The exaggerated acting of Lillian Gish depicting Elsie Stoneman embracing the bedpost and of certain other scenes, particularly those involving the love stories, is partly attributable to Griffith's sentimental strain. Griffith did not follow a detailed scenario. Having only a rough mental outline of the action, he improvised as he went along. In directing the scenes in which Elsie Stoneman visits Ben in the military hospital, Griffith noticed that a young studio worker named William Freeman was watching Lillian Gish with an expression of adoration on his face. He told Bitzer to get that expression onto the film. Assigned the part of the sentry standing guard at the entrance to the ward, Freeman interpreted the role so expressively that he steals the scenes in which he appears with Miss Gish. Then there is the scene in which Ben comes home from the war and is welcomed by his sister and his mother. The first part of the scene, between Ben and the Little Sister, is sentimental enough. But we do not see Mrs. Cameron. Instead, as Ben goes into the house, we see her arm as it goes about his shoulder.

There were more than 1,500 shots in the print of *The Birth of a Nation* at its premiere. As a result of objection to scenes of Negroes amuck in Piedmont, Griffith deleted some of these scenes, and the number of shots is now 1,375. However, no film before had contained even as many as 1,375 shots, nor so many different kinds. There are 28 shots in *Queen Elizabeth,* all of the same spatial length. The shots in *The Birth of a Nation* vary from close shots of objects—such as an eye seen through a small hole in a door, a cotton blossom, a pistol, and parched corn in a pan—to shots across great expanses of countryside. Griffith moves the camera less than contemporary directors, although he moves it when it suits his purpose, tilting, for example, to take in the puppies at Dr. Cameron's feet, panning to encompass a battlefield, or tracking ahead of the Little Colonel making a charge or the clansmen riding down a road.

This care for composition is reminiscent of Griffith's early films. A fence extending across the bottom of the frame of a scene enclosed by the sides of a valley or by tree trunks looks back, for example, to that leafy branch against which a love scene is played in *The Lonedale Operator.* Seymour Stern singles out two shots in *The Lonely Villa* —"shot of a long, empty road, with a horse and wagon dashing down the middle: shot of horse and wagon, swinging into main road from lonely side road"—as "anticipating the landscape style in the climax of *The Birth of a Nation.*"[5] The shot of the clansmen side-by-side on horseback, viewed in a line extending far into the background, is as studied a composition as the rural scenes in *A Corner in Wheat.* During the

scene in which Lincoln signs the proclamation calling for volunteers and that in which Lee surrenders to Grant, the actors pose in tableaux suggestive of certain paintings of those events.

Griffith also composes by shaping the frame itself. He has a predilection—the Ford's Theatre sequence is illustrative—for rounding the frame at the corners or edges and for limiting the size of the frame by the iris, also called a mask, whereby all but the essential part of a shot is blacked out, or by the vignette, similar to the mask except that the edges, as in a studio photograph, fade gradually into the surrounding ground. A round mask encircles the shot following the title "The masked batteries." An arched vignette frames scenes illustrating "The North victorious." The riding clansmen are masked in an elliptical shape, emphasizing horizontal extent. An iris encircles a distant shot of the cabin, thereby made prominent —and isolated—by separation from its surroundings. On the other hand, a close shot of an eye peering through a hole in a door is masked by the door itself. To present the burning of Atlanta—"The bombardment and flight"—Griffith cuts the screen diagonally between the scene of "bombardment" that occupies the upper triangle and that of "flight" in the lower. Called the split screen, the device similarly composes two scenes in the epilogue.

Now that the making of motion pictures has become a specialized but diversified process, a director is favored if he is permitted to edit his own films. That part of the process is usually assigned to a specialist in editing. But Griffith, who, like Méliès, epitomized the industry that motion pictures have become, was his own editor. It is difficult to imagine how his films could have been edited otherwise, for not only did he shoot his pictures without a prepared script, but only he knew how the parts were to be fitted together. The greatness of *The Birth of a Nation* depends on the exact order in which the 1,375 shots appear on the screen.

In arranging the shots, Griffith continues the development of editing that marks his

SCENE 444: Elsie and her brother come to seats—speak to acquaintances.

SCENE 445: She looks through her opera glasses.

early films. From the one-shot scenes in *The Lonely Villa* to the slight cutting within scenes in *A Corner in Wheat* and *The Lonedale Operator* to the further breaking down of scenes in *The New York Hat,* it is only a step to the multiple-shot scenes in *The Birth of a Nation*—a giant step but the path is the same and the progress sure. The hat-shop sequence—in fourteen shots, including three intercut shots—in *The New York Hat* anticipates, for example, the Ford's Theatre sequence—in fifty-five shots, including eight intercuts. In the former, Griffith concentrates on individual characters and the objects of the characters' attention—the heroine admiring the hat, the hat itself, the minister noticing her admiring it, the minister purchasing the hat, the gossips noticing the minister purchasing the hat, and so forth. In the Ford's Theatre sequence, here represented in the continuity prepared by Theodore Huff,[6] Griffith also concentrates on individual characters and the objects of their attention, and he edits accordingly: the Stonemans watching the play, the Stonemans applauding Lincoln, Lincoln bowing to the audience, Lincoln watching the play, the Stonemans noticing Booth in the gallery, the bodyguard watching the play, and the play being performed on the stage. The preface

to the continuity explains that "the figure at the right of each scene is the footage; it also can be taken as the number of seconds the scene lasts. When scenes were under three feet, they were measured exactly—the figure in parentheses being the number of *frames.* Thus 2 (4) means 2 feet plus 4 frames, or a total of 36 frames. (16 frames per foot-second)."

TITLE:
A gala performance to celebrate the surrender of Lee, attended by the President and staff.
THE YOUNG STONEMANS PRESENT.
AN HISTORICAL FACSIMILE of Ford's Theatre as on that night, exact in size and detail with the recorded incidents, after Nicolay and Hay in "Lincoln, a History." 24 ft.

SCENE 444
Iris-in to Circle Bottom of Screen
Elsie and her brother come to seats—
speak to acquaintances—
Iris Opens to Full Screen to Long Shot of Theatre (from above one side showing stage—orchestra, boxes, gallery, etc.) 18 ft.

SCENE 445
Semi Close-up of Phil and Elsie
She looks through her opera glasses. 3 ft.

SCENE 446: The painted curtain rises—maid dusting table.

SCENE 452: Stairs dark and shadowy—guard leads man, two women, and Lincoln up stairs.

SCENE 455: Lincoln comes forward in box.

TITLE:
The play: "Our American Cousin," starring Laura Keene.   4 ft.

SCENE 446
As 444
The painted curtain rises—maid dusting table.   7 ft.

SCENE 447
Medium-Long Shot of Stage
Star enters grandly.   3 ft.

SCENE 448
As 446
Star bows to audience's applause.   4½ ft.

SCENE 449
As 445
Elsie with fan—applauds—smiles at brother.   6 ft.

SCENE 450
As 447
Star blows kisses to audience—bows.   3½ ft.

SCENE 451
As 448
Star comes forward to footlights—receives flowers—applause—   9 ft.

TITLE:
Time, 8:30
The arrival of the President, Mrs. Lincoln, and party.   4½ ft.

SCENE 452
3/4 Shot of Stairs Back of Box (Sides Rounded)
Stairs dark and shadowy—guard leads man, two women, and Lincoln up stairs.   8 ft.

SCENE 453
Medium Shot of Theatre Box
First of party enter.   3 ft.

SCENE 454
As 452
Lincoln hands hat and coat to man—enters box door r.   5 ft.

SCENE 455
As 453
Lincoln comes forward in box.   4½ ft.

SCENE 456
Semi Close-Up of Phil and Elsie
They see Lincoln—applaud—rise.   6 ft.

SCENE 457
Long Shot of Theatre
Audience standing up, cheering.   2½ ft.

SCENE 458
As 453
Lincoln bows.   2 (6)

SCENE 459
As 457
Audience cheering.   2½ ft.

SCENE 460
As 458
Lincoln and party sit down.   6½ ft.

TITLE:
Mr. Lincoln's personal bodyguard takes
his post outside the Presidential box.   6 ft.

SCENE 461
*3/4 Shot of Hall Back of Box (Corners
Rounded)*
Guard enters—sits in chair in front of
box door.   10½ ft.

SCENE 462
As 459
Audience still standing—play tries to go
on—   4 ft.

SCENE 463
As 460
The box—President and Mrs. Lincoln
bowing.   8 ft.

SCENE 464
*Medium-Long Shot of Audience and
Box (Corners Soft)*
Cheers—waving handkerchiefs.   3 ft.

SCENE 465
Medium Shot of Stage
Old style footlights—painted scenery—
people leave stage—couple alone, come
forward—spotlight follows them.   9 ft.

TITLE:
To get a view of the play, the bodyguard
leaves his post.

SCENE 464: Cheers—waving handkerchiefs.

SCENE 465: Old style footlights—painted scenery.

SCENE 466
*Medium Shot of Hall, Rear of Box
(Edges Rounded)*
Guard tries to see play.   3½ ft.

SCENE 467
Medium Shot of Stage   3 ft.

SCENE 468
As 466
Guard gets up—opens rear door to
gallery.   6½ ft.

SCENE 470: The guard seats himself at edge.

SCENE 473: Booth (Napolean pose) in the shadows of gallery.

SCENE 478: Comedy line—man waves arms.

SCENE 469
Long shot of Theatre   Iris Up Toward Boxes and Gallery
Guard comes.   3 ft.

SCENE 470
Medium Shot of Gallery (Circle)
The guard seats himself at edge.   4 ft.

TITLE:
Time, 10:13
Act III, scene 2   2 ft.

SCENE 471
Long Shot of Theatre   Iris at Upper Right Corner of Screen
The gallery—man in shadows.   4 ft.

SCENE 472
Semi Close-Up of Phil and Elsie
Watching play—Elsie laughing behind fan—points with fan to man in balcony—asks who he is.   7 ft.

TITLE:
John Wilkes Booth   (14)

SCENE 473
Semi Close-Up of Booth (Circle Iris)
(Napoleon pose) in the shadows of gallery.   2 (2)

SCENE 474
As 472
Elsie is amused by his mysterious appearance—laughs behind fan—looks at him thru opera glasses.   6 ft.

SCENE 475
As 473
Booth waiting.   2 (3)

SCENE 476
Medium-Long Shot of Gallery and Audience (Sides Rounded)
Booth waiting.   5½ ft.

SCENE 477
As 475
Booth waiting.   4 ft.

SCENE 478
Medium Shot of Stage Play
Comedy line—man waves arms.   3½ ft.

SCENE 479
Medium Shot of Lincoln's Box
They laugh—Lincoln feels draught—
reaches for shawl.   6½ ft.

SCENE 480
As 477
Booth watches.   3 ft.

SCENE 481
As 479
The box—Lincoln drawing shawl around
shoulders.   5½ ft.

SCENE 482
Long Shot of Theatre As 471   *Iris Opens*
Booth goes to box door.   5 ft.

SCENE 483
Medium Shot (Circle)
Guard in gallery—Booth opens door be-
hind him.   1 (7)

SCENE 484
*Medium Shot of Hall Back of Box
(Corners Softened)*
Heavy shadows—Booth enters softly—
closes and locks door—peeks thru keyhole at box door—stands up majestically
—pulls out pistol—tosses head back—
—actor-like—   12½ ft.

SCENE 485
Close-Up of Pistol (Circle Vignette)
He cocks it.   3 ft.

SCENE 486
As 484
Booth comes forward—opens door to
box—enters.   9 ft.

SCENE 487
The Box As 479
Booth creeps in behind Lincoln.   4½ ft.

SCENE 488
The Play As 478
The comic chases woman out—cheers.   4 ft.

SCENE 489
Medium Shot of Box
Lincoln is shot—Booth jumps from left
side of box.   4½ ft.

SCENE 484: Heavy shadows—Booth enters softly.

SCENE 485: He cocks it.

SCENE 490
Long Shot of Theatre
Booth jumps on stage—shouts.   2½ ft.

TITLE:
"Sic semper tyrannis!"   2 ft.

SCENE 491
Medium Shot of Booth on Stage
Holds arms out—limps back quickly.   3 ft.

SCENE 492
Medium Shot of Box
Lincoln slumped down—Mrs. Lincoln
calls for help.   2 (6)

SCENE 493
Semi Close-Up of Phil and Elsie
They hardly realize what has happened
—rise—   4½ ft.

SCENE 494
Long Shot of Theatre
Audience standing up in turmoil—Elsie
in foreground faints—Phil supports
her—   4 ft.

SCENE 495
As 492
Man climbs up into box to Lincoln's aid.   5 ft.

SCENE 496
Medium-Long Shot of Theatre and Boxes
Audience agitated.   3½ ft.

SCENE 497
Long Shot of Excited Throng
Phil and Elsie leave. *Fade-Out*   11½ ft.

SCENE 498
Medium Shot of Box
They carry Lincoln out. *Fade-Out*   10½ ft.

Although the method is that of the hat-shop sequence, the increased number of shots admits of subtleties and nuances in the treatment of an action more complex and grave than the purchase of a hat. One of the results of Griffith's recreation of the assassination of Abraham Lincoln is dramatic irony. Only we and Booth are conscious of the terrible deed about to be committed. Thus shot after shot not only creates suspense but points up the irony: the very presence of Lincoln in Ford's Theatre, the Stonemans noticing that the man posing in the gallery is John Wilkes Booth, the bodyguard leaving his post, the audience enjoying the play, Lincoln enjoying the play, and so on. Such details as Elsie looking through her opera glasses or pointing with her fan, Lincoln drawing the shawl about his shoulders, and Booth cocking his pistol would go unnoticed if the sequence were not edited. The occasion being the performance of *Our American Cousin,* the inclusion of the play is relevant if not obligatory, but the point is that Griffith includes it cinematically by alternating shots of the performance with those of the various characters whose attention is on the stage.

The presence of Phil and Elsie Stoneman in Ford's Theatre on this fateful evening serves as one of the links between the fictional stories and the historical background, and Griffith presents more of the action from the Stonemans' point of view than from that of any other character. First he calls attention to the Stonemans in the title prefacing the sequence: THE YOUNG STONEMANS PRESENT. Then he begins the sequence with an iris-in (a gradual appearance of a scene through an expanding circle) on Phil and Elsie taking their seats. By following the second shot—Elsie looking through her opera glasses—with two shots of the stage—the curtain rising and the star entering—he establishes a point of view that he immediately reinforces by cutting to the Stonemans again, Elsie now applauding. A glance at the continuity will reveal not only the extent to which Griffith presents the sequence subjectively but the way in which he does so, that is, by following every shot of the Stonemans with a shot of the stage or of Booth or of Lincoln. After the assassination he directs attention to the Stonemans again, first as Elsie faints and Phil supports her and again as they leave the theatre. Furthermore, as they leave, Griffith fades out the scene. Although he reopens it for a final shot, the rest is anticlimax.

Throughout the sequence the primary motion is that of editing. There is no motion of the camera, and there is as comparatively little motion within the shots as in the rescue sequences in *The Lonely Villa* and *The Lonedale Operator* or in the church-board scene in *The New York Hat.* Laura Keene receiving flowers at the footlights, Lincoln bowing, the audience waving handkerchiefs, Booth posing in the gallery (so nearly motionless that the shots could be stills), Lincoln watching the play, the bodyguard watching the play,—some of this is enhanced by acting, but what brings the sequence alive and creates suspense is the order in which Griffith arranges the shots. Notice, for example, this arrangement:

SHOT 479: *Medium Shot of Lincoln's Box*
     . . . Lincoln laughs—reaches for shawl.
SHOT 480: *Semi Close-Up of Booth (Circle Iris).*
     Booth watches.
SHOT 481: *As* 479.
     The box—Lincoln drawing shawl a-round shoulders.

A writer would say, "Booth watched Lincoln drawing his shawl around his shoulders." Griffith says it cinematically.

To a considerable extent the sequence epitomizes the method throughout the film. Griffith usually begins a sequence with a long shot—long both spatially and temporally. Spatially long, it establishes the locale in which subsequent action is to take place —an establishing shot. Temporally long, it gives the audience time to familiarize itself with the locale. Griffith appreciates the difference, in this respect, between a film and a play. Whereas in a play the distance between actors and audience remains comparatively constant, and a play may begin, and usually does, with an intimate scene, a film usually takes us into the scene gradually. Although Phil and Elsie appear in the foreground at the beginning of the sequence, they are, like the robbers in the foreground of the establishing shot of *The Lonely Villa,* only part of the whole scene to which the camera directs our attention —or, as in the Ford's Theatre sequence, the camera together with the iris-in. As the sequence progresses, Griffith decreases the temporal length—a pattern which, modified by a variety in spatial length, gives the sequence its rhythm.

The shot of the pistol as Booth cocks it is one of the many close shots in the film. The effectiveness of a close shot depends of course on its relation to other shots. That of the pistol is preceded by a medium shot of Booth drawing the pistol. The pattern has its antecedent, for example, in *The Lonedale Operator,* when the close shot of the wrench is preceded by the medium shot of the girl holding the robbers at bay with what

Long shot: Two slaves picking cotton.

Medium shot: The slaves.

Close shot: The slaves' hands picking cotton.

Long shot: The Camerons and the Stonemans in the cotton field.

Medium shot: The Camerons and the Stonemans, Ben holding a cotton blossom.

Close shot: The cotton blossom in Ben's hand.

appears to be a pistol; or in *The New York Hat,* when the close shot of the hat is preceded by the medium shot of the clerk putting the hat in the window. At the beginning of the scene in the cotton field in *The Birth of a Nation,* Griffith extends the pattern by editing three shots in order of decreasing spatial length:

Long shot: Two slaves picking cotton
Medium shot: The slaves
Close shot: The slaves' hands picking cotton

The effect is comparable to that of a dolly shot in which the camera moves up close to an object from a distance. But instead of moving the camera, Griffith obtains motion by editing, and by so doing he also compresses time. Then he immediately repeats the pattern:

Long shot: The Camerons and the Stonemans in the cotton field
Medium shot: The Camerons and the Stonemans, Ben holding a cotton blossom
Close shot: The cotton blossom in Ben's hand

Intercutting in the Ford's Theatre sequence—between the auditorium and the hall leading to the president's box—represents one of the most familiar of Griffith's editing patterns. Intercutting relates scenes occurring simultaneously, for example, the ball in Piedmont and the bonfire celebrations in the streets, or Ben on the battlefield and the Camerons at home. Intercutting creates suspense in the sequence in which the guerillas break into the Cameron house, the women meanwhile hiding in the cellar and, also meanwhile, the Confederates coming to the rescue; or Gus pursuing Flora Cameron while Flora flees from him through the woods and while her brother comes looking for her. And it shapes the climax of the film—a Griffith last-minute rescue —or, rather, two rescues—simultaneous action in an office, an adjoining room, a street, the exterior and the interior of the cabin, and various parts of the countryside.

In the rescue of the Camerons, who have taken refuge in the cabin, Griffith prolongs suspense in the manner of *The Lonely Villa* and *The Lonedale Operator*. As in those earlier films, the attackers have to break down first one door and then another to reach their intended victims, the Camerons barricading themselves in the back room while the blacks are breaking into the main room.

From the crosscut it is only a step to the flashback, whereby a scene is interrupted, not for the presentation of simultaneous action, but of past action. When the Little Colonel "relates a series of outrages that have occurred," flashbacks take the place of subtitles to represent what he is relating. When Phil Stoneman proposes to Margaret Cameron, Griffith interrupts the scene by a flashback to Margaret's brother, dead on the battlefield. Griffith used to say, "You can photograph thought." The interruption illustrates what he meant. When the proposal scene resumes, no subtitle is needed to explain what Margaret is thinking and therefore why she turns away.

Whereas Méliès, having by chance discovered the dissolve, included it in his films as part of the trickery, Griffith adopted it as a special kind of linking device. Although the dissolves in *A Trip to the Moon* may be said to link the scenes, they add nothing to the meaning, the scenes following one another in chronological order. But in *The Birth of a Nation,* by prefacing the Master's Hall sequence with a still photograph of the empty hall and then dissolving it to the hall filled with his actors, Griffith presents visible evidence of his fidelity to history, and the accompanying subtitle leaves no doubt as to the purpose of the dissolve: "AN HISTORICAL FACSIMILE of the State House of Representatives of South Carolina as it was in 1870. After photograph by 'The Columbia State.'"

Griffith depends considerably on the iris-in and the iris-out, whereby, in reverse order to that of the iris-in, a scene gradually disappears through a contracting circle. One does not notice everything in a full-screen shot simultaneously, nor does everyone notice details in the same order. The iris not only controls the attention of the spectator absolutely but compels all spectators to see similarly. The iris-in on the Ford's Theatre sequence singles out the young Stonemans and, opening to full screen, relates them to the locale. An iris-out on the scene of the riot in the Master's Hall centers attention on the cheering spectators at the right end of the gallery. The iris also has the possibility of other implications. The sequence prefaced by the subtitle "While the women and children weep, a great conqueror marches to the sea" opens with an iris-in on a woman and three children huddled beside the ruin of their burned-down house; then, the camera panning right, the iris opens to a full-screen shot of Sherman's men in the valley below. And to reinforce the relationship, Griffith reverses the order by panning the camera left from the scene in the valley to an iris-out on the huddled group on the hillside. Of the scene in which Lincoln, surrounded by his advisors, signs the proclamation calling for volunteers, Fred Silva refers to "a sense of war-caused loneliness."[7] After the advisors withdraw, Lincoln weeps. As though to emphasize his loneliness, Griffith closes the scene with an iris-out on Lincoln.

Although the fade-in and the fade-out are the cinematic equivalent of a curtain opening and closing a scene on the stage, Griffith does not consistently depend on fades in this sense. Many of his scenes fade in, but comparatively few fade out. On the other hand, the Ford's Theatre sequence, which opens with an iris-in, concludes with a fade-out. Here and there Griffith ends a scene in a fade-out only to reopen the scene in the following shot. Again the Ford's Theatre sequence is illustrative.

Titles are not inherent in the cinematic method—the first films had no titles—but Griffith incorporates them variously and effectively in *The Birth of a Nation*. There are continuity titles, that is, titles to link scenes or indicate action to follow. Griffith effects irony by following the title "War's Peace" with stills of the corpse-strewn battlefield, as in *A Corner in Wheat* he effects irony by following the title "Little thinking of the misery and suffering his so-called genius has induced" with a still of the poor at the bakery. Then there are subtitles which indicate dialogue, but Griffith depends on these sparingly. The Grim-Reaping episode, introduced by Lynch saying, "See, my people fill the streets," and constituting sixty-six shots, contains only two other subtitles.

Whatever the purpose of editing—to emphasize a particular detail, to increase suspense, to recall the past, to symbolize, to effect irony, to represent speech, or to "photograph thought"—the result must be clear to the observer. Editing must not be obvious, but it must not be obtuse. The observer should be impressed by the result rather than by the way the result is obtained. Even though successive shots may have been photographed days apart and in widely separated places, their arrangement can merge them into a coherent effect, and it is this effect which Griffith gets in his film.

Griffith made *The Birth of a Nation* before sound became an adjunct to the screen. But almost from the beginning, music had been an accompaniment to motion pictures. When the Lumière films were exhibited in New York in 1896, they were screened to a piano accompaniment. Méliès had a special score composed for *A Trip to the Moon*. Camille Saint-Saëns wrote his *Opus 128*, for strings, piano, and harmonium, expressly to accompany the first showing of *The Assassination of the Duc de Guise* in Paris in 1908. By 1915 scores had been composed for other films. But most films were screened to the accompaniment of whatever tunes the pianists chose, the piano being the standard musical instrument in motion-picture houses. There was an attempt, however, to match the mood of a film: lively music was played during lively scenes, solemn music during sad ones. Music publishing houses printed music to accord with various kinds of scenes. A book of sheet music for the motion-picture pianist would be indexed somewhat as follows:

Aeroplane	Chase
Band	Chatter
Battle	Children
Birds	Chimes
Calls	Dances

A piece of music entitled "Hurry No. 2" was intended "for scenes of great excitement, duels, fights, etc." Many of the tunes incorporated classical music. It was not Griffith's intention, however, to permit *The Birth of a Nation* to be screened to haphazard accompaniment. He and Joseph Carl Briel, who had composed music for *Queen Elizabeth* in 1912, composed a score for a full orchestra. Seymour Stern describes the music as follows:

The orchestral score as a whole was not original, consisting as it did of folk-tunes and symphonic selections. Some notable examples of the latter were *In the Hall of the Mountain King*, from the *Peer Gynt* Suite (played during the "evacuation of Atlanta" scenes); strains from the *Ride of the Valkyrie*, mingled with *Dixie* and also with other Wagnerian and other dramatic music (for the ride of the Clansmen); and innumerable fragments or mixed strains from Beethoven, Liszt, Rossini, Verdi, Tschaikovsky and other composers. However, the score did contain a number of original themes and tunes, especially composed by Griffith and Briel for the film, and of these, several have long since become famous: namely, a theme expressing barbarism, insolence and menace, played during the film-prologue, in the scenes depicting the introduction of Negro slavery into colonial America, and more especially during Part II, in virtually all scenes depicting the rise to power of the Negroes, after the Civil War; a somewhat related tune, expressing insolence, sadism and villany, played during the scenes featuring the Hon. Austin Stoneman, or his protégé, Silas Lynch; the love-theme music for the romantic "business" between the Little Colonel and Elsie Stoneman—(radio rights to the use of this motif were acquired by the comedians "Amos and Andy," who used it for years over the air as the opening bars of a musical introduction to their programme)—and, most famous of all, that weird blend of reed-whistles and horn-blasts, the Clan call, composed by Joseph Carl Briel, and played during the scenes showing the birth of the Ku Klux Klan, the summoning of the Clans and the ride of the Clansmen.[8]

Griffith worked with Briel and the orchestra to get the music just right. The orchestra was synchronized with bugle calls, artillery fire, and dance scenes to imitate sounds implied in the pictures. Karl Brown, Bitzer's assistant, recalls the imitative effect of the music when the sentry at the military hospital sighs. "The sigh," he says, "uttered by the cellos and the muted trombones softly sliding down in a discordant glissando, drove the audience into gales of laughter."[9] The musical score was thus a part of the editing. Years later, Griffith told an interviewer, Otis L. Guernsey, Jr., of the New York *Herald Tribune:*

The only pure art, if pure art exists, is music, and the sound pictures can't use it to best advantage. No sound track will reproduce the true melodic interrelation of instruments in an orchestra. We used to take films on tour with an orchestra to play the score, and we'd charge as much for admission as a regular legitimate road show. The music was very important—I can remember rehearsing a whole day to make the instruments give just the right sort of hysterical laugh for a scene in *Broken Blossoms.*[10]

The Birth of a Nation is an exciting film to watch. No other treatment of this ambitious theme equals it. Making allowances for the unfortunate bias in Griffith's interpretation of history, one can enjoy the film for its immensity of scope, the construction of its narrative, and its spectacular scenes. Even the sentimental love stories do not seriously distract from the realistic background on which they are imposed. Never had the motion-picture camera been used more boldly or with more variety, nor had there been such an effective use of close shots, close-ups, distance shots, and camera movement. But *The Birth of a Nation* is most fascinating for its editing. Griffith boldly cuts scenes before they are ended to transport the spectator at once in time and space. He juxtaposes long, medium, and close shots and varies the shots spatially and temporally while effecting variety in the objects of his camera. Woodrow Wilson said, "It is like writing history with lightning."

The greatness of the film is all the more impressive because it was almost independent of anything the art had produced.

Before *The Birth of a Nation* was released, Griffith had started work on a film called *The Mother and the Law,* which originated in his sense of irony in the activities of certain do-gooders. Meantime, however, having become involved in controversy over *The Birth of a Nation,* Griffith decided not to release *The Mother and the Law* by itself but to work it into a larger film that would have intolerance as the theme. Accordingly, he added to *The Mother and the Law* three other stories which purport to show intolerance in three other periods in history. Intolerance, Griffith says in the film, is the motivation of tyrants, groups and individuals, uplifters in all ages everywhere. It is the cause of persecution, torture, and war. Its only counterforce is love. The theme became the title, and Griffith produced *Intolerance* the year after *The Birth of a Nation.*

After the introductory titles, which announce that the "play," as the film is called, is made up of four separate stories, laid in different periods of history, and that the play turns from one story to another as the theme unfolds, the modern story—originally *The Mother and the Law*—begins. "In a western city," as the first title in the story states, "we can find certain ambitious ladies banded together for the uplift of humanity." The uplifters persuade Miss Jenkins, spinster sister of a wealthy manufacturer, to contribute to their cause. Miss Jenkins obtains the money from her brother, who, in self-compensation, reduces the wages of his employees. In the resulting strike some of the workers are shot. Another result of the strike is that the Boy and Dear One, as the hero and heroine are sentimentally called, leave for the city, where they meet and are married. Meantime, however, the Boy has become a victim of the Musketeer of the Slums. When he attempts to free himself from his evil environment, the Musketeer arranges circumstances so that he is sent to prison for a theft that he has not committed. The uplifters from the Jenkins Foundation take away Dear One's baby. Released from prison, the Boy is again charged with a crime of which he is innocent—of murdering the Musketeer—and is sentenced to be hanged. Through the confession of the murderess he is proved innocent, and through the efforts of Dear One he is saved from the gallows in a last-minute rescue.

The second story, the least developed of the four, opens in Judea in A.D. 27. In it the Crucifixion of Jesus is shown to be instigated by the Pharisees and other intolerant groups.

The massacre of the Huguenots in France on St. Bartholomew's Day, 1572, the subject of the third story, is made the result of religious intolerance. Catherine de Médici persuades her son Charles IX to order the massacre, reminding him of the massacre of the Catholics by the Protestants at Nîmes. As a result Brown Eyes, the heroine, is killed in spite of the hero's attempt at a last-minute rescue.

In the Babylonian story intolerance is depicted as the cause of Belshazzar's downfall in 539 B.C. The priests of Bel, intolerant of Belshazzar's worship of Ishtar, goddess of love, betray Belshazzar to Cyrus. Again an attempt at a last-minute rescue fails when the Mountain Girl warns Belshazzar too late that Cyrus is leading his army against the city.

The multiple plot enables Griffith to increase suspense in the modern story even beyond that engendered by the chase: before presenting the climax of the modern story, he ends the French story with the failure of Prosper to cross the city in time to save the heroine, the Babylonian story with the death of Belshazzar and the Princess, and the Judean story with the Crucifixion.

The four stories, which are told simultaneously, are united by the symbol of a woman rocking a cradle. Repeatedly during the film, particularly when cutting from one story to another, Griffith inserts in a vignette this symbol of the cradle, suggested by Walt Whitman's lines in *Leaves of Grass*:

Out of the cradle endlessly rocking,
I, chanter of pains and joys, uniter of here and
* hereafter.*
A reminiscence sing.

Griffith paraphrases Whitman for a title:

"Today as yesterday, endlessly rocking, ever bringing the same human passions, the same joys and sorrows."

In some of the cradle-rocking scenes, the Three Fates appear in the background.

Like *The Birth of a Nation, Intolerance* has a symbolic epilogue. Images of "canon and prison bars wrought in the fires of intolerance" dissolve into "flowery fields," the cross in soft focus appears on a split screen, and the film ends with the cradle-rocking scene.

Intolerance is also like *The Birth of a Nation* in its sentimentality. The epithets "Little Dear One," "Brown Eyes," "the Kindly Heart," "the Friendless One," are in keeping with Griffith's oversimplification of character. On the other hand there are bits of crude realism, as in the cutting off of the Persian soldier's head—reminiscent of the kinetoscope film, *The Execution of Mary Queen of Scots*—and in details of the massacre of the Huguenots.

The style is characteristically Griffith's. There is the studiedly developed suspense, not only in individual incidents, such as Charles IX's hesitancy in signing the fatal decree and the uncertainty over the outcome of the Boy's trial, but in the events leading up to the climaxes: Will Latour cross the city in time to save Brown Eyes from the mercenaries? Will the Mountain Girl reach Babylon in time to save Belshazzar from the Persians? Will Dear One reach the governor, and then the prison, in time to save the Boy from the gallows? The suspense in the climaxes is developed, of course, by the Griffith last-minute rescue, although in only one of the stories is the rescue accomplished.

There are not only the obvious comparisons among the four stories in *Intolerance,* which, in fact, Griffith called "A Drama of Comparisons," but also comparisons and contrasts in details. There are, for example, the two trials, the one in the Judean story and the one in the modern. The uplifters are the modern counterparts of the Pharisees. There is irony in the episode of the strike at Jenkins's plant: the reformers, led by the industrialist's sister, go to the workers' homes to keep the workers from sin; the company guards, called out by the industrialist, shoot the workers to keep the workers from striking. Here the ironic parallelism extends even to details:

"the reformers" vs. *"the guards"*
"led by" vs. *"called out by"*
"the industrialist's sister" vs. *"the industrialist"*
"go to the workers' homes" vs. *"shoot the workers"*
"to keep the workers from sin" vs. *"to keep the workers from striking"*

After the workers have been shot down, the camera, panning across the dead and wounded in the street, takes in a billboard on which is written the legend "The Same Today as Yesterday." It is said that this legend on a billboard, which Griffith saw from a train window as he was on his way from California to New York for the premiere of *The Birth of a Nation,* gave him the idea for *Intolerance.* "What a wonderful man, the Admiral Coligny, if he only thought as *we do!"* a courtier of Charles IX whispers to another courtier. "What a wonderful king, if he only thought as *we do!"* a Huguenot whispers to another Huguenot. The scene in which the uplifters take away Dear One's baby is concluded by the scriptural injunction quoted as a title: "Suffer little children to come unto me." The parallel shots in *A Corner in Wheat*—the poor people at the baker's unable to buy bread and the lavish banquet of the wheat king—anticipated similar ironic contrasts in *Intolerance,* as, for example, the lavishness of the Jenkins's home contrasted with the simplicity of Dear One's, or Egibi, "Babylon's greatest noble," served wine at Belshazzar's feast contrasted with the Mountain Girl milking a goat in the tenement district to obtain a drink for herself.

Symbolism, another favorite device of Griffith's, is as pronounced in *Intolerance* as in *The Birth of a Nation.* There is the familiar use of animals to represent attitudes and traits of people. Inanimate objects are made symbolic. A shot of Belshazzar's guard, the Mighty Man of Valor, sword in hand, is followed by a masked shot of the sword. Some of the continuity titles are superimposed on shots of a book entitled *Intolerance,* the leaves turning, of an emblem decorated with a crown and the fleur-de-lis, and of a bas-relief on stone. A long shot of the industrialist sitting alone in his office symbolizes his dominance, which is emphasized by the bare foreground.

Griffith worked even less from a script in making *Intolerance* than in *The Birth of a Nation.* The scenario for the film was entirely his own, but it existed only in his notes, which he destroyed before filming began. He seems to have depended on the inspiration of the moment for much of the direction. The actors were ignorant not only of the whole plan of the film but even of the plots of the stories in which they appeared.

Intolerance, which cost about half a million dollars, is not only more spectacular than *The Birth of a Nation* but more spectacular than any film that had been made previously, and in some ways its spectacle has not been equalled. In addition to the principals in the four stories, the cast numbered in the thousands. The film calls for settings representing widely different times and places. Whereas today such effects as these are more often than not obtained by models and process shots, Griffith had full-size sets built. The walls of Babylon were erected on a ten-acre plot near the present juncture of Hollywood Boulevard and Sunset Boulevard in Hollywood. Billy Bitzer, in a letter to Seymour Stern, recounted the building of the sets:

Imagine laying out what were to be the mammoth, stupendous sets for "Intolerance," without

Babylon during the siege (Griffith, *Intolerance*). *Courtesy of the Museum of Modern Art*

sketches, plans or blueprints at the beginning. . . . Mr. Griffith, "Huck" Wortman and myself would have a pow-wow as to how the sun might be, its approximate arc-position months hence —and that was the beginning of a set for "Intolerance," to which, as it progressed and became a fifty-foot-high structure, a hundred or more feet long. Mr. Griffith kept continually adding. So that eventually these walls and towers soared to a height of well over a hundred and fifty feet, although at the beginning their foundations were intended only for a fifty-foot height. Huck had to continually reinforce their bases for the ever-increasing height, which perturbed Huck a whole lot, and also shot my light-direction plans all to pieces.[11]

In variety of shots, no other film had equalled *Intolerance*. From its space-filling distance shot of the Persian army to a close shot of the sword of the Mighty Man of Valor, from a view of Belshazzar's feast as the observer looks down onto the court far below to close-ups of the feasters, it contains shots of varying distances and angles. To introduce the feast the camera shoots the court from a distance and from above—an establishing shot; then it comes down toward the court and tracks up the steps. In the modern story, it tilts up the wall of the Musketeer's room to reveal pictures rep-

Judea (Griffith, *Intolerance*). *Courtesy of the Museum of Modern Art*

resenting the Musketeer's taste. For the pursuit-of-the-train sequence, it was mounted on an automobile, as it had been for tracking ahead of the riding clansmen in *The Birth of a Nation*. A close shot of Mae Marsh's clenched hands expresses the Dear One's anxiety as to the outcome of the trial. The original print of *Intolerance* was tinted in shades of blue, red, yellow, green, and amber.

Observing that Griffith had modeled the farm scene in *A Corner in Wheat* after Millet, Bernard Hanson also sees similarity between the Babylonian set in *Intolerance* and John Martin's *Belshazzar's Feast*. Hanson points out that Griffith adopted not only the architecture and space of Martin's painting but the dramatic atmosphere, and he cites the shot in which the High Priest of Bel looks down upon the city he is planning to betray to Cyrus:

The High Priest (Tully Marshall) looks out of a rectangular window upon the city of Babylon. He sees an open square surrounded by low buildings and containing a colossal statue of Ishtar. But above this is a wild sky of dark moving clouds that scurry across a brilliant moon. The effect is strikingly close to Martin's painting except

The French court (Griffith, *Intolerance*). *Courtesy of the Museum of Modern Art*

that it comprises actual movement and change of light.[12]

Griffith gives careful attention to the composition of his shots. The camera in the modern story is directed across the row of prone soldiers, their guns pointed in parallel lines, and makes a composition comparable to that of the line of mounted clansmen in *The Birth of a Nation*. In the French story, the white of candles in the Huguenot home and of the headdresses of the Huguenot women contrasts strikingly with the dark background. Architectural features of the sets frame shots in the Babylonian scenes.

For example, when the High Priest looks down on the city, Griffith relates the character and the object of the character's attention by placing the camera to photograph the Priest in the foreground and Babylon, framed by an opening in a wall, in the background. The opening thus at once serves the purpose of a mask and is an inherent part of the scene. In the Judean story, a shot is framed by the arch of a gate.

Intolerance is important primarily for its editing. As in *The Birth of a Nation,* Griffith makes use of crosscuts, flashbacks, fades, irises, and dissolves. Catherine de Médici says, "Remember, gentlemen, when hun-

Belshazzar's feast (Griffith, *Intolerance*)

dreds of our faith perished at the hands of the Huguenots," whereupon a flashback depicts what is to be remembered. A flashback photographs the thoughts of the Friendless One as she is about to shoot the Musketeer. In the trial scene, a flashback gives the Boy's reply to the evidence against him. The iris is used, as in *The Birth of a Nation,* to open and close sequences. An iris-in on the great gate of Imgur-Bel introduces the Babylonian story. Comparing this use of the iris-in with its use in introducing Sherman's March-to-the-Sea sequence in *The Birth of a Nation,* Seymour Stern writes that "the camera retreats through the ages and time rolls backward."[13] A fade-out followed by a fade-in denotes a lapse of time in the scene in which the Dear One and the Boy are praying. The dissolve links the scene of the empty headquarters of the uplifters to a similar scene of the headquarters occupied, as in the two comparable shots of the Master's Hall in *The Birth of a Nation.* A dissolve makes a transition from a long to a medium shot of the uplifters, from a medium to a close shot of an alcohol still, and from a shot of the bell tower of St. Germain to that of a single bell. There are also dissolves in the epilogue. Griffith sought composition not only in the arrangement of photographed

Griffith (right) and Bitzer on platform; Mae Marsh and Miriam Cooper in car. *Courtesy of the Museum of Modern Art*

objects but also by editing. There is, for example, the masked shot of the Persian warrior falling from the wall, the shot blacked out at the sides to emphasize height. Processing gives the shot of the onrushing Persians a menacingly dark sky for a background.

The famous shots of Mae Marsh's hands in the courtroom scenes are alternated with shots of the Judge and of the Boy to depict the wife's anguish. Griffith was the first to appreciate the close shot as particularly cinematic—a means of emphasizing some-

thing already shown and of directing attention to it as the stage cannot. Any one of the sequences illustrates how editing guides the attention of the audience precisely as the director wishes. The scene in the death chamber in the modern story is made up of shots varying in spatial and temporal length, in angle, and in a subject—of the knives cutting ropes, of the guards' faces, of the Boy in his cell, of the trap falling. This is the method of a film, not of a play. It effects its purpose in a way that no other medium can. It is purely cinematic.

The High Priest looks down on the city (Griffith, *Intolerance*)

As in *The Birth of a Nation,* titles describe action to follow, comment, and indicate dialogue, and footnotes to titles document references to history. Continuity titles are superimposed on backgrounds suggestive, as pointed out, of the four stories. Titles underline Griffith's theme: "Brown Eyes and her family ignorant of the web intolerance is weaving around them"; "Cyrus repeats the world-old prayer to kill, kill, kill, and to God be the glory, world without end"; "Intolerance burning and slaying"; and "Returning to our story of today we find Miss Jenkins aligning herself with the Pharisees." In the final sequences, the titles are few. Relationships between situations having been established, explanatory titles would be redundant.

If it was necessary to establish that the unit of motion-picture construction is not, as in *Queen Elizabeth,* the scene but the shot, *The Birth of a Nation* accomplished it. *Intolerance* expanded editing, particularly in the presentation of simultaneous action. Griffith crosscuts not only within each of his four stories but from one story to another. At the beginning of the film he spends several consecutive minutes in getting each story under way—seven minutes on the modern story, four on the Judean, five on the French and, after a return for three minutes to the modern story, nine on the Babylonian. As he progresses, he cuts more and more frequently from one story to another. Toward the end of the film some of these cuts are lightninglike. In the climax, some of the shots are only one-fifth of a second in duration.

Although Griffith did not plan *Intolerance* or give it that title until he had made the modern story as *The Mother and the Law,* the modern story is the basis of the film. Each of the other stories is related to it. It not only introduces—and ends—the film but is the only story that Griffith returns to before he has introduced all of the others; that is, after beginning the third story, the French, he returns to the modern story before beginning the Babylonian. Furthermore, he devotes more of his film to the modern story than to any of the others. Ironically, however, only in an incidental way can its theme be considered intolerance at all. It is significant that the modern story had been a separate film with a conventional happy ending before Griffith decided to combine it with three other stories also purporting to be based on the same theme. Even if the ending were not happy, the story would not be primarily one of intolerance. The uplifters are intolerant, but they are only links in chains of circumstance. By securing Miss Jenkins's money, they indirectly cause the strike, and the strike indirectly causes the Boy to get into trouble. Later, the uplifters take away Dear One's baby, but the baby is of so little importance that Griffith does not have it returned to its mother at the end of the story. (According to Arthur Lennig, the final scene in the originally released print of *Intolerance* shows mother and baby reunited.)[14]

Neither is the Babylonian story, the second longest and most spectacular of the four and the *raison d'être* of the film, any more strongly based on intolerance than the modern story. Because the priests are jealous of Ishtar, they betray Belshazzar to Cyrus. But even if the priests' jealousy were intolerance, it is not the cause of the war but only, indirectly, of Belshazzar's losing the war. However, one does not really care which side wins. As Julian Johnson has observed, it is just a great show.

The weaving together of the four stories does not then produce the effect that Griffith intended. Nor does the cradle-rocking symbol overcome this weakness. The symbol is only a literary one, depending on the accompanying paraphrase of lines in *Leaves of Grass* for its meaning. As John Howard Lawson points out, nothing happens to the woman rocking the cradle. She is still only a literary symbol at the end of the film.

The greatness of *Intolerance* does not lie in the development of its theme or in its spectacle. Its greatness is in Griffith's execution of his plan. He appreciated, as no one else had, that in motion pictures, immeasurably more than in any other medium, there are means of compressing time, place, and action. He effects this compression in *The Birth of a Nation. Intolerance,* says Terry Ramsaye, was "the first and only film fugue." Its weaknesses, including the four separate stories told as one, make it a monstrosity, but the bold use of cinematic techniques by which the stories are told overcomes the weakness by greatness.

Intolerance had its premiere at the Liberty Theatre in New York on September 5, 1916. Because of the fame of *The Birth of a Nation,* the interest in the gigantic sets Griffith had built in California, and the announcements in the New York newspapers of "D. W. Griffith's Colossal Spectacle," the opening attracted even more attention and a larger crowd than had the earlier picture. The released print, 13,000 feet long, took almost three and one-half hours to screen, not including two intermissions. Deletions, some of them due to censorship, have since reduced the length of this time. The print distributed by the Museum of Modern Art Film Library runs 170 minutes.

As they had for *The Birth of a Nation,* Briel and Griffith composed a special orchestral score incorporating familiar music and played by the orchestra of the Metropolitan Opera House. The music was varied as well as familiar—Beethoven's *Minuet in G* for the peaceful scene in the Huguenot home before the massacre, Handel's *Largo* for the scene in which Jesus is scorned by the Pharisees, "In the Good Old Summer Time" for a day at Coney Island, and so forth. The film provides opportunity for considerable use of imitative music, such as bugle calls, bells, and gongs, as well as accompaniment to the various dance scenes.

In its first four weeks at the Liberty Theatre, *Intolerance* drew larger audiences than *The Birth of a Nation* during the same length of time, but attendance fell off thereafter, and the run at the Liberty was concluded after twenty-two weeks.

Financially, *Intolerance* was a failure. Although after the New York run the film toured the United States and Europe, Griffith never recouped the vast sums of money that he had poured into its production. The cause for the failure is said to have been that audiences were baffled by the rapid cutting among the four stories. Actually, however, Griffith introduces and develops the stories so clearly that the increased rate of cutting as the film nears its end can hardly hide the meaning. If the meaning is hidden, it is in the stories themselves, not in the way in which they are told.

Griffith continued to make films until after the coming of sound; his most famous ones, in addition to *The Birth of a Nation*

and *Intolerance*, are *Hearts of the World* (1918), *Broken Blossoms* (1919), *Way Down East* (1920), *Orphans of the Storm* (1922), *America* (1924), and *Abraham Lincoln* (1930). Like Méliès, Griffith was ignored in his later years by the industry for which he had done more than anyone else. Almost forgotten, he died in Hollywood on July 23, 1948. As if in atonement for neglect of their master, motion-picture people gathered for his funeral and testified to his greatness. The evaluation by his fellow director René Clair still holds: "Nothing essential has been added to the art of the motion pictures since Griffith."[15] Some of Griffith's successors have told more sophisticated stories in motion pictures, but Griffith created the way to tell them. His films reveal not only the growth of an artist but the process of creation.

7.
Expressionism

Because of Dickson, Edison, and other Americans, the motion-picture machine originated in the United States, and because of Porter and Griffith, motion-picture art also, but the evolution of motion pictures has been international. As early as 1898, five years before Porter made *The Great Train Robbery,* a German film called *Excursion* shows the rudiments of editing. *Excursion* is a short film of some bicycle riders but, unlike films of the time on comparable subjects—traffic scenes, waves breaking, trains approaching—*Excursion* is composed of several shots: a long shot of bicycles in the distance, a closer shot of bicycles winding along a road, a shot of the cyclists' faces, a shot of their legs in motion, and finally the cyclists in full shot. But the Germans did not continue to contribute to the rise of the art during its earliest years.

At the time of World War I, however, they struck out in an interesting direction. Some of the young Germans working in experimental theatres—directors, actors, scene designers—started experimenting with motion pictures. The style that their work took was expressionism. The most famous of all the German expressionistic films is *The Cabinet of Dr. Caligari,* directed by Robert Wiene and released in 1920.

This film originated in the experiences of its scenarists, Hans Janowitz and Carl Mayer.

At a fair in Hamburg in 1913, Janowitz, a young Czech, observed quite closely the suspicious actions of a shadowy figure in a park on the Holstenwall. The next day Janowitz read in the newspaper of a murder at the fair. Attending the funeral of the victim, he suddenly had the sensation of having discovered the murderer. After the war Janowitz met Mayer in Berlin and told him of his experience. Mayer, who had been an infantry officer in the German army and had come out of the war a pacifist, told Janowitz of having become embittered by a military psychiatrist who had examined him. The two discussed the possibility of making a film based on Janowitz's experience at Hamburg and Mayer's experience with the psychiatrist. Then one evening at a fair in Berlin they visited a sideshow in which a hypnotized strong man foretold the future. The collaborators now had their story. The title was the result of Mayer's happening on the name *Caligari* in looking through *Unknown Letters of Stendhal.*

The subject of their scenario is a mountebank, Dr. Caligari, who comes to a North German town called Holstenwall and obtains a permit to operate a concession at a fair. Ostensibly, Caligari's show is the exhibition of a somnambulist, Cesare, who answers questions about the future, but actually Caligari uses Cesare as an agent for committing murders. Finally detected by a student named Francis, whose friend Alan was one of Caligari's victims and whose fiancée, Jane, was kidnapped by Cesare, Caligari seeks refuge in an insane asylum. Pursuing him there, Francis discovers that the superintendent of the asylum and Caligari are the same person. With the assistance of members of the asylum staff, Francis finds in the director's office a book about an eleventh-century homicidal showman named Caligari whose agent is Cesare. Faced with the evidence that he has been emulating the original Caligari, the mountebank becomes violent and is placed in a straitjacket.

In undertaking the direction of the film, Robert Wiene put Janowitz and Mayer's story into a frame so that it is told by Francis as an inmate of the insane asylum. As the film opens, Francis and a fellow inmate are sitting on a bench in the garden of the asylum. Jane, who is also an inmate, passes by. "What she and I have experienced," Francis says, "is yet more remarkable than the story you have told me. I will tell you." As Francis goes on, "In Holstenwall, where I was born . . .", an iris-out on the asylum scene is followed by an iris-in on a picture of Holstenwall, and Janowitz and Mayer's story begins. And at the end of the story, when Caligari has been put into the straitjacket, the scene becomes the garden again. Francis is saying to his fellow inmate, "Today he is a raving madman chained to his cell." Francis and his companion then get up and walk into the courtyard of the asylum. Meeting Caligari there, Francis becomes hysterical and is overpowered by attendants, who carry him into the same room where Caligari was restrained. After examining Francis, Caligari announces, "At last I recognize his mania. He believes me to be the mythical Caligari. Astonishing! But I think I know how to cure him now." Thus the film ends, the frame device, it turns out, framing the story only at the beginning. Siegfried Kracauer makes the point that in representing the story of Caligari as told by a madman, Wiene changes the meaning, that whereas in Janowitz and Mayer's original scenario

madness is shown to be inherent in authority, in the revised version authority is glorified, and its antagonist is mad. The film, Kracauer concludes, thus mirrors the eagerness of the Germans, after the war, to withdraw into a shell.[1]

Wiene had chosen three scene designers to do the sets for *The Cabinet of Dr. Caligari*—Hermann Warm, Walter Röhrig, and Walter Reimann—and it was Warm's suggestion to paint light and shadows instead of representing them realistically. *The Cabinet of Dr. Caligari* evidences not only this distortion of reality but other manifestations of expressionism too.

Expressionism results from the attempt of the artist to express meaning beyond objective reality. The result is studied distortion. In expressionistic drama, which developed in Germany at the end of World War I, the resulting distortion is manifested in various ways: type—or even abstract—characters, kaleidoscopic sequence, unrealistic dialogue, frank use of the aside and the soliloquy, monodrama, symbolism, telescopic characterization, and so forth. The staging of expressionistic plays calls for a corresponding distortion that takes the form of expression of the medium of the stage itself: scenery and properties painted on backdrops, abstract settings, arbitrary lighting, vaudevillelike use of spotlights, robotlike stage movement and gesture, the extension of the acting area to include the auditorium as well as the stage, and so forth.

Some of these manifestations are evident in *The Cabinet of Dr. Caligari*. Not only are light and shadow painted on the sets, but the sets are deliberately distorted in perspective—in keeping with the madman's imagination. The shadows are painted to fall unnaturally. The opening scene of the story within the frame—the town of Holstenwall—is a painted one. The town clerk's desk and chair are unnaturally high to symbolize authority and to dwarf Caligari. There is sharp contrast between Cesare's black, tight-fitting costume and Jane's white, flowing gown to emphasize the girl's helplessness. Caligari's makeup gives the impression of

Expressionistic staging (Wiene, *The Cabinet of Dr. Caligari*). *Courtesy of the Museum of Modern Art*

camera moves, as, for example, in panning the faces of the men in the asylum office examining Caligari's book. There is cross-cutting between Cesare and Jane when Cesare approaches Jane's house and between Caligari and Francis when Francis, having become suspicious of Caligari, is investigating him. There is a flashback to show Cesare being admitted to the asylum. The story within the frame is, in fact, a flashback too. In making the transition from the frame to the story, Wiene cuts several times between Francis telling the story to his fellow inmate and the beginning of the story itself. Some of the transitions here, as in other parts of the film, are effected by the iris-out and the iris-in. "In Holstenwall, where I was born," reads the subtitle. An iris-out on Francis is then followed by an iris-in on a scene of the painted town on the hill. In an iris-out on Caligari, the circle contracts to the black stripes on the back of Caligari's light-colored gloves. The iris is used freely throughout.

The reason that *The Cabinet of Dr. Caligari* has had little effect on the development of motion-picture art is that the conspicuous characteristic of the film—expressionism—is almost entirely a matter of staging. Expressionism in *The Cabinet of Dr. Caligari* is effected no more cinematically than are the "arranged scenes" of *A Trip to the Moon.* For example, although there is expressionistic symbolism in the height of the town clerk's desk and chair, the effect is obtained as it would be in the production of a play on the stage: the camera merely photographs the scene. Similarly, the other elements of expressionism in the film are effected not by the camera but by the scene designers. Although the camera offers possibilities for distortion of reality quite as much as stage-craft does, if not more, Wiene chose to effect expressionism in the film as though the camera were only a recording instrument. *The Cabinet of Dr. Caligari* is famous for its expressionism, but the expressionism in *The Cabinet of Dr. Caligari* is of the theatre. The film implies the motion pictures primarily as a machine.

having been carelessly applied. Here and there the acting is stylized, particularly that of Werner Krauss as Dr. Caligari and of Conrad Veidt as Cesare. As Cesare attempts to escape, Veidt's body seems to lean against the wall as if, as Kracauer observes, the wall had exuded him.[2] The titles and subtitles in the original print of the film were represented in crooked letters.

Although expressionism in *The Cabinet of Dr. Caligari* is primarily a matter of staging, there are expressionistic elements in the story itself: telescopic characterization is represented in the identity of Caligari with the superintendent of the asylum, for example, and thus both characters are portrayed in the film by only one actor. In keeping with another expressionistic manifestation, all of the characters are types.

For all its stagelike methods, *The Cabinet of Dr. Caligari* has certain cinematic elements. Although most of the scenes are in medium shots, comparable to the method of *Queen Elizabeth,* there are cuts to close-ups and even close shots. Occasionally the

8.
Naturalism

When in 1923 Erich von Stroheim persuaded the Goldwyn Company to give him the opportunity to film Frank Norris's novel *McTeague,* the project seemed appropriate. In films that he had already made, von Stroheim had demonstrated the possibilities of motion pictures for realistic treatment of material. In assuming that he would appreciate the naturalistic *McTeague* and, as a gifted director, translate it properly into screen terms, the producers failed to take sufficiently into account that von Stroheim was an artist who refused to be bound by the conventions of his art. They were dismayed by his adaptation of *McTeague,* the colossal motion picture *Greed.*

Von Stroheim was born in Vienna on September 22, 1885. Until after his death, on May 12, 1957, it was supposed—because of the legend he had fabricated—that he was of noble Austrian birth, that he had been graduated from the Imperial and Royal Military Academy, and that he had held commissions in the Austrian army. It is now known that his parents were of the Jewish lower-middle class, that his merchant father was from Gliwice, in Prussia, and his mother from Prague. The prefix *von* was, accordingly, part of the legend. He came to the United States in 1909 after serving as a private in the Austrian army. Until he arrived in Hollywood in 1914 he was engaged in a variety of occupations, which would account, at least in part, for the realism in his films. He is said to have been a peddler of flypaper, a dishwasher, a railroad section hand, a book agent, a lifeguard, and a member of the New York National Guard. During World War I he was a familiar figure in films as a Prussian officer, monocled, stiff-necked, and aggressively unpleasant. In Griffith's *Hearts of the World* he not only was assistant director of the production but played this kind of part.

Von Stroheim ended his career as an actor rather than a director. As a refugee in the United States during World War II he acted in several films, in some of them resuming his German-officer roles—now Nazi. For two and a half years during the war he acted on the stage as the psychopathic brother in *Arsenic and Old Lace.* Then he returned to Paris, which had been his home for several years, and appeared in French films, including his own adaptation of Strindberg's *The Dance of Death.* In 1950 he was the butler in the Hollywood-made *Sunset Boulevard,* an ironic story of a faded star of the silent screen who cannot believe that she is no longer glamorous. There is another kind of irony in the role von Stroheim plays: that of the butler who was formerly not only the husband of the now-deranged actress but also a great director (in the concluding scene, to humor her, he pretends that he is directing her in a new picture), for von Stroheim's greatest contribution to motion pictures is as a director, although he made only nine films. There is further irony in *Sunset Boulevard* when the actress, played by Gloria Swanson, shows the hero a clip from one of her films. Arthur Lennig points out that the clip is from *Queen Kelly* (1928), which von Stroheim directed and in which Gloria Swanson played the title role.[1]

For all his flamboyance von Stroheim was a serious artist, and he was never more serious than when he made *Greed.* Although his previous films had been marked by their Continental background and sophisticated society, he had been fascinated by Norris's naturalistic *McTeague,* about working-class life in San Francisco at the turn of the century, and for years had wished for an opportunity to put it on the screen—drabness and all. Evidence of his seriousness is his dedication of *Greed* to his mother. It was not out of mere pique that he refused to see the film after the producers radically cut it. Having adapted *McTeague* to the screen as he believed a novel should be adapted, he considered the deletions a violence to his film and to his theory. Years later he told Peter Noble:

I had always been against cutting great chunks out of a novel to fit it into screen time. Some of the world's masterpieces have been hacked in this way to make a film director's holiday, but I always believed in putting a novel *completely* on the screen just as it was originally written.[2]

This is what he tried to do when the Goldwyn Company gave him carte blanche in 1923. To accomplish his purpose, he filmed *McTeague* almost paragraph by paragraph and with added narration of his own.

Filming a novel in this way would obviously result in a picture much too long. There is, however, nothing in the cinematic method of storytelling that determines how long a film should be. On the other hand, a film maker knows that an audience is in a theatre to see the film at one sitting—or

at one sitting with an intermission, as Griffith arranged to have provided for his audience in *The Birth of a Nation* and *Intolerance.* In this respect a film is comparable to a play. In *Alice-Sit-by-the-Fire,* James Barrie, who was a novelist as well as a playwright, makes a distinction between a novel and a play:

In a play we must tell little that is not revealed by the spoken words; you must ferret out all you want to know from them, although of course now and then you may whisper a conjecture in brackets; there is no weather even in plays except in melodrama; the novelist can have sixteen chapters about the hero's grandparents, but there can be very little rummaging in the past for us; we are expected merely to present our characters as they toe the mark; then the handkerchief falls, and off they go.[3]

Here Barrie the playwright is pointing out, in a stage direction very much in the manner of Barrie, the limitations that the stage imposes on the drama. A play is shorter than a novel because an audience can be expected to be attentive in a theatre for only a limited time, and it has been determined that this time is not much more than three hours. Since a film likewise depends on holding the attention of an audience in a theatre, the running time of most films does not exceed that of plays.

Von Stroheim's attempt to put *McTeague* completely on the screen resulted in a film of 42 reels, which would have meant a running time of about ten hours. The studio insisted that it be shortened; von Stroheim reduced it to 24 reels, and then permitted a further reduction to 18 reels, to be shown in two parts. Finally Metro-Goldwyn-Mayer, which the Goldwyn Company had become, turned the print over to a studio worker who cut it to 10 reels by eliminating not only the subplots but parts of the main plot as well, and by bridging gaps with subtitles. In the process McTeague's fight with Marcus in Frena's saloon was transposed so that in the released print it occurs after, instead of before, the wedding. The studio burned all the parts that had been cut, but the extant reels together with von Stroheim's script for the original film illustrate what von Stroheim meant by "putting a novel *completely* on the screen just as it was originally written." That *Greed* is not *McTeague* so reproduced can be seen from von Stroheim's own alterations, and that it could not have been is patent because the media of novel and film are different.

In the first place, von Stroheim changes the historical period of *McTeague*. His story commences in 1908, whereas Norris began writing *McTeague* in 1892 or 1893 and had completed it by 1898. Von Stroheim's purpose was apparently to bring the outcome of the story down more nearly to the time *Greed* was filmed—1923. Inasmuch as *Greed* includes actual shots of San Francisco streets and environs, von Stroheim may have decided on this change for the sake of verisimilitude, but in making the change he sacrificed absolute verisimilitude to the novel and thus compromised his theory.

Whereas Norris begins the novel by presenting the hero as an already established dentist, *Greed* opens with McTeague as a young man working in the gold mine. In the novel the gold mine episode is introduced indirectly and only briefly. Sitting in his dental chair in that scene at the beginning of the novel, McTeague is reminded by the tunes he is playing on his concertina of his life ten years earlier. In the film these recollections are presented directly; had von Stroheim put the novel on the screen just as it was originally written, these scenes would have been presented by flashbacks. This change to an earlier point of attack is significant, for it is characteristic of films to begin their stories at the beginning. *Greed* begins with an iris-in on the title "The Big Dipper Gold Mine, 1908, Placer County, California." For about ten minutes (an hour in the original print) and in contrast to the hardly more than two hundred words that Norris devoted to this part, the film presents McTeague's early life before it brings McTeague up to the point in the story at which the novel begins. Like many other films, *Greed* therefore requires no exposition.

Greed deviates from *McTeague* in the presentation of events near the climax. Chapter 21, which narrates McTeague's flight across Death Valley, ends as follows:

> He tramped forward a little farther, then paused at length in a hollow between two breaks, resolving to make camp there.
> Suddenly there was a shout.
> "Hands up. By damn, I got the drop on you!"
> McTeague looked up.
> It was Marcus.

The first part of chapter 22, the concluding chapter of the novel, tells of Marcus joining the posse to track down McTeague, of the rest of the posse giving up, and of Marcus going on alone. A third of the way through the chapter the action is brought up as follows to the point at which the preceding chapter ends: "'If he ain't got water with um,' he said to himself as he pushed on, 'if he ain't got water with um, by damn! I'll be in a bad way. I will for a fact.' . . . At Marcus's shout McTeague looked up . . ." This is the novelistic method of presenting simultaneous action. But, Griffith having shown him how motion pictures can manipulate time and space to an extent beyond that possible in a novel, von Stroheim rearranges the order of these incidents so that action in separate places is more nearly simultaneous. The flight-and-pursuit sequence opens with a continuity title: "McTeague had been missing from San Francisco for weeks when—" There follows an insert of a poster announcing a reward of a hundred dollars for the capture of "John 'Doc' McTeague." Then after a medium-long shot of a crowd in western gear looking at the poster, there is a close-up of an individual in the crowd; it is Marcus. After a few more shots to emphasize Marcus's connection with the crowd and its interest in the poster, there is another continuity title—"The fugitive." The next shots are of a valley and of McTeague leading his mule. The film now cuts back to Marcus and his associates. It is night. A brief sequence shows Marcus joining the posse to track down McTeague.

Again there is a continuity title—"That night desolation lay around Mac." A series of shots pictures the fugitive, unnerved, firing at imaginary pursuers, and then throwing his rifle away. Again the film cuts back to Marcus, who is starting out with the posse. This cut is made without a continuity title, for now the relationship between the two lines of action has been established. The sequence continues in this manner for fifteen minutes, crosscutting seventeen times between the pursuer and the pursued, before the lines of action are united by Marcus catching up with McTeague.

Such deviations from the novel are inherent in the difference between the epic and cinematic methods of narration. There are also arbitrary deviations, illustrating not only this difference but von Stroheim's failure to put *McTeague completely* on the screen. Mortimer Adler points out that "if a novel be adapted to the screen, it must be contracted in the direction of dramatic magnitude."[4] (By "dramatic magnitude" Adler means the limited number of characters and incidents in a play as contrasted to the larger number in a novel.) Even in its original 42 reels *Greed* illustrated Adler's dictum. For example, in narrating the events of the picnic, Norris writes:

In the afternoon Mr. Sieppe disappeared. They heard the reports of his rifle on the range. The others swarmed over the park, now around the swings, now in the Casino, now in the museum, now invading the merry-go-round.

Of the locales Norris mentions in this passage, von Stroheim included only the merry-go-round in his film, intercutting it with a scene in a shooting gallery as though to represent what "they heard." The merry-go-round would offer more interesting possibilities for filming than the other locales, and von Stroheim may have selected it for this reason. The point, however, is not that he selected the merry-go-round but that he selected. In the novel McTeague celebrates his engagement to Trina by taking the Sieppes to a variety show. Norris describes not only most of the acts in considerable detail but also their effect on the unsophisti-

cated theatre party. Von Stroheim filmed only one of the acts—a pair of knock-a-bouts—deleted in the abridgement. As in the picnic sequence, he selects, and by selecting he not only fails to put the novel completely on the screen but again demonstrates the impracticality, if not the impossibility, of succeeding. In the truncated print, the contraction in the direction of dramatic magnitude is of course only greater. The deletion of the subplots is part of this kind of contraction. And the deletion of the subplots results in the deletion of characters except those who appear in the main plot. Both the Old Grannis–Miss Baker affair and the Zerkow–Maria affair are deleted. Zerkow is left out entirely. Miss Baker remains as the patient in the dental chair when Marcus brings Trina to see McTeague and as a guest at the wedding, at which Old Grannis may be identified as best man. Maria sells Trina the lottery ticket and, at the wedding, waits on the table. Parts of the main plot are also curtailed, as, for example, details of McTeague's early life in San Francisco and some of the incidents after the murder of Trina.

On the other hand, here and there von Stroheim expands even the scope of the novel. Whereas, for example, Norris has Marcus tell McTeague about Trina's falling out of a swing and breaking a tooth, von Stroheim includes two scenes that were deleted when the film was cut—one of Marcus telling McTeague about the accident and another depicting the accident itself. Similarly he filmed not only the scene in which McTeague tells Trina about losing his job at the surgical instrument factory but, to precede it, a scene—not retained in the extant print—in which he is dismissed and paid off. In the novel the last appearance of the Sieppes is at the wedding. As they are saying their good-byes, Mr. Sieppe keeps calling, "Gome, gome, we miss der drain." Taking "der drain" as a cue, von Stroheim planned a sequence—not retained in the cut version—that began with an iris-in of the Sieppes at the Santa Fe Railroad Station loaded with boxes, satchels, and valises, pushing their way through the crowd into the main entrance. Then a series of shots shows them going through the station, out to the platform, and onto the train. Von Stroheim planned the sequence with his usual detail: Mr. Sieppe neglects to present tickets to the ticket taker at the gate and has to come back and put down four boxes to find the tickets, other travelers say good-bye to friends and relatives, Mr. and Mrs. Sieppe get on the train and enter the day coach but have to go back to help the children up, the car gives a lurch and Mrs. Sieppe drops her hatbox, which falls under the wheels, Mr. Sieppe retrieves the box. The sequence ends with an iris-out on a long shot of the departing train.

Scenes such as these seem to originate in von Stroheim's compulsion to tell everything, as though he, had he written *McTeague,* would have included them. In this respect there is a revealing sequence in *Foolish Wives* in which two people escape from a burning building by leaping from a balcony into a net held by firemen. Making a Griffith last-minute rescue out of the incident, von Stroheim intercuts the scene on the balcony with shots reminiscent of those in *The Life of an American Fireman:* a close shot of a fire-alarm box, a hand pulling down the knob; firemen sliding down the pole and climbing aboard the fire engines; a hook and ladder coming out of the enginehouse; fire engines on the way to the fire; and finally the arrival of the firemen at the scene.

The deletions in *Greed* that reduce the magnitude of *McTeague* illustrate the kind of contraction to which Adler refers. But Adler also observes about the adaptation of a novel to the screen that "it must be expanded with respect to dramatic detail."[5] (By "dramatic detail" Adler means the amount of detail in the development of single incidents.) Although the presentational nature of motion pictures makes this kind of expansion inevitable, the extent of the expansion depends on the director. That von Stroheim expanded Norris's two hundred words on McTeague's early life into an hour-long prologue is illustrative. Even the curtailed prologue illustrates this kind of expansion. McTeague recalls the episode

that led to his becoming a dentist, Norris narrating it in two sentences:

Two or three years later a travelling dentist visited the mine and put up his tent near the bunk-house. He was more or less of a charlatan, but he fired Mrs. McTeague's ambition, and young McTeague went away with him to learn his profession.

In the extant version of *Greed* the two sentences are represented in twenty-six shots. The expansion of the five words "he fired Mrs. McTeague's ambition" illustrates the difference between the epic and the cinematic methods of storytelling. A continuity title announces what is to be depicted: "Filled with the one idea of having her son enter a profession and rise in life . . . the chance came at last to Mother McTeague." These shots follow:

Fade-in to medium-long shot. A crowd in front of Mike's Saloon.

Medium shot. The crowd surrounds the dentist and the dental chair, in which is seated a Chinaman.

Medium-close shot. The patient in the chair. McTeague stands at right. The dentist extracts a tooth and holds it up for the crowd to see.

Full shot. Mrs. McTeague watches.

Medium-close shot. McTeague.

Close-up. Mrs. McTeague.

Medium shot. The patient leans over and spits, the dentist standing beside him.

Dissolve to scene of preceding shot. McTeague, in a black frock coat, is in the dentist's place. The patient stands up, reaches into his pocket for a coin, and pays McTeague.

Dissolve to scene of preceding shot. The dentist is in McTeague's place. The patient pays the dentist.

Close-up. Mrs. McTeague.

Medium shot. The crowd around the chair. *Fade-out.*

Von Stroheim filmed *Greed* before sound became an adjunct to the screen. In describing the wedding of Trina and McTeague, Norris writes:

Then Trina and the dentist were married. The guests stood in constrained attitudes, looking furtively out of the corners of their eyes. Mr. Sieppe never moved a muscle; Mrs. Sieppe cried into her handkerchief all the time. At the melodeon Selina played "Call Me Thine Own," very softly, the tremolo stop pulled out. She looked over her shoulder from time to time. Between the pauses of the music one could hear the low tones of the minister, the responses of the participants, and the suppressed sounds of Mrs. Sieppe's weeping. Outside the noises of the street rose to the windows in muffled undertones, a cable car rumbled past, a newsboy went by chanting the evening papers; from somewhere in the building itself came a persistent noise of sawing.

The predominant image in that passage is sound: the sounds in the room itself, the sounds from the street, and, finally, a sound from somewhere in the building—"a persistent noise of sawing." Without specifically naming it, Norris implies that, in spite of the immediate concern of the characters with a momentous event, the everyday world is going on just the same, and in "a persistent noise of sawing" he implies a premonition of discord in this marriage.

How would von Stroheim express in pictures the idea that Norris expresses in the noise of sawing? A similar problem arose when *What Price Glory?* was filmed three years later. The problem in *What Price Glory?* is solved by a title which reads: "Deafening roar of guns . . . shrieks of shells." Von Stroheim's solution is different. Recognizing that the street noises and the sawing are symbolic, von Stroheim changes the audio symbols into a visual one. During the wedding scene he points his camera over the shoulders of the bridal couple and past the face of the minister to the window. Through the window is seen, passing in the street below, a funeral procession. Lest there be any doubt as to his intention, he interpolates three more shots of the procession, one of them at close range and at street level. And

in his zeal to put *McTeague* completely on the screen, he represented the noise of sawing itself by a medium-close shot of "a hand holding a piece of hard wood while the other hand works a saw."[6] Among the deletions when the film was cut are six interpolations of this shot during the wedding.

Although this and other shots of the sources of sound—a train whistle, a bird singing, seals barking, the keyboard of the melodeon as Selina, playing, pulls out the stop labeled "Tremolo," a clock striking nine—were also cut out, comparable shots remain—a piano player (its open front showing the levers moving), the bellows of the concertina moving as McTeague plays, the bell in McTeague's office ringing, and so forth. To show that Trina, secretly polishing her gold coins, hears McTeague coming, von Stroheim cuts from a medium-long shot of Trina at a table to a close shot of McTeague's feet approaching along the hall, to Trina looking frightened, to McTeague's feet again, to Trina hurriedly picking up the coins, to a medium-close shot of McTeague reaching the door, to Trina hiding the coins in a trunk, to McTeague banging on the door, to Trina's going toward the door, and, after all this crosscutting, to a long shot of the room as Trina opens the door and McTeague enters.

The changes resulting from the translation of *McTeague* to *Greed* might be expected of an appreciative and imaginative director, particularly a director who had been an assistant to Griffith. Von Stroheim had learned, for example, the cinematic values in the varying distances of the camera from the photographed objects. *Greed* contains Griffithlike close-ups. There are close shots, comparable to those in *The Birth of a Nation* and *Intolerance,* of a bird's beak against McTeague's lips, of the McTeague cat, of McTeague's feet approaching along the hallway, of McTeague's feet—and the mule's—wearily treading the dry, cracked floor of Death Valley, of Marcus Scholer's clenched fist, of the gila monsters, of the rattlesnake, and of inanimate objects, such as part of an ore crusher, a jackknife, a watch fob, and so on. In the tracking away from the wedding group or in a pan shot emphasizing the vastness of Death Valley, movement of the camera in *Greed* is no less effective than Griffith's. The shots are carefully composed, whether in an iris-out on the buggy disappearing up the road into the distant hills or in a studied arrangement of actors, furniture, and wall decoration. As Mrs. McTeague watches, the dentist in his long white coat becomes her son in a long black coat. In the murder scene the doorway, draped in Christmas tinsel, ironically frames McTeague. The white of Trina's apron and of McTeague's jacket standing out against the otherwise dark costumes and dark background are reminiscent of the black and white contrast in the Huguenot home in *Intolerance.*

In its editing, *Greed* is no less Griffithlike. Crosscutting during the murder sequence not only effects dramatic irony but suddenly relates the immediate and horrible action to the everyday world, with which the murderer sooner or later will have to reckon. The crosscutting in the climax is in the manner of the Griffith last-minute rescue. Also suggestive of Griffith are some of the contrasting and parallel shots: Marcus getting "four bits" from McTeague and Trina counting her hoarded wealth; Trina fondling the gold coins and the mottled arms reaching down into the treasure chest; the empty canteen and the gold coins spilled out on the ground, and so forth. In its transitions, *Greed* is evidence that von Stroheim had learned from Griffith the effective use of the dissolve, the fade, and the iris.

The naturalists said that they were trying to write the truth. A prefatory title to *Greed* is a quotation from Frank Norris:

I never truckled. I never took off the hat to fashion and held it out for pennies. By God, I told them the truth. They liked it, or they didn't like it. What had that to do with me? I knew it for the truth then, and I know it for the truth now.

In its naturalistic motivation, von Stroheim's film is true to Norris's novel. Man, according to the naturalists, is the product of his heredity and his environment. In keeping with this sociological approach, *McTeague* is a story of disintegration of character. McTeague's downfall is partly caused by fate—that, for example, he meets and marries Trina, whose character is also weak. A continuity title in *Greed* reads: "First, chance had brought them together. Now mysterious instincts as ungovernable as the winds of heaven were uniting them." Since Norris implies that the hero's heredity is also responsible, von Stroheim, paraphrasing a passage in the novel, inserts this subtitle: "But below the fine fabric bred of his mother ran the foul stream of hereditary evil, a taint given him by his father." The prologue of the original film details the degeneracy of McTeague's father and his death from alcoholic poisoning. Fate is against the characters. There is always the chance that they may escape, but there is also the chance that they may not.

The film is also faithful to the naturalism of the novel in its detailed picture of working-class life in California at the turn of the century. The neighborhood in which McTeague lives on Polk Street in San Francisco is photographed with documentarylike realism. Von Stroheim is no less realistic in his picture of the dental parlors and McTeague at work in them than Norris, who is said to have studied *A Textbook of Operative Dentistry* to get McTeague's dental procedures just right. The wedding feast is filmed in scrupulous accord with Norris's description. Nor is von Stroheim any less realistic in making up scenes of his own, for example, the scene in the shooting gallery, for which his script specifies "all kinds of Dutchmen, in funny hats, with moustaches, with and without glasses, beer-bellies and mush faces; plenty of tin and brass medals decorate their manly chests."[7] Vividly recording the mores of a people at a particular time and place, *Greed* is no less a sociological document than *McTeague.*

The tendency of the naturalists to emphasize drabness of environment characterizes *Greed* as much as it does *McTeague.* The film by no means glamorizes. Von Stroheim

Naturalism (von Stroheim, *Greed*). *Courtesy of the Museum of Modern Art*

even outdoes Norris in drabness. In the courtship scene in the novel, Trina and Mc-Teague sit on the roadbed of the railroad along the muddy shore of San Francisco Bay. Von Stroheim, in still another deviation from Norris, has them perch on a concrete block over the sewer outlet, Trina having suggested, "Let's go over and sit on the sewer." The scene of the marriage proposal, the little railway station to which they return in the rain, could not have been represented on the screen less glamorously. Von Stroheim declared once:

I had graduated from the D. W. Griffith school of film making and intended to go the Master one better as regards film realism. In real cities . . . with real street-cars, buses and automobiles, through real winding alleys, with real dirt and foulness, in the gutters as well as in real castles and palaces. I was going to people my scenes with real men, women and children, as we meet them every day in real life. I was going to dress them as they actually dressed in life, in bad as well as in good taste, clean and dirty, faultless and ragged, but without exaggeration, without modification, and without the then currently popular concession to the conventions of the stage and screen.[8]

Although the Polk Street that Norris describes in *McTeague* (which he had considered entitling *The People of Polk Street*) had been destroyed in the earthquake and fire of 1906, a comparable neighborhood near the waterfront had remained the same since the nineteenth century, and here von Stroheim filmed the Polk Street scenes, including those in a house which stood on the corner of Hayes and Laguna streets and which he recognized as resembling the one that Norris describes as McTeague's. Norris based the murder of Trina on a San Francisco murder that he had read about. Von Stroheim filmed the murder scene in the house where the real murder had occurred. He also filmed other scenes in actual locations such as San Francisco Bay, the Santa Fe railroad tracks, the picnic grounds of Shell Mount Park, the Cliff House, and Death Valley. But he had an expensive set built to represent a San Francisco street because of the alterations that time had made in the real one. (Rodney Ackland points out an anachronism in the street scenes: although the cast is costumed according to the time of the story, the passersby wear clothes of the time of the filming.) The drearily realistic butcher shop with the fat butcher in his bloody apron, the saloon, the dental parlors, the Cliff House with its piano player—everything looks authentic. The camera again and again focuses on naturalistic detail such as the cracked washbowl, unemptied, and the bed, unmade, in the McTeague flat; the patch on the face of the man who announces that Trina has won the lottery; Marcus picking his ear—and his nose; the ragged bandages on Trina's fingers; and August Sieppe's agonized fidgeting after the theatre. Norris would have appreciated the faithfulness of von Stroheim's film to the slice-of-life treatment implicit in his novel.

Greed shows von Stroheim appreciative of another naturalistic trait of *McTeague,* and that is its irony. The introduction of the funeral procession during the wedding is a departure in fact from the novel but not from its ironic intent. Norris's irony is even heightened by the visual images in the film, as for example, Trina's gold pieces in contrast to the personal appearance of the McTeagues and their surroundings, the Christmas setting for the grisly murder—no less grisly for being presented indirectly—and the coins spread out on the floor of Death Valley as Marcus says, "We are all dead men."

Romanticism is, paradoxically, a characteristic of naturalism, and the romantic elements in *McTeague* appear as well in *Greed:* the heroine who wins five thousand dollars in a lottery and becomes a miser, the revenge motive that leads the villain into the desert after the hero, and the melodramatic ending are presented in detail and emphasized by subtitles.

Von Stroheim makes quite as much of symbolism, another paradoxical characteristic of naturalism, as Norris does. Many of the symbols are inherent in the naturalistic elements of the story. There is, for example, the rain. *Greed* is not a picture of sunny California. Rain interrupts the courtship scene, and rain makes the scene of the marriage proposal even drearier. Looking for symbolism in a work of art is precarious, but it is more than probable that symbolism is intended in details such as the tear in the photograph of the bridal couple or in the express train roaring by as McTeague embraces Trina. Here and there von Stroheim introduces symbols of his own, such as the canary fluttering in its cage as McTeague contemplates the anesthetized Trina, the cat leaping at the canary as McTeague reads the forbidding letter, and the cat's eye winking when Marcus tells the McTeagues that he is going away. If *Greed* seems to depend on symbolism even more than *McTeague,* it is because von Stroheim attempts to represent by visual images passages in the novel that he could not otherwise represent so readily on the silent screen. That some of

Filming the funeral procession (von Stroheim, *Greed*). *Courtesy of the Museum of Modern Art*

his symbols involve animals may be ascribed to his having been a pupil of Griffith. In the first scene of the film McTeague fondles a bird and, in the last, he frees the canary from its cage. In the original prints the gold-colored objects—the huge tooth, the bird cage and the canaries, the ore, the dinner service, the gold coins—were tinted yellow. The use of concrete objects as symbols is also reminiscent of Griffith. The unrealistic shot of mottled arms reaching down into the treasure chest is as obvious a symbol as the cradle-rocking shots in *Intolerance.*

The theme of *Greed* is that of *McTeague.* It is pointed up in incident after incident and emphasized by subtitles. The film, like the novel, shows the effect of greed not only on the hero but on the other two main characters. Greed causes the death of each of them. The one-word title that von Stroheim chose for his version of *McTeague* seems to have been almost inevitable.

But *Greed* is an anomaly. The way in which it is true to *McTeague* is at once its flaw and its virtue. Von Stroheim's theory of completeness in the transference of a

Gibson Gowland as McTeague in von Stroheim's *Greed:* In the murder scene the doorway, draped in Christmas tinsel, ironically frames McTeague. *Courtesy of the Museum of Modern Art*

novel to the screen resulted in a film monstrosity. The significance of *Greed,* however, is not so much in the extent to which von Stroheim compromised in his translation of novelistic terms into cinematic ones, original and interesting as these translations are, but in the extent to which he actually succeeded in his purpose.

9.
Montage

Sergei Eisenstein's approach to motion pictures was, like Méliès's, through the theatre. When Méliès first saw the Lumière films, he realized that the *cinématographe* was a means of expanding his performance of magic at the Théâtre Robert-Houdin. Eisenstein, also a theatre director, saw in motion pictures not just a means of expanding stage performances but a means of expression far beyond anything the stage could effect.

Although the films of Eisentein and those of Méliès could hardly be more different, there is a similarity in the backgrounds and early inclinations of these famous directors. Sergei Mikhailovich Eisenstein was born January 23, 1898 in Riga, Latvia. His father, of German-Jewish descent, was an engineer and architect; his mother was a Russian lady of independent means. At an early age Eisenstein showed an aptitude for drawing. Because his father wanted him to become an engineer, he enrolled at the Institute of Civil Engineering at the University in St. Petersburg, but chose a course within engineering that led, he said, "not to mechanical, technical fields but to one closely allied to art—to architecture."[1] When the Russian Revolution broke out, Eisenstein, having left the university to join the Red Army, contributed his artistic skill to the cause not only by decorating military supply trains with banners and posters satirizing the old

regime and glorifying the revolution but by directing propaganda plays. Early in 1920 he joined the Proletkult Theatre as a scene painter, but he was soon directing. By the time he was twenty-four years old, he had become one of the major directors of the Proletkult. It would seem that here was another Méliès—the prosperous middle-class background, the early inclination to art, particularly drawing, the parental wish that the son would follow the father's practical profession but, instead, the following of the original bent, the satiric spirit expressed in caricature for political purposes, the attraction to the theatre, and the attainment, at a youthful age, of a theatre directorship.

Here, however, the similarity ends. Méliès adapted motion pictures to the confines of the stage. Eisenstein, who found the stage too confining, seized on motion pictures as a means of breaking the confines entirely.

By the time Eisenstein saw Griffith's films, he had definite ideas about the difference between a play and a production of the play on a stage. "A written play," he said, "belongs to literature, and those who are interested only in its content should read it in the privacy of their rooms." The stage, he contended on the other hand, "belongs to the performers, for whom the play is merely, or, at most, a stenciled material on which their art is embroidered." He held that the director's function is to coordinate their efforts. Eisenstein used to say that he wished he could dispense with actors and use puppets instead. At the Proletkult he made the stage a circuslike arena, the audience on three sides. Indeed, his production of *The Wise Man* at the Proletkult in 1923 was more circuslike than theatrelike. In her biography of Eisenstein, Marie Seton refers to Eisenstein's stage at the Proletkult as "acrobatic." Her description of the production of *The Wise Man* implies not only the extent to which Eisenstein had broken with theatre convention but also a groping toward the kind of editing that was to characterize his films—montage:

The stage properties were unique. The floor of the arena was covered with a soft carpet, as necessary physical protection for the actors. Attached to the ceiling was the high trapeze. Scattered about for easy use were rings, horizontal poles, vaulting horses, slack wire, and other instruments used as the contiguous extension of a stage gesture. Thus, the actors, commencing a line of dialogue with relative dramatic formality, ended with a gymnastic twist. In place of the dramatically formalized expression of rage as hitherto employed in the theatre (even in the Meyerhold Theatre), the climax of the rage became the lightning flash of a somersault; while exaltation found expression in a *salto-mortale,* and lyricism in a delicate pirouette along a tightrope.[2]

When he saw Griffith's films, Eisenstein realized that motion pictures offered possibilities far greater than those hemmed in by the puny scope of the stage, even of his acrobatic stage, and that he had found the way to resolve his problem.

Eisenstein set about seriously studying motion pictures. Boris Ingster, who was one of his associates, says that during the day Eisenstein studied motion-picture photography and at night attended the only motion-picture theatre in Moscow showing American films. "We joined him behind the screen," says Ingster, "because none of us could afford to pay our way into the theatre night after night, and fortunately the friendly manager permitted the young film enthu-

siasts to watch the show from the vantage point of Eisenstein—a vantage point that gave one a rather distorted view of the proceedings." Eisenstein was impressed by the editing, but he saw something more in editing than, for example, the linking of scenes to effect flashbacks or crosscutting. He saw that, through joining together strips of film, it would be possible to link scenes different not just in time and space but in content as well. Then he evolved his theory of montage.

Soviet film directors found that they could join pieces of film, only a few frames in length, and obtain effects not inherent in individual pieces. It will be remembered that Porter made parts of *The Life of an American Fireman* from bits of film he found in the Edison factory. The Soviet directors, however, obtained their effects from joining unrelated shots—a theory that Eisenstein perfected, as Griffith had perfected Porter's.

Eisenstein came to realize that unrelated shots might be combined to imply something other than merely the sum of the concepts of the shots. He explains his theory in his books *The Film Sense* and *Film Form*. Citing a passage in Pushkin's *Poltava,* he says that "the poet magically causes the image of nocturnal flight to rise before the reader in all its picturesque and emotional possibilities":[3]

But no one knew just how or when
She vanished. A lone fisherman
In that night heard the clack of horses' hoofs,
Cossack speech and a woman's whisper.

Eisenstein points out that there are three shots in this passage: (1) clack of horses' hoofs, (2) Cossack speech, and (3) a woman's whisper, and that these three representations—they are sounds—are combined to evoke an emotional experience in the reader. To these three sound pictures, Eisenstein observes, Pushkin adds a visual picture, which has the effect of a full stop. It is a close shot:

And eight horseshoes had left their traces
Over the meadow morning dew.

Eisenstein's point is that Pushkin gives the reader more than the information that a woman has vanished—he has, in fact, said as much in the first line and a half—that, by combining the objective images, he gives the reader the *experience* of vanishing and that he does so by montage.

Eisenstein likens montage to the trope, that is, he says, quoting *The Shorter Oxford English Dictionary,* "a figure of speech which consists in the use of a word or phrase in a sense other than that which is proper to it," and he cites "a *sharp* wit (normally, a *sharp* sword)" as an example. Although of course montage is editing, it is editing of a particular kind. "To the parallelism and alternating close-ups of America," Eisenstein writes in reference to editing in American films, "we offer the contrast of uniting these in fusion, the montage trope."[4] He points out that Griffith's films do not contain "this type of montage construction," that although Griffith's close-ups create atmosphere and outline traits of character and although the close-ups of the chaser and the chased speed up the tempo of the chase, "Griffith at all times remains on a level of *representation* and *objectivity* and nowhere does he try through the *juxtaposition* of shots to shape *import* and *image.*"[5] He observes that in *Intolerance* Griffith attempted montage. But, he says, citing Griffith's description of *Intolerance* as "a drama of comparisons," that is all it remains—a drama of comparisons. And he explains why the attempt to unite the four stories by the cradle-rocking shot is unsuccessful: Griffith had been inspired to translate the lines of Walt Whitman, "not in the structure, nor in the *harmonic recurrence of montage expressiveness,* but in *an isolated picture,* with the result that the cradle could not possibly be *abstracted into an image of eternally reborn epochs* and remained inevitably simply a *lifelike cradle,* calling forth derision, surprise or vexation in the spectator."[6]

Akin to Eisenstein's conception of montage is the device in films whereby an interpolation of a shot of a speeding train, or of only the driving wheels, indicates a journey, or that of the hands of a clock rapidly turning, leaves being torn from a calendar, or a succession of shots of the same scene in different seasons of the year indicates passage of time. This kind of interpolation, or, as it is called, Hollywood montage, conveys only fact. True montage, on the other hand, implies, as Eisenstein says, "a juxtaposition of shots to shape import and image."

Montage implies that the way the film is built up, that is, the arrangement of the shots, is as important as, if not more important than, the content of the shots. Eisenstein, like Griffith, directed the taking of the pictures in a series of scenes bearing little similarity to the form the pictures would take in the completed film. The most important work in the making of *The Birth of a Nation* and, particularly of *The Battleship Potemkin* was not in photographing the scenes but in breaking them down and rearranging the pieces according to an artistic plan. In 1930 Eisenstein went to Mexico to make a film that he was going to call *Que Viva Mexico!* Because of a misunderstanding with Upton Sinclair, who was financing the undertaking, Eisenstein was not permitted to complete the film. Instead it was taken out of his hands, edited in separate parts, and released under separate titles, including *Thunder Over Mexico* and *Death Day.* But these films are ineffective because the editors did not know how Eisenstein had planned to cut the scenes into pieces and arrange the shots.

Eisenstein elaborated his theory of montage. It is significant that the passage he cites from Pushkin involves images of sound, because even before sound became an established adjunct to the screen, Eisenstein was already explaining how montage could be applied to sound in relation to pictures. In his books he distinguishes nine kinds of montage, including what he calls "chromophonic," or color-sound, montage. In an essay published in 1929 he discusses two kinds of montage he incorporated in *Potemkin*: rhythmic montage and tonal montage.

In rhythmic montage, he explains, "formal tension by acceleration is obtained . . . by shortening the pieces not only in accordance with the fundamental plan, but also by violating this plan."[7] Contending that "the most affective violation is by the introduction of material more intense in an easily distinguished tempo," he cites the Odessa-steps sequence in *Potemkin*:

In this the rhythmic drum of the soldiers' feet as they descend the steps violates all *metrical* demands. Unsynchronized with the beat of the cutting, this drumming comes in *off-beat* each time, and the shot itself is entirely different in its solution with each of these appearances. The final pull of tension is supplied by the transfer from the rhythm of the descending feet to another rhythm—a new kind of downward movement—the next intensity level of the same activity —the baby-carriage rolling down the steps. The carriage functions as a directly progressing accelerator of the advancing feet. The stepping descent passes into a rolling descent.[8]

Whereas in rhythmic montage, Eisenstein says, "it is movement within the frame that impels the montage movement from frame to frame," in tonal montage, movement "embraces *all affects* of the montage piece. [Tonal montage] is based on the characteristic *emotional sound* of the piece—of its dominant. The general *tone* of a piece." A typical use of tonal montage would be, he says, "working with the combinations of varying degrees of soft focus or varying degrees of 'shrillness,'"[9] and he cites as an example the fog sequence in *Potemkin,* that part of the film in which the harbor is photographed through the fog:

Here the montage was based exclusively on the emotional "sound" of the pieces—on rhythmic vibrations that do not affect spatial alterations. In this example it is interesting that, alongside the basic tonal dominant, a secondary, accessory *rhythmic* dominant is also operating. This links the tonal construction of the scene with the tradition of rhythmic montage, the furthest development of which is tonal montage. And, like rhythmic montage, this is also a special variation of metric montage.

This secondary dominant is expressed in barely perceptible changing movements: the agitation of the water; the slight rocking of the anchored vessels and buoys; the slowly ascending vapor; the sea-gulls settling gently onto the water.[10]

Appreciating the screen as a powerful means of propaganda, the Soviets nationalized the motion-picture industry in 1919. "Of all the arts," declared Lenin, "the most important for us in my opinion is the film." The nationalization of the industry was at once an advantage and a disadvantage to the Russian directors—an advantage in that it freed them from commercialism and allowed them to experiment whether their films made money or not and a disadvantage in that they were expected to make films glorifying the Revolution and the new ideology. Such were the conditions under which Eisenstein set out on his career as a director of motion pictures.

His first film was *Strike,* completed in 1924. *Strike,* which treats of the activities of the Russian working class in the days before the Revolution, is not a story so much as a mood. If there is a hero in *Strike,* it is the masses.

The next year Eisenstein completed *Potemkin,* and then in 1928 he made *October* —or, as the film was entitled outside of Russia, *Ten Days that Shook the World* —to commemorate the tenth anniversary of the October Revolution. *October,* like *Strike* and *Potemkin,* has no conventional story. The subject is the flight of Kerensky, the attack on the Winter Palace, and the victory of Lenin. Again the hero is the masses. That the cast was drawn largely from among the people of Leningrad, where most of the scenes were shot, represents both the experimental and the didactic in Eisenstein's films. To Eisenstein, actors are of the theatre, and motion pictures should depend upon them as little as possible. The hero being the masses, the masses are appropriately the actors. *October* thus has a documentarylike quality which is characteristic of all of Eisenstein's films.

Before he made *October,* Eisenstein started a film to have been called *The General Line,* but after completing *October* he reorganized and rephotographed *The General Line* and brought it out in 1929 as *The Old and the New.* Propaganda for collective farming, it depicts the advantages of modern methods and modern machines over primitive agriculture.

By the time he completed his next film, *Alexander Nevsky,* it was 1938. The screen had been talking for a decade, Eisenstein had visited Hollywood and had made his ill-fated expedition into Mexico to film *Que Viva Mexico!* and he had returned to Russia to find himself out of favor with the government. He was accused of being a bourgeois individualist and formalist. But either the political climate changed, or it was believed that Eisenstein had, and he was commissioned to make *Alexander Nevsky.* Although *Alexander Nevsky* is a sound film—with a musical score by Sergei Prokofiev—its best parts do not depend on speech, as for example, the charge of the Teutonic knights across the ice of Lake Ladoga. The sequence of the charge of the Teutonic knights is said to have been the inspiration for Laurence Olivier's filming of the charge of the French knights in *Henry V.*

Eisenstein's last film was *Ivan the Terrible* (1944), even greater in pictorial quality than *Alexander Nevsky.* Part 2 of *Ivan the Terrible* (completed in 1946 but not released until 1958), however, was criticized as not following the party line. But Eisenstein admitted error, and Stalin consented to his making the third part of the film, in which certain sequences from part 2 were to be included. Part 3 was never completed. On the morning of February 10, 1948, Eisenstein was found dead in his study in Moscow.

The most famous of Eisenstein's films is *The Battleship Potemkin.* Eisenstein had been commissioned to make a film about Russia's earlier, unsuccessful revolution of 1905. It was in fact to have been called *1905.* But after shooting scenes in Moscow and St. Petersburg, he was not satisfied with the results. Part of the trouble is said to have been that the weather in the north of Russia was unfavorable for photography. Then Eisenstein's cameraman, Edward Tisse,

came back from Odessa with reports of sunshine and the beauty of that city on the Black Sea. He was particularly enthusiastic over the great marble steps leading down to the shore and the curving quay. So Eisenstein changed his base of operations to Odessa. One of the incidents in the 1905 revolution had taken place off Odessa anyway—the mutiny aboard the armored cruiser *Potemkin* during the last days of the Russo-Japanese War. When Eisenstein arrived in Odessa, and saw for the first time the steps and the beach where the Tsarist troops had massacred the citizens, the scene so appealed to his imagination that he decided to discard the work he had already done on *1905* and limit the subject to the mutiny aboard ship and the immediately related events in the city. The original cruiser *Potemkin* had been scrapped, but for the scene of the meeting Eisenstein obtained the use of a ship of the same class—the *Twelve Apostles.* Since the superstructure of the *Twelve Apostles* had been dismantled, Eisenstein had it replaced by a replica of lath and plywood. The other shipboard scenes he shot on the cruiser *Komintern.* Most of the actors in the film were residents of Odessa and sailors of the Russian navy. Before he began shooting, Eisenstein reconstructed the Odessa incident of twenty years before. He talked to survivors of the massacre. "The only thing I need is contact with the people," Marie Seton quotes him. "How many times I have gone out with a preconceived plan of execution, all thought out, with sketches and drawings, and then, on feeling their nearness, I have changed the idea completely. It is they, in their spontaneity, who actually imprint on the film the great tone of reality."[11] The shooting of the scenes at Odessa and on shipboard in the harbor at Sevastopol took only twenty-three days. By the end of 1925 the film was completed and, Eisenstein having changed its title from *1905* to *The Battleship Potemkin,* it had its premiere on December 21, 1925, at the Bolshoi Theatre in Moscow.

Eisenstein builds the film in five parts, each part indicated by a subtitle. The hundreds of shots from which he composes the parts may be summarized as follows:

PART 1. *Men and Maggots.* The night watch aboard the *Potemkin.* . . . The off-duty watch (the crew's quarters). Vakulinchuk haranguing the sailors: "Comrades, the time has come to act.". . . Morning. Shipboard routine. . . . Sailors gathered about a chunk of maggoty meat: "We've had enough garbage to eat. Ship's doctor Smirnov: "The meat is good. No further discussion." . . . The cook preparing the meat. . . . The bowls of steaming soup set on the chain-suspended, swaying tables in the sailors' mess. . . . The sailors buying food from the canteen. . . . The galley. Sailors washing dishes. A sailor examining the motto on a plate: "Give us this day our daily bread." The sailor smashing the plate.

PART 2. *Drama on the Quarterdeck.* A Bugler. . . . The crew lining up on deck. Captain Golikov coming on deck. Officers lined up. "Those satisfied with the food . . . two steps forward!" Officers stepping forward. A few members of the crew stepping forward. "All others will hang from the yardarm!" Matyushenko rallies some of the men to the gun turrets. . . . Captain Golikov calling for the marines. Doomed sailors huddled at the edge of the deck. "Cover them with a tarpaulin!" The priest: "Lord, reveal Thyself to the unruly!" Executive Officer Giliarovsky: "At the tarpaulin —Fire!" Vakulinchuk: "Brothers! Do you realize who you are shooting!" Giliarovsky: "Shoot!" The marines lowering their rifles. . . . The crew taking over the ship. Officers thrown overboard. Vakulinchuk killed. . . . His comrades taking Vakulinchuk's body ashore in the ship's tender. . . . Vakulinchuk's body in a tent near the pier.

PART 3. *An Appeal from the Dead.* Fog over the harbor. . . . The dead sailor in the tent. . . . Citizens coming to view the body of the fallen hero. "We will remember!" A placard on Vakulinchuk's body: "For a spoonful of soup." . . . A message from the *Potemkin:* "Death to the oppressors!" . . . The crowd on the great steps watching the *Potemkin.*

PART 4. *The Odessa Steps.* White winged boats flying out to the *Potemkin.* . . . Food being passed aboard. . . . Rejoicing on shore. . . . People on the great steps. Suddenly, the Cossacks. The crowd being mowed down. . . . The brutal military power answered by the guns of the battleship. . . . The headquarters of the generals bombarded.

PART 5. *The Meeting of the Squadron.* Night aboard the *Potemkin.* . . . "Landing impossible. The squadron is on its way." The sailors' decision: "With one voice they decide to meet the squadron." . . . Shipboard activity. A bugler: "To battle stations!" . . . Sailors in the engine room. . . . An ammunition hoist. . . . Dials, the indicators moving. . . . A gun manned. . . . Shells handled. . . . "Full speed ahead!" . . . The ship's engines turning. . . . Water flowing past the side. . . . Black smoke from a funnel. . . . The ship's wake. . . . The engines. . . . The wave cast by the bow. . . . Smoke. . . . A ship's gun rising, the muzzle close up. . . . "The enemy is within range!" Signals from the *Potemkin* to the squadron: "Brothers!" The gun lowering. . . . The squadron sailing past. . . . Sailors at the rail cheering. . . . The *Potemkin* coming head on, its bow blacking out the screen.

Typical of Eisenstein, *Potemkin* presents a theme more than a story. The theme, symbolized by the ship, is resistance to oppression. The theme is inherent in the film from its beginning. The first few shots are of water flowing over a jetty and of water breaking over rocks, after which appears the first subtitle, a quotation from Lenin: "Revolution is the only lawful, equal, effectual war. It was in Russia that this war was declared and begun." There is, of course, the story of the mutiny, and the mutiny is led at first by an individual, the sailor Vakulinchuk. But Vakulinchuk is killed, and he too becomes a symbol, round which the people gather, and which makes the sailors only the more determined to throw off their oppressors. The hero is no longer Vakulinchuk, except as he exists as a symbol. The hero is the masses.

Thus the characters in *Potemkin* are not individualized. Here, in another way, Eisenstein's work is documentarylike. Eisenstein deliberately selected his actors to represent types. He used the word *typage* to describe his selection of a nonactor to play a particular role because the person seemed to him to represent the characteristics the role

The ship's surgeon in Eisenstein's *The Battleship Potemkin. Courtesy of the Museum of Modern Art*

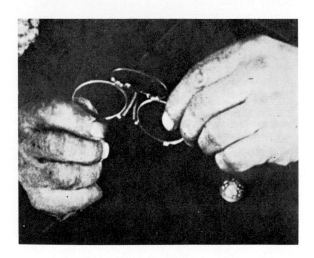

"The doctor with his sharp beard, nearsighted eyes, and nearsighted mind is perfectly epitomized by the pince-nez." *Courtesy of the Museum of Modern Art*

called for. Eisenstein's typage is comparable to what in the theatre is called type casting. Eisenstein once explained to Marie Seton how he applied his theory:

When he wanted to create a character, a street cleaner, for example, he went out into the streets and there observed the characteristics of people who were engaged in cleaning the streets. From the general characteristics he observed, he formed a composite image of a typical street cleaner. Then he searched for the individual who possessed the greatest number of traits observed in the many street cleaners, though he might in fact not be a street cleaner. When he found that person, he considered him as the best and the truest image of the "type."[12]

When he was filming *Potemkin,* he could not find anyone in Odessa who seemed to him to be the type of Smirnov, the ship's surgeon. But when he was in Sevastopol, where he had gone to shoot the shipboard scenes, he recognized in a hotel porter, who had become one of his prop men, the type he had in mind. The perky little doctor wears a pince-nez, which he takes off and folds together as a magnifying glass to examine the controversial meat. "The doctor with his sharp beard, nearsighted eyes and nearsighted mind," Eisenstein says, "is perfectly epitomized by the pince-nez in the 1905 style which is held in place, like a fox terrier, by a thin metal chain attached to his ear."[13] Eisenstein had also decided exactly what the priest, the ship's chaplain, should be like, and he found a gardener who fitted the type. He did not even need makeup. Eisenstein said: "A thirty-year-old actor may be called upon to play an old man of sixty. He may have a few days' or a few hours' rehearsal. But an old man of sixty will have had sixty years' rehearsal."[14]

The documentary quality in *Potemkin* is not in the characters alone. The staging is documentarylike for its background of Odessa and the Black Sea coast. In the scenes at sea, however, there is a lack of reality. Although the film is about a ship, the sea is slighted. The oncoming squadron, for example, is ridiculously close when it

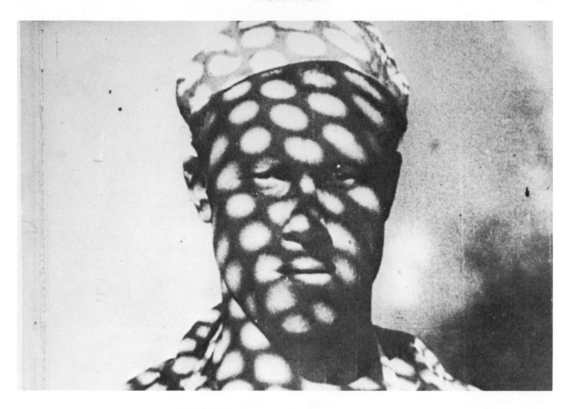

Composition (Eisenstein, *The Battleship Potemkin*)

is first sighted by the crew of the *Potemkin*. Eisenstein does not have the feeling for the sea that Robert Flaherty does. On the other hand, the harbor scenes are effective—the tender bringing Vakulinchuk's body ashore, the fog, the ships at anchor, and the gulls. Particularly documentarylike are the scenes aboard ship—the sequence of shots, at the beginning of the film, of the crew's quarters, shots of shipboard routine in the sequence before the mutiny and, in the last part of the film, the variety of shots as the *Potemkin* is got under way—the engines beginning to turn, the signal light flashing, the bugler sounding the alarm, and sailors manning the ammunition hoist, handling shells, and loading guns. Interspersed with these are other shots—of the water rushing past the side, of the ship's wake, and of smoke pouring from the funnels.

There is a great variety in the temporal and spatial length of shots and in angles. There are distance shots of the harbor, the Odessa shore, and the quay. There are close shots of a ship's dial, a candelabrum, a life preserver. It is a tendency of the Russian directors not to move the camera, and Eisenstein is no exception. In the scenes on the Odessa steps, however, Eisenstein had a trolley built large enough to hold himself, Tisse, the assistants, and the camera and carry them up and down the side of the steps to photograph the massacre. In making this sequence Eisenstein had a camera attached to a man's waist to photograph the scene as the man falls. There are tracking

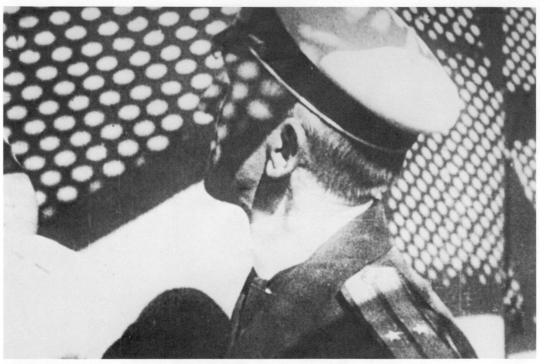

Composition (Eisenstein, *The Battleship Potemkin*)

Composition (Eisenstein, *The Battleship Potemkin*)

Composition (Eisenstein, *The Battleship Potemkin*)

shots of the tender moving through the harbor and a tilting and panning of the camera to show the people marching on the quay. But otherwise the camera is stationary. Eisenstein had Tisse change lenses instead of moving the camera, saying he did not want to disconcert his inexperienced actors.

Documentarylike as *Potemkin* is, there is hardly a shot in the film that is not carefully composed. The sailors' hammocks form a variety of geometric patterns. A ship's grating casts a checkered shadow on a sailor's face, emphasized by a close-up. The little boats on their way out to the *Potemkin* are photographed through a colonnade on the shore. The masts of the sailboats tied up at the curving quay fill a scene from foreground

to background, suggestive of the composition in the line of the hooded horsemen in *The Birth of a Nation*. The opening of a tent, through which the camera photographs the harbor, masks the shot triangularly. Two of the *Potemkin's* guns symmetrically frame the deck. The film is brought to a close as the great bow of the ship comes directly head-on until it blacks out the screen.

Eisenstein is a master not only in directing crowd scenes but in moving groups of people in studied composition. For example, he had Tisse set up his camera aboard ship to catch sailors simultaneously running in opposite directions at different levels, a ship's rail forming a dividing line from lower left to upper right in the manner of a split screen. Taking advantage of the steep slope from

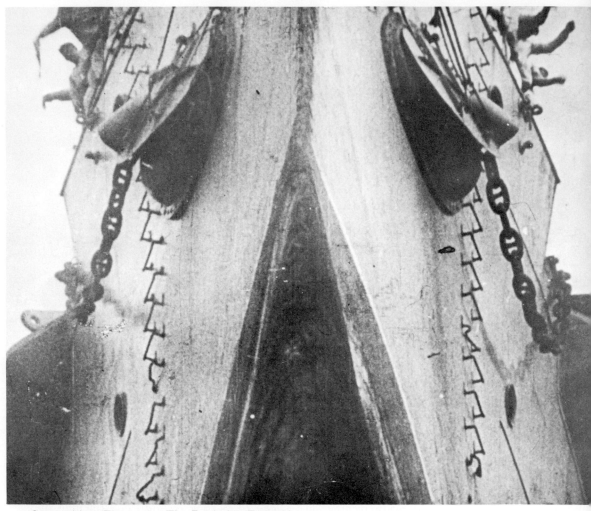

Composition (Eisenstein, *The Battleship Potemkin*)

The Battleship Potemkin

. . . masked to emphasize height.

Odessa down to the shore and of bridges, walls, steps, and other architectural features of the city, Eisenstein moves crowds in more than one direction in individual shots. A line of people moves down an incline from upper right to lower left while another line is crossing the scene from left to right at the bottom. In another shot the pattern of movement represents a line moving from right to left at the top while a second line comes in from center to left at the bottom. One of the lines may represent a curve, or two curves, or three. A crowd moves from lower left toward upper right through the arch of a bridge; joining this line, another group comes in from the left and moves toward lower center; at the same time a line marches across the bridge from right to left at the top.

Although Eisenstein seldom resorts to the dissolve, there are several dissolves in *Potemkin*. When Captain Golikov threatens the sailors with hanging, he points up. Then follows a shot of the yardarm as seen from the deck. After several shots of men and officers turning their heads to look—here again time is expanded—the shot of the yardarm is repeated. This then dissolves to a similar shot of the arm, except that now six men are hanging there. Here, of course,

Above, left, and facing page: Motion effected solely by editing. (Eisenstein, *The Battleship Potemkin*). *Courtesy of the Museum of Modern Art*

Eisenstein is effecting what Griffith meant when he said that "you can photograph thought." Two other dissolves in *Potemkin* are also reminiscent of Griffith. In the sequence in which citizens come to pay their respects to the dead dailor, a long flight of steps extends down the center of the screen, masked at the sides to emphasize height. This scene dissolves to that of the same steps crowded with people descending them. The coming of night aboard ship is implied by a dissolve from a shot of the deck massed with sailors to that of the empty deck. One is reminded of the photograph of the interior of the Master's Hall in *The Birth of a Nation* dissolving to the shot of Griffith's replica of the hall occupied by the Negro legislature or of the shot of the empty office in the modern story of *Intolerance* dissolving to that of the office bustling with uplifters.

But *Potemkin* is important most of all for its montage. Few films depend less on movement of the camera. Few depend as little even on movement within the scene. No other film depends so much on the arrangement of shots. Consider, for example, the prologue. Its two scenes—water flowing over a smooth jetty and splashing up in sheets and water dashing roughly over rocks —are separated into five shots, arranged alternately. They symbolize Lenin's words, quoted as the first subtitle. The scene in the sailors' quarters is built up by thirty-nine separate shots, on the screen an average of four seconds each. The action in this sequence depends almost entirely, except for five brief titles, on the arrangement of the shots.

The most cited example of montage in *Potemkin* is in the shots of the marble lions interpolated in the scene of the massacre on the Odessa steps. On a visit to the Alupka Palace in the Crimea, Eisenstein and Tisse were impressed by statues of lions decorating the steps from the palace down to the garden. Tisse photographed three of the statues, each representing a lion in a different posture—asleep, awake, and rising—and, together with a shot of a smoke-billowing gun on the *Potemkin,* Eisenstein added the shots of the lions to the massacre scene. Arranged in rapid succession—ten frames for the first lion, fourteen for the second, and seventeen for the third—the three shots give the impression of a single lion in motion—motion effected solely by editing. But the point is that, arranged with the other shots, they become a metaphor. "In the thunder of the *Potemkin's* guns," as Eisenstein says, "a marble lion leaps up in protest against the bloodshed on the Odessa steps."[15]

In the sequence of the mutiny, montage effects another kind of trope—a cinematic synecdoche. To show that the Russian church supports the Tsarist oppression of the common people, Eisenstein follows a shot of the priest tapping his crucifix against his palm with that of an officer fingering the hilt of his sword. And as though pointing up the synecdoche, the shots of these symbols—the crucifix and the sword—are close shots.

The shots interrupt the action at a crucial moment. The marines, lined up on deck, have been given the command to fire on the sailors massed under the tarpaulin in

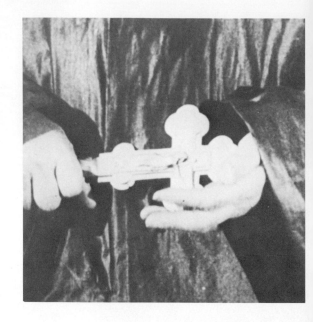

the bow. Eisenstein then, as it were, makes time stand still while he digresses to call attention to the affinity of the church with the military. He expands time even further by other digressions here. The incident, beginning with the officer's command "Attention!" and continuing until the marines lower their rifles, would in actuality be a matter of but a few seconds, but it lasts on the screen for nearly three minutes. The time is expanded by the interpolation of a series of shots, varying in spatial as well as in temporal length: a medium-close shot of two officers; a close shot of the executive officer; a long shot of the deck, the sea in the background; a medium-close shot of the marines; a long shot of the deck, the turret in the background; a distance shot of the ship on the water; a full shot of the tarpaulin over the sailors; a two-shot of Vakulinchuk and another sailor; a close shot of a life preserver; a long shot of the ship's bow head-on; a close shot of a bugle; and so on. The incident is edited in fifty-seven shots. Editing similarly expands time in

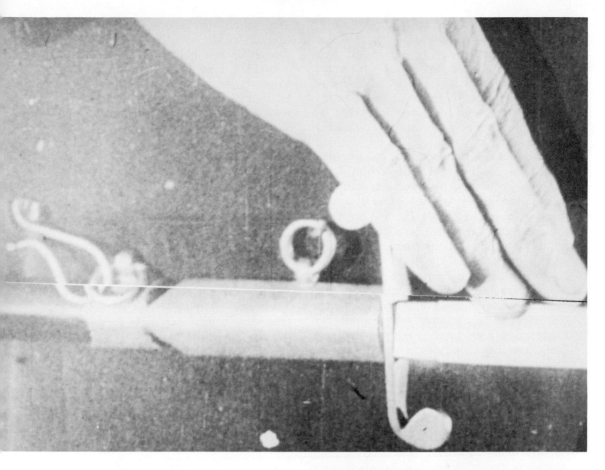

Above and facing page: Cinematic synecdoche
(Eisenstein, *The Battleship Potemkin*)

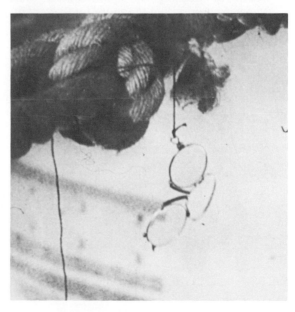

other parts of the film, particularly in the
scene of the massacre on the Odessa steps.

When the doctor is tossed overboard,
there follows a shot of his pince-nez caught
by its chain on a ship's line. The shot, constituting a cinematic synecdoche—the part
(the pince-nez) for the whole (the doctor)
—makes for even more effective montage
than the shots of the three lions because
the pince-nez is inherent in the action, not
imposed upon it. And it is effective for

"... taking the place of a whole surgeon."

another reason. As Eisenstein points out, "The prince-nez, taking the place of a whole surgeon, not only completely fills his role and place, but does so with a huge sensual-emotional increase in the intensity of the impression, to an extent considerably greater than could have been obtained by the reappearance of the surgeon-character himself."[16]

Potemkin is so cinematic that, watching it, one forgets that it is a silent film. It is, of course, enhanced by musical accompaniment, although, as Arthur Kleiner observes, it is "so completely absorbing and powerful a picture that anything could be played or nothing at all."[17] At the premiere the film was accompanied by the Bolshoi Orchestra. In preparation for the release of *Potemkin* in Germany in 1926, Edmund Meisel, a pioneer in film music, composed an orchestral score in accordance with Eisenstein's suggestions. Kurt London records that several European countries which permitted the showing of *Potemkin* forbade Meisel's score to be played with it because the provocative rhythms were liable to incite revolutionary instincts. "The rhythms which mark the departure of the mutinous ship, as the engines begin to move," London says, "have become famous and have since been imitated countless times."[18] His collaboration with Meisel in composing the score for *Potemkin* —reminiscent of Griffith's with Joseph Carl Briel in composing the score for *The Birth*

of a Nation—led Eisenstein to see the possibilities of the creative use of sound, although he was not to make a sound film until 1937. Lost from the time Hitler came to power, Meisel's score was found by Jay Leyda in 1971 in the Eisenstein Archives in Russia and, under the direction of Arthur Kleiner, was played to accompany a showing of *Potemkin* over television the next year.

Potemkin is the opposite of *A Trip to the Moon* because of montage. Whereas in Méliès's film the values are primarily in the photographed objects, in Eisenstein's they reside primarily in the way the photographs are arranged. Arrangement is the province of the artist. Willa Cather says in "The Novel Démeublé":

Whatever is felt upon the page without being specifically named there—that, it seems to me, is created. It is the inexplicable presence of the thing not named, of the overtone divined by the ear but not heard by it, the verbal mood, the emotional aura of the fact or the thing or the deed, that gives high quality to the novel or the drama, as well as to poetry itself.

For "page" may be substituted "screen." In *Potemkin,* as in any truly cinematic film, "the inexplicable presence of the thing not named" is effected by arrangement. Griffith established the principle of arrangement in motion pictures as *editing*. Eisenstein extended it as *montage*.

10.
Sound

"It is because the moving picture has per-force to do without the potent appeal of the spoken word that it can never be really a rival of the drama." Thus declared Brander Matthews in 1917.[1] And in 1917 most people would have agreed. Within a decade, how-ever, the premise would no longer hold, for in 1927 the screen began to talk.

Actually it had been talking before. From the time the motion-picture machine was invented, attempts had been made to match the pictures with sound. In fact, the idea of moving pictures, it may be remembered, first occurred to Edison as a device for recording and reproducing motion and sound simultaneously. Dickson said that in 1889, in his experiments which were to lead to the kinetoscope, he had synchronized a phonograph record of his voice with his image projected onto a screen. Some of the kinetoscopes were equipped with phono-graphs so that by means of earphones a viewer could hear the sound as though it were emanating from the picture. After the introduction of the *cinématographe* and other projectors, by which time phonographs were equipped with horns, a phonograph was sometimes linked with the projector. At the 1900 Paris Exposition, Sarah Bern-hardt was thereby both seen and heard reciting from *Hamlet,* and Coquelin from *Cyrano de Bergerac.*

But the combining of phonograph records with silent films was less than satisfactory, not only because it was difficult to synchro-nize sound with pictures exactly but because the sound from the phonograph could not be amplified. Although in 1906 Eugene Lauste, who had been associated with Dick-son in the Edison laboratory and had assisted the Lathams in building their camera, took out a patent in England for the recording of sound on film, his patent did not attract attention. In 1920 Charles Hoxie demon-strated a sound-on-film device in a labora-tory of the General Electric Company.

Meantime Lee De Forest had interested himself in sound films. Hearing that Earl Sponable, who, while employed by Theodore Case, had perfected tubes for recording sound on film, De Forest leased the Case-Sponable system, including a small pent-house in which sound was recorded while the film was being shot. With this equip-ment, together with his Bell and Howell camera and a microphone borrowed from the Western Electric Company, De Forest's cameraman, Freeman Owens, set up a studio for making talking pictures. Enclosing the camera in a padded telephone booth—to prevent the noise of the mechanism from reaching the microphone—he attached it to the penthouse and hung the microphone over the acting area. Then, on a printer which he himself had invented, Owens photographed the sound in striations along the film strip.[2] De Forest called the films phonofilms. Popular entertainers came to the phonofilm studio to be recorded in one-reel phonofilms, as entertainers of an earlier time had come to the Black Maria. When the phonofilm was first publicly shown—on April 15, 1923, at the Rivoli Theatre in New York, together with *Bella Donna,* a silent feature film—it was billed, like the original showing of the vitascope, as a device. "First showing of De Forest PHONOFILM the perfected talking pictures," read the advertisement in the *Times,* nor did the *Times* review of *Bella Donna* indicate the subject of the talking pictures.

Hollywood was unimpressed, or pretended to be. In the mid-twenties the big motion-picture companies were making money with silent pictures and did not wish to risk their profits by experimenting with sound.

But one of the companies was not making so much money as some of the others. In 1906 three sons of a Russian immigrant family—Sam, Harry, and Albert Warner—had given up the operation of a bicycle repair shop to open a motion-picture theatre in New Castle, Pennsylvania. Then, following the lead of the Mileses, they set up a film exchange. By 1912 the enterprising Warners, joined now by a younger brother, Jack, were producing motion pictures themselves. Their company, Warner Brothers, prospered, but by the mid-twenties it was outranked by Paramount, Fox, First National, and Metro-Goldwyn. The Warners were willing to try something different. So they tried sound.

In 1925, Warner Brothers signed an agreement with the Western Electric Company to make sound films. The project was called vitaphone, a device whereby electrically recorded sound on discs was synchronized with the motion-picture projector, and on the evening of August 6, 1926, Warner's introduced vitaphone at the Warner Theatre in New York. The program consisted of half a dozen shorts—including Will Hays, President of the Motion Picture Producers and Distributors of America, speaking; the New York Philharmonic Orchestra playing the Overture from *Tannhäuser,* and Giovanni Martinelli singing; and a feature film, *Don Juan,* starring John Barrymore. *Don Juan* was silent, but synchronized with it, by means of vitaphone, was a musical score. As at the initial showing of the vitascope, the machine was the thing. "A marvelous device known as the vitaphone, which synchronizes sound with motion pictures," Mordaunt Hall began his review in the *New York Times.*[3] Warner's produced two more programs of the same kind, one in the fall including *The Better 'Ole,* starring Sydney Chaplin, and another the following February—*When a Man Loves,* with John Barrymore and Dolores Costello.

Meanwhile William Fox inaugurated movietone, a sound-on-film device, with the presentation in January, 1927, of a short in which Raquel Meller was seen—and heard—singing. In May movietone presented a short incorporating spoken dialogue—*They're Coming to Get Me,* starring Chic Sale. With the filming of the departure of Charles Lindbergh on his transatlantic flight, Fox began the production of movietone newsreels.

Then on October 6, 1927, Warner Brothers presented *The Jazz Singer,* a feature film. The method of most of *The Jazz Singer* is that of earlier experiments with vitaphone, that is, music recorded on discs but dialogue represented by subtitles. In *The Jazz Singer,* however, not only is the sound of Al Jolson's singing synchronized with his image on the screen, but Jolson and Eugene Besserer are seen and heard talking. The few audible lines which they speak seem ad-libbed but, ad-libbed or not, they make of *The Jazz Singer* the first feature film incorporating spoken dialogue. One wonders, however, whether the very first of these lines was impromptu. It is Jolson's: "Wait a minute, wait a minute, you ain't heard nothing yet!"

Although *The Jazz Singer* did not at once convince the other companies, some of the exhibitors who had not been presenting vitaphone or movietone shorts began equipping their theatres with sound, and before the end of the year nine producers were licensed by the Western Electric Company to make sound films. The big companies, however, went on making silent films. Sound, they reasoned, might be just a novelty and, even if it did last, it was not certain that it would replace the silent screen. But in July of 1928 Warner's presented *Lights of New York*— the first "all-talking" feature picture.

Warner Brothers had won. Motion-picture theatres all over the country rushed to install sound equipment. Whereas in July of 1928 only 220 theatres in the United States were showing sound pictures, by the end of the year 1,000 theatres had sound equipment and, by the end of 1929, 4,000. Signs went up on theatre marquees: THIS THEATRE IS WIRED FOR SOUND. Attendance at motion pictures nearly doubled. Within a year after the release of *Lights of New York* Warner's obtained a controlling interest in First National and were on an equal footing with the other companies.

Warner's had produced not only *The Jazz Singer* and *Lights of New York* but a revolution in the motion-picture industry. And thus, indirectly, they were to revolutionize the art itself. In giving the screen a voice, they had made possible an aesthetic use of sound comparable to editing. The artistic linking of sound to pictures, however, was to take time, as the discovery of editing had taken time. Out of the machine had evolved an art. Now, by means of another mechanical device, the art was to be expanded.

Although there were those who, like Eisenstein, appreciated the significance of this new dimension and had, in fact, anticipated it and foreseen some of its possibilities, sound at first was exploited almost for its own sake, like a novelty. The introduction of sound was reminiscent of the introduction of the motion-picture machine, which had also been a novelty. Audiences were fascinated by the vitaphone much as, thirty years before, they had been fascinated by the vitascope. Their interest in the first sound films was in the sound, the voice matched with the actor, the sound with the source. The *New York Times* reported that in *Old San Francisco* (1927) "the earthquake episodes are embellished by the shouts of men and screams of women via Vitaphone."[4] But novelty was not enough, not for long. Only a year later the *Times* critic wrote of *Lights of New York:* "The only evidence of careful direction is in a cabaret scene when a door opens and the music seems louder. Then when it closes again, the music grows dim."[5]

Like the first motion-picture machines, the new device had mechanical limitations. To keep the whirring noise of the mechanism from reaching the microphones, the camera was housed in a thickly padded booth, a soundproof window in front, a padded door at the back. Whereas long before 1927 the camera had become flexible, the booth gave it a rigidity comparable to that of Edison's camera in the Black Maria and Méliès's in the studio at Montreuil. As a result the actors were once more confined to a limited playing space, as on a stage. In the early sound films shots are reminiscent of those in *Queen Elizabeth*. In fact, because of the microphone, stage movement was even more contained than in *Queen Elizabeth*. Microphones were hidden under tables, in lamps, in vases, and in other stage props, and an actor had to maneuver himself close to a microphone when it was his turn to speak. Motion pictures were hardly more than a mechanical device again.

If *Lights of New York* was a success, it was because of its novelty. Other "all-talking" films were rushed into production, and the phrase "100% all-talking" lured audiences into theatres in ever-increasing numbers. The term "movies" became "talkies," an appropriate epithet because in the new films the microphone overcame the camera.

Producers enticed actors from Broadway, for now the voice was the chief criterion, and not all of the actors who were experienced in appearing in silent films could adapt themselves to the new device. A voice at variance with screen personality, a speech defect, a regional accent, or even just inability to memorize lines lost some of the

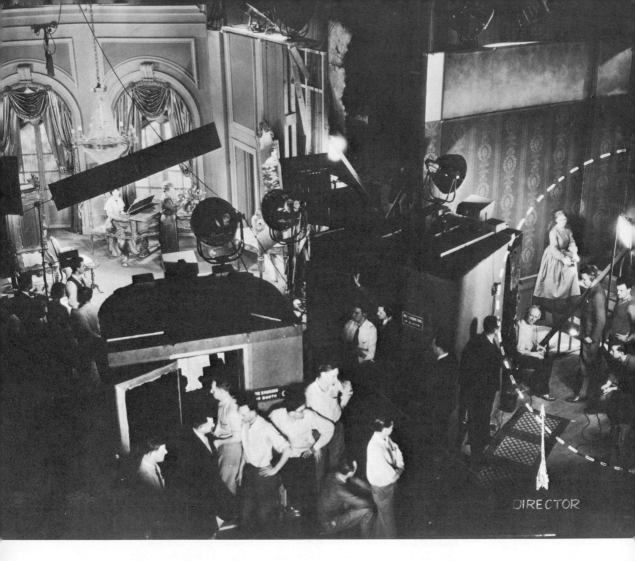

Camera booths—simultaneous rehearsal of two scenes from *Lummox,* 1930.
Courtesy of John & Susan Edwards Harvith

former screen stars the battle with the microphone. Furthermore, whereas in the silent
days the director could make the actor
almost entirely dependent upon him, audibly
directing every move and gesture, now the
actor was more on his own, and stage actors
had had experience in this kind of independence.

Producers also turned to Broadway for
scripts. Plays, which depend primarily on
dialogue, seemed even more suitable for

adaptation to the screen than before. They
seemed so suitable, in fact, that there was
a tendency to photograph them rather than
to adapt them. Not only had Brander Matthews's premise been upset, but the rivalry
to which Matthews had referred was, ironically, being reduced to mimicry, and the
art of the motion pictures to the machine.

Directors, however, began taking advantage of the possibilities of sound. Early in
1929 Fox released Raol Walsh's *In Old*

A movable camera in 1929—filming *The Taming of the Shrew* (Sam Taylor in beret; Carl Struss at his right). *Courtesy of John & Susan Edwards Harvith*

Arizona, not only its first all-talking feature film but the first of the kind to be shot out of doors. Mordaunt Hall declared in the *Times:*

The incidental sounds help in the unfurling of this yarn. They may be the appealing notes of mission bells, the tick-tock of a clock, the smacking of lips after a drink has been imbibed, the braying of a jackass, the plop-plop of horses' hoofs on the desert sands and other noises of sounds that help in adding to the naturalness of this adventure and avoiding, to a great extent, the disturbing sudden hushes that have marked so many talking pictures. Occasionally there is a notable silence, even in this film, but it is evident that much has been done to fill in with auxiliary sounds. . . .

In this film for the first time there is taken into consideration the fact that sounds grow fainter as the object is distanced. Horses' hoofs at first are distinct, but as the Cisco Kid or others gallop off the sound becomes fainter and fainter until it dies away.[6]

Of *The Ghost Talks,* Fox's second all-talking feature, produced a month later, Hall reported:

This picture begins with the arrival of the train, the sound of which is very true and without the grating that usually accompanies the beginning of such productions. There is then heard the greetings from passengers and those on the platform to meet them and eventually four of the characters start the real talking. Following the noises of automobiles the scene passes to the relative quiet of the interior of a hotel.[7]

"The shackles of sound," declares Frank Capra, whose career as a director spanned the coming-of-sound period, "set back film-making thirty years."[8] It set it back not only because the camera had become immobile but because the immobility of the camera inhibited motion of the actors. Once more art had to wait for the machine. It had to wait for the invention of devices to replace the padded booth and the set microphones. Capra writes cogently about the invention:

The cumbersome microphones hidden all over the set—with dead spots in between—were replaced with one sensitive mike on the end of an overhead movable boom, which followed actors everywhere, freeing them from static immobility. The Mitchell Camera people made a "silent" camera usable *outside* that prehistoric "fixed" monstrosity—the camera booth. May it rust in pieces. Once more the camera was free as a bird.[9]

Although the shackles of sound may have set back film making thirty years, film making was not long in recovering. Even before the advent of the silent camera, means were improvised to circumvent the limitations imposed by the booth. Scenes incorporating dialogue were filmed from the booth but filmed with a camera equipped with interchangeable lenses, which offset the effect of immobility. Spectacular scenes, such as those calling for crowds of extras but not necessitating dialogue, were filmed by a movable camera outside the booth—movable because it was mounted on a dolly—sound

effects for the scenes being added later. Karl Struss used such a contrivance in filming *The Taming of the Shrew* in 1929. Nor were all booths so inhibiting as Capra implies. Although Struss filmed most of the scenes in *The Taming of the Shrew* from within a booth, the booth itself was movable. In listing his choice of the ten best films of 1928, Mordaunt Hall explained, "The first ten films picked by this department for 1928 are silent films, and those among the number that were synchronized with sound effects cannot be said to have gained anything by the new device."[10] But the next year Hall included only one silent film in his best-ten list for 1929, and that one (*The Passion of Jeanne D'Arc*) had been produced in 1927. Films produced in 1929 would have been made under the limitations imposed by a camera not completely freed from its booth. As one of these, *The Taming of the Shrew* is particularly interesting for the extent to which it conceals the limitations.

The Taming of the Shrew resulted from the decision of Mary Pickford and Douglas Fairbanks to costar in a film. In 1929 a film based on a play would have been a natural choice. Half the films on Hall's 1929 list were adaptations of plays. Both Miss Pickford and Fairbanks had begun their careers on the stage. Both had reputations for comedy. Why not, then, a comedy offering them costarring roles? Why not for this well-known pair of actors, no less well known as a married couple, a comedy about marriage? Why not *The Taming of the Shrew?* The part of Petruchio would be well suited to Fairbanks, who was famous for swashbuckling roles exploiting his prowess in scaling castle walls, leaping from great heights, and fencing a dozen opponents in *The Mark of Zorro, The Thief of Bagdad, The Black Pirate,* and other such films. Calling him "a one-man circus who gave a three-times-three-ring performance and then jumped through all the rings at once," his biographers record that to prepare himself for his stunts in *Don Q, Son of Zorro,* in which he was to wield an Australian stockwhip as a weapon, "he brought an expert whip man from Australia and for six weeks he practiced whip-popping until he could use it like a twenty-foot extension of his own arm."[11] In *The Taming of the Shrew* not only Petruchio but also Katherine wields such a whip. Fairbanks and Miss Pickford financed the venture and released the film through United Artists, a company that they had formed together, with Charlie Chaplin and D. W. Griffith, in 1919.

Sam Taylor was chosen not only to direct *The Taming of the Shrew* but to adapt the play to the screen. The choice seemed a logical one. Taylor had directed Harold Lloyd films, for some of which he had also written the scripts, and Fairbanks's acting, like Lloyd's, was of a flamboyant, if less farcical, kind. Taylor had also directed Miss Pickford in two films; one of them, *Coquette,* he had helped to adapt from the George Abbott-Ann Preston Bridgers play.

Taylor's adaptation accords with the principal enunciated by Mortimer Adler; namely, that "if a play be adapted to the screen, it must be expanded in the direction of epic magnitude, but contracted with respect to dramatic detail."[12] (By "epic magnitude" Adler means the scope, for example of a novel, admitting of many incidents, scenes, and characters, and by "dramatic detail," the amount of detail in the development of a single incident, a play effecting detail by dialogue.) Although Taylor expands and contracts Shakespeare's play accordingly, he interprets is appreciatively.

The Taming of the Shrew is of doubtful Shakespearean origin; scholarly opinion is that Shakespeare may have been rewriting, or assisting in rewriting, an earlier play, *The Taming of a Shrew.* Its structural peculiarity is the induction. In the older play Christopher Sly's domestic relations are brought in, and at the end Sly says that he no longer fears his wife because he has learned how to tame a shrew. In the version ascribed, at least in part, to Shakespeare, the induction frames the play only at the beginning, Sly and the other characters in it never appearing again, with the exception of the few lines "the Presenters above speak." In the old play both the main plot and the subplot, about Bianca and her suitors, are farcical. Shakespeare does not change the almost extraneous subplot much. (John Masefield remarked that the subplot "seems to be by a dull man who did not know his craft as a dramatist.")[13] But Shakespeare cares about Petruchio and Katherine, and with them he turns farce into comedy of character. The situations remain farcical, but the clash of wills is comic.

The taming of a wife is not a theme that fits the modern world—or the Elizabethan world. It is a medieval theme. Dramatized in Shakespeare's time, it was played for fun, and that is the way Taylor plays it. As Katherine ends her speech on wifely duty on the word "obey," the shot changes to a close-up: Mary Pickford winks.

The film represents considerable contraction with respect to dramatic detail. Taylor deletes the induction and all but deletes the subplot. Bianca and the suitors are retained, except for Lucentio. whose part is combined with Hortensio's, but they are retained only to the extent that they motivate Petruchio's decision to woo Katherine. Also deleted is the scene in which Petruchio berates the tailor and the haberdasher. The scene on the road to Padua is contracted to the lines in which Petruchio and Katherine dispute about the sun and the moon and, altered to conform to nighttime, these lines are transferred to another scene. The scene about the wager is contracted to thirteen lines of Katherine's long speech on wifely duty and Petruchio's ". . . there's a wench! Come and kiss me, Kate." These and other contractions result in a script of hardly more than a quarter of the lines of the play.

In compensation for the contractions is the expansion in the direction of epic magnitude. The opening sequence illustrates this kind of expansion. From a close shot of a Punch and Judy performance, Punch pummeling Judy into submission, the camera tracks back to discover spectators standing in front of the miniature stage, continues back, and pans to encompass the crowd-

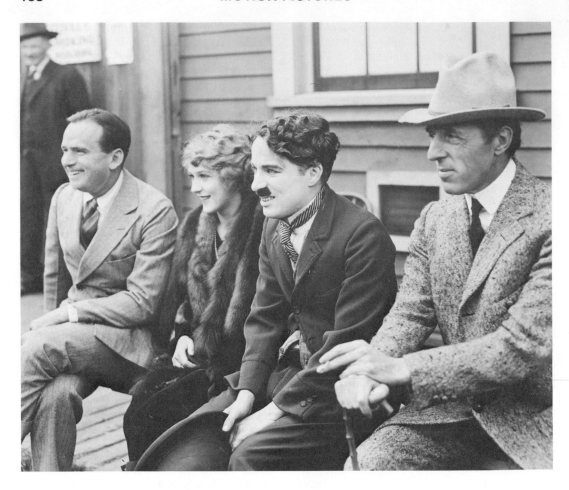

United Artists (Fairbanks, Pickford, Chaplin, and Griffith), February, 1919. *Courtesy of the Museum of Modern Art*

filled square in Padua—an establishing shot. Now the camera takes in a little band of musicians playing—and, of course, heard playing. Then, tracking forward at a different angle, it moves toward a street leading out of the square. In the second shot, which dissolves quickly from the first, the camera tracks up the street toward a doorway beyond which Hortensio is embracing Bianca, continues to a medium close shot of the couple, and then pulls back and pans left to reveal Baptista watching. Before Katherine is introduced, the camera looks past

a flight of steps toward an arched door at the top. Suddenly the glass in the door is shattered, the door opens, and, the camera pulling back, a servant falls through the doorway and starts tumbling down the steps. A reaction shot of Baptista intervening, the camera takes in the bottom of the steps as the servant lands sprawling on the floor. Now follow shots of varying spatial length —of bric-a-brac, a three-legged stool, and other props flying through the doorway, of Baptista being struck in the face by a large cushion, of servants rushing about to escape

Spectacle (Taylor, *The Taming of the Shrew*). *Courtesy of the Mary Pickford Company*

the barrage, of a dog running by, of a cat leaping from a chair to a desk and from the desk to an overhead shelf, the camera tilting up accordingly, of a painting ripped as its frame comes to rest over a servant's shoulders, and so on. Finally the camera moves up the steps and through the doorway and, slowly panning left, reveals the source of the violence—Katherine.

In thus expanding the scope of the play, Taylor depends not only on pictures instead of dialogue but on motion effected by editing and on motion of the camera itself. We see man and beast in motion, but the liveliness of the scene depends primarily on rapid cutting and the moving camera. The camera's tracking back at the beginning of the establishing shot links the close shot of Punch and Judy—epitomizing *The Taming of the Shrew*—with the rest of the scene. The introduction of the heroine effectively contrasts with all the motion in the preceding part of the sequence. When the camera finally comes to rest on Katherine, she stands all but motionless.

Some of the expansion results from direct

presentation of offstage action. In the play, for example, Grumio reports Katherine's falling off her horse into the mire. In the film the "report" is the basis for a slapstick scene. In the play Gremio tells Tranio (whom Gremio takes to be Lucentio) about Petruchio's behavior at the wedding:

I'll tell thee, Sir Lucentio: when the priest
Should ask if Katherine should be his wife,
"Ay, by gogs wouns!" quoth he; and swore so loud
That, all amazed, the priest let fall the book,
And, as he stooped again to take it up,
This mad-brained bridegroom took him such a
    cuff
That down fell priest and book and book and
    priest.

....

But after many ceremonies done,
He calls for wine: "A health!" quoth he, as if
He had been aboard, carousing to his mates
After a storm; quaffed off the muscatel
And threw the sops all in the sexton's face,
Having no other reason
But that his beard grew thin and hungerly,
And seemed to ask him sops as he was drinking.
This done, he took the bride about the neck
And kissed her lips with such a clamorous smack
That at the parting all the church did echo,
And I, seeing this, came thence for very shame;
And after me, I know, the rout is coming.

Gremio's description serves as an amusing interlude in the play. Directly presented, it would be ineffective or, at best, only farcical. In making the wedding not only part of his expansion of the play but the most spectacular sequence in the film, Taylor changes farce into conflict of characters. Accordingly he does not include Petruchio's most outrageous behavior—nor, it should be noticed, does Shakespeare—knocking the priest down and throwing sops in the sexton's face. Instead, he makes substitutions. The only detail he retains is Petruchio's profane reply to the priest, but even this he makes something other than farce. Of the instances of Petruchio's reported behavior, one in particular depends on sound: "And kissed her lips with such a clamorous smack/That at the parting all the church did echo." Only reported, the sound is literary. Futhermore, it is hyperbolic. Although it would have

been possible by means of the new device of the sound track to simulate the clamorous smack—Mordaunt Hall mentions the smacking of lips as one of the incidental sounds in *In Old Arizona*—and even the echo, Taylor substitutes another sound, that of Petruchio eating an apple. One advantage of the substituted sound is that it can be made continual—and is. The other is the way in which Taylor uses it.

The sequence begins with a screen-filling shot of bells ringing in the cathedral tower. This shot dissolves to a long shot of the facade of the cathedral, the camera tracking up to the door. Another dissolve takes us inside. Now the camera tracks ahead of the wedding procession, presented in shots of varying spatial length, and intervening are shots of Petruchio leaning against a pillar and loudly munching the apple. The procession reaches the altar and, as Katherine waits impatiently and the priest beckons to Petruchio to join them, Petruchio pretends not to notice. Finally, having eaten the apple, he strides across to the altar, slips the core into Gremio's hand—motivating stage business as Gremio attempts to dispose of the core—and takes his place beside Katherine. Now it is Katherine's turn to assert her will. In contrast to Petruchio's emphatic "Ay, by gogs wouns!" Katherine, when asked by the priest if she takes Petruchio for her husband, refuses to answer. A two-shot of bride and groom, the face of the former fixed in determination, cuts to a medium-close shot of Petruchio's foot stamping on Katherine's, whereupon comes an instantaneous "I do." At the conclusion of the sequence, we are again outside the cathedral. On the cathedral steps Petruchio and Katherine dispute, as in the play, whether they shall stay for "the wedding cheer." In the play Petruchio calls for his horse. In the film, by means of stop-motion, Petruchio—with Katherine in his arms—vaults onto the back of his horse and rides away. (Earlier in the film stop-motion also exaggerates Fairbanks's gymnastic ability as Petruchio leans over a balustrade and, with one hand, hoists Grumio up and swings him in an arc overhead.)

Depending as much on image as on dialogue, Pickford and Fairbanks in *The Taming of the Shrew*. *Courtesy of the Mary Pickford Company*

In the play Petruchio soliloquizes as to how he will tame Katherine:

Last night she slept not, nor tonight she shall not:
As with the meat, some undeserved fault
I'll find about the making of the bed,
And here I'll fling the pillow, there the bolster,
This way the coverlet, another way the sheets.
Ay, and amid this hurly I intend
That all is done in reverend care of her,
And in conclusion she shall watch all night;
And if she chance to nod I'll rail and brawl
And with the clamor keep her still awake.

Here again are lines that suggested to Taylor a scene by which to expand the play. And again, in creating the scene, he shows an appreciation of the difference between verbal narration and depiction on the screen. Instead of presenting Petruchio's plan in action—ineffective, if not impractical, as a scene in a film—he has Petruchio attempt to put the plan into action but fail because Katherine is made aware of the plan and thwarts him by outdoing him. When Petruchio pulls the coverlet from the bed, Katherine pulls off the mattress; when Petruchio opens a casement, and the curtains billow in a blast of wind, Katherine opens another casement; when Petruchio brawls—in loud but inarticulate sound—Katherine applauds, and so forth. In preparation for the scene Taylor has Petruchio speak the lines of the soliloquy, but he also has Katherine overhear him. Furthermore, he makes the soliloquy realistic by having Petruchio address it to his dog. ("It is probable," Strindberg writes in the preface to *Miss Julie,* "that a servant girl may talk to her cat, that a mother may prattle to her child, that an old spinster may chatter to her parrot.") Depending only slightly on dialogue—the few lines transposed from the scene on the road to Padua—the bedroom scene is amusing not only for its slapstick but for its dramatic irony, but the point is that both slapstick and irony depend on what we *see.*

Situations in Shakespeare's play also depend considerably on what we see, and the play lends itself to adaptation to the screen. Griffith chose *The Taming of the Shrew* as the basis for one of his early films, and there were a dozen other screen adaptations before the coming of sound. (Even Taylor's film was released in a silent as well as a sound version.) In contracting the play, Taylor tends to retain those parts depending as much on image as on dialogue. The combination of the credit titles—"By William Shakespeare/Additional dialogue by Sam Taylor"—on the original print naturally caused derision, but except for the lines spoken by the priest and an interpolated phrase here and there, the dialogue is Shakespeare's.[14] Taylor's additions are not so much dialogue as scenes, and the additional scenes depend primarily on pictures. Taking advantage of the innovation of sound, Taylor does not permit sound to take advantage of the film. The first Shakespearean play to be adapted to the screen after the coming of sound, *The Taming of the Shrew* represents not only the way motion pictures in that transitional period overcame the inadequacies of the machine but illustrates the principle by which a play is adapted.

If motion pictures were to rival the drama, they would have to do so on their own terms. If *The Taming of the Shrew* is more cinematic than *Queen Elizabeth,* the reason is not in the extent to which it depends on spoken dialogue, but the extent to which it does not. It is significant that the term "talkies" did not stick. For whereas drama depends primarily on dialogue, motion pictures depend primarily on pictures. Sound was to become established as a legitimate adjunct to the screen, but only as an adjunct, an embellishment to the pictures, not as a substitute for them.

11.
Creative Use
of Sound

The first great motion picture was not made until twenty years after the motion-picture machine was invented. Although *The Birth of a Nation* was filmed with equipment which represented an improvement over the *cinématographe,* the motion-picture camera had become flexible well before its flexibility was artistically exploited. Now that a device had been invented for recording sound on film, the art once more was to grope its way to the proper use of the machine. But this time it was not to grope so long. If there was any doubt that Brander Matthews had been mistaken in his pronouncement that the moving picture could never rival the drama because it lacked the potent appeal of the spoken word, the doubt should have been dispelled with the production of John Ford's film *The Informer* in 1935, less than eight years after the screen had begun to talk.

Ford said that *The Informer,* which he had filmed in only three weeks, was "the easiest picture" he had ever directed, adding, "No wonder. I had been dreaming of it for five years."[1] Ford, who has that quality of Eisenstein's, a social consciousness, is more concerned with the worth of the story itself. It is not chance that many of his films are adaptations of works of literary merit. He declared that a good story is one that tells of real people and real problems—a story

that has social meaning. Thus he was impressed by the cinematic possibilities in Liam O'Flaherty's tragedy of an Irishman involved in the Black and Tan troubles in Dublin in 1922. The background of the story appealed to him too, for although he was born in Maine (at Cape Elizabeth, February 1, 1894), his parents were Irish, and Ford had an affection for Ireland and the Irish people.

Ford was born John Martin Feeney, Feeney being the name his father had taken as an anglicization of the family name O'Fidne. In June of 1914, after graduation from high school in Portland, where the family had moved from nearby Cape Elizabeth, he went to Hollywood. There his older brother Francis, who had changed his last name to Ford, was already acting and directing. Ford began his career in motion pictures as an assistant property man and as a stunt actor. That summer of 1914 Griffith was filming *The Birth of a Nation* and Ford became an extra in it. "I rode with the Klansmen," he told Peter Bogdanovich years later. "I was the one with the glasses. I was riding with one hand holding the hood up so I could see because the damn thing kept slipping over my glasses."[2] In 1917, under the name of Jack Ford, he directed his first film *(The Tornado).* In a career that spanned more than half a century he made 130 films, some of them among the greatest in motion-picture history. Ford died on August 31, 1973.

Although it was ten years before he was known outside the industry, the trade papers from the beginning took note of the impact of his films and of his photography. Knowledgeable in all phases of motion-picture production, he had a firm conviction of the contrasting provinces of the director and the producer. "A producer's function has always seemed to me a casual one," he declared. "Pictures should be the result of a writer and a director getting together with the producer merely standing by in a fatherly way to chide them if they spend too much money."[3] Robert Parrish, who plays a soldier in *The Informer*, records that they were half way through the last day's shooting when Cliff Reid, the associate producer, ventured onto the set to praise Ford for the previous day's rushes. Ford called Joe August, the cameraman. "Joe, the front office likes the rushes, so there must be something wrong. We'll have to keep shooting until we find out what it is. We won't finish tonight after all." According to Parrish, Ford shot for two more days at an additional cost to RKO of about $25,000.[4] Ford, in a way, was his own editor. He expected his editors to know the way he had shot a sequence. "Indeed," declared Andrew Sinclair, "he often shot it only one way, without any cover shots to provide an alternative for cutting."[5]

Although Ford had become established as a director of silent films, he adapted himself, as Griffith somehow did not, to the changed nature of motion-picture art. "I use a minimum of dialogue," he says. "I believe the movies are primarily pictures, so I play them that way. Let the pictures do the talking for you." Although Ford's conception of the relationship of sound to pictures, thus succinctly stated, is not what Brander Matthews had in mind, it is the only relationship whereby sound can embellish the art without detracting from it. The convincing evidence of the validity of this conception is *The Informer*. In no film up to that time had sound been so considerably more than just a realistic accompaniment to the pictures.

Ford is said to have sneaked *The Informer* over on the producers, who were not fully aware of what he was doing. He had agreed to make the film without salary, taking instead a percentage of the profits. It was what Hollywood would have termed a "B" picture. The whole production cost only $218,000. It seemed at first as though Ford had miscalculated. For although *The Informer* opened at the Radio City Music Hall in New York (on May 9, 1935), it failed to attract large enough audiences and was withdrawn after only a week. But when it was shown in theatres throughout the country, it suddenly became popular, and its success was assured. The New York film critics voted it the best film of the year. The Academy of Motion Picture Arts and Sciences singled it out for several awards, including one to Ford for the direction, to Dudley Nichols for the adaptation, to Max Steiner for the musical score, and to Victor McLaglen, who plays the title role, for his acting.

The Informer is the story of a man's temptation, transgression, fear, remorse, retribution, forgiveness, and death—all within the hours of a foggy Dublin night during the exciting times of the Black and Tan troubles in 1922. Thus it has the unity of a Greek tragedy. A continuity title at the beginning, the only one in the film, reads simply: "A Certain Night in Strife-Torn Dublin—1922." As in O'Flaherty's novel, Gypo Nolan, a befuddled lout, has been expelled from the Revolutionary Organization for dereliction of duty. In need of money, he is tempted by a twenty-pound reward to inform on his friend Francis McPhillip, wanted by the British for the murder of a secretary of the Farmers' Union during a strike. Gypo informs, and Frankie, trying to escape from the Black and Tans, is killed. Now helpless without his more intelligent companion, Gypo becomes panic-stricken and is doomed. The rest of the film presents the course of his downfall, which culminates in his being tracked down by members of the Revolutionary Organization and shot. Dying, he is forgiven by the mother of the man he betrayed.

The Informer illustrates what Ford means when he says, "Let the pictures do the talking for you." As the film opens, Gypo appears out of the fog and approaches one of the reward posters, bearing Frankie's photograph. While Gypo is looking at the poster, there is superimposed on it a shot of him and Frankie in a bar singing and laughing. Then the superimposition fades out. Gypo pats the photograph affectionately, looks cautiously around, rips the poster from the wall, and throws it down. But as he walks away, the poster blows after him. Now he comes upon a little group around a street singer. As Gypo, leaning on the seat of a jaunting car, stands listening to the song, the crumpled poster blows against his leg. He looks down and, seeing the poster, tries to kick it loose. The singing continues. Gypo dislodges the poster, and it blows away. Before the song ends some Black and Tans appear, Gypo and the other listeners quickly disperse, and the soldiers frisk the singer. In the next scene Katie is being watched by the dandy. Seen in a close-up, her shawl over her head, she has a Madonnalike look. Then she jerks the shawl down over her shoulders and, as the camera pulls back, she is revealed as the streetwalker that she is. (Later she is to say to Frankie's sister, "I'm not the kind of girl you are. There was a time when I was . . .") Now the poster blows along the sidewalk and lodges against her feet. She kicks it loose. As the dandy comes up to Katie, Gypo appears. Gypo picks up the dandy and tosses him into the street. At this point Katie speaks the first word in the film: "Gypo!" Thus, in the first five minutes of *The Informer* there are established the mood of a foggy night in "strife-torn Dublin;" the situation on which the plot is to be based; the identity of three of the principal characters; the relationship of Gypo to Frankie and of Gypo to Katie; and the foreboding that Gypo may inform

on his friend. And during those five minutes not a word of dialogue is spoken.

A further relationship of Gypo to Frankie, particularly in regard to the twenty-pound reward, is also established without dialogue. As Gypo dislodges the poster, the camera, in a medium-close shot, concentrates on it against Gypo's feet and then shows it blowing off to the right. A few minutes later, with only the brief scene in which the poster blows against Katie's feet intervening, the poster appears again, this time blowing against the feet of some passerby: hands reach down for the poster, and the camera tilts up to reveal Frankie. In the next shot, as Frankie holds the poster in his hands, the camera points over his shoulder to emphasize that he is looking at his own picture. Then as he crumples up the poster and throws it away, he is startled by the approach of a squad of soldiers and darts into an archway to hide. When the soldiers flash their lights into the archway, one of the lights comes to rest on a poster, and Frankie's picture is spotlighted.

Nothing in this film is extraneous. Even the clocks tell part of the story. Because *The Informer* presents the almost uninterrupted experiences of a single night, transitions are not effected by fades but by dissolves, the only fades being those at the beginning and the ends of the film. One of the transitions is that from the scene in the Black and Tan headquarters to the scene in the McPhillip kitchen. Gypo has informed, and soldiers have been sent out to capture Frankie. As Gypo sits with his back to the camera, looking up at the clock on the wall of the police office, the camera looks up at the clock too. The hands indicate six minutes after six. Then the scene dissolves to one showing another clock, at the left of which is a closed door. In this scene, instead of pointing up at the clock, the camera points down. According to this clock it is sixteen minutes after six. The door slowly opens, and Frankie comes in.

In the novel the motivation for Gypo's betrayal of Frankie is expressed introspectively, O'Flaherty describing what is going on in Gypo's mind:

He seemed to be deep in thought but he was not thinking. At least there was no concrete idea fixed in his mind. Two facts rumbled about in his brain, making that primeval noise, which is the beginning of thought and which tired people experience when the jaded brain has spun out the last threads of its energy. There were two facts in his brain. First, the fact of his meeting with McPhillip. Second, the fact of his having no money to buy a bed for the night.

It would of course be possible to present these two facts cinematically. But Ford and Nichols decided on a different solution: they have Gypo inform so that he can get money to take Katie to America.

The motivation is presented almost as subjectively as in the novel. When Katie remarks, "Twenty pounds and the world is ours," Gypo grabs her and asks furiously, "What are ye sayin' that for?"

"Sayin' what—twenty pounds?"

"What are ye drivin' at?"

"Oh, Gypo, what's the matter with you? Twenty pounds! Might as well be a million."

As they speak these lines, they are standing in front of the sign on the window of the shipping offices:

Ⱡ 10
to
America
Information
Within

The dramatic irony is clear, because it has been established that Gypo has another sign in mind:

Ⱡ 20 Reward
Wanted for Murder
Frankie McPhillip

Furthermore, it has thus been made possible to represent cinematically the reason for Gypo's speechlessness at the sudden appearance of Frankie at Dunboy House. Superimposed over Frankie, as Gypo stares at him, is a printing from the poster:

Ⱡ 20 Reward

The printing dissolves out, but, after Frankie leaves, it reappears on the wall. Then follow two equally cinematic shots. They not only narrate the action from this point of the story up to Gypo's arrival at police headquarters to inform but, without a word of dialogue, present Gypo's thoughts. After the poster dissolves out, the whole scene at Dunboy House dissolves to that of the front of the shipping offices, the camera catching the printing on the window:

Ⱡ 10
to
America

Gypo comes on slowly, stops at the window, and looks in. The next shot is of the window from the inside. Gypo is now facing the camera. He looks down thoughtfully and rubs his face with his hands. The scene then dissolves to the exterior of the police headquarters as Gypo approaches.

Thought is somewhat similarly photographed when Gypo imagines that the girl at Aunt Betty's is Katie. The girl stands in the corner and Gypo, his back to the camera, in the foreground. As the spectator is thus made to look at the girl from Gypo's point of view, the girl's figure dissolves to that of Katie. Thought is photographed too when Gypo contemplates the ship model in the window of the shipping offices. Gypo's reflection is seen in the glass, and over it —and the model—is superimposed a scene representing Gypo and Katie on the deck of a ship, Katie wearing a bridal gown. Heard on the sound track are a few notes of "The Bridal Chorus."

In composing the music for *The Informer,* Max Steiner adopted what Oscar Levant has called "the Mickey Mouse technique." A chord of music imitates a door slamming, a few notes the falling of coins onto the floor, a run on a harp the blowing of cigarette smoke. Gypo swaggers along to the accompaniment of a march tune. When he rips the poster from the wall, a run of rough music imitates the action. The dandy strikes a match against the lamp post: music imitates the scratching sound. Gypo picks up the dandy and tosses him into the street: again music imitates. This imitative use of music is what Griffith had in mind when he rehearsed a whole day to make the instruments give just the right sort of hysterical-laugh accompaniment for a scene in the silent film *Broken Blossoms*.

The background music is evocative when Gypo stands looking at the printing on the window of the shipping offices:

$$£10$$
$$to$$
$$America$$

Accompanying this scene are a few bars of "Yankee Doodle." Also evocative are the notes of "The Bridal Chorus."

A money theme running through the film has a commentarial effect. It is expressed, as William Wooten has pointed out, in four descending notes, usually on a bassoon, against a background of woodwinds.[6]

Much of the music is inherent in the action. It is inherent, subjectively, when the shot of Gypo and Frankie singing in the bar is superimposed on the poster. The young street singer to whom Gypo stops to listen is singing "The Rose of Tralee" to violin accompaniment. The contrast between this singing and the menacing music heard shortly before—during the screening of the credit titles—is emphasized by a corresponding contrast of visual images as Ford cuts back and forth between the slight, sensitive-looking boy singing and the hulking, callous-looking Gypo listening. It is one of the unifying elements of the film that the same singer, still accompanied by the violin, sings at Frankie's wake. There is ironic contrast in the scene at Aunt Betty's as the raucous company earnestly sings Thomas Moore's Irish melody "Believe Me, If All Those Endearing Young Charms."

Here and there a situation is heightened by the very absence of sound. While the soldiers are flashing their lights into the archway and along the wall against which

Frankie is trying to hide, there is silence. A silence preceding a sound gives the sound added effect when, after Gypo has stood nervously—and in silence—in front of the major's desk in the police headquarters, the major snaps, "Yes!" The audience is as startled as Gypo. Conversely, an abrupt secession of sound may point up a situation. Shortly after Gypo has read the poster advertising a twenty-pound reward for information about Frankie, he is standing with Katie in front of the window of the shipping offices contemplating the sign which advertises passage to America for ten pounds. "Ten pounds to America," Katie reads aloud. And then as she adds, "Twenty pounds and the world is ours," the music suddenly stops. It stops suddenly when Gypo is surprised at seeing Frankie and, again, when Bartley's entrance interrupts the noisy scene at Aunt Betty's, and when Gallagher, concluding his enumeration of how Gypo has spent the money, speaks the meaningful words: "That makes just twenty pounds."

The addition of sound to motion pictures increased the possibilities of montage. It is not merely the use of sound to record literal dialogue that has made the screen the rival of the stage but the use of sound, together with pictures, to create "the inexplicable presence of the thing not named." The statement that a film tells its story primarily by pictures has had to be modified to include in "pictures" sound used cinematically, that is, montage. Furthermore "sound" should be taken to mean not only inarticulate sounds but speech used in any nonrepresentational way.

Speech may be used nonrepresentationally by a separation of sound from image and may thus photograph thought. As Gypo sits alone in the pub after he has received the money for informing, he whispers to himself, "I've got to have a plan! I've got to have a plan!" Then while the camera remains on Gypo, Frankie's voice is heard:

"Ah, Gypo, I'm your brain. You can't think without me. You're lost. You're lost."

The subjective point of view is effected cinematically in other ways. When Frankie runs into the archway to hide from the patrol, the camera, instead of pointing into the archway to show Frankie hiding there, photographs the scene from within the archway looking out. Thus the spectator is given Frankie's point of view. Frankie's death is also subjectively presented. As Frankie climbs out the window to escape, the camera points down at him and, still farther down, at the soldiers rushing into the yard and hurriedly setting up a machine gun. The soldiers aim the gun up at Frankie and thus at the camera—and the audience. The gun is fired, and the camera, still looking down on Frankie and the soldiers below him, catches, in a medium-close shot, Frankie's hand as it loses its grip and slips slowly over the ledge, the only sound the scratching of Frankie's fingernails. The shooting of Gypo is made subjective in a slightly different way. Gypo emerges from the house, stops, looks toward the foreground frightened and, as Bartley comes on at right, yells, "Bartley!" Then the scene cuts to a medium shot of Bartley looking toward the foreground, gun and hand in pocket. Bartley fires toward the foreground. Gypo is not in the picture at all. The shot is reminiscent of that in *The Great Train Robbery* when the outlaw fires "point-blank at the audience." In each the purpose is the same—to bring the audience into the situation.

Nichols says that he "sought and found a series of symbols to make visual the tragic psychology of the informer." Thus in another way, by an emphasis on the visual, the film is made subjective. The fog itself is subjective, for it represents what Nichols calls the groping primitive mind—the mental fog in which Gypo moves and dies. The officer's pushing the blood money to Gypo with a stick symbolizes contempt. The blind man represents, as Nichols says, the brute conscience. The first time he encounters the blind man, Gypo lurches at him and grabs his throat. When he realizes that he is blind, he lets him go. But the tapping of the blind man's stick follows him. Now just the sound has become a symbol—another effective use of sound separated from image. Later that night Gypo tries to buy off his conscience by giving the blind man a pound note. George Bluestone points out that Gypo's cap symbolizes security, that when Gypo is self-assured he wears his cap at a jaunty angle, but that when he is nervous and unsure, as in the Tan headquarters and at the court of inquiry, he twists it in his hand or wipes his face with it, and that from the time he is condemned, he goes bareheaded.[7]

The posters not only help to tell the story but symbolize the betrayal. The poster that Gypo tears from the wall follows him. At first he is not aware that it has become lodged against his leg, and, as soon as he is, he tries to kick it away. But it has impressed him, and he visualizes it when he sees Frankie a few minutes later. When he comes out of the police headquarters after receiving the money, he stops and looks at a bare wall: then there is superimposed on the wall one of the posters. In this poster Frankie's face is scowling. When the poster is burned in the grate, the firelight is reflected on Gypo's face. And when Gypo breaks out of the Bogey Hole, he imagines again that he sees one of the posters. As he looks at the wall of a building, the poster appears. Then as the poster disappears, Gypo clutches at the wall, calling out Frankie's name.

In predicting that the moving picture could never be really a rival of the drama, Brander Matthews implied that if the screen could talk, the rivalry would be based on dramatic terms. But the use of the sound track merely to synchronize sound with image does not represent art; it represents the machine. If *The Informer* errs in being less than realistic, its flaws are not due to its use of sound. No film had shown so widely and so well how sound may be used creatively.

12.
Documentary

Robert Flaherty's film *Nanook of the North* (1922), which had been financed by a fur company, so appealed to the Famous Players Company that Flaherty was sent to the South Pacific to photograph the life of the islanders there as he had photographed the Eskimos in *Nanook*. Flaherty called his film *Moana of the South Seas* (1926), and in reviewing it John Grierson referred to its value as "documentary"—the first time the word had been used in this way.[1] It comes from *documentaire*, a term by which the French described travel pictures. A travel picture is a documentary in the sense that it implies that the camera is present on the actual locale. In this sense newsreels are documentaries. In the same sense so were the first films of the Lumières.

A documentary, however, is more than an actual representation of life; it is an interpretation as well. A documentary is like a fictional film in that it is narrative. It is like a travelogue in that it is factual. It is also a unified record with a theme. Grierson calls it "the creative treatment of actuality."[2] Thus it implies motion pictures as not only a machine but an art.

Nanook is typical of Flaherty's films in that its subject is outside the pale of what is considered civilization. Like *Man of Aran* (1934) and *Moana,* it illustrates Flaherty's concern with man in a comparatively primitive state.

Flaherty's life was itself somewhat of a revolt against civilization. Flaherty was born in 1884 in the little community of Iron Mountain, in the Upper Michigan Peninsula, the son of a mining engineer. He attended the Iron Mountain School, but only when he felt like it and, when he did, likely as not, it is said, would show up at eleven o'clock smoking a cigar. When he was twelve he accompanied his father to the Rainy Lake region of Canada, where the elder Flaherty was manager of a gold mine. The settlement was made up of a rough element—miners, Chippewa Indians, gamblers, and other hangers-on of mining camps. Robert Flaherty's companions were young Chippewas. After two years of this life and a similar one in the heart of the Lake of the Woods country, where his father was next employed, young Flaherty attended Upper Canada College, a fashionable preparatory school in Toronto. He remained there only a little more than a year. Then, because he had shown an aptitude for mining, his parents sent him to the Michigan College of Mines. But academic study, even of mining, was not to his liking and after seven months he was dropped from college.

He undertook several jobs—working with

some Finns in a Michigan copper mine, and then in the gold fields again, and exploring with his father for iron in Canada. He traveled over the northern part of the continent, much of the way with an Indian and by canoe. At Hudson Bay he was told by the Eskimos of some great islands out in the bay, indicated on the charts as little reefs called the Belcher Group. At this time he was employed by the Canadian Northern Railroad, and he got the backing of one of the officials to explore these islands. On his first attempt his boat was wrecked in a storm, but, on returning to Toronto to report, he was encouraged to try again. In preparation for this expedition he went to Rochester, New York, and bought one of the early Bell and Howell motion-picture cameras so that he could record his discovery.

Back at Hudson Bay he set out on his voyage. He reached the islands and found that the Eskimos had been right. The main island in the group he discovered to be more than seventy-five miles in length. After staying so long on the island exploring that the ship was burned for fuel, he and the crew came back to the mainland in the whaleboat, a journey of ten days through the icy waters of Hudson Bay.

He had shot 70,000 feet of film and, having returned to Toronto, spent several weeks editing it. Then one evening, on completing the editing, he lit a cigarette and threw the match onto the floor. In a flash the film was destroyed. A positive print, however, escaped the fire. Flaherty showed it to the American Geographical Society, to the Explorers' Club, and to his friends. Then he realized how bad it was. It was just a series of disconnected scenes. Flaherty said it was boring.

Flaherty realized that it was bad because it was like a travelogue. He decided that if he went back north where he had lived for ten years and where he knew the people, he could make a film that would be different. It would be a film about a typical Eskimo and his family—a story of their

lives during one year. No motion-picture producer was interested, but finally in 1920 Flaherty persuaded the French fur company Revillon Frères to finance it. The subject was to be life in the vicinity of their trading station in northern Canada, and they would use the film for advertising in their competition with the Hudson's Bay Company. The scene of operations was Port Harrison, an outpost on the northeast shore of Hudson Bay. Flaherty took with him two Akeley cameras, which delighted him because of their gyro movement. Flaherty believed that he was a pioneer in the use of the Akeley, which could pan or tilt without a distracting jar or vibration and which he used in making all of his films.

On his arrival at Port Harrison in August of 1920, Flaherty followed what was to be his procedure in making documentaries—he became acquainted with the natives. They were to be his actors. He wanted to know them and he wanted them to know him so that they could work together. He established himself in a fifteen-by-twenty-foot hut, set up his generator, and invited the Eskimos in. His phonograph, which he kept continually going, fascinated them. The leading hunter in the community, an Eskimo named Nanook, meaning "the bear," was so pleased with the phonograph that he tried to eat a Harry Lauder record. When Flaherty told the Eskimos that he had come to live with them for a year to take their pictures, they roared with laughter. And when he showed Nanook some stills he had made of him, Nanook held them upside down, because the only image he had ever seen of himself had been his reflection in pools. Flaherty selected Nanook as the central figure in the film.

At the Eastman Kodak Company Flaherty had been shown how to do his own printing. He would project the day's rushes for the Eskimos so that they could see what was expected of them. Working without script, he allowed incidents that happened in the course of the filming to suggest the way to proceed. Thus his story developed out of the lives of the people and their environment.

The first incident he shot was that of a walrus hunt led by Nanook. When this sequence was printed, Flaherty invited the Eskimos into the hut to see the rushes, which he projected onto a Hudson's Bay blanket for a screen. The Eskimos kept looking back at the projector, the source of the light, until suddenly one of them shouted "ivuik," the Eskimo word for *walrus.* Then as the scene showed Nanook and his crew creeping down on the herd and Nanook throwing his harpoon, pandemonium broke loose. Here was a struggle for food, and as the harppon struck and the impaled walrus dove into the sea, the Eskimos shouted "Hold him!" and "Pull!" and clambered over the chairs to reach the screen and help Nanook with the harpoon line. From then on Nanook was constantly thinking up new hunting scenes to film.

Flaherty followed Nanook with a camera for two months hoping to get a picture of him harpooning a seal through a breathing hole in the ice. Finally a dead seal had to be used for this sequence. Lines were rigged to it under the ice, and a group of Eskimos out of camera range yanked on the lines while Nanook, together with his wife and three children, struggled with the harpoon rope. And this is the scene which Flaherty shot. "One often has to distort a thing," he used to say, "to catch its true spirit."

In his sixteen months in the north country filming *Nanook,* which he completed in 1921, Flaherty himself faced the dangers the Eskimos undergo. On one expedition in search of bear they were caught in a drifter, a northern storm so fierce that the flying snow can choke an Eskimo dog to death. They built an igloo and holed in for eight days. On this same expedition, in which they traveled 600 miles over sea ice, Flaherty nearly starved to death. Two years before his death (in 1951), Flaherty told an interviewer:

An Eskimo lives with menace. It is always ahead of him, over the next white ridge. A storm may be waiting, the game may be gone. The trip on sea ice may leave him on drifting pans. His dogs are dangerous. Eskimo Huskies are like wolves, of course, and they'll round on children that fall down within reach. The wife of a Northwest Mountie was torn apart and killed one year when I was up there. She just slipped. Indians are the Eskimos' constant enemy. Up to a few years ago, the Indians, who had guns first, used to hunt Eskimos for sport, as we hunt bear or deer. I came across an entry in an old journal at one post: "Party of Indians in canoes passed going north at 11 A.M. today hunting Eskimos." When eventually the Eskimos got guns, the Indians let them alone. In those days, one Eskimo was worth about twenty Indians. I like Eskimos. They were always dependable, helpful, and loyal. Nanook was my friend. He starved to death, you know. It was two years after I finished the movie. His family were hungry, he went after game, and a drifter caught him. I felt terrible about it. Nanook was a great man.[3]

Nanook of the North is an ideal documentary. It is a nonfictional, narrative film about the real world. Flaherty said that his film was to be a story about a man who has fewer resources than any other man in the world, a man whose life is a constant struggle against starvation in a land where nothing grows and where he must depend on what he can kill—all in the bitterest of climates. The theme, then, is that of several of Flaherty's documentaries—the will to live. In documenting the lives of a typical Eskimo and his family during one year, *Nanook* gets its unity and its construction. The story opens in the spring and concludes in the following winter.

The technique of *Nanook* is simple. The film is characterized almost by absence of technique. There is no trick photography. There is no studied composition. There is not a single dissolve. The camera does not even pan unless to enlarge the scope of a scene without cutting. One of the first shots is that of the icy waters of Hudson Bay. The whole scene has an undulating motion as though the camera were in a boat riding the swells—as it undoubtedly was. Although the camera thus moves, the movement results naturally from the circumstances of the filming. It is not made to move just for "effect," but it is effective. The simplicity of Flaherty's technique implies an almost complete dependence on the subject of each shot and the order in which the shots are arranged. Of the part showing Nanook building an igloo, Paul Rotha writes, "The screen has probably no more simply treated, yet brilliantly instructive, sequence."[4]

Nanook is no patronizing excursion into a quaint and far-off place. Flaherty is not showing that the Eskimo is different from ourselves, but rather that he is like us. Although it is a rare kind of ingenuity, fortitude, and bravery which the chief character in the film possesses, the subject is universal —dependence on oneself. In *Nanook* the dependence is quite physical—the dependence of man on himself to keep alive. As in all of his films, Flaherty is concerned with reality not coated over by the veneer of civilization. Flaherty is not only the father of the documentary but the first director to show how the camera can document nature.

Whereas *Nanook of the North* is about primitive man in conflict with nature, *Night Mail,* a documentary directed by Basil Wright and Harry Watt, has to do with civilization and the familiar. Produced in 1936 by John Grierson for the General Post Office Film Unit (of England), it records the nightly run of the *Postal Special* from London to Glasgow. The *Postal* is an express train which carries no passengers, only mail, and for which all other trains are sidetracked.

A propaganda film, *Night Mail* depicts the importance of the Post Office to the people it serves. Propaganda and theme are one, expressed in a line in the commentary: "All Scotland waits for her." Its construction, inherent in its subject, is simple: the run of the *Postal* from the time it leaves Euston Station at eight-thirty in the evening until it glides down into the railroad yard of Glasgow the next morning.

Dealing with the familiar, the directors have made the familiar interesting by select-

ing relevant details and putting them together to tell a story. There is even suspense in the routine business of the delivery of a mail sack from the speeding train to a trap net suspended beside the track. The directors humanize the incident by pointing up the apprehension of a novice clerk being shown how to strap a mail sack, tie it to a hinged bar, and swing the bar out the door at the proper second—all to the amusement of his fellow clerks.

A variety of shots shows the *Postal* being dispatched from the London station, a switchman in a tower speeding it on its way, a passenger train being backed onto a sliding, the *Postal* stopping at Crewe, the main junction of the Midlands, to take on mail and change crews and locomotives, clerks sorting letters, the train picking up and delivering mail by means of the trap nets. Humdrum routine is given meaning: a track gang standing clear at the approach of the train, the dispatcher at Crewe requesting and (after a cut to another office, where an official consults a schedule) receiving permission to hold the *Postal* four minutes because the connecting train from Holyhead is late, a mail clerk questioning his supervisor about the address on a letter.

In keeping with the purpose of the film, there are shots from another point of view, that of life along the right-of-way. A sequence presents a farmer climbing the embankment to the track and picking up his newspaper, tossed from the passing train. We catch glimpses of industrial plants identified in the commentary: the mines of Whickham, the steel mills of Warrington, the machine shops of Preston. The film is interspersed with shots of the landscape seen from the moving train, ranging from distant shots of the countryside to a shot of the near horizon, above eye level, as the train passes through a cut. There is a pan shot of Glasgow. Some of the most beautiful shots in *Night Mail* are of the train seen from various distances and at various angles. We see it from above as though the camera were on a bridge and, in longer shots, as though in an airplane. Panning across some hills, the camera catches, near the horizon, a moving plume of white smoke. The train not only gives these pictures meaning, by relating the mail to the parts of the country through which the *Postal* passes, but adds aesthetically to composition.

Although *Night Mail* is about a speeding train, the primary motion comes from the editing. Few other films are comprised proportionately of so many shots—290 in its twenty-four-minute running time. In this respect it is reminiscent of *The Battleship Potemkin.* There are shots of varying spatial length and angles as the camera sights along the sides of the cars. There is a shot from the front of the locomotive as it passes over a switch. The camera looks forward from the rear of the tender in the manner of that remarkable shot in *The Great Train Robbery.* Also reminiscent of *Potemkin* are the many close shots. In the sequence in which the novice prepares the mail bag for the trap net, nearly a third of the shots are close shots. There are close shots of the centers of driving wheels, of a piston rod, of the wheels of the foretruck. When the Scottish locomotive is backed onto the train at Crewe, we are given a close view, from above, of the couplings.

There is a spoken commentary, but it is slight and unobtrusive, that is, with the exception of the reciting of W. H. Auden's poem about a train and the letters it brings. The rhythm of the poem is intended to imitate the pulsation of the driving wheels, varying as the train labors up a grade and coasts down the other side:

This is the night mail crossing the border,
Bringing the cheque and the postal order,
Letters for the rich, letters for the poor,
The shop at the corner and the girl next door,
Pulling up Beattock, a steady climb—
The gradient's against her but she's on time.

Past cotton grass and moorland boulder,
Shovelling white steam over her shoulder,
Snorting noisily as she passes
Silent miles of wind-swept grasses;
Birds turn their heads as she approaches,
Stare from the bushes at her blank-faced coaches;

Sheep dogs cannot turn her course,
They slumber on with paws across.
In the farm she passes no one wakes,
But a jug in the bedroom gently shakes.

Dawn freshens, the climb is done.
Down towards Glasgow she descends
Towards the steam tugs, yelping down the glade
of cranes
Towards the fields of apparatus, the furnaces
Set on the dark plain like gigantic chessmen.
All Scotland waits for her;
In the dark glens, beside the pale-green sea lochs,
Men long for news.

Letters of thanks, letters from banks,
Letters of joy from the girl and boy,
Receipted bills and invitations
To inspect new stock or visit relations,
And applications for situations,
And timid lovers' declarations,
And gossip, gossip from all the nations,
News circumstantial, news financial,
Letters with holiday snaps to enlarge in,
Letters with faces scrawled on the margin.

Letters from uncles, cousins and aunts,
Letters to Scotland from the South of France,
Letters of condolence to Highlands and Lowlands,
Notes from overseas to the Hebrides;
Written on paper of every hue,
The pink, the violet, the white and the blue,
The chatty, the catty, the boring, adoring,
The cold and official and the heart's outpouring,
Clever, stupid, short and long,
The typed and the printed and the spelt all wrong.

Thousands are still asleep
Dreaming of terrifying monsters
Or a friendly tea beside the band at Cranston's
or Crawford's;
Asleep in working Glasgow, asleep in well-set
Edinburgh,
Asleep in granite Aberdeen.
They continue their dreams

But shall wake soon and long for letters.
And none will hear the postman's knock
Without a quickening of the heart,
For who can bear to feel himself forgotten?

The way in which the recitation is linked to the pictures has been indicated by Karel Reisz as follows:

		Ft.	fr.
1. Mountain scenery. Nearer dawn. *Camera pans slowly* to reveal a train coming up through the valley.	*(Wind)* COMMENTATOR (VOICE A): *This is the night mail crossing the border, bringing the cheque and the postal order, Letters for the rich, letters for the poor, (Slow rhythmic music fades in very gently.)*	24	
2. *LS* Train coming across the valley.	*The shop at the corner and the girl next door, Pulling up Beattock, a steady climb—The gradient's against her but she's on time. (Over the last line of commentary music is turned sharply up.)*	11	
3. *MS* Stoker and driver shovelling coal into the boiler.	*(Music continues: harsh, rhythmic; as if in time with the sound of engine pistons.)*	9	7
4. *CS* Boiler gate as shovel of coal enters.	*(Music continues.)*	6	
5. *MS* Stoker and driver. As in 3.	*(Music continues.)*	3	6
6. *CS* Hands on handle of shovel as they swing forward.	*(Music continues.)*	1	14
7. *CS* Engine driver looking on.	*(Music continues.)*	3	3
8. Front of engine, as seen from driver's cabin.	*(Music fades down.) Past cotton grass and moorland boulder,*	3	8
9. *LS* Train. *Tracking shot,* keeping train locomotive just *in frame to the left.*	*Shovelling white steam over her shoulder, Snorting noisily as she passes Silent miles of windswept grasses; Birds turn their heads—*	12	3
10. *CS* Locomotive wheels.	*—as she approaches,*	2	12
11. Passing trees, as seen from moving train.	*Stare from the bushes—*	1	12
12. Front of locomotive; from left side of driver's cabin as the train goes under a bridge.	*—at her blank-faced coaches; Sheep dogs cannot turn her course, They slumber on with paws across.*	7	14
13. Looking over engine driver's cabin. *Camera facing* in direction of train's movement.	*In the farm she passes no one wakes, But a jug in the bedroom gently shakes. (Tempo of music slows down to long calm phrases.)*	10	10
14. *Slow panning shot* of clouds at dawn.	*(Music continues calm.) Dawn freshens—*	12	2
15. *CS* Driver as he lifts his cap and wipes his brow with a handkerchief. *Dissolve to*:	*—the climb is done. (Music continues calm to end of shot 20.)*	5	7
16. Engine driver's panel. *Camera pans to left* to take in scenery as train speeds by. *Dissolve to*:	COMMENTATOR (VOICE B): *Down towards Glasgow she descends Towards the steam tugs, yelping down the glade of cranes Towards the fields of apparatus—*	15	5
17. *LS* Furnaces and chimneys. *Dissolve to*:	*—the furnaces Set on the dark plain like gigantic chessmen.*	6	6
18. *LS* Valley with hills in background. *Dissolve to*:	*All Scotland waits for her;*	5	14
19. Cottage in the valley. *Dissolve to*:	*In the dark glens, beside the pale-green sea lochs,*	3	11
20. Valley with hills in background.	*Men long for news.*	3	8
21. *CS* Wheels of engine; fast rhythmic motion of pistols.	COMMENTATOR (VOICE A): *Letters of thanks, letters from banks, Letters of joy from the girl and boy. . .*[5]	4	5

Reisz points out that in the first part of the recitation there are four separate phases as follows:[6]

1. SHOTS 1–13: *"The gradient's against her."* During the first two shots the rhythm is established by the commentary. During shots 3–7 music and accelerated cutting produce the beat. In 8–13 the commentary takes up the beat again.

2. SHOTS 13–15: *"The climb is done."* These shots represent a transition between the climb and the descent. The music, the irregular line *"Dawn freshens, the climb is done"* and Shot 15, that of the engineer wiping his brow, suggests the loosened tension after the climb.

3. SHOTS 15–20: *"All Scotland waits for her."* Here the descriptive commentary calls particular attention to itself, the pictures being subordinated to the verse and the shots linked by dissolves.

4. SHOT 21: *"Letters . . . Letters."* The rapid motion of the piston is matched by the staccato beat of the commentary as the train speeds downhill.

The variations in rhythm, Reisz observes, explain the sense of the sequence. During shot 21, for example, it is the accelerated rhythm of the verse, rather than the content of the commentary or the pictures, which suggests the downhill speed of the train.

More effective than the recitation of Auden's poem about the letters is what the directors have done with sounds peculiar to railroading. The comparative quiet in which the track crew works—the only sounds the click of tools on metal and stone, the piping of the foreman's whistle, and the warning call, "Stand by, stand clear!"—is broken as the train rounds a curve and comes toward the camera. There are sounds of wheels on the track—and the sounds are varied by distance and speed—of wheels passing over switch points, of the locomotive whistle. There are railroad-station sounds. Sorting mail, the clerks converse in that drone that characterizes voices made inarticulate by a more insistent noise, such as that of a train heard inside a car. The story of a train, *Night Mail* would be incomplete without sound. And the sounds in it are effective for being actual.

The year before Pare Lorentz wrote and directed *The River* (1937), he made a documentary film for the United States Department of Agriculture—*The Plow that Broke the Plains,* documenting the mistreatment of the lands in the West and the resulting dust storms. *The Plow that Broke the Plains* was successful, and the department had Lorentz make another documentary to show how deforestation and other mistreatment of the land in the Mississippi River basin caused millions of dollars of damage by floods. The result was *The River,* similar to *Nanook of the North* in that its subject is man and his conflict with nature, and to *Night Mail* in that its subject is man and his use of civilization.

It is said that when Lorentz saw the Mississippi River, he threw away his scenario: the Mississippi seemed dull to him—just a vast flow of brownish water between flat, uninteresting shores. Then he realized that the subject should not be so much the river as its people; it should be about what they had done to the river and what the river had done to them. Lorentz and his cameraman traveled 26,000 miles, and then, when he thought he had completed the footage, there came the disastrous floods of 1936. So he commandeered space in coast-guard boats and airplanes, and when he was through he had 80,000 feet of film. This he cut to 2,900 feet. Richard Barsam points out that *The River* includes some footage from two Hollywood films, *Come and Get It* and *Showboat,* as well as considerable newsreel footage.[7] Of all of it, Lorentz makes a beautifully unified epic.

In the preface to the published text of *The River* Lorentz names three books which he says he found essential to any understanding of the Mississippi: Mark Twain's *Life on the Mississippi,* "still the most accurate book ever written on the subject"; the Mississippi Valley Committee's Report (Department of the Interior, 1934), "the best written government report" Lorentz had ever read; and

"Black spruce and Norway pine,
Douglas fir and red cedar,
Scarlet oak and shagbark hickory,
Hemlock and aspen—
There was lumber in the North."
(Lorentz, *The River*). *Courtesy of Pare Lorentz*

"Black spruce and Norway pine,
Douglas fir and red cedar,
Scarlet oak and shagbark hickory.
We built a hundred cities and a thousand towns—
But at what a cost!"
(Lorentz, *The River*). *Courtesy of Pare Lorentz*

Lyle Saxon's *Father Mississippi.* Lorentz was soundly prepared to direct *The River.*

The film opens with a titled prologue, which states the subject and implies the theme:

This is the story of a river;
A record of the Mississippi:
Where it comes from, where it goes;
What it has meant to us . . .
And what it has cost us.

The story is told chronologically, beginning with the river and its tributaries flowing naturally within their banks—the state of the basin before the land was despoiled. Then are shown the growing of cotton, the impoverishment of the South by the Civil War, lumbering and steel-making and, finally, the results—the denuded land, the floods, the effects of the floods on the land, and the effects on the inhabitants of the valley. An epilogue documents the way in which the Tennessee Valley Authority has started to put the valley together again.

The pictures in *The River* are so beautifully composed that they could almost stand by themselves without a sound track. But the sound track adds immeasurably to them —a blending of natural sounds, a musical score composed by Virgil Thomson and incorporating American folk tunes, and Lorentz' commentary spoken by the actor Thomas Chalmers. The generalizing chapters in John Steinbeck's novel on a corresponding subject—*The Grapes of Wrath*— have been compared to the sound track in *The River* because in each the rhythm pervades the story. Effective use is made of natural sounds merely by repetition. For example, the sounds of the steel mill early in the film are imitated in the frantic whistle of a coast-guard boat later. Even in the commentary there is effective repetition— the names of the tributary rivers recited as the rivers are shown in flood. "Black spruce and Norway pine . . . ," Chalmers's voice is heard accompanying a shot of trees silhouetted against white clouds. "Black spruce and Norway pine . . . ," recited later is made

Pare Lorentz, *The River*

ironic by the now accompanying shot of charred tree trunks and stumps.

The commentary which Lorentz wrote to emphasize his shots has a different relationship to the shots than Auden's poem has to *Night Mail.* Auden's poem is complete in itself. The pictures of the train are, as Ernest Lindgren points out, not even necessary to illustrate it. For the most part, in fact, the pictures do not illustrate it, except in a general way. The commentary for *The River,* on the other hand, is only a comment on the pictures. The commentary is always *under* the pictures, never, as in *Night Mail, over* them. "The water comes down hill, spring and fall . . . ," Chalmers recites, as the sequence of tributaries in flood begins with a shot of a charred stump, from which icicles drip water.

Affective in its sound and rhythm, the commentary is one with the natural sounds and the background music. But it is none the less literary. James Joyce called it the most beautiful prose he had heard in years. If the text is prose—in the published version it is represented as verse—it is poetic prose. In the manner of Walt Whitman and Thomas Wolfe, Lorentz effects much of his poetry by naming place names of the nation— words which are in themselves poetic:

From as far West as Idaho,
Down from the glacier peaks of the Rockies—
From as far East as New York,
Down from the turkey ridges of the Alleghenies
Down from Minnesota, twenty-five hundred miles,
The Mississippi River runs to the Gulf.
Carrying every drop of water that flows down
    two-thirds the continent,
Carrying every brook and rill, rivulet and creek,
Carrying all the rivers that run down two-thirds
    the continent,
The Mississippi runs to the Gulf of Mexico.

Down the Yellowstone, the Milk, the White and
    Cheyenne;
The Cannonball, the Musselshell, the James and
    the Sioux;
Down the Judith, the Grand, the Osage, and the
    Platte,
The Skunk, the Salt, the Black, and Minnesota;
Down the Rock, the Illinois, and the Kankakee,
The Allegheny, the Monongahela, Kanawha, and
    Muskingum;
Down the Miami, the Wabash, the Licking and
    the Green,
The Cumberland, the Kentucky, and the
    Tennessee;
Down the Ouachita, the Wichita, the Red, and
    Yazoo—
Down the Missouri three thousand miles from
    the Rockies;
Down the Ohio a thousand miles from the
    Alleghenies;
Down the Arkansas fifteen hundred miles from
    the Great Divide;
Down the Red, a thousand miles from Texas;
Down the great Valley, twenty-five hundred miles
    from Minnesota,
Carrying every rivulet and brook, creek and rill,
Carrying all the rivers that run down two-thirds
    the continent—
The Mississippi runs to the Gulf.

Like *Night Mail, The River* was produced as propaganda. *The River* is the story of how we despoiled the Mississippi basin by ruthlessly cutting timber, greedily mining for coal and iron, and unscientifically exploiting the land for cotton.

And we made cotton king!
We rolled a million bales down the river for
    Liverpool and Leeds . . .
Rolled them off Alabama,
Rolled them off Mississippi,
Rolled them off Louisiana,
Rolled them down the river!

The pictures and the text—in the first person plural—are accusatory:

We built a hundred cities and a thousand towns—
But at what a cost!
We cut the top off the Alleghenies and sent it
    down the river.
We cut the top off Minnesota and sent it down
    the river.
We cut the top off Wisconsin and sent it down
    the river.
We left the mountains and the hills slashed and
    burned,
And moved on.

We made cotton king, but we made the land poor. It is also the story of the river's savage retaliation. The purpose of the film is to show how we may repair the damage we have done, how, in fact, we have begun reclaiming the Mississippi basin by reforesting the burned-over land, properly cultivating the soil, and building dams in the tributaries.

Also like *Night Mail, The River* is an exemplary documentary in spite of its propaganda. Incidentally—and ironically—the propaganda that presents the building of dams as a way of repairing the damage we did to nature has become dated, for now we are damaging nature by building dams. But the film is not dated, its message so applicable to our pollution of nature today. Taking for its subject the natural world— nature and man's misuse of it—*The River* has a theme: nature's retaliatory power and man being forced to reckon with it.

"We rolled a million barrels down the river . . ." Cotton loading south of New Orleans, January, 1937 (Lorentz, *The River*)

And it has unity: it is not only the story of a river, where it comes from and where it goes, but also the story of how it was, how it became despoiled, and how it can be restored. And it tells this story in pictures embellished by sound—sound incorporated actually and creatively. Although it was made more than forty years ago, it has been surpassed by no other documentary.

In the early forties the Standard Oil Company, happening to learn that *Nanook of the North* had been sponsored by a commercial firm, commissioned Robert Flaherty to make a film about the oil industry—a film that would dramatize the heroism of the men who drill for oil. Flaherty's first problem was to find a way to make oil interesting. He and his wife Frances drove through the Southwest, where they found limitless plains dotted with oil derricks. But the derricks just stood rigid against the sky. The Flahertys kept reminding themselves that, even in westerns, horses galloped. Then

"And poor land makes poor people.
Poor people make poor land." (Lorentz, *The River*)

they came to the bayou country of Louisiana.
One day they stopped the car for lunch
near the edge of a bayou.

Suddenly over the heads of the marsh grass,
Flaherty says, an oil derrick came into our view.
It was moving up the bayou, towed by a launch.
In motion, this familiar structure suddenly be-
came poetry, its slim lines rising clean and taut
above the unending flatness of the marshes.

I looked at Frances. She looked at me. We
knew that we had our picture.[8]

The picture, *Louisiana Story* (1948), would
seem to satisfy the assignment by Standard
Oil, which stipulated that its name not be
included in the credit titles. Typical of
Flaherty because its subject is man in a
primitive state but different in that it represents the primitive invaded by civilization, it shows some oil drillers bringing their
equipment into a Louisiana bayou to the
surprise and wonder of a thirteen-year-old
Cajun boy, drilling for oil, capping the well,
and moving out, leaving no trace of their
having been there except for the well cap,
or "Christmas tree," sticking out of the
water. It seems to say that the machine is
not a harmful intruder in primitive life, that
oil drillers are skillful and human, and that
an oil company does not exploit the people
on whose property it drills. Flaherty calls
his theme "the impact of industry."[9]

Like *Nanook, Night Mail,* and *The River,
Louisiana Story,* then, is propaganda. But
as in them, the propaganda turns out to be
only incidental. Oil drilling is not even the

center of interest. The complete title implies something else:

LOUISIANA STORY
being an account
of certain adventures
of a cajun (Acadian)
boy who lives in the
marshlands of Petit
Anse Bayou in Louisiana

For the boy the arrival of the derrick, a strange intruder in his world of the bayou, is an adventure. He paddles out to it in his pirogue and becomes acquainted with the drillers, who are friendly to him. Later he ventures out to the derrick again, accepts an invitation to come aboard, and watches the drilling. After the well blows, the news is that it may be abandoned. But the boy, who carries a little bag of salt at his waist to ward off werewolves, pours salt down the well, which then bubbles oil. Alternating with these adventures are his adventures in the wilds of the swamp, the most exciting of them being an encounter with an alligator. His pet raccoon disappears and, convinced that an alligator has eaten him, the boy sets out to kill the alligator in revenge. But having caught the alligator on a hook and line, he is dragged into the water. Now intercutting includes his father, who is searching the swamp for him, and who arrives on the scene in a Griffith last-minute rescue. As the story ends, the boy is perched on the Christmas tree with his pet raccoon—it turns out that the raccoon was not eaten by the alligator after all—waving goodbye to the friendly oil drillers moving out of the bayou with their machinery.

Having concocted a story, Flaherty, in a way reminiscent of Eisenstein's typage, went about finding the right people to enact it. "For our hero," he says, "we dreamed up a half-wild Cajun boy of the woods and bayous."[10] Frances Flaherty and Richard Leacock, the cameraman for the film, heard about a promising boy in a distant parish, but on the way there, stopping at a cabin for directions, they saw on top of a radio a photograph of a boy who fitted the type.

He is Joseph Boudreaux, the Alexander Napoleon Ulysses Latour of the story. "Almost at once," Flaherty says, "we ran into Lionel Le Blanc, who was a natural both in manner and looks to play the old trapper who was to be the father of our boy hero."[11] An old trapper himself and overseer of Avery Island, where some of the scenes were shot, Le Blanc bears a remarkable resemblance to Flaherty. For the oil driller who would personalize the impact of industry and make friends with the boy, they chose a Texan working on a nearby rig. The other drillers were the crew of Humble Petite Anse No. 1, put at Flaherty's disposal by Humble Oil and Refining Company, an affiliate of Standard Oil.

Immediately the film begins, a mood is established—a mood of tranquilty, which is to be shattered by the arrival of the drilling machinery. The script described the first shot:

			Ft.
1	After a *very slow fade in (eight feet)* during which the *camera pans upwards slowly* we open on an enormous lotus leaf undulating slowly. The leaf itself and some mud-patches form black reflections in the water-surface in which also bright white clouds are reflected. Tiny bugs skim over the water-surface.[12]	*Music begins.*	13

"A different shot," Karel Reisz observes, "—of a sleeping animal, a gently swaying branch, or a shaft of sunlight on the bank —might have served equally well if it conveyed a similar emotional meaning." The mood continues:

		Ft.
2	*L. S.* Black, silhouette-like form of an alligator swimming very slowly. Again clear white clouds are reflected in the water.	11
3	The surface of the water with reflections of several lotus-leaves and branches with	8

"We open on an enormous lotus leaf undulating slowly." (Flaherty, *Louisiana Story*). *Courtesy of International Film Seminars*

a bird on it. *Camera pans upward,* revealing what we have seen before in the reflections.

4   The surface of the lily-pond, lotus-   12
    leaves here and there in the water.
    An alligator crawls slowly on a
    cypress-log.

5   *C. U.* Lotus-leaf, the shadow of   3
    unseen branches on it. In the foreground
    of the leaf: dewdrops.

6   *C. U.* Dewdrop on the lotus-leaf.   3

7   *M. L. S.* Magnificent bird, perched on
    the branch of a tree.[13]

The images in the shots have no real connection with one another—no *real* connection. We make the connection as we watch the shots in this order. Helen van Dongen, who edited the film, observes that the slow upward movement of the camera in the first shot coincides with the slow movement of the swimming alligator, that a sense of direction is created "because in the first shot the leaf cups slightly towards the right and also bends over in the same direction in which the alligator is swimming," and that "the slight rippling in the water in shot 1 is continued in shot 2."[14] The shots constitute montage of Eisenstein's kind. A lotus leaf, an alligator, clouds, a bird, and so forth, become more than the sum of seven images. They become an eighth image: the tranquility of a primitive country untouched by civilization. The mood not only continues in shot 8 but prepares for the content of the shot:

8   L. S. of the forest in the swamp. The trunks of trees are standing in the dark water, silvery spanish moss dangles from the branches. *(Shot from a floating raft which moved slowly along, while the camera itself pans very slowly in the opposite direction, thus creating an almost three-dimensional effect.) After approximately 25* feet we discover from very far behind the trees a little boy paddling his priogue. He disappears and reappears again far behind the enormous trees in the foreground.[15]

In keeping with the slow motion of the preceding shots, we come upon the boy slowly. If he were introduced to us abruptly, for example, in a comparatively close shot, the mood would be shattered. He would seem like an intruder instead of a part of the swamp.

Most of the story is told from the boy's point of view. We are introduced to the boy as the film begins and, when the derrick moves up the bayou, towering impressively above the trees, editing makes us see it as he sees it. Editing picks out details for the boy to notice, such as parts of the tower, the tugs, members of the crew, and the stake marking the spot where the derrick is to drill. Van Dongen points out that the well-drilling sequence is composed of the elements of admiration for the skill of the drillers, of danger in the drilling operation (a mishandling of the slashing chain could be fatal), of awe, and of excitement and magic—to the boy the magic is one with the magic of the swamp.[16]   Again it is the editing that makes the point of view subjective so that these elements appeal alike to the boy and to us. A critic took exception to the well-drilling sequence for being edited in a way that prevents us from absorbing the action, that keeps us straining to

see what the drillers are about. But *Louisiana Story* is not an educational film on how to drill for oil. The sequence expresses a mood composed of the elements van Dongen points out. "There is no place for a purely technical explanation," she says. "Instead it should be the 'observation of men and machine at work.'"[17]

Louisiana Story is the first film for which Flaherty had the sound recorded on location. He composed some dialogue for his actors but, finding that they spoke their lines woodenly, told them the context and allowed them to use their own words. Consequently some of the speech is in French. What little dialogue is spoken during the film consists for the most part of chitchat of no importance to the advancement of the story. In fact, one of the cinematic values of *Louisiana Story* is the slightness of its dependence on dialogue. It is, as van Dongen observes, "essentially a silent film."[18] For the sounds of the derrick van Dongen applied the same breakdown of elements that she used for the selection and continuity of images. Flaherty says that from the very first they were fascinated with the sound that a derrick makes: "The mighty clash and ring of the steel pipe, the clatter of the block and the cables, with the steady throb of the engines running underneath it all, had the qualities of a great symphony" he says, adding that, "this sound proved to be an inspiration to Virgil Thomson, too, when he came to write the music for the film."[19] By means of seven sound tracks, van Dongen picks out individual sounds as accompaniment or counterpart to details in the pictures. For example, as the chain whips dangerously around the pipe, she emphasizes the danger by isolating the clattering noise against a background of silence. Or she has us hear the chain but see the pump —a separation of sound from image as in *The Informer*. Flaherty says that their last job was to gather "wild sounds"—animal and bird cries, water lapping, and so forth. "We had but to approach the alligator," he says, "and he emitted his terrifying sound like the hiss of escaping steam."[20]

Thomson explains that the music he wrote

for the film is of three kinds—"folk music, scenery music, and noise-music."[21] As he did for *The River,* he reset folk music, here the music of the Cajun people, their waltzes, their square dances, and the tunes they sing. For "scenery music" he adapted Mendelssohn, Debussy, and other landscape composers. For "noise-music" he used the recorded sound of the derrick—his inspiration, as Flaherty says. "I call it music," Thomson writes in his autobiography, "because, as compounded and shaped by Helen van Dongen into a rich and deafening accompaniment for a passage of well-digging one whole reel (nine minutes) long, these noises make a composition."[22] Referring to the music for the first scene as "the binding agent that gives continuity to the atmosphere which surrounds lotus-leaves, birds, snakes, and the boy in his pirogue," Frederick W. Sternfield points out that "its motion sublimates the motion of the photography," and that "the result is cinema in the original sense, not stills."[23] In keeping with the predominance of mood in the film, much of the music is evocative. It is at once evocative and commentarial when it rises in a chorale in accompaniment to the derrick's moving impressively up the bayou. And it is imitative in accompanying, for example, the rapid swimming of the raccoon, a launch speeding past the trapper's cabin, and the alligator's lunge. Music of the accordion is prominent in the score, Sternfield observing that "no other instrument conveys the appeal of the Cajun tunes so aptly."[24] Thomson has extracted from his score two suites which, he says, have been played more than any other of his orchestral works.[25]

Louisiana Story is indeed a story, but a different kind of story than "the story of a river" which constitutes Lorentz's documentary. When we first see the boy in his pirogue appearing and disappearing behind the trees of the swamp, we hear Flaherty's voice on the sound track: "His name is Alexander—Napoleon—Ulysses—Latour." The name, as van Dongen observes, "spoken with a soft, almost mysterious voice—the combination of pictures and words evokes the mystery which Flaherty wanted to surround the scene. The mood is established, the basis for the fairy-tale set. From now on all is acceptable."[26] It is acceptable when, in accompaniment to a close shot of bubbles rising to the surface, Flaherty's voice continues: "Mermaids—their hair is green he says—swim up these waters from the sea. He's seen their bubbles—often." It is acceptable that the bayou is a vague locale and that the relationship of its parts and its extent are also vague. In *Night Mail* and *The River* geography is specific. In *The River* we are even oriented by a map. In a documentary about oil, not only geography but geology would be relevant, but in *Louisiana Story* it is acceptable merely that a surveyor signal where the derrick is to anchor and that a stake be put down to mark the spot. We see the company launches speeding past as though on important missions, but what the missions are or where the launches are coming from or where they are going, we do not know. The cypress swamp in which the boy appears to be far away in the background is deceptive. "In reality," van Dongen reveals, "it is nothing but a little pond with a few cypress trees." It is acceptable that the oil-drilling sequence not be explicit as an engineering process. Had Flaherty been intent on documenting oil drilling, he would not have filmed the sequence at night. He was intent on something else:

We worked day after day, he says, shooting reams of stuff. But somehow we never could seem to make that pesky derrick come alive. We could not recapture that exhilaration we had felt when we first saw it slowly moving up the bayou.

Then we hit on it. At night! That's when it was alive!

At night, with the derrick lights dancing and flickering on the dark surface of the water, the excitement that is the very essence of drilling for oil became visual. So we threw our daytime footage into the ashcan and started in all over again to shoot out drilling scenes against a night background.[27]

The battle with the alligator is partly arranged. Editing makes it appear that an alligator caught on a line is pulling the boy into the water. Helen van Dongen remembers, however, that it was not possible at the time to film the alligator struggling and slashing the water with his powerful tail. "Therefore, some months later," she says, "shots were made of fighting alligators in the 'Sabine Refuge' during an alligator hunt by professional trappers."[28] There is less than realism in the assignment itself—a film to depict the romance of oil drilling. In subsidizing the film, Standard Oil did not intend that Flaherty should call attention to it being in the bayou for commercial exploitation. It may be noticed that, in those shots of the boy perched on the Christmas tree and waving goodbye to the friendly oil drillers, the Christmas tree is equipped with valves. The oil company will return; the bayou will not remain in its primitive state after all. But the return of the oil company and the future of the bayou together with the future of the boy are another story. *Louisiana Story,* as Flaherty himself says, is a fantasy.[29] There is, incidentally, an ironic twist in that other story: Joseph Boudreaux grew up to be an oil driller.

13.
From Play
to Film

It might be asked why, now that the motion-picture machine has taken on the dimension of sound, plays should not be reproduced on the screen as literally as the medium permits. Particularly today, when color and stereoscopic film make possible still closer approximation to reality, it would seem that the machine is admirably suited to this purpose. And of course it is. Plays literally recorded are justifiable because wide audiences are thus enabled to see them. For a comparable reason symphonic music is recorded on phonograph records. On the other hand, the more literally a play is reproduced on the screen, the more the motion pictures constitute only a machine.

What then is the proper use of the machine in the adaptation of a play? The answer lies in the difference between the drama and motion pictures, between a play and a film.

That a play is written to be performed determines what it is like. Because it is written, it involves images suggested by words. Because it is performed, it involves actors who speak the words. Because a performance involves stage settings, it is limited in the number of scenes. (Although the comparatively bare stage of the Elizabethan theatre permitted plays of many scenes, even the number of these was limited by the time required to establish the locale of each scene and to get actors on and off the stage as well as by other elements of dramatic narration.) And because a performance also involves an audience, it is limited in its length. These characteristics in turn determine others. A play, for example, narrates in the present tense. It does not readily shift to the past except by resorting to exposition. It does not admit of lapse of time unless indicated by a device such as the lowering and raising of the curtain or the stage lights. It does not naturally present simultaneous events in more than one place. It tends to have a late point of attack. It has few characters in comparison, for example, to those in a novel. It contains comparatively few incidents. And, except for the old drama, which depended on soliloquies, it is objective in point of view. (Exceptions to these generalizations are represented by expressionistic plays or plays incorporating expressionistic devices, which circumvent some of the restrictions imposed by the stage.)

A film is limited by only one of these restrictions, namely, length. Because the medium of motion pictures is pictures—and, since 1927, pictures with sound—words, of primary importance in a play, are of secondary importance in a film. As René Clair says, "A blind man in a regular theatre and deaf mute in a movie theatre should still

166

get the essentials from the performance."[1] Scene shifting not occupying time on the screen, a film is comparatively unlimited as to number of scenes. A film shifts easily between the present and the past, and even to the future; it admits of frequent lapses of time; and in it time may be compressed or extended. It can present simultaneous actions in more than one place. The point of attack in a film may be early, since all action is readily presented directly. The greater number of scenes makes possible a correspondingly larger number of characters and incidents. Furthermore, because motion pictures can photograph thought, a film can be more subjective than a play.

However, if a play were adapted to the screen only by increasing the number of scenes, characters, and incidents, the resulting film would be too long. Since a film is restricted in its length, something must be deleted in the adaptation. Since a play has few scenes, the scenes are developed in detail, in more detail, for example, than in a novel. What is deleted, then, in the adaptation is some of the detail. Thus it is that when a play is adapted to the screen it is not only expanded but contracted. The expansion gives the screen version the characteristics of a novel: many scenes, characters, and incidents, a wide diversity in time, and early point of attack—or at least a flashback method to reveal the past—the presentation of parallel action, and subjectivity not germane to the drama. The contraction makes the film less dramatic than the play and, correspondingly, more like a novel, because the deletion of detail requires a corresponding deletion of dialogue, which is the basis of the dramatic method. The principle of expansion and contraction is that enunciated by Mortimer Adler—"expanded in the direction of epic magnitude but contracted with respect to dramatic detail." In other words a play adapted to the screen becomes more like a novel than a play, except that whereas a novel effects description and narration by words, a film effects them by pictures. Dialogue, the method of the play, does not, of course, admit

of representation in pictures. Dialogue in a film depends on the machine—the microphone. The play does not, however, become *completely* like a novel. (Even von Stroheim failed to put a novel "*completely*" on the screen.") It becomes a motion picture.

Although both film and play tell their stories by presenting them, the manner of presentation differs. A film that presents its story in the manner of the play tends to be only a photograph of the play. If a play is to be adapted to the screen, that is, if it is to become a film with an aesthetic entity of its own and not a mechanical reproduction, it must be adapted cinematically. It should not be bound by the restrictions imposed by the stage but exploit the freedom implicit in motion pictures by virtue of the flexibility, actual and figurative, of the camera and of editing. How these changes should be made is illustrated by the adaptation, in 1940, of Robert E. Sherwood's play *Abe Lincoln in Illinois* and, in 1946, of Noel Coward's one-act play *Still Life.*

In his supplementary notes to *Abe Lincoln in Illinois,* Sherwood makes the point that Lincoln's great achievement was "the solidification of the American ideal." But his play, Sherwood says, is not about Lincoln's achievement but rather about the "solidification of Lincoln himself—a long, uncertain process, effected by influences some of which came from his own reasoning mind, some from his surrounding circumstances, some from sources which we cannot comprehend." It was to be "a play about the development of the extraordinary character of Abraham Lincoln." Observing that a playwright is allowed poetic license when his subject is a character out of history, Sherwood says, "The Cleopatra who actually existed may have borne no resemblance to the Cleopatra of Shakespeare's creation nor to the entirely different one of Shaw's, but no one now cares about that, even in Egypt." In presenting the character of Lincoln, however, Sherwood felt that it was not only obligatory to eschew poetic license but desirable because, he says, Lincoln's life was "a work of art," and "his character needs no romanticizing, no sentimentalizing, no dramatizing." As Sherwood realized, however, the development of Lincoln's character was not only a much longer process than that which is usually encompassed within the limits of dramatic action but a process resulting from more influences than those operating on a fictitious character in a play. Since Sherwood proposed to present this process and these influences, the problem was to fit them into a form not readily adaptable to so broad a scope.

As a result *Abe Lincoln in Illinois* represents twenty-eight years in the life of the hero, from 1833, shortly after Abe has arrived in New Salem, a backwoods boy from a cabin home on the Sangamon River, to 1861, when, on the eve of his fifty-second birthday, he leaves Springfield for Washington to be inaugurated president of the United States. The incidents which Sherwood has selected as contributing to the development of Lincoln's character during these twenty-eight years are presented in twelve separate scenes, most of them widely separated in time and involving varied settings and a large cast of characters. It is therefore not surprising that *Abe Lincoln in Illinois* has been criticized as loosely constructed.

Actually the play is more compact than this criticism implies. Sherwood points out in his notes that Lincoln's life formed "a veritable allegory of the growth of the democratic spirit, with its humble origins, its inward struggles, its seemingly timid policy of 'live and let live' and 'mind your own business,' its slow awakening to the dreadful problems, its death at the hands of a crazed assassin, and its perpetual renewal caused by the perpetual human need for it." In declaring that Lincoln's character needs no dramatizing, Sherwood means not only that it contains the materials of drama itself but that its actual development is dramatic. He finds in the chronology of events as history presents them to him a conflict, a crisis, a climax, and even a denouement.

Abe Lincoln in Illinois is more than a series of loosely connected scenes depicting incidents in the life of a great national figure. It is a well-constructed play, dramatically presenting the "long, uncertain process" by which the hero resolves an inner conflict and the momentous consequences of his resolution of it. In adapting history to his purpose, Sherwood contracts the process. In spite of the contraction, however, the play remains epical, and it is this epic quality which largely accounts for its successful adaptation to the screen.

A play is not usually epical, tending rather to center on a single point. St. John Hankin described his method of playwriting as follows:

This is what I do with my plays. I select an episode in the life of one of my characters or of a group of characters when something of importance to their future has to be decided, and I ring up my curtain. Having shown how it was decided and why it was so decided, I ring it down again. The episode is over and with it the play.

An episode, however, is not isolated, and frequently an understanding of it depends on an understanding of previous happenings. These happenings the playwright is therefore obliged to present. He does not, however, always present them directly. Mrs. Fiske used to say, "Ibsen gives us the last hours." By this she meant that an Ibsen play observes the unity of time, antecedent action being presented indirectly and the crisis and the climax coming close together. Although most plays are not so nearly unified as Ibsen's, plays tend to be more nearly unified than, for example, novels, which usually narrate most of their stories directly and thus contain many scenes, incidents, and characters.

To be successfully adapted to the screen a play must give up its characteristic unity. When Sherwood rewrote *Abe Lincoln in Illinois* for the screen and Grover Jones made the adaptation, they were at an advantage, for the epic story of nearly thirty years in the life of a great national hero is particularly suited to screen terms, in fact, even better suited than to the stage. For whereas in writing the play Sherwood had to compress the story into comparatively few incidents and scenes, in the film he had a medium which by its very nature would enable him to present it with less sacrifice of its broad scope.

The film gets some of its epic quality from an earlier point of attack than in the play and from a direct presentation of incidents that in the play are only referred to—incidents that happen before the action of the play begins and incidents that are represented as happening offstage between or during scenes. Whereas the play begins after Abe has become established in New Salem and is part owner of the store, the film opens with a scene in his earlier home on the Sangamon. In the play Josh Speed tells the Bowling Greens that the first time he ever saw Abe Lincoln was when Abe was piloting the steamboat *Talisman:*

You remember how she ran into trouble at the dam. I had a valuable load of goods aboard for my father's store, and I was sure that steamboat, goods, and all were a total loss. But Abe got her through. It was a great piece of work.

In the film this incident, somewhat altered, is presented directly. Furthermore it is made the occasion of Abe's first meeting Ann Rutledge. The steamboat *Talisman* becomes in the film a flatboat passing New Salem. The valuable load of goods is pigs. In this version Abe's seamanship is less successful. The prow of the boat drops over the dam, and the cargo is spilled into the stream. Next, Abe is shown chasing a pig through the woods. Making a flying leap, he catches the animal by a hind leg and, as he lies prone, holding the squealing pig, Ann Rutledge enters the scene. In the play Abe has already bested Jack Armstrong in a fight. In the film the fight is presented directly. Action represented as occurring between scenes is further material for the film. For example, Ann Rutledge's death, only referred to in the play, is the occasion in the film for two sequences totaling seven minutes. In the first, Ann becomes ill at a dance in connection with the political campaign.

The sequence opens with a close shot of a sign:

ABE LINCOLN
Our Candidate to the Assembly

The sign hangs in the background of the dance scene. This sequence is concluded after Ann collapses and is taken home. After an intervening sequence, in which Abe makes a political speech, the scene shifts to the Rutledge cottage, where the death scene is presented. Other examples of this kind of expansion are Abe's winning the election to the Assembly, the resulting celebration, and a dance at the Edwardses', where Abe is presented to Mary Todd.

Sherwood draws on history itself to expand the scope of his play. For example, Lincoln's part in the Black Hawk War is represented by a scene in which Abe is drilling a company of volunteers. The time between Lincoln's marriage, in 1842, and the Lincoln-Douglas debates, in 1858, is bridged for the most part by Hollywood montage—a series of shots and inserts, linked by dissolves and superimposition. The sequence illustrates a continuity title, superimposed over some of these shots, "And then—years that marked the growth of a man and of a nation": a man swinging a pick, a man digging, men building a fence, a mason laying brick, a street in Springfield and a sign

LINCOLN & HERNDON
COUNSELLORS AT LAW

being nailed up, a telegraph pole rising, a newspaper headline reporting the coming of the telegraph service to the West, a train crossing the prairie, Lincoln speaking in the House of Representatives, and headlines implying a growing dissension between North and South. The montage is concluded by an insert reading

ARMED REBELLION
IN VIRGINIA
John Brown
Leads Insurrection
Against Slaveholders

The insert dissolves to a shot of an arch over a doorway. Across the arch is a sign:

HARPERS FERRY
ENGINE HOUSE

Then follows a sequence presenting the arrest of John Brown.

This kind of expansion not only broadens the scope of the play but by bridging gaps in time—as, for instance, the sixteen years between acts 2 and 3—gives the film a continuity that the play lacks. The film includes all but one of the scenes of the play. But so smoothly are the gaps bridged that the scenes seem less like individual units than, uninterrupted parts of a continuous picture. For example, the Hollywood montage referred to does not start abruptly after the scene in which Abe asks Mary to take him back. That scene is concluded by a dissolve to a close shot of a family Bible, which opens to a marriage certificate for Abraham Lincoln and Mary Todd Lincoln. A hand is filling in the date: November 4, 1842. Then, as the background music rises, there is a dissolve to a double exposure—a medium-close shot of the man swinging the pick. This shot, superimposed on that of a scene in which a mule team moves toward the foreground, unobtrusively begins the montage.

In the play the first scene after the sixteen-year gap is that of the Lincoln-Douglas debate. In the film the debate scene is more smoothly led up to. After the John Brown scene fades out, there is a fade-in to a scene in which Douglas learns that Lincoln is to run against him for election to the senate. Announcing that he will go to Springfield, Douglas orders a reception with "a brass band at the station and liquor for all." The next scene is that of Abe and his family sitting for their photograph. The children are restless, and the photographer is having difficulty. Then as the picture is finally about to be taken, a band is heard, and the children rush to the window. A distance shot reveals Douglas arriving at the station. The following scene is that of the debate.

Nor after the debate scene is there an abrupt break, as there is in the play, in which the next scene, that of the committee waiting on Lincoln in the parlor of the Edwards house in Springfield, is represented as taking place two years later. In the film, shots intervening between these two scenes give the impression of continuous action. At the end of the debate scene there is an insert of shorthand notes. (During the debate the reporters have been shown writing at a table beside the debating platform.) Then there is a cut to a scene that represents Horace Greeley in his newspaper office reading a news dispatch. He reads aloud the last words of Lincoln's rebuttal: "'A house divided against itself cannot stand.' This government cannot endure permanently half slave and half free!"

"Lincoln? I've never heard of him," observes one of Greeley's assistants.

"You will," says Greeley, and there begins a sequence of inserts of newspaper headlines.

Then follows a scene in which the politicians are talking about Abe. "Anyway," says one of them, "I ask you gentlemen to look him over," whereupon the scene dissolves to that of the parlor: Abe is awaiting the arrival of the committee.

A dissolve also helps to bridge the gap between two of the interpolated sequences —the flatboat episode and Abe's arrival in New Salem. After the scene in which Abe first meets Ann Rutledge, the film shows the flatboat once more on its way downstream. Abe, at the tiller, is looking longingly in the direction of New Salem, which they are drifting past. Then the camera pans from the boat to the river. This shot, of the rippling water, dissolves to a close shot of a wagon wheel turning. Tilting up, the camera reveals the lettering SPRINGFIELD STAGE on the front part of a stagecoach and, continuing to tilt, Abe seated beside the driver. The stagecoach is entering New Salem.

The debate scene represents another kind of expansion. In the play the debate scene is not only adequate for its purpose but particularly effective. Much of its effectiveness results from Sherwood's resorting to the expressionistic device of bringing the audience into the scene, that is, figuratively extending the stage. The stage becomes the debating platform, the audience becomes the crowd listening to the debate in 1848, and accordingly the actors address this audience. But if presented in the same way on the screen, the scene would be not only incongruous, because of the method of the rest of the film, but uncinematic, because of dependence on dialogue. Accordingly the long speeches in the scene in the play are considerably cut—that is, detail is contracted —and the scene is made to include more than the speakers on the platform—that is, scope is expanded within the scene itself.

These are the kinds of expansion implicit in Adler's dictum that "if a play be adapted to the screen, it must be expanded in the direction of epic magnitude." They represent the tendency of the adapted play to be novellike because of an increased number and variety of scenes, incidents, and characters. The increase entails more dependence on the camera than on the microphone. For whereas the method of the play is dialogue, that of the novel is primarily narration and description. Narration and description, which can be represented pictorially, are, unlike dialogue, the essence of motion pictures. But Sherwood's play requires nearly three hours for presentation on the stage, and the running time of the film is only 100 minutes, part of which is represented by expansion in scope. It is therefore obvious that a considerable part of the play must have been deleted when it was adapted to the screen. The deletions accord with the principle expressed in the concluding phrase of Adler's dictum: "but contracted with respect to dramatic detail." As illustrated in Chapter 10, contraction with respect to dramatic detail implies deletions in dialogue.

In the adaptation of *Abe Lincoln in Illinois* some of the deletions are more than compensated for by direct presentation of allusions in the play. Most of the deletions, however, are absolute. In the debate scene,

for example, each of the two long speeches by Abe and Douglas is considerably cut. The scene in which Abe receives the committee is contracted by a reduction in the number of questions that the members of the committee ask the prospective candidate. The film limits this interview, for the most part, to Barrick's questioning Abe about church-going and to Abe's reply.

All of the contractions, however, are not so simple. One of the most effective in the film involves a substitution for the crisis scene. It is the scene on the prairie—which Sherwood calls "the most completely fictitious" of all the twelve scenes. "Lincoln's astounding metamorphosis from a man of doubt and indecision—even to indifference —to a man of passionate conviction and decisive action," Sherwood points out, "was not accomplished in one stroke, by one magnificent act of God." Since Sherwood was writing a play, however, he needed to condense the crisis so that it could be presented dramatically. Accordingly he wrote this scene, in which Abe, impressed by the courage of Seth Gale and his family in braving the dangers of the wilderness to help establish a free territory in Oregon, suddenly realizes his own lack of courage and decides to accept his destiny:

ABE *(suddenly rises)*: You mustn't be scared, Seth. I know I'm a poor one to be telling you that—because I've been scared all my life. But —seeing you now—and thinking of the big thing you've set out to do—well, it's made me feel pretty small. It's made me feel that I've got to do something, too, to keep you and your kind in the United States of America.

Seth's little boy is ill, and Seth has asked Abe to speak a prayer for his recovery. Abe has demurred with the excuse that he "couldn't think of a blessed thing that would be of any comfort." But now that he has accepted his destiny, his negative attitude changes, and the first evidence of the change is his offer to speak the prayer. He prays for the boy but also, indirectly, for himself: "Spare him and give him his father's strength —give us all strength, O God, to do the work that is before us." The substitution is not made because the scene is fictitious but because it is dramatic.

In preparation for the change, the opening scene of the film has Sarah Lincoln say to Abe as he leaves home: "Wherever you go, whatever you do, remember what the Good Book says: 'The world passeth, but he that doeth the will of God abideth forever.'" Also in preparation for the change, the setting of Abe's proposal to Ann Rutledge is not, as in the play, the Rutledge tavern, but the woods near the edge of the clearing where Abe, having seen Ann leave the tavern, has followed her.

The substitute crisis scene occurs, as in the play, after Abe has broken his engagement to Mary Todd. It shows him, bewildered and perplexed, returning to the now deserted New Salem. He leads his horse down the empty street, past the vacant houses, ties it up in front of the tavern, and goes inside. As he looks out across the clearing there is a cut to what he sees, or imagines he sees: the figure of Ann Rutledge walking away from the tavern as on that other day. Abe follows the ethereal form across the clearing and into the woods. As he stands by the same tree under which the proposal scene took place, Sarah Lincoln's voice is heard: "'The world passeth, but he that doeth the will of God abideth forever.'" The scene fades out, and in the next one, fading in, Abe is walking briskly along a Springfield street on his way to call on Mary Todd. Thus without dialogue the film accomplishes in less than three minutes what in the play takes a whole scene.

Sarah Lincoln's voice heard on the sound track while the camera remains on Abe is comparable to the separation of sound from image in *The Informer.* Depending for its meaning, not only on the sound and the image, but also on the two incidents previously inserted, it exemplifies "the inexplicable presence of the thing not named." It is entirely cinematic.

The substituted crisis scene results, of necessity, in a contraction of dramatic detail in the scene in which Abe asks Mary to take

him back. In the play the value of the latter scene is that it emphasizes the significance of the scene on the prairie. There is no doubt now that Abe has accepted his destiny. Furthermore it makes clear, as though everyone in the audience would not otherwise get the point, how Abe came to make his fateful decision. "What was it that brought you to this change of heart and mind?" Mary asks him.

ABE: On the prairie, I met an old friend of mine who was moving West, with his wife and child, in a covered wagon. He asked me to go with him, and I was strongly tempted to do so. *(There is great sadness in his tone—but he seems to collect himself, and turns to her again, speaking with a sort of resignation.)* But then I knew that was not my direction. The way I must go is the way you have always wanted me to go.

Obviously this dialogue had to be deleted in the adaptation, but the cinematic way of presenting the crisis makes the reason for Abe's changed attitude so clear that no substitution is necessary.

Although the crisis is thus altered, the climax—Abe's election to the presidency—and the denouement—the departure from Illinois—are based on the same facts as the play. The only changes in the climax and the denouement are the expansion and contraction resulting from the cinematic method of storytelling.

When a play is adapted to the screen, each scene is usually represented in more than one shot. After the problem of the microphone had been solved and the camera had once more become flexible, scenes incorporating sound could be built up, as Ford showed in *The Informer,* by as many shots taken from as many different angles and distances as in any scene in *The Birth of a Nation.* Although this change is not essential to the cinematic method, it is peculiar to it. In fact, to avoid it is to effect a tour de force. Alfred Hitchcock filmed *Rope* (1948) ostensibly in a single shot, but he guided the attention of the spectator by a continual movement of the camera. In the production of a play a director depends on grouping of actors and sheer acting ability to force attention. In a play, however, attention cannot be absolute. There is no physical barrier to its wandering. It may be diverted by the idle glance of the spectator. It may be diverted by an actor stealing a scene. The motion-picture director, on the other hand, has absolute control over the spectator's attention.

All of *Abe Lincoln in Illinois* is edited in this way. The first scene is that in which Abe leaves his home on the Sangamon. One can imagine how, if this scene were in Sherwood's original play, it would be done on the stage. In the film its parts are related by cutting and movement of the camera. The first shot is that of an exterior of the cabin. It is an establishing shot. But even this establishing shot has been prepared for by the pictures which form a background to the credit titles that immediately precede it, for they too are of pioneer scenes. The film itself begins with a fade-in on the Lincoln cabin. Superimposed large over it are the figures 1831. They fade out, and there is a cut to a closer shot of the cabin—a window, through which Tom Lincoln is looking. It is raining. The next shot is of the interior—a medium shot of Tom as he turns from the window and moves right, the camera panning with him. As Tom walks past the fireplace, the camera centers attention on Abe lying on the floor in front of the fire, reading. Panning still farther right, it reveals Sarah Lincoln. There is a cut to a medium-close shot of Sarah, and then to a medium shot of Abe, Tom standing at the right. Reaching down for a brand to light his pipe, Tom speaks the first words of the film: "It's raining, but you wouldn't notice—your nose everlastin' stuck in some book." Thus in a few brief shots the mood and the situation are established.

Editing can emphasize detailed action or gesture that would be ineffective or even unnoticed on a stage. During the debate Mary and the Lincoln children wave to Abe from a second-story window of a nearby building, and Abe, seated on the platform, acknowledges the greeting. If the scene were done in the same way on the stage, it would be difficult to direct the audience's attention away from the speaker to the window at the proper moment and then immediately from the window to Abe. Furthermore, since Abe is sitting at the back of the platform, the speaker would hide him from part of the audience. And it would be difficult to make this exchange of salutations noticeable and yet not seem impolite under the circumstances and therefore out of character. But in the film the incident is made effective by editing. It is done in four brief shots: of the crowd listening to Ninian Edwards, of Abe glancing up to the left, of the group at the window waving, and of Abe's responding by a slight motion of his hand.

The film is remarkably faithful to the characterization in the play. Although in the adaptation to the screen the characters are deprived of considerable dialogue, this loss is somehow compensated for in the expansion in scope. In the play Sherwood intended to show that "the long uncertain process" in the development of the hero's character was effected, as he said, by influences some of which came from the hero's "own reasoning mind." Because motion pictures can photograph thought, the method by which the film presents, for example, Abe's resolution of an inner conflict is a satisfactory substitute for the crisis scene in the play. The long uncertain process was also effected, Sherwood says, by some influences that came from the hero's surrounding circumstances, and the circumstances are largely represented by the other characters. Billy Herndon, berating Abe for failure to do his "own great duty," is as much the raisonneur of the film as of the play. And Mary Todd, whose role in the play could be, according to Sherwood, "only that of a symbol of her husband's glorious, tragic destiny," is quite as much this symbol in the film. "And how far do you think you will go with anyone like Abe Lincoln, who is lazy and shiftless and prefers to stop constantly along the way to tell jokes?" Elizabeth Edwards rhetorically asks her sister. But Mary, who is determined to marry Abe, is no less determined that he shall not stop along the way. In one of the transition scenes in the film, that of a party at the Edwards house, Abe is telling a joke to a group of men in the hall. The symbolic effectiveness of the scene is almost entirely pictorial. It does not even matter what the joke is. In fact, Abe does not finish telling it, for at this moment Mary Todd comes up. The camera picks her out in the background, approaching slowly but, the symbol of Abe's destiny, determinedly. And no less determinedly she links her arm in Abe's and leads Abe away.

A particular kind of dramatic irony characterizes Sherwood's play, because from a vantage point in time an audience catches meanings beyond those that the characters can appreciate. "You go into politics, and you may get elected," Abe tells Mentor Graham. "And if you get elected, you've got to go to the city. I don't want none of that." "I'm a conservative, all right," he assures Ninian Edwards, who wants the young postmaster to run for the legislature. "If I go into the legislature, you'd never catch me starting any movement for reform or progress." And there is Elizabeth's rhetorical question, "And how far do you think you will go with any one like Abe Lincoln . . . ?" These examples, depending as they do on dialogue, are of course more germane to the drama than to the motion pictures. But in one of the interpolated scenes in the adaptation, the irony is effected as much by the camera as by the microphone. It occurs when Abe, on his first arrival in New Salem, is sworn in as a clerk in the election. The irony is implicit not only in what is heard— Abe's repeating the oath, "I, Abraham Lincoln, do solemnly swear to uphold the Constitution of the United States of America" —but even more in what is seen—the serious-faced young man in pioneer clothes, right hand upraised—in a medium-close shot with which the scene fades out.

It is not to disparge the fine acting in this film to point out that the acting is of no more than secondary importance, of considerably less importance, for example, than in the production of the play. It may be said in general that the better a film, the less important the actors. For the better the film, the less it depends on the method of the stage. It is conceivable that a film might be made without actors at all. *The Titan* (1950), which has been described as pure cinema, was made in just that way. It should be observed that many of the shots in *Abe Lincoln in Illinois* contain no actors and that many that do, call for no particular acting ability. Because *Abe Lincoln in Illinois* has been adapted cinematically, the film depends more on the arrangement of shots than on the acting in them. It is of course not to be inferred that acting does not contribute to a film. It contributes if only because the content of the shots is important.

A one-act play is adapted to the screen somewhat differently than a full-length play. For whereas in the adaptation of a full-length play scope is expanded, in the adaptation of a one-act play it is expanded even more. And whereas in the adaptation of the full-length play detail is contracted, in that of a one-act play it is contracted less, if at all. This variation is well illustrated by *Brief Encounter,* adapted from Noel Coward's *Still Life.*

Noel Coward himself wrote the adaptation; so to begin with, the adapter was at an advantage. A playwright knows more about the lives of his characters than he can present in the brief time of a play, of a one-act play in particular. In giving *Still Life* the scope of his film, Coward drew on this kind of knowledge. The two main characters in his realistic little play meet by chance in the refreshment room of a railway station, continue to meet, fall in love, and finally separate. The action, in five scenes spaced out to represent a year's time, takes place in one setting—the refreshment room with its background of travelers, station attendants, and the activity and noise relative to the arrival and departure of the local trains and the roaring past of the expresses. There are allusions in the play to situations and incidents not directly presented. For example, Laura says, "I'm a respectable married woman with a husband

and a home and three children." In the film Laura's home is the focus of the story; Laura's husband, only sketchily described in *Still Life,* is presented directly, and so are the children. In the play allusions such as "an accidental meeting—then a little lunch—then the movies" are the bases for sequences in the film. These sequences result in the creation of additional characters: in *Still Life* there are eleven characters: in *Brief Encounter* there are, not including extras, twenty-one.

Several of the sequences whereby the scope is expanded not only elaborate the abortive love affair but symbolize its frustration. In the play the last meeting of Laura and Alec is interrupted by Laura's gossipy acquaintance, Dolly Messiter. In the film comparable discords mark all of the lovers' meetings. They meet by chance at a café, where a ladies' orchestra plays squeakily and loudly, and Laura is embarrassed about the check. They escape from the noise of the café and go the the movies. But the organist, playing loudly at the movies, is the cellist from the orchestra at the café. They go to the movies again, but it is "a terribly bad picture," and they leave before it is over. They go boating, but Alec does not row well and, in an encounter with a low bridge, falls out of the boat. Alec takes Laura to the Grand Hotel for lunch and orders a bottle of champagne, but Laura is disconcerted because two of her acquaintances have been watching them. They drive out into the country in a little two-seater car, but the sun does not shine and Laura is shivering and "not really happy." They return to Stephen Lynn's flat, but the flat is bare and cold and when Alec tries to make a fire, it only smokes. "I hope the fire will perk up," says Alec, but Stephen unexpectedly returns, and Laura has to escape through the kitchen.

Inasmuch as *Brief Encounter* is the adaptation of a one-act play, detail is expanded too. Some of the dialogue of the minor characters is deleted in the adaptation because the minor characters are made less important in the film than in the play. But the film includes most of the original dialogue and all but two of the characters.

Furthermore, since the additional scenes involve additional dialogue, there is more dialogue in the film than in the play. Whereas *Still Life* can be acted in less than three quarters of an hour, the running time of *Brief Encounter* is an hour and a half.

In adapting *Still Life* to the screen, Coward puts the action of the play into a frame whereby most of *Brief Encounter* becomes a presentation of Laura's recollection of the abortive affair. That the story should be told from Laura's point of view is implied in *Still Life,* for it is Laura's inner conflict that is stronger, and it is Laura who makes the final decision between love and duty. Alec is for compromise. Realizing that there can be no compromise, Laura chooses duty. Accordingly the film includes scenes in Laura's family life, but not in Alec's.

With the exception of a few brief incidents, the story within the frame is told consistently from Laura's point of view. The film opens with a night scene on the platform of the Milford Junction Station and then cuts to the refreshment room, where Laura and Alec are sitting at a table and where the action is that of the last scene of the play. This frame part of the film continues past the action of *Still Life,* which ends as Laura and Dolly are about to leave the refreshment room. The film goes on to show them leaving the room, taking the train, riding to Ketchworth and arriving there, and continues up to the point where Laura, having returned home, is sewing in the library while her husband, Fred, sits opposite her, working a crossword puzzle. Falling into a reverie, Laura narrates the story of her love affair as though she were speaking her thoughts out loud to Fred—at first, speaking in interior monologue (that is, her voice heard on the sound track but her lips not moving), and then in voice-over (speaking as narrator while the pictures and other sounds continue). As she says, "It all started on an ordinary day, in the most ordinary place in the world," the scene dissolves to the refreshment room. Laura is seated at one of the tables, and Alec enters, as he does about midway through scene 1 of *Still Life.* From here on the action includes that of the play, with the exception of a few incidents involving minor characters. Most of the last scene of the play is represented twice in the film—at the beginning, as part of the frame, and toward the end, as the conclusion to Laura's reverie. The second enactment of the scene, however, continues only to that point at which Laura comes back into the refreshment room, having rushed out to throw herself under the express. At that point there is a return to the frame, with which the film ends.

The frame intrudes at one other point. About midway in the film Laura comes out of her reverie for a moment and realizes that she is at home, seated in the library with her husband. This brief intrusion of reality not only reminds us of the story-within-the-story method of the film but points up the conflict.

Part of the frame itself is presented subjectively. In the first scene on the train Laura is so preoccupied that she does not hear what Dolly is saying. Accordingly Dolly's voice is made to fade away on the sound track and, while the camera pictures Dolly still talking, Laura's voice is heard in interior monologue.

The story-within-the-story method is complicated by reveries *within* Laura's reverie. For example, Laura recollects that when she was riding home on the train she imagined herself and Alec "in all sorts of glamorous circumstances." As Laura turns to look out of the window, the camera tracks and pans slowly forward until a back projection of the darkened countryside fills the screen. Laura's face is faintly reflected in the window as she narrates in voice-over: "I stared out of that railway carriage window into the dark and watched the dim trees and the telegraph posts slipping by, and through them I saw Alec and me." Then as the view of the countryside dissolves to that of a ballroom in which Laura and Alec are dancing, the noise of the train recedes and is replaced by music. Again Laura's voice is heard: "Alec and me—perhaps a little youn-

ger than we are now." The sound of the train returns and the dancing figures dissolve to the passing countryside. Again the train noise dies away and is replaced by the sound of an orchestra tuning up while the countryside changes to a picture of Laura and Alec in a theatre box. Several more imagined scenes are similarly presented. As the last one dissolves to the passing countryside, Laura's reflection appears on the window too. Then the camera pulls back. The window, which has been one with the screen, is now again only the window, beside which Laura is still sitting. In this sequence the primary reverie is represented by Laura, by Laura's reflection in the window, by the landscape outside, by Laura's voice, and by the sound of the train. The inner reverie is represented by the series of scenes Laura imagines and by the music.

The subjective-within-the-subjective occurs again when Laura recalls that as she was sitting alone in the refreshment room she was preoccupied by what she and Alec had said to each other a few moments before about going back to Stephen's flat. As Laura sits at the table recollecting their conversation, the camera shows her in a medium-close shot. The loudspeaker announces her train. Then as the camera remains on Laura, her voice and Alec's are heard on the sound track, Laura's voice repeating, "I must go home," and Alec saying, "I'm going back to the flat."

The difference between objective and subjective narration is strikingly illustrated by two presentations of the same scene. The last scene in the refreshment room is a reenactment of the first scene there except that now it is presented, not from an objective point of view, but from Laura's. Laura is now remembering what happened in that earlier scene; so there are differences in the way the scene is filmed. In the first place, the reenacted scene is partly a condensation of the original one, since Laura does not recollect the scene in every detail, in fact, could not, because she goes out onto the platform during it. In the reenactment Laura is heard in voice-over: "Dolly went on talking, but I wasn't listening to her." Accordingly Dolly's voice fades out while Laura's, narrating the scene, is heard above it. In the original scene Laura is not shown rushing out to throw herself under the express, the camera remaining on Dolly. Now not only does the camera concentrate on Laura but photographs off level—a cinematic equivalent of studied distortion in expressionistic drama to manifest strong emotion. A sequence of five shots begins with a close-up of Laura as the camera starts to revolve. In the next shot, as Laura gets up and runs to the door, the camera, panning to follow her, remains off level, so that she seems to be running uphill. There is a cut to the platform, and Laura runs out the door and toward the tracks, the camera again photographing off level. A shot of the tracks from above is similarly titled. The next shot, also tilted, is a close-up of Laura as she sways on the edge of the platform and the lights from the train streak past her face. The roar of the train is deafening. Then, as the lights stop flashing and the sound rapidly dies away, the camera slowly returns to horizontal.

The deletion of the only two characters who appear in *Still Life* but not in *Brief Encounter* is in keeping with the change from the objective to the subjective point of view. These characters are minor. One of them is the girl who comes in with a message for Beryl, the assistant at the lunch counter, and the other is the young man who orders coffee and a sandwich. Although in the film Laura and Alec are amused by some of the conversation and byplay of the station people, they are not seriously concerned in Beryl's private affairs. To include in the film, then, the business of the message would involve both a violation of the subjective point of view and an irrelevancy. The young man ordering coffee and a sandwich interrupts the colloquy between Albert Godby, the ticket taker, and Myrtle Bagot, the manageress of the refreshment room. In the play the progress of Albert's affair with Myrtle is continually checked by the official duties of the participants and re-

stricted by its being carried on in public. This low-comedy affair parodies the affair between Laura and Alec. The parody is kept in the adaptation, but the subjective point of view of the film reduces the importance of the station attendants. Since the young man is not necessary, he is left out.

There is another result of the changed point of view. In the play the station attendants are aware of the affair between Laura and Alec and make allusions to it when the principals are not on the scene. But since, in the film, the story is told from Laura's point of view, this aspect of it is deleted in the adaptation. Also deleted are other bits of dialogue which take place in the station but which Laura would not hear.

The device of the story told within a frame admits readily of cinematic treatment. It is, in effect, the old device of the flashback. The conventional means of bridging the gap between a frame and a story within the frame is the dissolve. In *Brief Encounter,* however, the gap is bridged by more than the dissolve. In the first place, the subjective point of view has been introduced during a scene in the frame at the beginning of the film when Laura's thoughts are expressed out loud on the sound track. But even in this scene, which presents Laura and Dolly in the train compartment, the intrusion of the subjective is effected smoothly by a separation of the visual from the audio image. Dolly's incessant chatter and Laura's nervous condition make the separation of the images seem natural—Dolly's moving lips but no sound from them, Laura's closed lips but Laura's voice. The subjective having thus been established, it does not seem awkward when the images are again separated in the transition from the frame to the story within it. Furthermore the dissolve does not occur at once, but only after Laura's voice has been heard for a minute or so while movement of the camera and cutting keep Laura's speech from seeming stagy. As the library dissolves into the refreshment room, the image of Laura in the library does not fade out with the rest of the scene. Consequently Laura is represented as being at once in the library and in the refreshment room; that is, she is watching herself. Finally, there is the music which comes over the radio. Laura has tuned in on the Rachmaninoff Concerto in C Minor. The music, which lulls her into a reverie, helps to bridge the gap between the frame and the subjective part of the film, not only at this point, but also later when the frame intrudes again, that is, when Laura is roused from her reverie by Fred's calling out to her because the radio has become too loud.

The music serves also as an accompaniment to the reverie itself. It becomes, in effect, the background music to the subjective part of the film. Familiar music originating in the story adds to the realism, as for example, that of the barrel organ, the ladies' orchestra in the restaurant, and the organ in the motion-picture theatre. But the use of familiar music as background music is usually avoided in films because of conflicting associations it would set up in the minds of the audience, the attention of which the director is trying to control. In *Brief Encounter,* however, the Rachmaninoff Concerto is more than background music. Because it has been introduced naturally in the frame, it subtly relates the realistic to the subjective part of the film. The use of the Concerto is also evocative, for as Roger Manvell has pointed out, the heavily emotional music enables the film to get away from the expression of emotion through open words and deeds.

The relation becomes less subtle, but no less effective, when, about midway in the film, Laura is momentarily roused from her reverie:

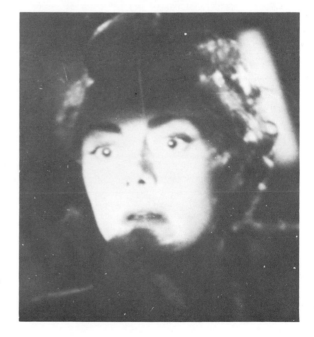

> *In the foreground of the picture the dim outline of Laura can be seen watching herself and Alec as they walk along the subway towards Number 4 platform. The sound of an express train roaring overhead becomes the sound of loud music. Fred's voice is heard.*

Fred is calling out to Laura about the loudness of the music coming over the radio. Then the scene dissolves into the library —a long shot over Laura's shoulder, Laura

in the same position as that of the dim outline in the preceding shot. The use of the
simultaneous images of Laura—Laura in
the subway and the dim outline of Laura in
the foreground—is comparable to that in
the reverse transition earlier in the film—
from the frame to the subjective part, when
the image of Laura in the library remains
on the screen in the foreground for several
seconds after the dissolve to Laura in the
refreshment room is completed. The sound
in the transition is natural, in that sounds
imagined in dreams have realistic counterparts, and it is germane, in that the loudness
of the music which induces Laura to imagine
the sound of the train is that of the radio
playing the Concerto.

Transition in which the means are inte-
grated with content is, in fact, characteristic
of *Brief Encounter.* When Laura looks out
the window and imagines herself and Alec
in glamorous settings, the imagined scenes
are linked not merely by dissolves but also
by the interpolated shots of the landscape
outside, by Laura's voice, and by the inter-
changing of the sound of the train with that
of music. When the camera tracks and pans
forward, the car window becomes a motion-
picture screen itself, on which the imagined
scenes appear. After the last of these scenes
the return to the compartment is effected
not only by dissolves and a drawing back
of the camera but by elements inherent in
the content. Laura's voice on the sound
track implies what is happening: "Then the
palm trees changed into those pollarded
willows by the canal just before the level
crossing." The sound of the music fades
again into the sound of the train and, before
the camera pulls back, Laura's reflection
is seen in the window.

In the reverie in which Laura imagines
that she hears her voice and Alec's, sound
is the principal means of transition. There
is a close-up of Laura as she is sitting in
the refreshment room. *"A train bell goes.
She fumbles in her bag and finds a cigarette.
She lights it. There is the sound of her train
approaching."* After the loudspeaker has
announced the Ketchworth train and as the

camera remains on Laura, the voices are heard on the sound track. And the camera remains on Laura after the voices are heard. These transitions are thus made in a single shot, the scene not changing from the refreshment room.

When Laura again comes out of her reverie, the return to reality is effected, not by a dissolve, but by a cut and movement of the camera. Laura has just reentered the refreshment room, having rushed out to the platform to throw herself under the train. She shuts the door and leans back against it—in a medium shot, from which there is a cut to a close-up of her. But because of the lighting in the close-up, the door, against which she is supposedly leaning, is indistinguishable. Then the camera pulls back, the light comes up, and Laura is seen, not leaning against the door in the refreshment room, but sitting in her chair in the library.

Brief Encounter is faithful to the realism of *Still Life.* As in the play, the principal characters are middle-aged and middle class. They have the same commonplace names —Laura Jesson and Alec Harvey. There is no attempt to make them or their love affair more glamorous than in the play. Laura's clothes *"are not smart but obviously chosen with taste."* Laura's home is unpretentious, and the drab realism of the refreshment room in the station is accentuated by detail that would have satisfied von Stroheim. Laura and Alec go to the movies, go boating, take drives into the country, where they stop by a stone bridge over a little stream, meet clandestinely in a friend's flat—occasions which might imply a glamorous treatment. But the glamour is deliberately played down: the film they see at the Palladium so bad that it is a parody of bad films, the boating expedition on a wintry day and Alec's lack of oarsmanship resulting in minor disaster, the bleak scene at the bridge in the country, and the bare and cold flat with the smoldering fireplace. The lack of glamor makes Laura's reverie on the train all the more effective by contrast: Laura and Alec, a little younger than they are, "dancing a gay waltz . . . being together in

a box at the Opera . . . drifting along the Grand Canal in a gondola . . . driving through beautiful countryside . . . leaning on the rail of a ship . . . standing on some tropical beach in the moonlight."

Brief Encounter makes the most of possibilities for realism inherent in a railway station. Whereas in the play the trains are represented only by offstage noises, the film presents them directly and with a documentarylike quality. The train scenes, which were shot in the station at Carnforth in Lancashire, are reminiscent of *Night Mail.* The arrival and departure of the local trains and the roaring through of the expresses are made interesting, but not just for their own sake. Roger Manvell has pointed out that the express trains "gradually become symbolic of the lover's inability to fulfill their passion, confined as they were to catching the slow, necessary and useful locals." "The first awful feeling of danger swept over me," Laura is heard saying, and her statement is emphasized by a noise of escaping steam as a locomotive comes toward the foreground. In the scene in which Alec startles Laura by saying that he is going back to Stephen's flat, an express is heard approaching in the distance. As Laura and Alec look at each other, *"the noise of the express rises to a thundering crescendo out of which emerges the scream of the train whistle."* The scene cuts to the tunnel entrance. *"An express hurtles out of the tunnel."* The scene then cuts back to Laura and Alec: they are in each other's arms. This montage is comparable to the scene in *Greed* in which the express flashes past as McTeague embraces Trina.

This kind of "dramatized reality," as David Lean, the director of *Brief Encounter,* calls it, is evidenced even in the lighting. As the film opens, Albert Godby is clocking a train passing through the station. His face, beaming approval because the train is on time, is illuminated by flashes of light reflected from the windows of the passing coaches. Just before the end of the film, when Laura is also watching a train pass, similar flashes, together with the deafening noise, accentuate her distraught expression.

Some of the realistic touches in the film have ironic overtones. Laura has come home from her farewell meeting with Alec at the railroad station, and now she and Fred, in a scene in the dining room, are discussing the children. A train whistle is heard, whereupon *"Laura's eyes suddenly fill with tears."* In *Still Life* the station attendants become aware of the couple's weekly meetings in the refreshment room, but in *Brief Encounter* the ticket taker does not recognize Laura and Alec when they hand him their tickets. On the station platform, as Laura and Alec are discussing a momentous matter, three girls run giggling by. There is dramatic irony in the sequence in which Laura telephones Mary Norton. Although upset, Laura makes her voice sound natural, and thus Mary is unaware that "the most appalling domestic lie" in which Laura is asking her to back her up is not so appalling as the truth. The scene is intercut with a shot of Mary at her dressing table at the other end of the line. She is holding the telephone, over which Laura's voice is heard, but she shows no interest in what Laura is saying. Instead she is intent on her makeup as she leans forward to examine herself in the mirror.

Although *Brief Encounter* has been praised primarily for being about real people treated realistically, its chief contribution to motion pictures is something more. The critics called *Brief Encounter* adult. David Lean said, "We defied all the rules of box-office success. There were no big names. There was an unhappy ending to the main love story. The film was played in unglamorous surroundings. And the three leading characters were approaching middle age. A few years ago this would have been a recipe for box-office failure, but this wasn't the case with *Brief Encounter.*" Because it was not a box-office failure and because it has been continually revived, it should encourage the making of other films like it. An exemplary adaptation of a one-act play to the screen, it is inherently cinematic.

Adaptation of a play to the screen implies, then, a translation of the dramatic into the cinematic. To present the play in its own terms is not to adapt it. It is the adaptation that accounts for the effectiveness of *Abe Lincoln in Illinois* and *Brief Encounter.* Without violating the purpose and the spirit of the play, each of these films tells the story as a film should tell it. In telling it in this way, it represents not just the motion-picture machine but motion-picture art.

14.
From Novel to Film

Discussion of a film based on a novel or a play arrives sooner or later at a comparison of the film with its source. This kind of criticism may have its advantages. But somehow it leads to the mistaken conclusion that the excellence of the film depends on similarity to the novel or the play from which it is adapted.

It is relevant to observe that the method of the motion pictures is more like that of the novel than of the play. The way a novel tells a story—primarily by description and narration—is comparable to the way a film does—primarily by pictures—whereas the dramatic method of storytelling is primarily dialogue. It is true of course that a more literal adaptation can be made of a play than of a novel. A film resembles a play in manner of presentation; that is, it can be seen and heard. A play might therefore be so recorded by camera and microphone as to be almost identical to the play produced on the stage. The more faithfully a film "follows the play," the more like the play it becomes—and the less cinematic. A novel, on the other hand, is faithfully adapted to the screen by a translation of the novelistic terms into cinematic ones and thus by being different. For these reasons a film adapted from a play is seldom better than, or even as good as, the original play, whereas a film

adapted from a novel is frequently as good as the original novel, and occasionally better. With few exceptions, films made from novels are better than films made from plays. They are invariably better than films adapted from plays literally—and they are better because of the ways in which they are different.

Although a film made from a novel is sometimes praised for "following" the book, literal likeness is of course impossible. It is ironic, however, that frequently the conspicuous differences between a film and its source are due not to the cinematic way of storytelling, but to changes imposed arbitrarily. The changes may be as minor, for example, as the one in *Great Expectations* (1946) in which the sound of the mice rattling behind a panel in Miss Havisham's dining room in Dickens's novel becomes, in the film, a mouse seen nibbling the wedding cake on the table. Or the changes may be as radical as the one in *The Informer* in which the motivation for Gypo's informing, that is, a half-realized need of money for a night's lodging, becomes in the film Gypo's wanting money for two steamship tickets to America. Although it might be argued that on the screen a mouse is more effective seen than heard or that the hero's wanting to take his girl to America is a more plausible motive than wanting shelter, such changes are for the most part not dictated by the necessities of the medium.

Considerably less arbitrary, however, is the matter of style. In the adaptation of a play, the playwright's style can be retained only in whatever dialogue is carried over verbatim into the film. What, though, if the adaptation be that of a novel? The film *Great Expectations* begins with a shot of a book being opened and the voice of John Mills, the actor who plays the older Pip, reading the first paragraph of *Great Expectations* as Dickens wrote it. This literal injection of the paragraph into the film, however, is hardly cinematic. A film adapted from a novel cannot naturally retain the author's style. In describing a scene in the estuary Dickens writes:

. . . some ballast-lighters, shaped like a child's first rude imitation of a boat, lay low in the mud; and a little squat shoal-lighthouse on open piles, stood crippled in the mud on stilts and crutches; and slimy stakes stuck out of the mud, and slimy stones stuck out of the mud, and red landmarks and tidemarks stuck out of the mud, and an old landing-stage and an old roofless building slipped into the mud, and all about us was stagnation and mud.

But the scene in the estuary, for all its realism, cannot approximate the style in Dickens's description. On the other hand, if the passage were merely recited on the sound track, it would be as extrinsic as the recitation of Auden's poem in *Night Mail*.

The running time of *Great Expectations* is two hours. Dickens's novel runs to about five hundred pages. On the assumption that one can read a page a minute, it might be estimated that the reading time of *Great Expectations* is eight hours, although one would not ordinarily read five hundred pages continuously at this rate. In one respect it may be said, then, that the film adaptation of *Great Expectations* is only a quarter as long as the novel. What accounts for the contraction? Consider Dickens's description of Miss Havisham's dining room:

I crossed the staircase landing, and entered the room she indicated. From that room, too, the daylight was completely excluded, and it had an airless smell that was oppressive. A fire had been lately kindled in the damp old-fashioned grate, and it was more disposed to go out than to burn up, and the reluctant smoke which hung in the room seemed colder than the clearer air—like our own marsh mist. Certain wintry branches of candles on the high chimney-piece faintly lighted the chamber; or, it would be more expressive to say, faintly troubled its darkness. It was spacious, and I dare say had once been handsome, but every discernible thing in it was covered with dust and mould, and dropping to pieces. The most prominent object was a long table with a tablecloth spread on it, as if a feast had been in preparation when the house and the clocks all stopped together. An epergne or centre-piece of some kind was in the middle of this cloth; it was so heavily overhung with cobwebs that its form was quite indistinguishable.

Except for the airless smell and the temperature, not to mention Dickens's style, the description of Miss Havisham's dining room can be represented on the screen—and in only a few seconds. Although it happens that in depicting this particular scene in the film the camera probes about the room for more than a few seconds, the time could be reduced to nothing. For in a novel the action ceases when the novelist begins to describe, but in a film the description and narration can be simultaneous. For example, Dickens takes a page to describe Miss Havisham. In the film we *see* Miss Havisham while Pip is entering the room, and we continue to see her throughout most of the scene. Since a film takes less time to describe than a novel, it cannot be said that a film is shortened by a curtailing of description.

On the other hand, a film takes more time to narrate than a novel. Suppose, for example, the novelist writes that the hero went to London. The narration is effected as briefly as that. But if the hero's going to London were presented in a film, even if the action were reduced to a minimum, as for example, just the hero's departure and arrival, it would require more time than that for a reading of the statement. In *The*

David Lean, *Great Expectations. Courtesy of the J. Arthur Rank Organization*

Informer O'Flaherty narrates McPhillip's death in hardly more than a hundred words:

At thirty-five minutes past seven Francis Joseph McPhillip shot himself dead while trying to escape from No. 44 Titt Street, his father's house. The house had been surrounded by Detective Sergeant McCartney and ten men. Hanging by his left hand from the sill of the back-bedroom window on the second floor, McPhillip put two bullets into McCartney's left shoulder. While he was trying to fire again, his left hand slipped and lost its hold. The pistol muzzle struck the edge of the sill. The bullet shot upwards and entered McPhillip's brain through the right temple.

In the film this bit of narration comprises a sequence of more than three minutes. The clocks on the wall of the police station and on the wall of the McPhillip kitchen not only link the separate locales but expand the phrase "at thirty-five minutes past seven." Or take, for example, the statement "The house had been surrounded." It becomes, in screen terms, the soldiers getting into trucks at police headquarters, general indistinct talking, an officer giving a command, the trucks starting, the trucks arriving at the McPhillip house, the sergeant giving orders, a machine gun being set up, and so forth. Other statements in the novel are correspondingly expanded. Thus, although in the adaptation of a novel to the screen, description implies contraction, narration implies expansion. But a novel comprises more narration than description. Even the maximum length of time that an audience could be expected to sit watching a film would fall far short of the time required to include all of the narration in an average-length novel. A film adapted from a novel therefore implies deletions.

When *Great Expectations* was adapted to the screen, Orlick, Joe's journeyman, was left out and therefore all of that part of the plot which depends on him. Other characters were also omitted—Mr. Wopsle's great aunt, Trabb, Trabb's boy, the Avenger, Miss Skiffins, and Clara—and the film is accordingly narrower in scope than the novel. Episodes are abridged: Pumblechook's taking Pip to Miss Havisham's, Pip's preparation for leaving home, Mrs. Joe's death, and the return of Magwitch. In the novel Mr. Jaggers finds Pip and Joe at the Three Jolly Bargemen and then accompanies them home, where Pip's great expectations are revealed. In the film, all of the scenes at the public house having been deleted, the incident is compressed into a single scene at the forge.

This kind of contraction tends to make a film like a play not only in scope, for it results in fewer characters, scenes, incidents, and plots than in a novel, but also in detail, for when a novel is adapted to the screen, detail is elaborated as in a play. The brief passage in *The Informer* narrating Frankie's death is expanded in the film to present such details as Frankie's arriving home, his conversation with his mother and his sister, the police surrounding the house, and Frankie's attempt to escape. Furthermore the film presents the setting and the appearance of the characters in as much detail as in a play produced on the stage.

In being adapted to the screen a novel, then, is both contracted and expanded. It in contracted in scope and expanded in detail, according to Mortimer Adler's dictum. Whereas a play in being adapted to the screen takes on certain aspects of a novel, a novel in being adapted takes on certain aspects of a play. However, because the cinematic way is more like the novelistic than like the dramatic, a film is more like a novel than like a play. It cannot of course be exactly like a novel. It is something less than a novel. But it is also something more.

Although a film cannot "follow the book" in the matter of style, it can remain true to it in other ways. The most impressive parts of Dickens's *Great Expectations* are the descriptions of the marshes and the effect of the marshes on Pip. These are the Cooling Marshes in East Kent, where Dickens himself lived. He refers to them again and again, not just for the sake of description but for projection of character. Dickens was conscious of the effect of the marshes on himself, and he has them similarly affect Pip. The scene of the impressive opening sequence of the film is the marshes, and the marshes and the river are the backgrounds for other scenes too. The scenes were shot in the actual marsh country, the British Royal Navy providing a tank landing craft for the purpose. The film is true to the novel in another way in which character is delineated. Dickens has a good enough memory to see his own unhappy childhood clearly, and in *Great Expectations* he describes the treatment of a child from a child's point of view. The film, like the novel, shows Pip ordered about, nagged at, regarded condescendingly and, above all, having his dignity imposed upon. Mrs. Joe's experience with Orlick is left out of the film, but not Mrs. Joe's treatment of Pip. The Christmas dinner, as in the novel, is made the occasion for the grown-ups to torment the boy. Joe is the only one of the company to respect Pip's feelings. The film is also true to the autobiographical in the novel in its reflection of Dickens's consciousness of his own poverty-stricken background. As though ashamed of his early life, Dickens went to extremes to show that he was a gentleman. He dressed ostentatiously, to the point of vulgarity. Pip goes to London to learn to be a gentleman and is ashamed of his sister because she is married to a blacksmith. He is even ashamed of Joe. This attitude of Pip's is emphasized in scene after scene.

The theme of the novel is ingratitude. As a child Pip is told to be grateful. Magwitch's gratitude for Pip's little kindness results in Pip's great expectations. Later Pip is bothered by his conscience, but not enough to keep him from becoming a snob. It is not until he has lost his money that he really repents and begs forgiveness for his ingratitude. Mainly as a result of contraction in scope the emphasis on theme is lessened in the adaptation. For example, whereas in the novel Pip becomes snobbish before he leaves the forge, in the film his snobbishness is not evident until Joe visits him in London. But the film is true to the theme and to the irony implicit in it.

One of the reasons that *Great Expectations* is a promising source for a film is that its characters are depicted not so much by complex psychological makeup as by physical appearance, mannerisms, dress, and other outward manifestations. They are interesting as individuals, but they are types. Pumblechook is a pompous nincompoop, Mrs. Joe is a termagant, Joe is a likable rustic, Estella is a spoiled child, and Drummle is an adventurer. By acting, costuming, and makeup these characters can be faithfully translated to the screen. They are theatric themselves. On the screen they look as Dickensian as the Cruikshank drawings.

Even the incredible Miss Havisham is no less believable than in the novel. Although a novel can be more fantastic than a film, a film, as Adler has pointed out, can be at once more fantastic and more realistic than a novel. Miss Havisham, together with her impossible surroundings, is as credible in the film as the more realistic Pip. Dickens would be satisfied with Martita

Hunt's impersonation of his eccentric creation.

Dickens's novel is almost cinematic itself in its variety of striking and often spectacular scenes. These David Lean, director of the film, has made the most of—Pip's meeting the convict in the graveyard and other scenes on the marshes, Pip's visit to Satis House, the surprise return of Magwitch, and particularly the running down of the skiffs by the packet boat. The stagecoach scenes are no less fascinating in the film than in the novel.

The construction of *Great Expectations* is particularly well suited to screen adaptation. Having more sense of form than most of Dickens's novels, *Great Expectations* is put together like a fan. Pip is the handle, and the sticks are linked by his first meeting with the convict. As a result of the contraction in scope in the adaptation, some of the sticks are left out, as for example, Orlick's beating Mrs. Joc and Pip's adventures with Orlick. The adapters did not even find it necessary to make radical changes in the order of events.

Watching the film, however, one has the continual impression of being rushed through Dickens's novel—of pauses, now for one scene or episode, now another, but of pages and pages being flipped by. It is disconcerting to a Dickens reader who would have the film literally "follow the book." But it is not so disconcerting if one appreciates the impossibility of literal duplication and the necessity of "contraction in the direction of dramatic magnitude," that is, if one accepts the film on its own terms. As a matter of fact, though, the film does not disregard all of the flipped-by pages. Consider, for example, the gap between the scene in which Pip tells Miss Havisham that he can no longer "come to play," because he is going to be apprenticed to Joe—itself a condensation of a corresponding scene in the novel —and that in which, five chapters later, Jaggers informs Pip of "great expectations." Bridging the gap is only the more difficult because in the former scene Pip is played by a young actor, and in the latter an older

David Lean, *Great Expectations. Courtesy of the J. Arthur Rank Organization*

learning to become a gentleman. This time it is a montage of scenes in which Pip is taking dancing, fencing, and boxing lessons.

To the extent that the film reproduces the dialogue in Dickens's novel, the film may be said to "follow the book." Dickens, who had a flair for the dramatic, writes many of his scenes as though for the stage. The chapter in which Pip reproaches Miss Havisham for letting him suppose that she was his benefactor is like a scene from a play. It is composed largely of dialogue, which can be literally reproduced on the sound track. But to the extent to which it is so reproduced, the scene is dramatic rather than cinematic. It is no more cinematic than the comparatively static images of the actors permit. The ineffectiveness of this scene in the film is the extent to which it "follows the book."

There are in the novel, on the other hand, scenes which, although consisting primarily of dialogue, contain in the dialogue cues for cinematic treatment. There is, for example, the scene in which Herbert Pocket and Pip, having just met for the first time since childhood, are at dinner. Since in this scene Dickens has Herbert narrate antecedent action, the scene is talky. But Dickens interpolates Herbert's exposition with Herbert's criticism of Pip's table manners. In the novel Pip's manners are only implied; in the film they are visual as well, and camera and editing make the most of them.

The narrative passages in some of these scenes are themselves the cues for cinematic treatment. In the chapter in which Joe visits Pip and Herbert in London, Dickens includes, as it were, stage directions for the business with Joe's hat, which keeps falling off the mantelpiece. Similarly he writes cues for breaking up the dialogue between Pip and Wemmick at Wemmick's Castle—the exchange of exaggerated nods between Pip and the Aged Parent.

The visual elements in these scenes are as dramatic as they would be in a play, but because of editing they become cinematic as well. This distinction between the merely dramatic and the dramatic together with

one. The gap is bridged by the voice of the older Pip heard on the sound track. It is also bridged cinematically. As the latter scene opens, Pip is not directly visible; instead, his shadow is cast on the wall of the forge. And before Pip himself is seen, he is heard answering Jaggers's question. The shadow and the voice help to bridge the gap and make the change from the younger to the older Pip less sudden and less startling than it would be otherwise. Again pages are flipped by, as it were, until Pip is seen presenting himself at Satis House to pay his respects before leaving for London. Here editing and movement of the camera effect the transition. From a shot of Pip in his blacksmith's apron just after he has heard of his "great expectations," the film dissolves to another shot of Pip. At the beginning of this second shot only his feet are visible. Then the camera tilts slowly up, revealing Pip, fashionably dressed, standing at Miss Havisham's gate. Still another method condenses much that Dickens writes about Pip's

David Lean, *Great Expectations. Courtesy of the J. Arthur Rank Organization*

the cinematic is particularly evident in the way in which the film treats the scene of the Assembly Ball at Richmond. Dickens writes the scene almost entirely in dialogue, the background merely mentioned. Although the film includes much of this dialogue, it is presented as accompaniment to a variety of shots in which the background is the ballroom, the dancers, and the music. The scene is one of the most spectacular scenes in the film. Furthermore the dialogue is broken up by the announcement of the

dances—the announcer seen as well as heard—and by such other visual images as the dancing of the Spanish polka, during which Pip and Estella are continually being separated.

The kind of detail and emphasis that editing can effect is illustrated by what is called the "reaction shot." For example, when Mrs. Joe starts whipping Pip, there is a cut to a medium shot of Joe. We hear the swishes of the whip outside the scene, but we see Joe wince with each swish. When

Jaggers pours the gold pieces onto the table in the forge, there are reaction shots to show Pip's and Joe's amazement. When Herbert dashes into the room and suddenly sees the convict, the camera rushes at Herbert in a veritable zoom shot to catch his frightened expression. Particularly effective is the reaction shot in the scene of Jaggers's explanation to Pip that Magwitch is in danger of his life by returning to England. "Look out that window," Jaggers tells Pip. The scene cuts to the street below. Here has been erected a gallows, on which several prisoners are about to be hanged and around which is a crowd of people. The scene cuts back to a close-up of Pip watching the execution. Then, while the camera remains on Pip, a roar goes up from the crowd, out of the scene, and Pip's face contorts in revulsion.

Sound helps to tell the story far beyond its merely realistic accompaniment to the pictures. When Pip slowly opens the door to Miss Havisham's room and reveals the weird scene within, the background music swells to emphasize the startling effect. Music imitates the rocking motion of the stagecoach, and as the coach enters London the music is picked up by the ringing of the London church bells. In the scene in the estuary, when Pip sees the pursuing boat, we hear the screaming of the gulls. We have seen and heard the gulls in a preceding shot. The sound is now at once realistic and symbolic. Sound also links shots in another way. The steersman in the pursuing boat is calling the stroke. The scene cuts to Pip's boat, and Pip and Pocket are rowing in time to the steersman's count. A combination of sounds is made effective when Mrs. Joe, driving up to the forge with Pumblechook, opens her mouth to scream at Pip and is unheard because the sound of the wind drowns out what she is saying. It is a cinematic metaphor: Mrs. Joe's words and the wind are one. Absence of sound increases humor in the scene in which Pumblechook and Pip are driving to Miss Havisham's, the camera tracking along with them. Pumblechook is seen speaking to Pip, who holds

out his hands for inspection. Pumblechook fatuously nods approval. The only sound is that of the spirited background music in imitation of the brisk movement of the chaise.

The film may also be said to "follow the book" in that it tells the story from the same point of view as the novel, that is, in the first person, the narrator being the chief character. Consider, for example, the opening scene. Dickens begins the narration of it as follows:

Ours was the marsh country, down by the river, within, as the river wound, twenty miles of the sea. My first most vivid and broad impression of the identity of things, seems to me to have been gained on a memorable raw afternoon towards evening. At such a time I found out for certain, that this bleak place overgrown with nettles was the churchyard; and that Philip Pirrip, late of this parish, and also Georgiana wife of the above, were dead and buried; and that Alexander, Bartholomew, Abraham, Tobias, and Roger, infant children of the aforesaid, were also dead and buried; and that the dark flat wilderness beyond the churchyard, intersected with dykes and mounds and gates, with scattered cattle feeding on it, was the marshes; and that the low leaden line beyond was the river; and that the distant savage lair from which the wind was rushing, was the sea; and that the small bundle of shivers growing afraid of it all and beginning to cry, was Pip.

"Hold your noise!" cried a terrible voice, as a man started up from among the graves at the side of the church porch. "Keep still, you little devil, or I'll cut your throat!"

A fearful man, all in coarse grey, with a great iron on his leg. A man with no hat, and with broken shoes, and with an old rag tied round his head. A man who had been soaked in water, and smothered in mud, and lamed by stones, and cut by flints, and stung by nettles, and torn by briars; who limped, and shivered, and glared and and growled; and whose teeth chattered in his head as he seized me by the chin.

The problem in the adaptation was to present the incident from the point of view of the small frightened boy. The film resolves it in this way:

1. Exterior Thames Estuary. Sunset. The wind is making a high-pitched, ghostly whistling noise. VLS of a small boy—Pip running left to right along the bank of the Estuary. Camera tracks and pans with Pip as he runs round a bend in the pathway and comes toward camera. A gibbet is built on the edge of the path, camera right, and Pip glances up at it as he passes—he continues running and moves out of picture camera right. *Dissolve to:*

2. Exterior Churchyard. Wind continues. MS Pip. He is carrying a bunch of holly in his right hand. He climbs over a broken stone wall and camera pans right with him as he walks past the tombstones and old graves in the churchyard. Camera continues panning as he makes his way towards one of the tombstones and kneels in front of it—he is now in MLS.

3. MS of Pip kneeling at the foot of the grave. Wind continues. Pip pulls up an old rose bush, which he throws aside, pats down the earth again and then places his bunch of holly at the head of the grave near the engraved tombstone. Crackling of branches.

4. MCS Pip kneeling near the tombstone. Wind gets louder. Pip looks round nervously towards camera.

5. LS from Pip's eyeline of the leafless branches of a tree. Wind and crackling of branches. The wind is blowing the branches, which look to Pip like bony hands clutching at him.

6. MCS Pip looks round as in 4.

7. MS of the trunk of an old tree from Pip's eyeline. The tree makes a creaking sound. The tree looks sinister to Pip, like a distorted human body.

8. MS Pip. He jumps up from the grave and runs away right to left towards the stone wall. Camera pans with him, then becomes static as he runs into the arms of a large, dirty, uncouth and horrible-looking man. From his clothes and shackles it is obvious that he is an escaped convict. Pip screams loudly.

9. CS Pip. His mouth is open as he screams, but a large, dirty hand is clapped over it, silencing him.

10. CS of the Convict. His face is dirty and scowling, his hair is closely cut. He leers down at Pip.
CONVICT: Keep still, you little devil, or I'll cut your throat.[1]

The sudden appearance of the convict is made as frightening to us as to Pip, because the scene has been built up from Pip's point of view. Lean's method is similar to that in *The Informer* when the soldiers are photographed from the point of view of Frankie hiding in the archway. But the scene in *Great Expectations* is subtly subjective throughout. Pip's solitariness is indicated in the first shot—a very long shot of a small boy. The method is comparable to that in *Intolerance* when Griffith photographs the manager of the factory seated alone at the end of a room. The eeriness of the opening scene in *Great Expectations* is heightened by the lighting, the solitary marshes, the gibbet, the graveyard, the wind. In the medium-close shot of Pip kneeling near the tombstone, the camera, at Pip's height, makes the tombstone loom larger than it really is. At the sound of the crackling branches Pip looks nervously around, and we see the branches *from Pip's eyeline.* The interpolated shots of the bare branches, which *look like bony hands clutching at him,* and of the gnarled tree, which *looks sinister to Pip, like a distorted human body,* are pictorial counterparts of the sounds. The sound track singles out the crackling of the branches and the creaking of the tree so that we not only see, but *hear,* from Pip's point of view.

The empathy is so well established that when Pip can stand the frightening atmosphere no longer and starts to run away, we run with him, as it were. And we run with him into something still more frightening—the convict. As Pip starts to scream, there is an instantaneous cut to the close-up of Pip and the convict's hand clamping over Pip's mouth. Jack Harris, who edited the film, explains how the point of view is effected here:

The most difficult thing to get over by photography was the sudden appearance of the convict. The effect was finally obtained by panning with the boy until he runs straight into the stationary convict.

The difficulty in the editing was to decide on the exact frame up to which to leave the panning shot on the screen and to cut to the boy screaming. The effect aimed at was to leave the shot on the screen sufficiently long to let the audience see that the boy had run into a man—and

David Lean, *Great Expectations. Courtesy of the J. Arthur Rank Organization*

not a very nice man, at that—but not sufficiently long to get a good look and be able to decide that he was after all something recognisably human. As a matter of interest, there are fourteen frames from the time the convict appears to the close-up of Pip. The sound of Pip's scream starts four frames before the cut, at just the precise moment that the apparition is taken away from the audience's sight.[2]

A subjective point of view is somewhat similarly effected in other parts of the film. There is, for example, the scene in which Pip, ascending the stairs at Satis House, encounters the formidable Mr. Jaggers fumbling his way down. We see Jaggers as Pip does—in a low-angle shot. (A low-angle shot is a shot in which the camera photographs an image from below eye level.) The angle makes Jaggers appear all the more formidable to the small boy. Then there is the Christmas-dinner scene: when Pip can stand the table talk no longer, he gets up and starts to run out of the room—and runs directly

into a soldier standing in the doorway. Since we have not seen the soldier before, we are as startled as Pip. By dramatic irony the scene has built up Pip's apprehension that the theft of the pie will be discovered. Thus the apprehension is as intense for us as for Pip, and thus the sudden frustration of Pip's attempt to escape is vicariously ours. In the scene in which Magwitch visits Pip in London, subjectivity is effected in somewhat the same way. Magwitch's sudden appearance is prepared for, but it is not expected. The sequence opens with a view of the city at night—wind, mist, rain. Then Pip is seen in his lodgings, the sound of the wind and the rain continuing. When in response to a knock Pip opens the door, the camera is facing the black, muffled figure standing in the hall outside. We do not see Pip's expression of surprise. We see Magwitch—and are surprised ourselves.

The door opening to reveal Magwitch is comparable to an iris-in. But the use of the door for this purpose is more effective than an iris-in would be, because the door is part of the scene itself. Similarly when Pip timidly opens the door to Miss Havisham's room, the room is gradually revealed to us. Or a door can be closed on a scene in the manner of an iris-out. When Pip leaves Jaggers's office, he closes the door behind him. Since the camera is on the passage, the closing door shuts off our view of the office. But the opening and closing of these doors are not merely for effect. They represent Pip's point of view.

Point of view is also effected by sound used creatively, as in *The Informer*. In the opening scene in the graveyard, Dickens has the convict threaten Pip:

"You bring me, to-morrow early, that file and them wittles. You bring the lot to me, at that old Battery over yonder. You do it, and you never dare say a word or dare to make a sign concerning your having seen such a person as me, or any person sumever, and you shall be let to live. You fail, or you go from my words in any partickler, no matter how small it is, and your heart and liver shall be tore out, roasted and ate. Now, I ain't alone, as you may think

I am. There's a young man hid with me, in comparison with which young man I am a Angel. That young man hears the words I speak. That young man has a secret way pecooliar to himself, of getting at a boy, and at his heart, and at his liver. It is in wain for a boy to attempt to hide himself from that young man. A boy may lock his door, may be warm in bed, may tuck himself up, may draw the clothes over his head, may think himself comfortable and safe, but that young man will softly creep and creep his way to him and tear him open. I am keeping that young man from harming of you at the present moment, with great difficulty. I find it wery hard to hold that young man off of your inside. Now, what do you say?"

As a result Pip is in terror not only of the young man, but of himself, for having to rob Mrs. Joe of food to appease the convict:

If I slept at all that night, it was only to imagine myself drifting down the river on a strong spring-tide, to the Hulks; a ghostly pirate calling out to me through a speaking-trumpet, as I passed the gibbet-station, that I had better come ashore and be hanged at once, and not put it off. I was afraid to sleep, even if I had been inclined, for I knew that at the first faint dawn of morning I must rob the pantry. There was no doing it in the night, for there was no getting a light by easy friction then; to have got one, I must have struck it out of flint and steel, and have made a noise like the very pirate himself rattling his chains.

In the film the convict similarly threatens Pip, but it is part of the contraction in the adaptation that Pip's thoughts about the pirate, the necessity of robbing Mrs. Joe, and the difficulties concerning a light are left out. In their place a single image is substituted to represent Pip's fear. Although it would be possible to indicate cinematically all of Pip's thoughts as Dickens records them, to do so would mean an ineffective digression in the film. Instead the adapters chose an image which is not Dickens's but which is suggested by what Dickens has had the convict say to Pip. They have Pip imagine that he hears again the convict threatening him. The post-production script indicates how it is done:

Interior Pip's Bedroom—Dawn. Medium Close Shot Pip lying in bed awake—Music starts. He pushes the clothes off and sits up in bed—he is fully clothed in his outdoor clothes—he crawls down the bed and looks out of the window.

Exterior Joe Gargery's House—Dawn. Camera shooting on to Pip's bedroom window—Pip can be seen peering through one of the window-panes.

Long Shot of the marshes and the estuary from Pip's eyeline—a mist hangs over the water; a leafless tree waves its branches in foreground.

Interior Pip's Bedroom—Dawn. Medium Shot Pip quickly getting back into bed and pulling the clothes up tightly round his chin.

CONVICT'S VOICE (in Pip's thoughts): A Boy may be warm in bed. (Pip pulls the clothes right over his head.) He may pull his clothes right over his head (Camera tracks forward on to Close Shot of Pip's covered head)—but that young man will softly creep his way to him and Tear Him Open. . . .
Pip throws back the bedclothes with a breathless 'No' and jumps out on to the floor.

The substitution of Pip's recollection of the convict's threat for Pip's imaginings about the pirate is proper cinematic treatment. The repetition of the convict's words, which are actually heard—whereas of course they could not be in a novel—makes the substitution particularly effective. The effectiveness depends on our having heard the words before. It depends particularly on the separation of the convict's voice from its natural counterpart, the convict, and the linking of the voice with another visual image—Pip. It is pure cinema in that it constitutes the creative use of sound.

Sound is also used creatively in other ways to effect an introspective point of view. As Pip goes downstairs to steal the food, he imagines, as Dickens expresses it, "every board and every crack in every board" calling after him, "'Stop thief!' and 'Get up, Mrs. Joe!'" In reproducing this scene, the film is almost as near a literal version of the novel as the two mediums permit:

Interior Blacksmith's House Stairway—Dawn. Medium Shot of Pip's feet walking slowly down the stairs; the music in background is in an eerie theme. Camera pans down to the bottom of the stairs and then upwards to include Pip—he moves across the room towards the pantry door.

WHISPERED VOICE (as in Pip's mind): Wake up, Mrs. Joe. Wake up. Mrs. Joe, wake up.

Having obtained the provisions for the convict, Pip starts out across the marshes. Dickens's narration here is almost cinematic itself:

The mist was heavier yet when I got out upon the marshes, so that, instead of my running at everything, everything seemed to run at me. This was very disagreeable to a guilty mind. The gates and dykes and banks came bursting at me through the mist, as if they cried as plainly as could be, "A boy with Somebody-else's pork pie! Stop him!" The cattle came upon me with like suddenness, staring out of their eyes, and steaming out of their nostrils, "Holloa, young thief!" One black ox, with a white cravat on —who even had to my awakened conscience something of a clerical air—fixed me so obstinately with his eyes, and moved his blunt head round in such an accusatory manner as I moved round, that I blubbered out to him, "I couldn't help it, sir! It wasn't for myself I took it!" Upon which he put down his head, blew a cloud of smoke out of his nose, and vanished with a kick-up of his hind-legs and a flourish of his tail.

Recognizing that Dickens had written part of the scenario for them, the adapters took their cue accordingly:

Close Shot Pip running through fog, looking from right to left, camera panning with him.

Medium Shot cows looking towards Pip, out of picture. Mooing noise in background. *Camera panning* right to left from one cow to another.

FIRST COW: A boy with somebody else's brandy.
SECOND COW: With somebody else's file.
THIRD COW: With somebody else's pork pie.

Medium Shot Pip running through fog, camera panning with him.
THIRD COW (off): Stop him!
Pip stops and looks out of picture, *camera left.*

Close Shot Black Ox.
OX (to Pip): Halloa, young thief.

Medium Shot Pip looking out of picture, *camera left.*
PIP (to Ox): I couldn't help it, sir.
He runs out of picture, *camera right. Music swells,* sounding like ox bellowing.

The purpose in the film, according to David Lean, is to create the larger-than-life picture that is characteristic of Dickens. Lean points out that the scenes of Pip lying terrified in his bedroom, creeping downstairs, and stealing food for the convict are "something Dickens wrote as if he were right inside the boy himself," and that the film attempts "to make the audience share Pip's fear." If this had not been attempted, he says, the audience would have found the convicts merely funny. Accordingly everything in the film is made larger than life "as it is in a boy's imagination." The audience is made to "share Pip's own exaggerated experience." It is made to hear the voices which Pip imagines he hears. The convicts are made "figures of terror out of some childish nightmare."

Separation of sound from image effects introspection in the stagecoach scene when Pip is on his way from London to Rochester. His conscience bothers him because he is ashamed to stay at the forge. Accordingly, as he is seen riding on the coach, voices are heard commenting on his going to the Blue Boar—Joe's, Biddy's, Estella's, and Miss Havisham's.

After Magwitch's death, Pip walks in a daze through the London streets. The street noises are distorted on the sound track. They sound to us as they do to Pip.

Particulary effective is the creative use of sound in the final sequence of the film— Pip's last visit to Satis House. The adapters wish to show that Pip is thinking of his visits to the house as a child. Accordingly on the sound track lines are heard from previous scenes there. The speakers are recognized only by their voices—Estella and Pip as children, Pumblechook, Miss Havisham, and

Mr. Jaggers. We see Pip enter the gate where Pumblechook, years ago, turned him over to Estella, and we hear again:

"What name?"
"Pumblechook."
"Quite right."

In the courtyard Pip looks up at the clock tower and hears Miss Havisham's voice: "I know nothing of days of the week, nothing of weeks of the year." As Pip makes his way into the house, we hear Estella's voice: "Don't loiter, boy. . . . Come along, boy. . . . Take your hat off." On the stairs Pip remembers his first encounter with Mr. Jaggers:

"Whom have we here?'
"A boy."
"A boy of the neighborhood, eh?"

And he hears once more Miss Havisham's cruel aside to Estella: "You can break his heart." The method is that of *Brief Encounter* when Laura imagines that she hears again a conversation she has had with Alec.

In ways like these a film adapted from a novel can represent the novel on the screen. Here and there it can almost reproduce the novel. More often it compensates for what cannot be reproduced. If the adaptation is faithful to the intent of the novel, to its theme, and to its characters, it may be said that it "follows the book."

15.
From Short Story to Film

The short story lends itself readily to motion-picture adaptation. Whereas a novel adapted to the screen must be contracted in scope and a play must be expanded, a short story may be adapted with only slight change in scope, if any at all. Given the usual short story—that is, one dependent largely on narration—an adapter has for the most part only to translate epic terms into cinematic ones. It is not surprising that short stories were popular sources of early films. Many a short story was ready-made for representation in one or two reels.

Although films are now longer, short stories continue to be drawn on as source material. But the increased length of films has resulted in a different treatment. A short story made into a feature-length film must be expanded, although not in the same way as in the adaptation of a novel. For whereas a novel adapted to the screen is expanded in detail and contracted in scope, a short story is made into a feature-length film by an expansion of both scope and detail. A short story so adapted to the screen therefore implies a film more different from the story than a film adapted from a novel is different from the novel. But although this additional difference implies a correspondingly greater freedom in adaptation, the resulting film, if it is to be faithful to its source, must not distort subject, theme, characterizations, and so forth.

The greater freedom not only allowed but demanded in the adaptation of short stories has resulted in a variety of treatments. Ernest Hemingway's short story "The Killers," which tells about two gunmen waiting to kill a Swede called Ole Andreson and Andreson doing nothing to escape, was made into a film which begins by presenting Hemingway's story faithfully and then, after answering a question Hemingway purposely does not answer, that is, what happens next, answers in a flashback, which constitutes most of the film, other questions Hemingway also purposely leaves unanswered—who Andreson is, who the gunmen are, what Andreson has done, and why anyone should want him killed. The original story is thus represented as only a brief introduction to the film. F. Scott Fitzgerald's short story "Babylon Revisited" presents, like Hemingway's story, only the results of a long untold narrative except that, whereas Hemingway is not concerned with answers to questions, Fitzgerald implies the answers while he presents the result. In *The Last Time I Saw Paris,* adapted from "Babylon Revisited," the expansion constitutes the first part of the film, to which the original story is made the climax. A different treatment is represented in the adaptation of another Hemingway story, "The Snows of Kilimanjaro," about a writer dying of gangrene in a camp on the African veld and recollecting his lost opportunities. The film version expands the scope by a direct presentation of the stricken man's recollections, including not only those in Hemingway's story but others created by Casey Robinson, the author of the screen play.

Another kind of treatment is represented by *All That Money Can Buy* (1941), a film based on Stephen Vincent Benét's short story "The Devil and Daniel Webster." Benét's story is about Daniel Webster's defense of a New Hampshire farmer, Jabez Stone, whose opponent in an unearthly court trial is the devil, or Scratch, as he calls himself. Because Jabez had been having bad luck in farming, he sold his soul to Scratch in return for seven years of prosperity. Before payment was due, Jabez obtained a three-year extension and then to anticipate foreclosure got Daniel to defend him. In writing the film play Benét and Dan Totheroh retain most of the original story and expand the scope primarily by presenting what happens to Jabez after he makes the compact with Scratch.

What happens is the degeneration of Jabez's character. To depict the changes in Jabez, the film shows him in relation to, and his treatment of, other people. Thus it is that characters only referred to in the original story are presented directly and in detail. And the chief characters in the story are presented at even greater length in the film. Furthermore additional characters are created. The most important of these is Belle Dee, the mysterious woman from "over the mountain." Belle not only symbolizes but aggravates Jabez's degeneration.

All That Money Can Buy represents not only expansion in scope but expansion in detail, which naturally results in the adaptation of a short story or a novel to the screen. In the adaptation of "The Devil and Daniel Webster" some of this kind of expansion involves details which have been substituted

for those in the original story. In narrating in "The Devil and Daniel Webster" the immediate cause for Jabez's selling his soul, Benét writes:

He'd been plowing that morning and he'd just broke the plowshare on a rock that he could have sworn hadn't been there yesterday. And, as he stood looking at the plowshare, the off horse began to cough—that ropy kind of cough that means sickness and horse doctors. There were two children down with the measles, his wife was ailing, and he had a whitlow on his thumb. It was about the last straw for Jabez Stone. "I vow," he said, and he looked around him kind of desperate, "I vow it's enough to make a man want to sell his soul to the devil! And I would, too, for two cents!"

It would be possible to represent these details on the screen—the broken plowshare, the coughing horse, the sick children, the ailing wife, even the whitlow on Jabez's thumb—but the adapters chose other details and expanded them instead because they would be more effective pictorially. Thus they show Jabez chasing the pig and falling in the mud in his Sunday clothes, the pig breaking a leg, the sheriff warning Jabez that he must pay Miser Stevens, Mary falling off the wagon, and the seed bursting the sack and running into a puddle of dirty water. The substitution of these details for those in the short story is made for the same reason as that for the change, in the adaptation of *The Informer,* in Gypo's motivation for informing. Furthermore the changed details in *All That Money Can Buy* also introduce the characters and establish relationships and the situation from which the story is to proceed.

There are also changes in detail to represent Jabez's prosperity. According to the short story, Jabez's "cows got fat and his horses sleek, his crops were the envy of the neighborhood, and lightning might strike all over the valley, but it wouldn't strike his barn." In the film Jabez's uncanny prosperity is presented directly. Kicking loose a board in the barn floor, Scratch shows Jabez a pot of Hessian gold. Jabez accordingly pays off his mortgage to Miser Stevens and makes extensive purchases at the village store. A series of scenes show Jabez's fields in blossom, the barley and corn ripe and golden. An August hailstorm levels the fields of the neighbors but leaves Jabez's fields untouched, and the camera sights along the boundary line to show the marked and astonishing contrast. The neighbors are hired to help Jabez harvest his crops, hauling them by the wagonload into Jabez's big new barn. Jabez builds himself a mansion. These are details that lend themselves to pictorial representation. It would be possible to represent in the film, for example, the lightning striking other barns than Jabez's, but, like the substitution in the adaptation of *Great Expectations,* of the mice nibbling the cake on the table for the mice rattling behind the panel in the dining room, the shot of the contrasting fields in more effective for the purpose.

Such changes, which do not distort the theme or spirit of the original, are justifiable. But in the course of the adaptation of "The Devil and Daniel Webster" there are other changes too.

Back of the original story is Benét's recurring theme—the importance of freedom. In "The Devil and Daniel Webster" the kind of freedom Benét is writing about is personal freedom. The crisis is Daniel's realization that it is not only for Jabez Stone that the unearthly jury has come but for him. If he should fight them with their own weapons, he'd fall into their power. So he bases his appeal on the meaning of freedom and the sorrows of slavery. And he wins his case. Although in the film Daniel's speech to the jury is represented directly and specifically, its relation to the crisis is not established. In fact the crisis is changed too, for the subject of the film is not so much the conflict between the devil and Daniel Webster as the degeneration of the character of Jabez Stone. The trial is kept in the adaptation, is, in fact, expanded, but Daniel becomes primarily a *deus ex machina* who rescues the hero from perdition. The change in the

title accords with the change in theme—from "The Devil and Daniel Webster" to *All That Money Can Buy.*

The film also represents a change in the spirit, or mood, of the original story. If Daniel Webster has become an American legend, it is because Benét has created folktales about him. In "The Devil and Daniel Webster" Benét adapts the Faust legend to American characters in an American setting. Like the Faust legend "The Devil and Daniel Webster" shows that the most precious thing in the world—the soul —can be bought. The story is a fantasy, and the fantasy is effective because of Benét's artful simplicity and simple indirectness. The devil, who is called that only in the title and, by reference, in the frame in which Benét tells the story, is "a soft-spoken, dark-dressed stranger." He introduces himself to Daniel only as Scratch. Jabez "didn't like the looks of the stranger not the way he smiled with his teeth. They were white teeth, and plentiful—some say they were filed to a point, but," says Benét, heightening the indirectness, "I wouldn't vouch for that." Jabez never liked the looks of the stranger's boots either, "particularly the toes," nor did he like it "when the dog took one look at the stranger and ran away howling, with his tail between his legs." What Jabez saw fluttering out of the stranger's black pocketbook was "something that looked like a moth, but it wasn't a moth." When the stranger poured himself a drink from the jug, "the liquor was cold in the jug, but it came steaming into the glass."

This kind of indirectness cannot be expressed so well on the screen. A film can be fanciful, but not so naturally as a novel or a short story. Now and then in *All That Money Can Buy* the fanciful is attempted, but in direct terms of pictures and sound. When Scratch first appears in the film, he is represented by his shadow on the wall. Later he materializes out of a bright light. Similarly a bright light blurs Belle when she asks Miser Stevens to dance. Whereas in the story Benét tells what Daniel's speech to the jury is about, in the film the speech is actual; one hears Edward Arnold speak it. And whereas Benét only suggests what the jury is like, in the film the jury is represented by twelve actors. The jury is seen through a haze to suggest unearthliness, but the haze does not make the jury so unearthly as Benét's indirectness. Scratch sweeps his finger across the bark of a tree, and suddenly there is the date upon it: "April 7, 1847." But these are theatric devices, not essentially different from Méliès's abracadabra in *A Trip to the Moon*. They are no less real for being tricks. They are not comparable to Benét's indirectness, an approach to which is effected in the film in a different way when in the final scene Scratch points directly at the camera. It is the method of the final scene of *The Great Train Robbery* when the bandit fires point blank at the audience.

All That Money Can Buy might present the New England background more faithfully than it does. "It's a story they tell in the border country," Benét begins, "where Massachusetts joins New Hampshire and Vermont." Jabez's farm is at Cross Corners, New Hampshire. It's a New England farm, boulders and all. Jabez is a genuine New Hampshireman. Daniel is a New Hampshireman too, although he now lives in Massachusetts. Daniel and Jabez wait for Scratch in the farmhouse kitchen, not in the front parlor, because Daniel knows front parlors. When the trial is over, Daniel expresses the hope that there will be pie for breakfast. The adaptation of a novel or a short story is not expected to retain the author's style or the kind of fantasy which it is the province of words alone to create, but the allusions to New England in "The Devil and Daniel Webster" are cues for a background more authentic than most of the prettified and artificial scenes in *All That Money Can Buy*.

With a minor exception the background music for *All That Money Can Buy* is more appropriate than the sets. The singing of the harvest hymn incongruously accompanies the scene in which the neighbors help to fill Jabez's barn with crops made bountiful by the devil. Otherwise the score, composed by Bernard Herrmann, evokes the mood of the story. Based on the folk song "Springfield Mountain," the score is not only evocative of nineteenth-century New England but, as Lawrence Morton has pointed out, "powerful because in its creativity it goes beyond the mere evocation of time and place."

Pictures, however, cannot connote in the way that music or words can. In "The Devil and Daniel Webster" Benét creates fantasy through the connotative quality of language itself. Connotation effected through the editing of pictures is of a different kind. If a film is to attempt the fanciful, it should do so in cinematic terms or, indirectly, through realism. For the most part *All That Money Can Buy* is presented realistically, including even scenes involving Scratch. It is only now and then, as though a reminder that the story is not real, that theatric tricks are resorted to. On the surface Benét's story is represented by realistic images. These might have been translated intact and consistently into pictures and sound.

Whereas "The Devil and Daniel Webster," like "The Killers," "The Snows of Kilimanjaro," and "Babylon Revisited," is adapted to the screen by an expansion of scope as well as of detail, the film *Quartet* (1948) represents a different treatment.

Although *Quartet* is, as the title implies, a four-part film, it has unifying elements. The stories from which it is adapted are by one author, Somerset Maugham, and one author, R. C. Sherriff, wrote the film plays. Although each of the films which compose *Quartet* is the work of a different director, they were produced as a unit by one staff. Mr. Maugham appears on the screen and speaks a prologue to the whole film, and a narrator introduces each of the parts by reading the opening sentence or so of the story while an insert of the page is seen on the screen. Nevertheless, each of the films in *Quartet* is complete in itself.

The films are, however, similarly adapted. Sherriff implies in the foreword to the published text of *Quartet,* which includes both the stories and the film plays, that each of the plays is "allowed to run its natural course" with the result that each film, he says, "ends when the story is finished." In defending his method Sherriff declares that "it stands to reason that no story can be good if it appears on the screen stretched out beyond its natural length." He refers to "the padding and cutting that generally has to happen" in the process of adaptation. He admits, however, that "when the *Quartet* screenplays are compared with their originals . . . it may be said that we have defeated our purpose by leaving out parts of certain stories and adding scenes to others." A comparison of Sherriff's film plays with Maugham's short stories reveals, however, that the scope of the added "scenes" hardly compensates for that of "parts" left out. Furthermore, in the adaptation of the film plays to the screen, the scope is even narrower than Sherriff indicates in the script. And since detail is expanded in accordance with the difference in medium, the adaptation of these four stories is comparable to that of a novel. Although scope is not contracted to the extent that it is in the adaptation of a novel, the method is more nearly that of a novel than of a short story adapted in the manner of "The Devil and Daniel Webster."

In Maugham's story "The Facts of Life" irony is more important than characterization. The characters in "The Facts of Life" are hardly more than types. Henry Garnet is a clubman. His son Nicky is a callow youth. The girl—Maugham does not even give her a name—is an adventuress. The chief irony is that Nicky is successful by deliberately doing the three things his father warns him against. And the story ends ironically in the advice which the lawyer gives Henry. Maugham tells the story in a frame, which not only makes Nicky's adventure in Monte Carlo more than just a story but creates suspense. But the primary advantage of the frame is that it establishes a basis for the irony, which becomes dramatic as, step by step, Nicky is observed disregarding his father's advice and being successful.

The adaptation of "The Facts of Life" is true to the structure of the story and thus to the irony. Motion pictures lend themselves readily to the "frame" method of narration as illustrated by many films, from *The Cabinet of Dr. Caligari* to *Brief Encounter,* and in Maugham's short story Sherriff had the structure ready-made. He had only to adapt it as literally as possible.

But the "cutting" to which Sherriff takes exception is nevertheless evident in the adaptation of this story as in that of the other three in *Quartet.* For example, whereas Maugham begins "The Facts of Life" with a page of exposition about Henry Garnet, the film adaptation begins abruptly with the particular afternoon on which Henry tells the story about his son Nicky. And the film almost completely disregards Maugham's even longer exposition about Nicky. Maugham describes the baccara dealer in the casino at Monte Carlo, tells who he is, and narrates the effect on Nicky of the baccara game. He describes Monte Carlo in the early morning as Nicky walks through the deserted streets. But these and other "parts" of the story are presented only slightly in the film, if at all. On the other hand, if the scope were not so contracted in all four of the stories, the film would be unwieldy in length.

Detail is correspondingly expanded. Whereas, for example, Maugham writes, "Another rubber was begun and in the second game Henry denied a suit," the film presents the bridge game directly, including the concomitant dialogue. Maugham devotes less than a page to the scene at the nightclub; in the film the scene is of five minutes' duration. In these and other ways detail is expanded. The expansion is similar to that in the adaptation of a novel.

On the other hand, some of the changes Sherriff makes in Maugham's stories are arbitrary; that is, they are not implicit in the cinematic method but are made for reasons of effectiveness or simplicity. They are comparable to changes made in the adaptations of *The Informer, Great Expectations,* and "The Devil and Daniel Webster."

Whereas in "The Facts of Life" Maugham has a Colonel Brabazon, one of Henry Garnet's tennis friends, suggest to Henry at a

City dinner that Nicky enter the tournament at Monte Carlo, in the film Colonel Brabazon becomes Professor Branksome of Cambridge, and the City dinner a tennis match at Wimbledon. There is nothing in the cinematic method to prevent the adaptation to the screen of the former instead of the latter. But, a film being visual, a tennis match provides a more effective setting than a dinner. Sherriff indicates how the scene is to be staged:

2. Exterior Wimbledon Centre Court *(Stock)*. Day. This should be the best possible stock shot of Wimbledon during a match on the centre court —and if possible one which *pans over* to the crowd in the stands, or at least shows the crowd to some advantage.

3. Exterior Wimbledon Centre Court *(Stock)*. Day. *Another stock shot,* this time of the crowd in the stand watching the play, with their heads moving to and fro in unison, as they follow the flight of the ball. (NOTE: There are *several excellent stock shots* of this available.)

4. Exterior Wimbledon Centre Court (Studio). Day. A section of stand to match up to scene 3, with about twenty people following the play. We *move in* to concentrate on Henry. He is sitting with his wife on one side of him and a distinguished looking man of fifty or sixty on the other side. This is PROFESSOR BRANKSOME.[1]

The substitution also makes for simplicity. In his foreword Sherriff points out that an adaptation of a story to the screen makes the proper allowance for the different perspective of the reader lounging in his armchair and the people sitting upright in a cinema. "The reader, as it were," Sherriff says, "can see the story from a distance, with all its side shoots and wandering tendrils: there is nothing to distract him. Subconsciously the man in the cinema puts on blinkers to help him concentrate: his perspective is narrowed while vision sharpens his conception, so you have to prune the story to the main stem to save him getting lost among the side shoots." In changing the City dinner to a tennis match at Wimble-

don and Colonel Brabazon to Professor Branksome, Sherriff makes the proper allowance for the different perspective of the reader and the people at the cinema. A City dinner and a Colonel Brabazon would be side shoots. Nicky plays tennis; a tennis scene is to the point. Nicky is at Cambridge; Professor Branksome is, as Henry says, "the Poo Bah of tennis" there.

The substitution of the tennis scene for the dinner scene makes not only for simplicity and effectiveness but even for humor. Whereas Maugham narrates at considerable length and in detail what happens to make Henry change his mind about letting Nicky play in the tournament at Monte Carlo, Sherriff represents this action in one short scene. But in the final adaptation, the scope was further contracted: Sherriff's scene was deleted entirely. The deletion is appropriate, because to narrate how Henry is made to change his mind would involve another digression. The film instead merely implies how he is made to change his mind. Mrs. Garnet is not present at the City dinner in the story, but she is at the tennis match in the film, and after Professor Branksome leaves, she urges Henry to let Nicky play in the tournament at Monte Carlo. The scene ends as Henry declares flatly, "No, I've made up my mind and I'm not going to change it." There is a cut to the airport as Nicky is saying to Henry, "It's awfully decent of you to let me go, Dad."

Because of expansion of detail and the presentational method of narration, characters become specific in a film. In a novel or a short story they may be only vaguely represented. In "The Facts of Life" there are only four specifically named characters; in the film adaptation there are nine. In the story Nicky meets an acquaintance at the casino; in the film the acquaintance is Nicky's friend John. Sherriff uses John to avoid a subjective treatment. Maugham says that Nicky reflected that he hadn't promised his father not to gamble, he'd promised him not to forget his advice. It would of course be possible to present Nicky's thoughts on the screen. But Sherriff, who is a playwright, chooses a dramatic rather than a cinematic method, and thus a dialogue:

JOHN: Wotcha Nicky! Doing any good?
NICKY: I haven't been playing.
JOHN: You ought to have one little flutter before you go.
NICKY: I suppose so—but my father wasn't any too keen on my coming at all, and one of the things he particularly warned me against was gambling.
JOHN: It isn't gambling if you know when to stop. I had a go with a hundred francs and lost it, and that's that. You're crazy if you leave Monte Carlo without trying your luck once. Surely your father wouldn't mind you losing a hundred francs!
NICKY *(weakening)*: I don't suppose he would, really. After all, I didn't promise him not to gamble—I only promised not to forget his advice.

By means of the specific character John the film similarly dramatizes the anticlimax, which in the story is presented subjectively. Maugham has Nicky, riding in the car from Monte Carlo to the aerodrome, think about the twenty thousand francs:

He thought he would like to have a look at them. He had so nearly lost them that they had a double value for him. He took them out of his hip-pocket into which for safety's sake he had stuffed them when he put on the suit he was travelling in, and counted them one by one. Something very strange had happened to them. Instead of there being twenty notes as there should have been there were twenty-six. He couldn't make it out. He asked himself if it was possible that he had won more at the Sporting Club than he had realized. But no, that was out of the question, he distinctly remembered the man at the desk laying the notes out in four rows of five, and he had counted them himself. Suddenly the explanation occurred to him; when he had put his hand into the flower-pot, after taking out the cineraria, he had grabbed everything he felt there. The flower-pot was the little hussy's money-box and he had taken out not only his own money, but her savings as well. Nicky leant back in the car and burst into a roar of laughter. It was the funniest thing he had ever heard in his life.

Here again the film could present Nicky's thoughts, but Sherriff substitutes a dialogue between Nicky and John on the airplane taking them back to England:

JOHN: You don't say! You know she took *me* in when *I* saw her. I guessed she was a gambler—but she was decently dressed and not made up. I never thought she was just a rotten little thief.
NICKY: She took me in, too—at first.
JOHN: I bet she does that every night to some mug or another.
NICKY: She didn't get a mug last night, anyway. *They laugh. Nicky is feeling very proud of himself.*

JOHN: How much was it?
NICKY: Twenty thousand francs.
JOHN: I say!
NICKY: Enough for that motor bike.
JOHN: Is it all there?
NICKY: It must be.
JOHN: She might have taken some for safety and put it somewhere else.
NICKY: I don't think she'd have had time. . . . *But he looks worried at this. He fumbles in his pocket, and pulls out the wad of notes. He counts the notes quickly in fives.*

NICKY: Five thousand . . . ten thousand . . . fifteen . . . hey! there's more than twenty here. *counted to thirty but there are still several notes untouched.)* Well—I'll be damned!
JOHN: You know what? That flower pot was her money-box. You've got all her loot as well twenty . . . twenty-five . . . thirty . . . *(Nicky has . . . nearly enough to buy a car.*
They burst out laughing.

Other arbitrary changes are made for various reasons, not all of them obvious. Maugham says that Nicky is eighteen; in the film he is a year older. In the story Nicky wagers a hundred francs and wins twenty thousand; in the film these amounts are increased tenfold. In accordance with Maugham's story, Sherriff indicates that Jeanne and Nicky take a taxi to the hotel. In the film the taxi is a barouche, and the hotel "a quiet little place." And Jeanne's room becomes a suite, whereby the sleeping arrangements conform to censorship of the time. In the story Nicky is in a car on his way to the aerodrome when he discovers the additional franc notes; in the film the discovery takes place in the airplane. These and other variations, however, are minor, and the film remains essentially faithful to its source.

The longest of the four stories as Maugham wrote them is "The Alien Corn," more than twice as long as "The Facts of Life." On the screen "The Facts of Life" runs for twenty-two minutes and "The Alien Corn" is only four minutes longer. Obviously, then, in the adaptation of "The Alien Corn" scope is contracted even further than in that of "The Facts of Life." In "The Alien Corn" Maugham is concerned primarily with members of a wealthy Jewish family ashamed of their race. Intolerant of art, they are unhappy when the eldest son wants to make music his career. The scope is contracted largely by deletion of this character study; the film concentrates instead on George's failure to become a concert pianist. Maugham tells the story in the first person, represented as a friend of the family. Although this point of view could be effected cinematically, as it is, for example, in the adaptation of *Great Expectations,* the storyteller is among the characters deleted in the contraction in scope. Maugham has the storyteller visit George in Munich; in the film the visitor is a girl, Paula, created to introduce a love interest. The only suggestion of the subjective point of view is in the scene in which George plays for Lea Makart. While he plays, Paula's thoughts are represented by shots of Paula and George in previous dialogues, the shots superimposed on a close-up of Paula and the music fading so that the voices can be heard above it. But the subjective is not introduced so much to suggest the substitution of Paula for the first-person storyteller as to give the impression of extended time. *"As it is obvious that George's playing could not be fairly judged under at least twenty minutes,"* Sherriff notes in the script, *"some device will have to be used here to give an artistic impression of time-lapse."*

The other two stories, "The Kite" and "The Colonel's Lady," are adapted more in the manner of "The Facts of Life" than of "The Alien Corn" in that they undergo comparatively little contraction in scope. Each is expanded by a denouement for the sake of "a happy ending." Although Maugham implies in "The Kite" that the hero's love of freedom is so strong that, ironically, he prefers staying in jail to returning to his wife, in the film the wife is reconciled to the kite, and the husband to the wife. And whereas "The Colonel's Lady" has an enigmatic ending, Sherriff appends a sentimental denouement identifying the lover. As in "The Facts of Life" and "The Alien Corn," there are a few arbitrary changes.

With the exceptions noted, however, each of these films is as faithful to its source as "The Facts of Life." Staging, casting, and acting are in keeping with the intention and essence of the original stories. Here and there in the adaptation an incident is broadened or a subtle point is lost, but for the most part Maugham's satire of British manners, morals, and mores is as effective on the screen as on the printed page.

A short story, then, can be more faithfully adapted to the screen than a play or a novel. Whereas a film adapted from a play represents something more than the play, and a film adapted from a novel something less than the novel, a film adapted from a short story may be comparatively similar. But a film must be judged on its own merits. *All That Money Can Buy* might have been better if it had not expanded the scope of Benét's story. On the other hand, it might have been better if it had expanded the scope differently. The fact, however, remains that because the cinematic way of storytelling resembles that of the novel and the short story more than it does that of the play, and because the scope of a film is more nearly that of a short story than of a novel, the short story is promising material for adaptation to the screen.

16.
From Script to Film

Of all artists the most dependent is the motion-picture director. He is dependent not only on a machine but on the talents of assistants in a variety of callings, no one of whom is more important to him than the screenwriter. The screenwriter either may have written the script for the film or may have adapted it from a story or a novel or a play by another author. If the director is a Méliès or a Griffith or a von Stroheim, he may have been his own screenwriter, with or without assistance. The point is that in the beginning is a story.

In declaring that pictures should be the result of a writer and a director "getting together," Ford did not mean collaborating as, for example, playwrights usually collaborate. Ford's contemptuous treatment of screenwriters is legendary. According to Frank Nugent, Ford, noticing a reference to a Sharps repeater rifle in a script, said to the author, "I like the sound of Winchester repeater better." When the writer protested that "they didn't have Winchester repeaters then," Ford told him to leave "Sharps" in the script, adding, "But it's going to sound mighty like 'Winchester' on the sound track."[1] Andrew Sinclair recounts the time when Dudley Nichols, who used to toil at his screenplays in a forward cabin of Ford's yacht while, elsewhere aboard, Ford played poker with John Wayne and other cronies, interrupted a poker session to give Ford a completed script. Nichols asked him to be careful with it, saying that he didn't have a copy. "You bet," said Ford, leafing through the manuscript. Noticing that it contained too much dialogue, he weighed it in his hand and tossed it through an open porthole into the ocean.[2] It happens that what Ford took exception to is the only element of a script that he could literally reproduce in a film. Except for dialogue, a script is barely more than suggestions as to how a director should proceed.

The screenwriter, Nichols says, "creates an approximate continuity of scenes and images, suggesting cinematic touches where he can."[3] To appreciate what he means, compare any scene that he wrote for *The Informer* with the way Ford shot it. Consider, for example, the scene in the headquarters of the Black and Tans when word comes that, as a result of Gypo Nolan's information, Frankie McPhillip has been killed in trying to escape. In his script Nichols specified that after the officer says, "You may go now. I will let you out the back way," Gypo get up, looking at his hands, that a close-up of his hands dissolve to another view of the headquarters office, where a riding crop pushes the money across the table, a voice saying icily, "You might count it," and that Gypo stuff the money into his pocket. In filming the scene Ford elaborates the symbol of contempt represented by the business with the riding crop —one of the symbols that Nichols sought and found to make visual the tragic psychology of the informer. Ford has a major remove some bills from his wallet, toss them onto the table and go out at right. With a cane an officer pushes the bills toward Gypo, saying contemptuously, "Twenty pounds. You better count it," and then to a sentry, "Show him out the back way."

"Shoot as written," Thomas Ince used to write on a script before handing it to one of his directors. But a director of course cannot shoot as literally written: what is written is words and what is shot is pictures. Even if Nichols had specified in his description of the scene in the Black and Tan headquarters the way in which Ford refines the symbol of contempt—the major consigning to a subaltern the dirty business of pushing the money toward Gypo, and the subaltern then ordering a lower subaltern to show Gypo out—the description would still be only an approximation. The thousand words that a picture is said to be worth could not completely describe the scene in all its detail. Furthermore, however detailed a script might be, exigencies of filming, arbitrary changes not inherent in the cinematic method, editorial rearrangement or deletions, and so forth, would result in a film different from what one might visualize in reading the script. A comparison of the script on which Orson Welles collaborated with Herman J. Mankiewicz for *Citizen Kane* (1941) with the resulting film, which Welles directed and in which he played the title role, is particularly illuminating as a way of examining what happens when a gifted director adapts a script to the screen.[4]

Welles came to motion pictures from the theatre and from radio. A native of Wisconsin, where he was born in Kenosha on May 6, 1915, he began his stage career at the Gate Theatre in Dublin when he was sixteen. Two years later, after acting at both the Gate and the Abbey theatres, he toured in the United States with Katharine Cornell's company, playing Mercutio in *Romeo and Juliet,* Marchbanks in *Candida,* and Octavius Barrett in *The Barretts of Wimpole Street.* During the summer of 1934 he organized and managed the Woodstock Theatre Festival, in Woodstock, Illinois, and that fall made his first appearance on the New York stage, as the Chorus and Tybalt in *Romeo and Juliet.* He directed a black production of *Macbeth* in Harlem and, for the Mercury Theatre, which he had founded with John Houseman, a modern-dress *Julius Caesar* with an anti-fascist point of view. He wrote, directed, and acted in a weekly radio program called the Mercury Theatre of the Air. It was on this program that in October of 1938 he broadcast an adaptation of H. G. Wells's *The War of the Worlds* so convincingly that it caused a panic on the eastern seaboard. Except for some shorts which he had made for inclusion in the production of plays, *Citizen Kane* was his first film.

Citizen Kane is the story of a man named Charles Foster Kane, whose life and career resemble the life and career of the newspaper publisher William Randolph Hearst (1863–1951). Like Hearst, Kane inherits great wealth, including a newspaper. Like Hearst, he announces his intention of campaigning, through his paper, against special interests. But Hearstlike he practices yellow journalism, expands his publishing enterprise by acquiring a chain of newspapers, and becomes a demagogue. Like Hearst, he leaves his wife for a woman who has become his mistress, builds a seaside castle, and fills it with paintings, statues, furniture, and other objects collected from around the world. Welles declared that his film "is not based upon the life of Mr. Hearst or anyone else," adding, "on the other hand, had Mr. Hearst and similar financial barons not lived during the period we discuss, *Citizen Kane* could not have been made."[5] But there are too many similarities to make the disclaimer convincing. Here, for example, are a few: Kane's fortune originated in the Colorado

Lode (Hearst's in the Comstock Lode); sent a list of his inherited property, Kane finds only a newspaper, the New York *Inquirer,* of interest to him and writes his guardian that "it would be fun to run a newspaper" (Hearst's first paper, the San Francisco *Examiner,* was called "Hearst's plaything"); Kane begins his career by attacking the public transportation trust (Hearst editorially attacked the Southern Pacific Railroad). Through the *Inquirer* Kane urges war with Spain, and the Spanish-American War is called "Kane's War." When a correspondent cables from Cuba that he could write prose poems about scenery but that there is no war, Kane replies, "You provide the prose poems, I'll provide the war." (It was said that when Frederic Remington, whom Hearst had sent to Havana to sketch Spanish atrocities, cabled that there was no trouble in Cuba, that there would be no war, Hearst replied, "You furnish the pictures, and I'll furnish the war." The Spanish-American War was called "Hearst's War.") Kane promotes his second wife, formerly his mistress, Susan Alexander, as an opera singer. (Hearst was engaged to Sibyl Sanderson, who became an opera singer. He took as his mistress Marion Davies, whose career as a motion-picture actress he helped promote.) Kane loses an election for the governorship of New York (Hearst lost an election for the governorship of New York.) Kane builds his castle, Xanadu, on a man-made hill overlooking the Gulf of Mexico. (Hearst's Xanadu was San Simeon, on a hill overlooking the Pacific.)

The similarities caused a furor. A Hearst gossip columnist, Louella Parsons, previewed *Citizen Kane* and demanded its withdrawal. Although only halfheartedly approving of her objection, Hearst, it is said, out of deference to Miss Davies, forbade the heads of his newspapers to mention RKO (producer of *(Citizen Kane)* or its products. Louis Mayer, head of production at MGM, offered RKO $842,000 to destroy the negatives and all the prints. The film had been scheduled to open in Radio City Music Hall in New York, but the opening was canceled. When George Schaefer, head of RKO, telephoned Nelson Rockefeller to ask why the opening had been canceled, he was told that Louella Parsons had warned Rockefeller off, asking him how he would like to have the *American Weekly Magazine* run a spread on John D. Rockefeller. Welles warned RKO that unless his film was released he would sue. *Citizen Kane* was completed in October of 1940 and, after a press showing in New York on April 9, 1941, had its premiere in Hollywood on May 1.

In its construction *Citizen Kane* accords with the script. The story begins with the death of the hero and is told in flashbacks. Because he is dissatisfied with a newsreel that has been assembled on the occasion of the death of this famous man, the newsreel producer, a Mr. Rawlston, sends out a reporter, Thompson, to get in touch with people who knew Kane well. Kane had uttered the word "rosebud" when he died: If Thompson can find the meaning of that word, the clue to Kane's character will be clear. The script is so contrived that the order in which Thompson gets his information accords with the chronology of Kane's life: from the memoirs of Walter P. Thatcher, Kane's guardian, Kane from the time when as a child he is put into Thatcher's care until, having become of age, he acquires his first newspaper, attacks the trusts, and provokes the Spanish-American War; from Kane's business manager, Mr. Bernstein, the building of the newspaper empire and Kane's marriage to Emily Norton, niece of the President of the United States; from Kane's best friend, Jedediah Leland, the failure of the marriage, the loss of the election because of the revelation about Kane's affair with Susan Alexander, the second marriage, that with Susan, and the rift with Leland because Leland, as Kane's drama critic, writes deprecatingly about Susan's acting in her operatic debut; from Susan, her operatic career and its failure and the failure of her marriage; and from Kane's butler, Raymond, Susan's leaving her husband and, in frustration and anger, Kane's wrecking Susan's room. Thompson's interview with Raymond takes place at Xanadu as Kane's possessions are being catalogued and junk is being burned. Into the furnace is thrown a sled, on which is painted the word "Rosebud." The flashbacks overlap. Bernstein, for example, recollects the beginning of Kane's newspaper career, about which Thompson has read in Thatcher's memoirs, or Susan describes her operatic debut, previously reported to Thompson by Leland.

Some of the departures from the script are arbitrary, that is, not due to a difference between words and pictures. For example, whereas the script puts Kane at five years of age in the winter of 1870—although Thatcher has written "six years old" in his memoirs—the year is 1871 in the film, and Kane is eight. The change seems minor indeed except that in 1870 Hearst was six years old, and one accordingly wonders again at Welles's disclaimer. On the other hand the change may have been made merely because Buddy Swan, who plays the boy Kane, appears in the film to be more nearly eight than six.

Pauline Kael reports that Robert Wise, editor of *Citizen Kane,* ran a print of the film, with Welles's consent, for the heads of all the major companies and their lawyers, and that then for six weeks Wise and his assistant, Mark Robson, "fussed over the movie, making tiny, nervous changes—mostly a word here or there—that the executives and lawyers hoped would render the picture less objectionable to Hearst."[6] Hearst's name, mentioned twice in the script, was deleted.

The film accords with the script in the names of all of the principal characters but one, Boss Rogers, who brings about Kane's defeat in the gubernatorial election. In the film he is Boss Gettys. Did he become Gettys because, during the campaign for the governorship, Hearst publicly attacked a Colonel Rogers? Or did Welles like the sound of "Gettys" better? Although the script includes a scene at the Xanadu telegraph office, from which an announcement of Mrs. Kane's separation from her husband is sent out to Kane papers, that scene is omitted from the film. Censorship in the 1940s accounts for a bordello scene being changed—with proper modifications—to the scene of the *Inquirer* banquet. There are other digressions from the script, such as the scene in which Kane displaces Mr. Carter, the old-fashioned editor of the *Inquirer.* "Not that Charlie was brutal," Leland tells Thompson, "he just did brutal things." The scene with Carter accords with the intent of the script, but Welles changes the manner of Kane's brutality. In the script Carter, harassed by Kane's criticism of his editorship, warns Kane that he might feel obliged to ask that his resignation be accepted, and Kane replies, "It *is* accepted, Mr. Carter, with assurances of my deepest regret." Omitting the talk about resignation, Welles's Kane—insincerity in his tone of voice—thanks Carter for being "most understanding" and bids him good-bye.

In the scene in which Kane, speaking at Madison Square Garden, promises "to arrange for the indictment, prosecution, and conviction of Boss Jim W. Gettys," Welles interpolates a shot—not specified in the script—of Gettys, a shadowy figure standing high above the speaker's platform looking down at Kane and, during the roar that goes up from the crowd at this promise, putting on his hat and slipping out. In combining concepts to equal more than their sum, the shot is montagelike: image (a man) plus sound (the roar following Kane's promise) implying that the man is Gettys and that Kane may now be in trouble. Furthermore, the shot not only constitutes dramatic irony but anticipates the scene in which Kane and his wife arrive at Susan's. When Gettys steps into the hall after the Kanes have reached the top of the stairs, the situation is immediately clear.

Digression from a script or embellishment of it may occur to a director on the set. We do not know, for example, when it occurred to Welles to take advantage of constancy of size to make a whisky bottle loom large in front of the typewriter over which Leland has fallen asleep. When Kane rushes into Susan's room after Susan has taken too many sleeping tablets, the camera shoots across the bed to the door in the background. On the bedside table, a glass containing a spoon appears as large as Leland's whisky bottle because the table is near the camera. In the scene in which Kane assumes control of the *Inquirer,* Carter mistakes Leland for Kane. The script does not indicate this comic bit of stage business, which may or may not have been impromptu.

"Seventy years in a man's life . . ." and "that's a lot to try to get into a newsreel" are comments when the lights come on after the preview and Rawlston asks for opinions. It's also a lot to try to get into the 119 minutes of *Citizen Kane.* Obviously there are gaps in time to be bridged. The script would have them bridged by dissolves. Welles refines by bridging them in various other ways.

According to the script, the first such gap is from the time Charles leaves home until after he has become the publisher of the *Inquirer.* Following the scene in which Thatcher is about to take the boy away from his parents, the script would have the film interpolate a shot of sleeping-car wheels and a scene in which Charles in his berth in the car is crying for his mother, Thatcher standing helplessly by. An insert from Thatcher's manuscript intervening, the next scene would be the office of the *Inquirer* twenty-eight years later. In the film, in which the corresponding gap in Thatcher's account is hardly thirteen years, a shot of Charles's sled being covered with snow dissolves to a close shot of a sled being unwrapped. The camera pulls back to show Charles holding and looking at the sled, a Christmas tree in the background. "Well, Charles," says Thatcher offscreen, the camera tilting up to him, "Merry Christmas." In the next shot Charles, rising with the sled, replies, "Merry Christmas." "And a Happy New Year," says an older Thatcher in a close-up by a window. The camera pulls back, and Thatcher comes forward, dictating to a man seated at a desk a letter to Charles, reminding him that his twenty-first birthday, now approaching, marks his independence from Thatcher and

Company. In the next shot a secretary is reading to Thatcher a letter from Charles saying that, among his holdings, all that interests him is the *Inquirer,* and that he thinks it would be fun to run a newspaper. The transition from Thatcher at the window to Thatcher dictating in his office is of the kind that David Lean was to use five years later when, in *Brief Encounter,* he pulled the camera back from a close-up of Laura supposedly in the refreshment room of the railroad station to reveal her in a chair in her living room at home.

In Bernstein's account eight years are bridged by a photograph that turns out to be the *Chronicle* staff being photographed. First we see Kane, Leland, and Bernstein looking at the photograph in the window of the *Chronicle,* the camera then moving in to show the photograph in close shot. This shot dissolves to a medium shot of the same staff posing to have the photograph taken. The camera pulls back, Kane comes on at left, the photographer, at right, takes the picture, and the men rise. The picture of an object becoming the object itself was to be one of Resnais's transitions in *Last Year at Marienbad.* It happens that in this particular transition in *Citizen Kane* Welles takes a cue from the script but not entirely. The script, for example, would have Kane posed in the center of the group being photographed.

According to the script, as Leland starts to tell Thompson about Kane's first marriage, the scene dissolves from the hospital roof, where Thompson has found Leland, to a breakfast room. Then follow seven brief scenes, linked by dissolves, presenting Kane and Emily growing apart over a period of nine years. The scene remains the same, the only changes those in makeup, wardrobe, lighting, and special effects outside the window. In filming the sequence Welles follows the script in dissolving from scene to scene except that he combines the dissolves with panning motions of the camera so rapid that they blur the images. He also follows the script in dissolving from the scene on the roof to the breakfast room, but he elaborates on the script by having Leland's image, large at the left of the frame, remaining onscreen until after the breakfast scene has faded in. At the conclusion of the breakfast-room sequence Leland's image fades in, and the images are held in juxtaposition. Again the manner anticipates that of *Brief Encounter,* in which Laura's image in the living room remains after the refreshment-room scene fades in, the implication being that she is watching herself.

In departing from the script to bridge gaps in time in Leland's story, Welles ingeniously depends on the carrying over of sound from one shot to another. In four shots Welles takes us from the evening Kane meets Susan to the evening, a year later, when he is speaking in Madison Square Garden. In the script the gap is bridged only by inserts from the *Inquirer.* In the film the arrangement is as follows:

Medium shot of parlor of Susan's rooming house. SUSAN *at piano, left, playing, singing.* KANE *sitting in background, right. Dissolve.*

Medium-long shot of elegantly furnished room. SUSAN *at piano, left, playing, singing.* KANE *sitting in background, right. As* SUSAN *finishes,* KANE *applauds. Dissolve.*

Medium-long shot of street. Crowd around open car, from which LELAND *is speaking. Applause in preceding shot becomes that of crowd applauding* LELAND. . . . LELAND. . . . "I am speaking of Charles Foster Kane, the fighting liberal, . . . who entered upon this campaign . . .

Close shot of banner with picture of Kane, his name above it. KANE (off): . . . with one purpose only . . . *Camera tilts down to* KANE *speaking in Madison Square Garden.*

Note that the transition between the first two shots consists not only of continuation of sound together with the same relative positions of the characters in each shot but also of a change in settings whereby Welles implies all that we need to know about the change in Susan and Kane's relationship.

Welles amplifies the script in his treatment of the newsreel. In the film, but not in the script, there is counterpoint between clips in the newsreel and events later in the story. An insertion in the newsreel of a newspaper photograph of Kane, Emily, and their son outside Madison Square Garden, illustrating the announcer's statement that Emily and her son died in a motor accident in 1918, is repeated later when we see the photograph being taken. On the other hand, a clip in the newsreel of Kane and Susan coming out of the courthouse in Trenton, New Jersey, after their marriage—expanded as a scene in Susan's story—accords with the script. Not only is the newsreel, called "News on the March," a parody of a current popular newsreel, "The March of Time," (notice, for example, its *Time*-style backward syntax: "Legendary was Xanadu where Kubla Khan decreed his stately pleasure dome," that is here, ironically, in keeping with the syntax of Coleridge's poem: "In Xanadu did Kubla Khan . . ."), which is again in accordance with the script. Cedric Redford has pointed out that "scenes of Kane's earlier days are scratched as if the film were taken from newsreel archives, and a camera of earlier days has presumably been used, exposing fewer frames to the second than the camera of today."[7] Nor does the script indicate the parody in the plenipotent voice of the announcer. That voice, by the way, belongs to William Alland, who plays the effacing Thompson.

Only here and there does the script indicate composition and angles of shots. It suggests the staging of a scene in which Welles takes advantage of Gregg Toland's deep-focus photography, whereby figures in the background stand out as clearly as those in the foreground. The scene is that in the nightclub, from which Thompson telephones Rawlston that Susan will not talk. While we *hear* and see Thompson in the glass-enclosed telephone booth in the foreground, we also see Susan, her head resting on the spotlighted table in the background. On the other hand, whereas the script specifies that shots of Kane's parents talking to Thatcher be crosscut with shots of Kane playing outside in the snow, Welles films all of this portion of the sequence like the nightclub scene. We hear—and see—the parents and Thatcher in the house while, through a window, we see the subject of their conversation, the boy playing in the snow.

In the scene of the *Inquirer* banquet, Toland's photography makes figures at the far end of a long table distinct. The script does not mention such details as the larger-than-life-sized busts of Leland and Bernstein carved in ice, which frame the shot of the table and, by virtue of constancy of size, look even larger. In another elaboration on the script, Leland and Bernstein, in medium close-ups, converse by a window while Kane and chorus girls dance in a pinwheel pattern in the background. Alternating with these shots, the angle reversed, shots of the dancers are reflected in the window. Accordingly throughout we *hear* the conversation above the shouting and the music while we *see* the dancing. Low-angle shots of Kane emphasize his rise in power. After his defeat in the election, a high-angle shot of newspapers lying in the street creates the opposite effect.

Welles departs from the script in deleting some of the dialogue. Ford would have deleted more, but Ford would have approved of the wordless opening sequence, in which we are taken from the gate at the foot of the hill to Kane's bedroom high in a tower in the castle. Not until the fifteenth shot is the first word uttered—"Rosebud"—reminiscent of the wordless beginning of *The Informer*. It happens that here wordlessness accords with the script. But Welles curtails dialogue, for example, when Thatcher tries to reassure Charles about leaving home. The script has him say, "When we get to New York, Charles, we'll get you a sled that will—." Thatcher does not complete the line because Charles kicks him in the ankle. Welles deletes the line and, as Ford would say, lets the pictures do the talking, by cutting from the sled in the snow to the sled Charles is unwrapping in New York.

The film depends on sound not indicated in the script. In describing the vault room of the Thatcher Memorial Library as having the warmth and charm of Napoleon's tomb, the script specifies that the floor is marble, but it does not indicate that when, in the film, Thompson is led into the room, the predominant sound is echoes—echoes of footsteps, of a steel door clanging shut, of voices in a variety of intonations. As Charles is being taken away from his parents, his father tries to console him. Charles and Thatcher are to leave on Number Ten. "That's the train with all the lights," says the father. Although Welles deletes the shots of the car wheels and the scene aboard the train that are indicated in the script and dissolves instead from the sled in the snow to the sled being unwrapped, he interpolates during the dissolve the sound of a train whistle. As Kane is completing Leland's unfavorable review of Susan's acting in the opera, Leland comes in. "Hello, Jedediah," says Kane, typing rapidly.

"Hello, Charlie," Leland replies. "I didn't know we were speaking."

"Sure we're speaking, Jedediah. You're fired." The script does not mention that, with "You're fired," Kane swings the typewriter carriage back so that the sound is like an exclamation mark.

Nor, except for a reference to brassy music in the newsreel, is background music specified in the script. As the camera shoots through the window of the room where Kane is dying, the lights go out, and simultaneously the music abruptly stops. "Goodbye, everybody. Thanks for the use of the hall," Thompson calls out on leaving the Thatcher Memorial. The line approximates that in the script, but the script does not indicate that the line is accompanied by a run of satiric music. Music imitates Susan's voice dying out, marking the end of her operatic career. Accompanying the failing voice, the music winds down like an old phonograph. And Susan works one jigsaw puzzle after another in the great hall of Xanadu, music simulates the ticking of a clock.

Bernard Herrmann, who composed and

directed the score for *Citizen Kane* (shortly before he composed and directed music for *All That Money Can Buy*) incorporates music not only imitatively but commentarily. In describing the music, Herrmann points out that there are two main motifs—a simple four-note figure in the brass for Kane's power and a vibraphone solo for Rosebud—the power motif heard in the first two bars of the film and subsequently transformed into "a vigorous piece of ragtime, a hornpipe polka, and at the end of the picture, a final commentary of Kane's life," and the Rosebud motif, first heard during the death scene and "again and again throughout the film under various guises." The Rosebud motif, he contends, "if followed closely, is a clue to the ultimate identity of Rosebud itself."[8] Some of the music could not have been described in the script anyway. Contrary to the practice of matching music to film, Welles cut many of the sequences to match the music. Herrmann cites as an example the breakfast-table montage, the theme of which is a waltz in the style of Waldteufel. Heard during the first scene, it varies as discord creeps in, each scene a separate variation until finally "it is heard bleakly played in the high registers of the violins."[9]

Some of the music is evocative. For the scenes showing Kane's newspaper activities in the 1890s, Herrmann used, as he says, various dance forms popular at the time; for the montage showing the increase in the circulation of the *Inquirer,* a can-can scherzo; for the campaign against the traction trust, a gallop; and for the arrival of Kane and Leland at the newspaper office, a rhythm of early ragtime.

In addition to all of the background music, music inheres in the action. Most of the inherent music is that of Susan singing and the opera scenes. Herrmann himself wrote Susan's aria "Salammbo," composed, he says, "in the style of the nineteenth-century French Oriental operatic school."[10] Hermann obtained the newsreel music for "News on the March" from the RKO files. An ironic turn is given to music at the picnic. It is not indicated in the script that, while Susan and Kane quarrel in their tent, a professional entertainer is heard singing "This Can't Be Love."

Not only in these ways does the film depart from or augment the script. In scene after scene Welles exploits the freedom Nichols's script would allow a director, as implied in his reference to continuity as "approximate." It is illustrated in the scene representing Susan's recollection of her operatic debut. The continuity suggested by the script consists of eleven shots, five of them close-ups of Kane in the audience. It would begin with a dissolve from a shot of the stage, the curtain down, the camera angled toward it, to that of the same scene from the same angle, Susan alone downstage, the orchestra beginning to play, the curtain rising, and Susan starting to sing. Beyond her would be the prompter's box, in which appears the face of the prompter, and beyond that the conductor. Then would follow a close-up of Kane and a voice saying, "Really pathetic," which provokes tittering. A close-up of Susan singing would intervene, and in the next shot (a close-up of Kane, with slight applause heard), the camera would move back, revealing Bernstein and others in the Kane claque applauding loudly. Alternating with the other close-ups of Kane would be view of the stage from Kane's point of view: the stage, the curtain down, no one appearing; the stage again, Susan appearing for her bow; the stage, Susan finishing her bow and going out through the curtains, the light on the curtain going out, and the house lights coming up.

In filming the sequence, Welles increases the eleven shots to thirty-six. He adheres to the script in its attention to Kane; in fact, he increases the number of close-ups of him to nine, but he also shows the occasion to be an ordeal for Susan. The sequence opens on Susan practicing her aria before the curtain goes up. She has not sung two words before Signor Matisti, her coach, comes on, gesturing wildly and shouting, "No, no, no, no, no," and the prompter adds,

"I should say not." While they give Susan last-minute instructions, she is disconcerted by her maid and the other assistants who are fussing with her costume. As she is again trying the aria, a plumed hat is fitted to her head. Welles further adds to the script by interpolating reaction shots of Matisti in the prompter's box, nodding, closing one eye, gesturing, waving his arms, biting his fingers, and jumping up and down; of Leland examining his program as though in boredom, tearing it into strips, and blowing on them; of flowers being carried down to the stage and passed up to Susan; and of Susan awkwardly picking them up and backing through the curtains.

The film adheres to the script in not answering for Thompson the question conspicuously posed: What is the explanation for the character of Kane? "He had some sort of private greatness," Leland says, "but he kept it to himself." "Mr. Thatcher never did figure him out," Bernstein says. "Sometimes even I couldn't." Susan is evasive. "You wouldn't want to hear a lot of what comes to my mind about Mr. Charlie Kane," she says, and refers Thompson to Raymond, "who knows where all the bodies are buried." But Raymond is least revealing of all. Bernstein comes closest to the answer when he speculates, "Maybe it was something he lost."

What he lost, script and film imply, was his youth. Thompson does not see "Rosebud" lettered on the sled in the fire. Accordingly the sign on the Xanadu gate, NO TRESPASSING—on which the camera comes to rest in the last shot of the film, tracking down from the castle in reversal of the opening shots—constitutes dramatic irony. Kane's character, which Thompson's search attempts to penetrate, is impenetrable: the clue has gone up in smoke; Thompson's search is in vain. In this regard, *Citizen Kane* is a psychological film. It is about subconscious motivations. (In one of those elaborations on the script, Welles had anticipated this ironic effect by also beginning the film with the camera on the sign.) There is another clue. When Kane dies, a glass ball containing a snow scene—anticipating the scene of the eight-year-old boy with his sled—drops from his hand and shatters on the floor. The ball is associated not only with the lost youth but with Susan. It is the ball that Kane finds in the wreckage of Susan's room. In another elaboration on the script, Welles establishes that the ball was indeed originally Susan's: we first see it on her dresser in her rooming house.

Welles has called "Rosebud" a gimmick. It might be considered a gimmick because no one hears Kane utter the word when he dies. The script is vague as to whether the nurse is in the room, but in the film she enters only afterwards when she appears in distortion as though seen through the shattered glass. It might also be considered a gimmick because it motivates Thompson's search and thus the flashbacks, which tell most of the story. But it is primarily a gimmick because it purports to explain Kane. "I was on my way to the Western Manhattan Warehouse in search of my youth," Kane tells Susan when he first meets her. Lost youth might account for a man's character, but neither script nor film shows how Kane's lost youth accounts for Kane's character. Kane's youth is only a gap in time. Thus there is also dramatic irony in Thompson's conclusion at the end of his search: "I don't think any word can explain a man's life."

Had it been the intention to explain the character of Kane, the story might have been told from the point of view of the one person from whose point of view it is not told. But that would have been another story. *Citizen Kane* has been criticized as the picture of a man who is not really worth depicting, and here is the film's weakness.[11] The point is that the man is not really depicted, and here is the film's virtue. While adhering, in general, to the script, Welles adapts it so cinematically as to make the manner of telling the story worth more than the story.

17.
Point of View

From the time that Porter incorporated a dream balloon in *The Life of an American Fireman* to give "the impression that the fire chief dreams of his wife and child," directors have exploited motion pictures to narrate from a subjective point of view. Purposely or not, in *The Great Train Robbery* Porter puts us in the position of the posse when he has Barnes fire "point-blank at the audience." Margaret Cameron remembering her brother's death on the battlefield, Mother McTeague picturing her son a dentist, the *Potemkin* sailors imagining themselves hanging from the yardarm, and Gypo Nolan recollecting a barroom episode illustrate what Griffith meant when he said that you can photograph thought. Films like *Great Expectations* and *Brief Encounter* purport to narrate subjectively throughout, or almost throughout, by the device of a narrator who is one with the protagonist. Even *The Cabinet of Dr. Caligari,* for all its playlike manner, is in this category. But motion pictures have other ways of narrating subjectively, as illustrated by three notable films: Ingmar Bergman's *Wild Strawberries* (1957), Alain Resnais's *Last Year at Marienbad* (1961), and Federico Fellini's *8½* (1962).

Like Méliès, Griffith, Eisenstein, and others, Bergman, who was born July 14, 1918, in Uppsala, Sweden, came to motion pictures from the theatre. While he was a student at the University of Stockholm, he ran a youth-club theatre, and after he was graduated he directed plays in Stockholm. When he was twenty-six years old he was made director of the City Theatre in Hälsingborg. Other directorships followed, and he became recognized as one of the leading stage directors in Europe. Meanwhile he had been rewriting film scripts for Svensk Filmindustri. In 1944 he submitted to Svensk a script of his own called *Hets,* a novel intended as a film. It was produced that year (under the title *Torment* in the United States, and *Frenzy* in England). Although his distinguished career in motion pictures then began, he continues to be active in the theatre. And the manner of the theatre continues to manifest itself in his films.

In *Wild Strawberries* Bergman tells the story from the point of view of an eminent physician and professor of medicine named Isak Borg. On a certain day when Isak was seventy-eight years old, he returned to his old university at Lund to receive an honorary degree. (Among the several differences between script and film is Isak's age —seventy-six in the script. Victor Sjöstrom, who plays Isak, was seventy-eight in 1957, the year in which *Wild Strawberries* was filmed.) Now, not more than a year later,

Ingmar Bergman, *Wild Strawberries. Courtesy of Janus Films*

he is writing a true account, he tells us, of the events, dreams, and thoughts that befell him on that day.

The day begins for him when he wakes from a disturbing dream marked by distorted images (a clock, his watch without hands, a corpse that Isak recognizes as himself). Isak was going to fly to Lund, but he decides instead to drive. Accompanying him is his daughter-in-law, Marianne, who is returning home to see her estranged husband, Evald. They stop at a lakeside cottage where Isak spent every summer for the first twenty years of his life. Here he dreams again, this time of the long ago—of his brothers and sisters and of his cousin Sara, whom he loved but lost to his brother Sigfrid. He is awakened by a girl who perfectly resembles Sara and who introduces herself as Sara. Isak invites her and the two boys hiking with her to ride to Lund. They pick up a

married couple named Alman, but the Almans quarrel and Marianne has them get out of the car. They stop for petrol, and the petrol-station owner refuses payment out of gratitude for Dr. Borg's services to the community. After lunch on the terrace of an inn, Isak takes Marianne to visit his aged mother. Old Mrs. Borg talks about her children and shows Isak his grandfather's watch, which has lost its hands. Napping in the car while Marianne drives, Isak dreams of Sara and Sigfrid, of being examined by Alman on his qualifications as a physician, and of his wife being willingly seduced. When he wakes, the car is standing still. The youngsters have got out and are picking wild flowers. Before they return and present their flowers to Isak, Marianne tells Isak about her disagreement with Evald. At Lund they go to Evald's house and then to the cathedral for the academic ceremony. In the evening Isak is serenaded by the hikers and has a talk with Evald and Marianne. In his last dream Sara leads him to the lake. Here, across a stretch of water, he sees his father and mother.

The point of view is established at once, before the credit titles come and go. We see Isak writing at his desk in his study and, by voice-over, hear him describe himself and tell us about his family—that his nine brothers and sisters are dead, that his son, a physician in Lund, has been married for many years and is childless, that his mother is still living, that his wife died many years ago, and that his marriage was unhappy. Intermittently thereafter he also speaks in this way as narrator.

Bergman, however, seems deliberately to eschew a subjective point of view either by editing or by position of the camera whereby we share, for example, Laura's emotions in *Brief Encounter* or Pip's in *Great Expectations*. There are shots of objects of this or that character's attention but no more than in any film that does not purport to narrate subjectively. "Look at yourself in the mirror," Sara says, holding the mirror with Isak's face visible to us in it. But when Isak says, glancing up, that he looked at Sara in the rear-view mirror, the camera faces Isak and Sara, not the mirror. When Isak drives down the road to the scene of his boyhood, we do not approach the scene with him. Instead the camera pans with the car as it turns off the highway and disappears behind some trees. In the next shot the camera faces Isak and Marianne in the car; and in the next, the car is standing in a forest, and Isak and Marianne, having got out, come forward. When Isak looks in on his family assembling for breakfast in the dining room of the cottage, he stands in the hall while the camera tracks past him into the room. Accordingly for a moment we do indeed observe the lively scene approximately from his point of view, observing it, that is, over his shoulder. But only for a moment, because in the next shot the camera, panning from the opposite side of the room, reveals Isak facing forward in the background. The camera follows him up the steps to his mother's house, but when the door is opened the position of the camera is reversed, so that Isak comes forward as he enters. Similarly, as Alman leads him into the lecture room for the examination, the camera faces Isak coming into the room.

We have shot the final supplementary scenes of *Wild Strawberries* [Bergman recorded in his diary] — the final close-ups of Isak Borg as he is brought to clarity and reconciliation. His face shone with secretive light, as if reflected from another reality. His features became suddenly mild, almost effete. His look was open, smiling, tender.[1]

To present a character's emotion by facial expression is objective. It is the method of the stage. Although the close-ups of Isak narrow the distance between actor and audience, as it could not be narrowed in the production of a play, the close-ups are not subjective by being close-ups.

Bergman, who writes his own scripts, insists that the vital thing about a script is the dialogue.[2] Although dialogue may not be the vital thing about *Wild Strawberries* the film, it is of major importance. Isak's flaw is an unnatural coldness; in fact, Berg-

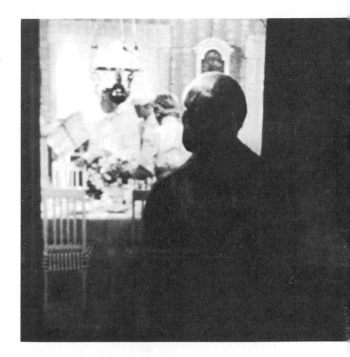

Ingmar Bergman, *Wild Strawberries. Courtesy of Janus Films*

man chose the name Isak because it seemed icy.³ He has been successful in his profession, but he is less than successful as a human being. In the dream about the seduction of his wife, he hears the wife say that she will tell Isak what she has done and ask forgiveness, that he will say he has nothing to forgive, but that he doesn't mean a word of it because he is completely cold. "What is the penalty?" he asks Alman. And the answer is "Loneliness." But even after the dreams and the happenings of the day, Isak does not find the penalty severe. "I have found myself rather alone in my old age," he says. "This is not a regret but a statement of fact. All I ask of life is to be left alone." If he is brought to clarity and reconciliation, it is in accepting his flaw, and his flaw is manifested by what he says and by what others say about him.

The scene in the car as Isak and Marianne set out for Lund not only reaffirms the impression Isak has given us in the preceding scene, in which he quarrels with Miss Agda, his housekeeper, but anticipates a reconciliation at the end of the day. The setting is the car, but the setting could be almost anywhere. The vital element, as in a play, is the dialogue, by which it is established that Marianne regards Isak only as a father-in-law and resents his asking why she is going home because, she says, the matter does not concern him, that Isak lent Evald money to complete his studies and that, although Isak knows that paying it back means a deprivation for both Evald and Marianne, he considers that a bargain is a bargain and that Evald understands and respects him. "That may be true," Marianne replies, "but he also hates you." Finally Isak asks what Marianne has against him.

MARIANNE: Shall I be frank?
ISAK: Please.
MARIANNE: You're an old egoist, Uncle Isak. You're utterly ruthless and listen to no one but yourself. But you hide it all behind your old-world manners and charm. Beneath your benevolent exterior, you're as hard as nails. But you can't fool us who have seen you at close quarters.

The scene anticipates that in which the petrol-station owner, who has *not* seen Isak at close quarters, speaks of him as a great humanitarian. The vital thing about the scene in Isak's bedroom in the evening is what is said in relation to what has been said during the day. Isak asks Evald what is going to happen between him and Marianne. After Evald tells him, Isak mentions the loan:

EVALD: Don't worry, you'll get your money.
ISAK: That's not what I mean.

Then Marianne comes in. If reconciliation between Isak and Evald is not complete, it is between Isak and Marianne:

ISAK: Thanks for coming with me. I like you, Marianne.
MARIANNE: I like you too, Uncle Isak.

Nevertheless, Marianne's earlier harsh but perceptive evaluation of Isak is enforced by what is said during the day. It is enforced, for example, in the scene in which Isak and Marianne visit Isak's aged mother. Hearing what old Mrs. Borg says, we realize that Isak's hardness is inherited. And when we hear what Evald says to Marianne, we realize that Isak has passed this trait on to his son. All of the Borg children, however, have not inherited hardness, as we infer from what they say in Isak's dream about his boyhood. In that dream what Sara says, in confiding in Isak's sister Charlotta, sets forth Isak's flaw in its incipiency:

Isak is so refined—so moral and sensitive. He wants us to read poetry and talk about the next life and play duets and he only likes to kiss me when it's dark and he talks about sin. He's frightfully far above me. I feel such a worm! I *am* a worm, there's no getting away from it. But sometimes I feel I'm much older than Isak, that he's just a child, although we're the same age.

When Marianne starts to tell Isak about her disagreement with Evald, there is a flashback. First, a medium close-up of Isak in his car is cut to a medium close-up of

Marianne sitting beside him. In the next shot the camera pulls back from a medium close-up of Evald—in Isak's place but in Evald's car—to reveal Marianne sitting next to him. At the end of the flashback the process is reversed. Kenneth Macgowan cites the flashback as exemplifying Bergman's ingeniousness—and success—in making an excursion into the past without benefit of the dissolve.[4] The transitions into and out of the past are indeed cinematic, but the value of the flashback lies in what Evald and Marianne say to each other during it.

Even the construction of *Wild Strawberries* is more dramatic than epic. The film observes the unities of time and action, if not of place—a day in the hero's life. The scenes are chronologically arranged, that is, except for the dreams, and each scene is played out to the end. There is no cross-cutting. For the most part, the stage is Isak's throughout. Other characters come and go, their entrances and exits well motivated or not. Marianne goes for a swim so that Isak can have a dream followed by a talk with Sara, and she returns when the talk is over. The hikers pick wild flowers so that Marianne can confide in Isak, and they stay out of hearing until called back. Marianne has broken the heel of her shoe so that she and Evald can return to the house for their final talk with Isak, and she and Evald leave to go to a dance so that Isak can dream again.

But Isak's story is presented more subjectively than elements such as these imply. In the first place there are the dreams, constituting more than half the running time of the film. The onset of each dream is marked by Isak speaking as narrator, and music foreshadows not only the beginnings but the endings of the dreams. Music also fades in now and then during the dreams. In the scenes depicting ordinary states of consciousness, however, there is almost no dependence on background music. During the dreams Isak does not speak as narrator. Some of the transitions from reality to dream and from dream to reality are effected by matched images. A close-up of Isak asleep is cut to a close-up of him as he walks through the street in the first dream. As the dream ends, a close-up of the corpse is cut to a close-up of Isak waking. When he begins to dream about his boyhood, a dissolve transforms the somber shuttered cottage into the cottage open and light. The distortions which make the first dream dreamlike are reminiscent of those in *The Cabinet of Dr. Caligari*. But the other dreams are also less than realistically presented. Isak moves through the cottage scenes unnoticed by the other characters. Sara cannot hear him when he speaks to her. The twins speak in unison. In the next dream, Isak approaches Sigfrid and Sara's house through a forest at night. Screeching birds fly about. The claw-shaped branches of a tree, like the tree that looks sinister to Pip in *Great Expectations*, look sinister to Isak, the editing—a cut from Isak to the branches—enforcing the subjective point of view. Reaching the house, he sees Sara and Sigfrid inside, and he raps on the window. But the window is opened by Alman, and Isak enters an empty room. In the last dream the shots of Isak's parents sitting on the shore are suggestive of impressionistic painting.

Jörn Donner aptly observes that Strindberg's *The Dream Play* inspired *Wild Strawberries* not only in several scenes but in its use of the technique of the dream, its free associations.[5] In the published text of the play Strindberg declares that he has tried to imitate the disconnected but seemingly logical form of the dream: "a medley of memories, experiences, free fancies, absurdities and improvisation."[6] The characters, Strindberg points out, "split, double, multiply, vanish, solidify, blur, clarify. But one consciousness reigns above them all—that of the dreamer."[7] With some modification the description fits the behaviour of the characters in Isak's dreams. And the consciousness that reigns above them all is Isak's.

In the script, but not in the film, Isak converses at the university with an old friend,

Ingmar Bergman, *Wild Strawberries. Courtesy of Janus Films*

a bishop, who quotes Schopenhauer as saying that dreams are a kind of lunacy, and that lunacy is a kind of dream. "But life is also supposed to be a kind of dream," adds the bishop, "isn't it?" During the ceremony in the cathedral, Isak tells us that it was then that he decided to write down everything that had happened during the day. In the script he says further, "I was beginning to see a remarkable causality in this chain of unexpected, entangled events. At the same time, I couldn't escape recalling the bishop's words." Dreams and events in *Wild Strawberries* are intertwined. Parts of the dreams are explained by previous happenings: Sara's objecting to Sigfrid's cigar and Sigfrid saying, "That's a man's smell, isn't it?" explained by Isak's having declared, in asking Marianne not to smoke in the car, that smoking cigars is a manly vice; Alman's examining Isak in the presence of the hikers, by the presence of Alman and the hikers in the car together; Alman's accusing Isak of indifference, selfishness, and lack of consideration, by Marianne's having told him that he is completely inconsiderate; or Alman's showing him the seduction of his wife, by Isak's having witnessed the quarrel of the Almans and being reminded of his own unhappy marriage. But it is remarkable that Mrs. Borg should talk about each of the children Isak has dreamed about that morning, and that Isak should notice that his grandfather's watch has lost its hands after dreaming about a clock and his own watch without hands, and particularly remarkable that, as he looks at the watch, a drum beats—a sound like that of the heartbeat he heard when he looked at his watch in the dream. It is indeed remarkable that, dreaming about his cousin Sara, he is awakened by an identical Sara. If the hikers seem less than plausible, it should be remembered that they are an image in an old man's recollection, in which dream and actuality merge. Isak envisions the hikers as modern youngsters. But even at the time the film was made, Bergman says, "the image was utterly outdated."[8]

There is also entanglement in that some

of the incidents in the dreams seem to constitute exposition. Isak tells us that his marriage was quite unhappy, and we hear Evald
say to Marianne: "Personally I was an un-
welcome child in a marriage which was a
nice imitation of hell. Is the old man really
sure that I'm his son?" (Strindberg again
—this time, *The Father*). Accordingly the
dream about the wife's infidelity may be
taken for reality. "Strange, isn't it?" Alman
says. "Tuesday, May 1, 1917, you stood
exactly here and heard and saw what that
woman and that man said and did." Isak was
the only one of the children not at breakfast that morning at the cottage. ("I think,"
the twins explain, "that Isak is out fishing
with Father, and they probably can't hear
the gong.") He witnesses the breakfast scene
only in his dream, but the implication is that
the happenings in the scene occurred.

Isak calls his story a true account of the
events, dreams, and thoughts which befell
him on a certain day. Which *befell* him.
He moves through the scenes of actuality
and dreams as an observer, a receiver more
than a doer. He is ministered to by Miss
Agda. He sees his brother take Sara away
from him. He endures the unpleasant Almans. (It is Marianne who puts them out
of the car.) He receives the praise of the
petrol-station owner. He submits to an examination by Alman. He observes the seduction of his wife. He is presented with flowers
by the hikers, and he is serenaded by them.
He receives an honorary degree. Isak is
incapable of becoming involved. "Let me
hear from you sometime," he says as the
hikers are calling their goodbyes under his
balcony. The script reads: "Those words I
said to myself and rather quietly."

The dreams are not represented as occurring but as Isak's recollection of having
dreamed them. They are one with the events
of the day, which he also recollects. "I have
found," he says, "that during the last few
years I glide rather easily into a twilight
world of memories and dreams." In that
world, images of memories and dreams
merge. With the image of Sara—both Saras

Ingmar Bergman, *Wild Strawberries. Courtesy of
Janus Films*

are played by the same actress—the merging
is complete.

Alain Robbe-Grillet, who wrote the script
for *Last Year at Marienbad,* calls it "the
story of a persuasion."[9] In an enormous
baroque chateau converted into a luxurious
hotel, a man pursues a young woman, attempting to persuade her that they met the
year before at Marienbad, or some other
resort, that they had an affair there, and
that she promised to meet him here a year
later and go away with him. The woman
seems to be under the guardianship of a
third character, who may be her husband.
She denies that she and the man ever met.
But he persists, describing incidents out
of the affair, until, apparently persuaded,
she walks out of the hotel with him.

Audiences have been puzzled by the film
because it seems to raise questions which
it fails to answer. Did the man and the woman
have an affair last year at Marienbad? Have
they ever met before? Does the woman
remember and only pretend not to? Or has

she forgotten? Such questions would seem logical, but Robbe-Grillet insists that they have no meaning because the film occurs in a world of a perpetual present. "This love story we were being told as a thing of the past," he explains, "was in fact actually happening before our eyes here and now. For of course an *elsewhere* is no more probable than a *formerly*."[10] His explanation implies an affinity of *Last Year at Marienbad* with that literary enterprise called the new novel, of which he is the chief exponent.

Noticeable at once about the new novel is its preoccupation with descriptions of objects, in particular, descriptions of seemingly insignificant objects, without any thought about them at all. Beginning his novel *The Voyeur* with an account of the docking of a steamer, Robbe-Grillet narrates the docking itself in hardly more than a hundred words, but before he has the steamer tied up, he has devoted twenty-five pages to a piece of string, the steamer's whistle ("objects" include sounds), the edge of the pier, the water in the slip, a piece of paper floating on the water, some rocks under the water, clumps of seaweed on the rocks, and so on. He sees geometric figures as objects: a rectangle, a cluster of parallel lines, a triangle, a figure eight formed by the piece of string, two small circles in a pair of glasses, smoke in equal small loops. The banana plantation in his novel *Jealousy* is laid out in rectangular and trapezoidal patches, the number of rows in each patch and the number of trees in each row enumerated.

The aim of the new novel is total subjectivity. The narrator, Robbe-Grillet says in his book *For a New Novel*, is "a man here, now." Declaring that objects in his novels never exist outside human perception, he holds that it is only natural that his books contain only objects, which he takes to include memory, intention, and every form of imagination. In this world of a perpetual present, a description starts from an insignificant point, creates objects, merges them, repeats itself, adds or subtracts details, or contradicts itself. In Robbe-Grillet's *In the Labyrinth* the description of a tavern scene represented in a painting hanging on a tavern wall becomes indistinguishable from the scene in the tavern. The description of a sea gull in *The Voyeur* is repeated. In *In the Labyrinth* a soldier notices a spray of ivy embossed on the conical cast-iron base of a lamppost. Robbe-Grillet has twice previously described the design minutely—the five-lobed palmate leaves, the attachment of the leaves to the stem, and the changing direction of the stem around the cone. The soldier having noticed the embossed spray, Robbe-Grillet describes it in detail again and in more detail than before. The narrator in *In the Labyrinth* tells us that it is raining and that the wind is blowing, the trees casting moving shadows, and, in the next sentence, that the sun is shining and that there is no tree or bush to cast a shadow. The new novelists intend that objects cancel themselves as the description proceeds so that at the end there is nothing—the interest, as Robbe-Grillet says, having shifted from the object described to the movement of the description.

Alain Resnais was a felicitous choice to direct *Last Year at Marienbad.* Although he had become prominent only two years before, with the production of his film *Hiroshima Mon Amour,* he had been devoting himself to motion pictures for fifteen years. Born in Brittany in 1922—he and Robbe-Grillet are the same age—he studied acting and was on the stage for a year and a half, an experience that has contributed to the theatrical style of acting in his films. From the time he was twenty-four years old until he directed *Hiroshima Mon Amour,* he edited not only his own films but films made by other directors. He is counted among the directors of the New Wave. (A journalistic term, "New Wave" refers not so much to a new style of directing as to a wave of young French directors whose talents were becoming manifest in the late fifties.) In the introduction to the published text of *Last Year at Marienbad,* Robbe-Grillet explains that he and Resnais were able to collaborate only because they saw the film in the same way, exactly in the construction of the least detail. The result is a remarkably faithful adaptation of Robbe-Grillet's script.

Subtitled "A Cine-novel," *Last Year at Marienbad* is a new novel in screen form. Whereas in the new novel the only important character is the reader, in the film the only important character is the spectator, in whose mind, Robbe-Grillet says, "unfolds the whole story, which is precisely imagined by him."[11] We are guided through the film by a narrator who not only speaks in the first person but is the hero of the story. He and the spectator are expected to be one and the same. Except for references to a character named Frank, who never appears, the characters are nameless. "Why persist," Robbe-Grillet asks, "in discovering what an individual's name is in a novel which does not supply it? Every day we meet people whose names we do not know, and we can talk to a stranger for a whole evening when we have not paid any attention to the introductions made by the hostess."[12] In the script Robbe-Grillet calls the woman A. (In *Jealousy* the heroine is also A, and "the other man" is Frank.) He calls the hero X, and the man who may be the husband M. "What is your name?" A asks X, and X replies, "It is of no importance."

Although Robbe-Grillet refers to *Last Year at Marienbad* as a story, he insists that "to tell a story has become strictly impossible."[13] The emphasis is on *tell,* with its implication of places elsewhere and of time past. The story in *Last Year at Marienbad* is happening here and now. "Once again—I walk on," the narrator begins, but soon he is narrating in the past tense. Nevertheless, the story takes place only as it is remembered or imagined. The order of incidents is the order in which they come to mind. The only time is the present, or the projection time. The presentational nature of motion pictures accords with a story recalled in a perpetual present. A film has no past—no real past. The flashback purports to take us into the past, but the flashback is only a device signaling us to *imagine* that we are in the past whereas what we see

on the screen and hear from the sound track continue to be happening in the present. The title *Last Year at Marienbad* is ironic. As Robbe-Grillet observes, there is no last year, and Marienbad is no longer on the map.

The film also reflects the new novel's preoccupation with objects. Opening with a loud burst of music, it begins with sound as an "object." Then follow a dozen shots of objects in a gallery, the narrator naming them: dark ornamental woodwork, moldings, dark paintings, framed drawings, heavy hangings, black mirrors, and sculptured door frames. The names are not consistently matched with the objects as we see them —in fact, the narrator begins naming them during the credit titles—nor are all of the objects named, and the shots are edited so as to give the impression of a single tracking shot. We are thus taken along a galley to a salon, where the characters are attending a play. Shot after shot of a statuary group is reminiscent of the repeated description of the design on the lamppost in *In the Labyrinth*. (Here, however, the film departs from the manner of the new novel, in which objects are described without any thought about them: X explains to A what he takes the group to represent, and M interrupts to offer a different explanation.) When A drops a glass and it shatters on the floor, the camera focuses on the broken pieces and continues focusing on them as an attendant, white napkin in hand, comes forward, picks them up one by one, and carefully places them in the napkin. Objects take geometric forms. In the play the actress's stance, as she raises her hand to the hollow of her shoulder, makes an acute angle. In a repeatedly played game four rows of cards are arranged in a triangle (seven, five, three, one), and the arrangement is repeated with other objects—dominoes, matches, photographs, and so on. Like the banana plantation in *Jealousy,* the garden is landscaped in geometric patterns—symmetrical plots, parallel paths intersecting at right angles, cubicle pedestals, and shrubbery clipped in the shape of cones, balls, and rectangles. The

Objects (Alain Robbe-Grillet's *Last Year at Marienbad,* directed by Alain Resnais). *Courtesy of Vauban Productions*

settings are baroque—baguettes, ogees, and friezes. In naming the objects in the gallery, the narrator repeats the word *baroque*. Resnais is given to the familiar device of photographing objects in mirrors, but he makes the baroque frames of the mirrors as prominent as the reflections.

In objectifying thought, *Last Year at Marienbad* distorts reality in ways limited only by the imaginations of its creators. Some photographs that A takes from a drawer are of scenes in the film, the last one filling the screen and thus becoming the scene itself, as in *In the Labyrinth* when the picture on the tavern wall becomes the scene in the tavern. This kind of transition is reversed when the statuary group in the garden becomes, as the camera pulls back, the group represented in a framed print in the gallery. A backdrop for the play vaguely represents some of the exterior scenes in the film. A repeatedly bends her arm in the angle assumed by the actress. Some of the objects in the garden cast shadows while others do not, nor do all objects cast shadows in the same direction. There is a dreamlike transposition in the way the film begins and ends. The loud burst of music at the beginning is of the kind, as the script specifies, "used at the end of films with powerfully emotional climaxes." At the beginning of the film we see the end of the play, and at the end, the play's beginning. At the beginning of the film, instead of an establishing shot, there are those close shots of inanimate objects. The establishing shot is at the end—a long shot of the garden with the chateau in the background.

What has attracted many of the new novelists to motion pictures, Robbe-Grillet says, is what has escaped the powers of literature: the sound track, the possibility of acting on the eye and the ear at once, the possibility of presenting "with all the appearance of incontestible objectivity what is, also, only dream or memory—in a word, what is only imagination."[14] Sound in *Last Year at Marienbad* not only matches the proper images but is so edited as to be separated from them. As the curtain comes down on the last

Alain Robbe-Grillet's *Last Year at Marienbad,* directed by Alain Resnais. *Courtesy of Vauban Productions*

act of the play, applause is heard but the audience is immobile—an immobility reflected in the actors, who take a curtain call without so much as a gesture. Organ music swells, stops, or becomes discordant as we see violins playing. We see the dancers dancing to music unrelated to the rhythm of their dancing. We see X playing cards but hear him narrating the action of another scene. We hear the crunching of gravel as A runs along a garden path, but we hear the same sound as she climbs the grand staircase in the chateau. A piece of balustrade falling into the garden sounds like distant thunder. M fires a pistol, but there is no detonation.

Such editing may represent the attraction of the new novelists to the possibilities of the sound track, but closer to description in the new novel is the editing of images so that objects do indeed cancel themselves, the interest shifting from the object to the movement, if not of description, then of its cinematic counterparts. When X mentions the mirror that we have seen in A's room, A insists that it is not a mirror but a snowscape, which it becomes in a subsequent shot. X imagines that M shoots A; M

Objects (Alain Robbe-Grillet's *Last Year at Marienbad,* directed by Alain Resnais). *Courtesy of Vauban Productions*

accordingly does so. Then X says, "No, this isn't the ending. . . . I must have you alive." Shortly there occurs another version of the affair: X rapes A. And again there is a correction. "That's wrong," says X. "It was not by force." Observing that three baroque castles—Nyphenburg, Schleissheim, and Amalienburg—served as locations for the filming, Roy Armes points out that Resnais edits in such a way that the same door opens into different rooms, and that the garden changes so that hedges and paths replace pools and fountains, and the statue appears in a variety of places.[15] Editing links images with the abruptness of transitions in the new novel. A and X conversing in a salon are instantaneously dancing in another salon. The scene in which A drops the glass is interrupted a dozen times by fraction-of-a-second shots of A in her bedroom. By means of no more than a cut (although here as elsewhere the script specifies a dissolve, there are no dissolves in the film) A, looking out the window, sees herself walking in the garden with X. *Last Year at Marienbad* may be reminiscent of *The Cabinet of Dr. Caligari,* in which thought is also objectified by studied distortion. But whereas the distortions in Weine's film are only those of the objects photographed, Resnais's editing distorts the medium itself.

Last Year at Marienbad has been variously

Objects (Alain Robbe-Grillet's *Last Year at Marienbad,* directed by Alain Resnais). *Courtesy of Vauban Productions*

interpreted. It has been proposed that the hotel is a sanitarium, X a psychiatrist, and A his patient. The story has been compared to the Breton legend in which Death comes after a year and a day to claim his victim. Although Robbe-Grillet specifies that the play named on the theatre poster have "a foreign meaningless title," the poster reads ROSMER. It has accordingly been deduced that the play is Ibsen's *Rosmersholm,* and that since persuasion in *Rosmersholm* leads to suicide, A is being so persuaded and, since incest is implied in *Rosmersholm,* M is

A's father or her brother. Or it is conjectured that M is A's husband because M stand for *mari.* Although such conjectures may seem plausible, they are in a category with questions that Robbe-Grillet calls meaningless. They are meaningless because they disregard the film's most significant resemblance to the new novel—point of view. The whole story unfolding in the spectator's mind, the only reality is what the spectator sees and hears. Asking, "Is he your husband?" X answers the question himself—and for us: "I don't know."

8½ is a comedy about a motion-picture director trying to make a motion picture. The director, Guido Anselmi, is so disconcerted by the banality of the script—about a spaceship in which survivors of a nuclear war leave the earth—that he enters a seaside spa to recover his equilibrium. But the spa hardly provides him with a rest cure. He is pursued by dreams, fancies, and obsessions with the past. He is also pursued by his work. The spa is the setting for the film he has begun, the production office adjoins his bedroom, a huge launching tower for the spaceship has been erected on the beach, and he cannot move about without being importuned by various people with various wants: Carini, a critic who wants to discuss the script; an actress who wants to know what her role in the film will be; a magazine storywriter who wants to know about Guido's private life; Pace, the producer, who wants to know when filming will start, and so forth. Guido's mistress, Carla, joins him at the spa, but he is bored by her. He sends for his wife, Luisa, who arrives with friends. Although he has put Carla up at an obscure hotel, she comes into an outdoor café where Luisa sees her. Guido denies that he knew of Carla's presence at the spa, but Luisa knows that he is lying, and Guido knows that she knows. Impatient with delay, Pace schedules a press conference on the site of the launching tower to announce the start of filming. Here Guido feels himself so badgered by reporters, photographers, Pace, and others that he crawls under a table and draws a gun. There is a shot. But the ending is not the death of the hero. Instead Guido reappears and, having decided not to make the film about a spaceship, orders the launching tower dismantled. Most of the characters we have seen in *8½* now converge at a circus ring, many of them trooping down the steps of the tower. Four clowns together with Guido as he was as a boy march about playing musical instruments. Picking up a bullhorn, Guido directs the characters in a dance. He asks Luisa to accept him as he is. The film that he will make is a film about himself—the film that we have seen.

Although Fellini shares credit for the script with other writers, the story is essentially his. Most of the events in it he admits are autobiographical. One of these takes place at his grandmother's farmhouse when Guido was a child, and where a nurse bathed him and his playmates in a wine vat. Then there is Guido's recollection of a Catholic school he attended, of running away from it with some of his schoolmates to see an obese prostitute called La Saraghina, who lived in a bunker near the sea, of being delighted when she danced on the beach for them, and, having been caught there by the priests, of being taken back to the school and punished.

Born in Rimini, in northern Italy, Fellini had a background similar to Guido's. He makes Guido his own age, 43 in 1963, the year the film was released. As a child Fellini spent the summers at his grandmother's house in the country near Rimini. Apropos of the bath in the wine vat, Deena Boyer tells us that it was an old custom in parts of northern Italy to immerse little boys in wine lees to make them strong.[16] Fellini attended a school run by the Carissimi Fathers. "It was a dull provincial college, miserable and squalid," he says. "We ate badly, were severely punished. When I got naught—which sometimes happened—I was pilloried and shown to all the classes, the 'naught' drawn on a sheet of paper and pinned to my chest."[17] Brought back to the school after he is caught watching La Saraghina, Guido is made to kneel on hard kernels, slapped, and paraded before his schoolmates, on his head a dunce cap and on his back a sheet of paper labeled SHAME. "Don't you know," a priest asks him rhetorically, "that Saraghina is the Devil?" La Saraghina, who Fellini acknowledges as an important figure in his childhood, lived in a hut on the beach at Rimini and, according to Boyer, was called La Saraghina because the Rimini fishermen to whom she sold herself paid her in the dregs of their sardine nets, sardines in that part of Italy being called *saraghine*.[18]

"I realize that *8½* is such a shameless and

brazen confession," Fellini told his auto-biographer, Angelo Solmi, "that it is futile to try and make people forget that it is about my own life."[19] It then becomes relevant, for example, that, two years before he made *8½*, Fellini was a patient at Chianciano, a seaside spa north of Rome, and that, because Guido consults a cardinal, Fellini, when he was making *The Nights of Cabiria* (1956), consulted Cardinal Siri, Archbishop of Genoa, concerning censorship. Fellini's having gone to school not only to the Carissimi Fathers but also to the Sisters of Saint Vincent may explain why Guido remembers that some of the priests at his school were women. Fellini's fascination with the circus and circus people accounts for the circus ring and the clowns. According to Solmi, Guido's quarrel with Luisa originated in Fellini's matrimonial quarrels with his wife, the actress Guiletta Masina, who, like Luisa, understood and forgave her husband.[20] Deena Boyer finds autobiography even in the nineteenth-century floral design in which the title *8½* appears on the screen, explaining that it reflects Fellini's childhood memory of drawing advertising posters for Rimini movie theatres in return for free admission to westerns.[21] The title refers to Fellini's having made six full-length films and parts of three others.

But *8½* is not an autobiography. On the occasion of its American premiere, Fellini told an interviewer for the *New Yorker*: "At the start I kept wondering, 'What shall we make the hero's occupation? Lawyer? Engineer? Doctor?' But they all seemed false; I didn't know these occupations well enough to make them true to the particular truth I was trying to tell. So at last I said, 'Let's make the hero a movie director, like me,' and everything instantly fell into place."[22] But everything is not autobiographical. "I love to improvise," Fellini says; "something unexpected and lucky in the scene opens the door to another, and then to another. In *8½*, I began with the idea of a man retreating from reality, and I wound up with a picture about a man confronting

half a dozen different problems at once."[23] Fellini, who declares that he works well only in the midst of confusion, makes confusion the immediate cause of Guido's downfall. As Fellini pointedly observes, Guido is a failure as a director.

Before he made the film, he told Deena Boyer that he "was trying to portray the three levels on which our minds live: the past, the present and, not the future, but the conditional—the realm of fantasy."[24] To materialize these levels, he depicts the world as it appears to Guido's disturbed mind, and he studiedly distorts reality accordingly.

8½ begins as we see Guido driving his automobile on a highway and entering a tunnel. Here he is stopped by traffic. As though he were suffocating, he struggles to get out of the closed car while other motorists either look on impassively or are oblivious of him. He escapes by floating out into the tunnel and then into the sky. Now he sees, tied to his ankle, a rope by which a man on a beach is pulling him down. About to plunge into the sea, he wakes in his bed at the spa. Soon thereafter, as he lines up with other patients for mineral water, a plain-looking attendant becomes a beautiful girl in white, Claudia, who subsequently materializes now and then as a figment of Guido's imagination. Waiting in a theatre for some screen tests to begin, Guido is so exasperated by Carini's criticism that he orders Carini hanged, whereupon the hanging takes place. Some of Guido's fantasies result from his attempt to avoid reality. The recurring figure of Claudia seems to represent an ideal that he is incapable of finding in real life. Instead of accepting the fact that Luisa sees Carla in the café, he imagines that wife and mistress greet each other affectionately. Unfortunate in his relations with women, he imagines his grandmother's house a harem where the women in his life bathe him in the wine vat and where, wielding a stockwhip, he orders them about.

Reality and unreality merge as in a dream. The geography of the spa is as indeterminate as that of the chateau in *Last Year at Marien-*

bad. We see Guido in his room, in Carla's room, at the railroad station, in the hotel lobby, and so forth, but nothing orients us, not so much as an establishing shot, as he appears now in one locale, now in another. As a matter of relevant fact, although Chianciano gave Fellini his setting, none of *8½* was filmed there or at any other spa, but instead was shot in motion-picture studios in Rome and in widely separated locales outside the city. Guido remembers a statue of the Virgin that stood in a hall of his school, but he remembers it as having the face of the Fashionable Unknown Woman, whom he has seen at the spa. In the screen tests, Carla, La Saraghina, and Luisa are different in appearance and acting than before. (They are even played by different actresses.) The cardinal in the tests is played by an actress — an entanglement comparable to Guido's recollection of some of the priests as women.

Among several motifs that merge actuality with fantasy, a predominant one is whiteness. There are, for example, sheets in which patients at the spa are wrapped, a sheet in which Carla envelopes herself, a sheet in which the nurse wraps the boy Guido after his bath in the wine vat, and a sheet in which the women in the harem scene wrap Guido after bathing him in the same vat. The Fashionable Unknown Woman wears a white veil, and, in Guido's recollection of returning to the beach to see La Saraghina again, a white veil billows from La Saraghina's shoulder. In the final sequence most of the characters wear white.

Fellini studiedly distorts reality in various ways. Guido expresses his thoughts in soliloquies and asides. "She didn't come. Better this way," he says aloud at the railroad station when he does not see Carla. Bored by what Carla is telling him, he says, "She's going to talk to you about her husband again," and, in an aside of inarticulate sound, mimics the rhythm of her chatter. On the other hand, when Guido asks Luisa to accept him as he is, he speaks in interior monologue, but Luisa replies as though she has heard him. The music, supposedly emanating from the little band playing at the spa, is that of a symphony orchestra. There is no natural source for the music heard at the screen tests. Like the rhumba, played by an offscreen accordion as an accompaniment to La Saraghina's dance on the desolate beach, the music is in Guido's mind. The year is 1962, and Guido and the other main characters are garbed in keeping with the fashion of the time—except that it is summer, and Guido wears a black suit and a black hat—but the extras wear clothes of the 1930s. Boyer tells us that the music played by the band is the kind heard at every Italian spa during the thirties. And she points out that the Fashionable Unknown Woman is Caterina Boratto, a star of the prewar Italian cinema. "Fellini wanted a real 'character out of the 1930's' for his film," she says, "and, to a man of his age, Caterina Boratto is precisely that: a lovely memory of adolescence come back to life."[25] Fantasy is compounded in the affinity between the film that Guido is trying to make and the film that we are seeing. There is the occasional sound of a buzzer of the kind heard in motion-picture studios. An alcove in the hotel lobby appears to be under construction. "I wanted something temporary looking in the hotel," Fellini explains. "That makes sense, doesn't it, with this character who doesn't know where he's going, who lives half in the past and half in his fantasies, all entangled in this film that's never going to be finished either."[26] The screen on which the screen tests are projected becomes the screen on which we are watching the film, as in *Brief Encounter* the railroad-car window and the screen become one. When Guido directs the cast in the dance around the circus ring, the fusion is complete. Pirandellolike, the film-within-the-film has become the film. Fellini even had his entire technical staff join in the dance.

In the manner of *Wild Strawberries* the order of some of the events is memorylike. During an audience with the cardinal, Guido is reminded of the Catholic school he attended and, noticing a large woman descending a bank, is then reminded of La

Federico Fellini, *8½. Courtesy of Rizzoli Film*

Saraghina and of the time he and some of his schoolmates ran away from school to watch her dance on the beach. Accordingly the scene cuts to a courtyard of the school. In the foreground stands the statue of a cleric, its right arm upraised. The camera is so placed that the boy Guido, in the courtyard below, is framed by the cleric's miter and the upraised arm. Calling to his friends, "I'm coming," Guido ducks out of this frame and runs off. Albert E. Benderson observes that when Guido runs out from under the cleric's arm, "this is rather a literal representation of the fact that Guido is now emerging for the first time in his life from the narrow confines of Catholic morality."[27] The shot is particularly effective not only because of what psychologists call constancy of size — whereby, for example, an object in the back-ground is smaller than it would be if it were in the foreground — but because the camera is photographing downward.[28] Constancy of size and the high angle of the shot combine to dwarf Guido in relation to the statue.

Everything that happens in *8½* happens to Guido or is recollected or imagined or dreamed by him. Not only does the camera include him or the object of his attention in every shot, but here and there its position enforces his point of view. In the scene in the tunnel, the camera photographs over his shoulder or through the windshield of his car. As he floats in the sky, the camera shoots along his leg to the rope tied to his ankle and to the shore far below. When he wakes in his room at the spa, the camera photographs the scene from the head of his bed. Some of the happenings have meaning

Federico Fellini, *8½. Courtesy of Rizzoli Film*

only in retrospect. We cannot know until later that the young woman who Guido dreams is being pawed by a motorist in the tunnel is Carla. Nor does the launching tower that Guido floats past have any significance at the time. It transpires only later that the man who pulls Guido earthward is Claudia's press representative, and that a horseman riding up at the moment is Claudia's agent.

Editing effects point of view in a variety of ways. Three successive shots make it clear that Guido, imagining Claudia to be offering him water at the spring, is brought back to reality by the sound of the attendant's voice: of Claudia holding a glass, of Guido, of the attendant holding the glass.

We see the production room as the door to it opens and the camera tracks through the doorway. As it tracks into the room, two men rise from their desks. The point of view is Guido's, but the point of view depends on the relationship of this tracking shot to the two preceding shots. In the first of these, Guido crosses the lobby in the direction of the grand staircase. The second is a straight-on view of the staircase as the camera tilts to the clock above. Guido's point of view thus established, it is Guido who enters the production room. At dinner in the farmhouse Guido sits at the head of the table. Because his back is to the camera, we view the scene from his point of view. The camera then pans to a medium close-up of Carla

Federico Fellini, *8½. Courtesy of Rizzoli Film*

playing the harp. The next shot is of the table scene again, except that now Guido is not in the scene. Instead, the camera photographs from where he was sitting in the previous shot. Here again the sequence of shots makes the point of view obvious. "What am I going to say to the Cardinal tomorrow?" Guido asks himself in interior monologue in Carla's room. Thereupon follow three shots in which the point of view depends not only on the position of the camera but on the arrangement of the shots and their relationship to the preceding shot:

1. *Wooded area. Camera tracks toward background. Voice on sound track:* Yes, I read the outline your producer sent us. Very interesting. *Camera continues tracking. Voice:* Do you have the hero meet the Cardinal while taking a mud bath?

2. *Same scene. The voice is that of the Cardinal's secretary, now seen in medium shot.* SECRETARY *(facing right and walking toward background, camera tracking after him):* That's impossible. A church dignitary would have a private cabana.

3. *Same scene.* GUIDO *(at right, in medium shot, back to camera, which tracks after him as he walks toward background):* I wanted to make the meeting unconventional.

In the scene in which Guido imagines himself on his way to an audience with the cardinal, we know that the characters who appear in front of the tracking camera are addressing him. We know that the camera and Guido are one not only by the dialogue —"Hurry, get dressed! The Cardinal is waiting! Tell him everything. Don't hide a thing." "What luck! Put on your socks! What luck!

Federico Fellini, *8½. Courtesy of Rizzoli Film*

The Cardinal! He can fix everything, even my Mexican divorce"—but by the dialogue in relation to the preceding shot, in which Guido, seated in the steam bath, hears an announcement: "Guido, His Eminence is waiting for you."

Guido does not appear at the beginning of the scene in which the patients at the spa congregate at a spring for mineral water. The patients move about in bright sunlight, some of them in the slow manner of the aged, while the band plays "The Ride of the Valkyries." A woman in white looks directly at the camera and waves. A woman holding a parasol blows a kiss at the camera. A nun faces the camera, giggles, and turns coquettishly away. Guido is not present, but the point of view is his by the linking of the scene with the preceding one, in which he turns on a light in a large white-walled bath. In a moment the light becomes

suddenly brighter, and the "Valkyries" music is heard. As Guido awkwardly bends his knees in imitation of the aged, there is an abrupt cut to the scene at the spring. The bright light, the music, and the knee-bending not only anticipate the scene but imply Guido's point of view in it.

It is a point of view that depends, like that in *Wild Strawberries,* not so much on the subjective camera as on a merging of reality in fantasy, that is, the fantasy of the protagonist. Fellini does not keep the camera continuously subjective in any scene. Guido's dream about being trapped in his car begins with a shot of the car, together with other cars, entering the tunnel. The shot is as objective as that in *Wild Strawberries* when Isak's car turns down a side road and disappears behind some trees. The scene in the tunnel includes only three shots from Guido's point of view, and in

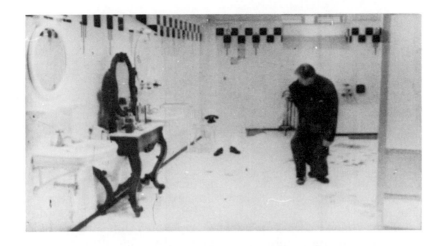

Frederico Fellini, *8½. Courtesy of Rizzoli Film*

one of these the camera tracks around to conclude the shot with a view, from outside the car, of the soles of Guido's shoes pressed against the misted window. The camera is subjective in the two shots of the rope tied to his ankle, but, when he is pulled earthward, the camera remains stationary and Guido falls away from it and dwindles into a speck far below.

8½ , like *Wild Strawberries* and *Last Year at Marienbad,* illustrates the possibilities of motion pictures to narrate subjectively. Here and there in these films we see this or that character or object as supposedly seen by Isak or X or Guido—but only here and there. In fact, it would be awkward if a film attempted to narrate continuously in this way. Yet the attempt was made in *Lady in the Lake* (1946), in which all of the scenes were photographed as though the camera and the protagonist were one. Interesting as it was for its novelty, the result was less than successful because, as Joseph P. Brinton

III has pointed out, the camera and the human eye do not record actuality alike, and to pretend that they do only calls attention to the difference.[29] Furthermore, the subjective point of view implies not only what one sees but what one thinks. The novelist can write subjectively because his medium is an immaterial one—images suggested by words. Motion pictures are immaterial as to words spoken by the actors or by a narrator, but they are material as to pictures and sound. In this respect they are closer to drama—a medium material as to stage and actor—than to the novel. Motion pictures, like drama, being presentational, the point of view in a film, as in a play, is characteristically objective. However, as point of view in a play can be made subjective, so can point of view in a film. But motion pictures can narrate subjectively in ways that drama cannot. They can do so by that kind of selection that is essentially cinematic.

Credit Titles

ABE LINCOLN IN ILLINOIS

Released by RKO Radio Pictures, 1940
Directed by John Cromwell
Produced by Max Gordon for the Plays and
    Pictures Corporation
Based on the Play by Robert E. Sherwood.
Screen Play by Mr. Sherwood
Adaptation by Grover Jones
Assistant Director: Dewey Starkey
Director of Photography: James Wong Howe
Musical Score by Roy Webb

Musical Effects by Vernon L. Walker
Art Director: Van Nest Polglase
Associate Art Director: Carroll Clark
Set Decorations by Casey Roberts
Wardrobe by Walter Plunkett
Dance Director: David Robel
Montage by Douglas Travers
Recorded by Hugh McDowell, Jr.
Edited by George Hively

Cast

Abe Lincoln	Raymond Massey	Dr. Chandler	George Rosener
Stephen Douglas	Gene Lockhart	John Hanks	Trevor Bardette
Mary Todd Lincoln	Ruth Gordon	Sarah Lincoln	Elizabeth Risdon
Ann Rutledge	Mary Howard	Gobey	Napoleon Simpson
Elizabeth Edwards	Dorothy Tree	Judge Bowling Green	Aldrich Bowker
Ninian Edwards	Harvey Stephens	Mentor Graham	Louis Jean Heydt
Joshua Speed	Minor Watson	Denton Offut	Harlan Briggs
Billy Herndon	Alan Baxter	Stage driver	Andy Clyde
Jack Armstrong	Howard da Silva	Mrs. Rutledge	Leona Roberts
John McNeill	Maurice Murphy	Mrs. Bowling Green	Florence Roberts
Ben Battling	Clem Bevans	Mrs. Seth Gale	Fay Helm
Seth Gale	Herbert Rudley	John Johnston	Syd Saylor
Mr. Crimmin	Roger Imhoff	Tom Lincoln	Charles Middleton
Mr. Rutledge	Edmund Elton	Trum Cogdall	Alec Craig

All That Money Can Buy

Released by RKO Radio Pictures, 1941
Produced and Directed by William Dieterle
Associate Producer: Charles L. Glett
Assistant Director: Argyle Nelson
Based on Stephen Vincent Benét's Short Story
    "The Devil and Daniel Webster"
Screen Play by Dan Totheroh and Mr. Benét
Director of Photography: Joseph August
Music Composed and Conducted by Bernard
    Herrmann

Art Director: Van Nest Polglase
Special Effects by Vernon L. Walker
Costumes by Edward Stevenson
Set Decorations by Darrell Silvera
Dialogue Director: Peter Berneis
Recorded by Hugh McDowell, Jr., and James G.
    Stewart
Edited by Robert Wise

Cast

Daniel Webster	Edward Arnold	Justice Hawthorne	H. B. Warner
Mr. Scratch	Walter Huston	Jabez Stone	James Craig
Ma Stone	Jane Darwell	Mary Stone	Anne Shirley
Belle	Simone Simon	Sheriff	Frank Conlan
Squire Slossum	Gene Lockhart	Daniel Stone	Lindy Wade
Miser Stevens	John Qualen	Cy Bibber	George Cleveland

The Battleship Potemkin

Produced by the First Studio of Goskino, Moscow, 1925
Directed by Sergei Eisenstein
Scenario by Eisenstein, from an Outline by Nina Agadjhanova
Photography by Edward Tisse
Assistant Director: Grigori Alexandrov
Assistants: A. Antonov, Mikhail Gomarov, A. Levshin, and Maxim Shtraukh
Supervisor: Yakov Bliokh
Subtitles by Nikolai Aseyev

Cast

Vakulinchuk	A. Antonov	Other Officers, Crew,	Sailors of the Red
Chief Officer		Citizens of Odessa,	Navy, Citizens of
Giliarovsky	Grigori Alexandrov	etc.	Odessa, and Members
Captain Golikov	Vladimir Barsky		of the Proletkult The-
Petty Officer	A. Levshin		atre
A Sailor	Mikhail Gomarov		

THE BIRTH OF A NATION

Produced by the Epoch Producing Corporation, 1915
Directed by D. W. Griffith
Based on *The Clansman,* by Thomas Dixon
Adaptation by D. W. Griffith and Frank Woods
Photography: G. W. Bitzer
Assistant Cameraman: Karl Brown
Music Composed by Joseph Carl Briel and D. W. Griffith

Cast

Benjamin Cameron (the "Little Colonel")	Henry B. Walthall
Flora Cameron, as a Child	Violet Wilkey
Flora, the Younger Sister	Mae Marsh
Margaret Cameron, the Older Sister	Miriam Cooper
Mrs. Cameron	Josephine Crowell
Dr. Cameron	Spottiswoode Aitken
Wade Cameron, the Second Son	Andre Beranger
Duke Cameron, the Youngest Son	Maxfield Stanley
Elsie Stoneman	Lillian Gish
The Hon. Austin Stoneman, Her Father	Ralph Lewis
Her Brother Phil	Elmer Clifton
Her Younger Brother, Tod	Robert Harron
Lydia Brown, Stoneman's Mulatto Housekeeper	Mary Alden
Silas Lynch, Leader of the Blacks	George Siegmann
Gus, the Negro Renegade	Walter Long
"White-Arm" Joe, Owner of the Gin Mill	Elmo Lincoln
Jeff, the Blacksmith	Wallace Reid
Abraham Lincoln	Joseph Henabery
Gen. U. S. Grant	Donald Crisp
Gen. Robert E. Lee	Howard Gaye
Sen. Charles Sumner	Sam de Grasse
John Wilkes Booth	Raoul Walsh
Laura Keene	Olga Grey
Slave Auctioneer	Elmo Lincoln
Stoneman's Negro Servant	Tom Wilson
Union Soldier	Eugene Pallette
Mrs. Lincoln	Alberta Lee
The Sentry	William Freeman
Volunteer	Charles Stevens
Piedmont Girl	Bessie Love
Jake, a Servant of the Camerons	William de Vaull
Cyndy (Mammy), Another Cameron Servant	Jennie Lee

BRIEF ENCOUNTER

Released by Universal Pictures Company, 1946
Directed by David Lean
Produced by Noel Coward
Presented by J. Arthur Rank
In Charge of Production: Anthony
    Havelock-Allan and Ronald Neame
Adapted by Noel Coward from His One-Act Play
    Still Life
Director of Photography: Robert Krasker
Art Director: L. P. Williams
Film Editor: Jack Harris
Art Supervisor to Noel Coward: G. E. Calthrop

Associate Editor: Margery Saunders
Sound Editor: Harry Miller
Sound Recordists: Stanley Lambourne and
    Desmond Dew
Production Manager: E. Holding
Assistant Director: George Pollock
Camera Operator: B. Francke
Continuity: Margaret Sibley
Rachmaninov Piano Concerto No. 2 Played by
    Eileen Joyce with the National Symphony
    Orchestra, Conducted by Muir Mathieson

Cast

Laura Jesson	Celia Johnson	Woman Organist	Irene Handl
Alec Harvey	Trevor Howard	Bill	Edward Hodge
Albert Godby	Stanley Holloway	Johnnie	Sydney Bromley
Myrtle Bagot	Joyce Carey	Policeman	Wilfred Babbage
Fred Jesson	Cyril Raymond	Waitress	Avis Scutt
Dolly Messiter	Everley Gregg	Margaret	Henrietta Vincent
Beryl Waters	Margaret Barton	Bobbie	Richard Thomas
Stanley	Dennis Harkin	Clergyman	George V. Sheldon
Stephen Lynn	Valentine Dyall	Doctor	Wally Bosco
Mary Norton	Marjorie Mars	Boatman	Jack Man
Mrs. Rolandson	Nuna Davey		

THE CABINET OF DR. CALIGARI

Released by Decla-Bioscop, 1920
Directed by Robert Wiene
Scenario by Carl Mayer and Hans Janowitz
Design by Hermann Warm, Walter Röhrig, and Walter Reimann
Photography by Willy Hameister

Cast

Dr. Caligari	Werner Krauss
Cesare	Conrad Veidt
Francis	Friedrich Feher
Jane	Lil Dagover
Alan	Hans von Twardowski
Dr. Olsen	Rudolf Lettinger
A Criminal	Rudolf Klein-Rogge

CITIZEN KANE

Produced by Orson Welles for RKO Radio
  Pictures, 1941
A Mercury Production
Directed by Orson Welles
Screenplay by Herman J. Mankiewicz and Orson
  Welles
Director of Photography: Gregg Toland
Camera Operator: Bert Shipman
Editors: Robert Wise and Mark Robson
Music Composed and Conducted by Bernard
  Herrmann

Art Director: Van Nest Polglase
Associate Art Director: Perry Ferguson
Set Director: Darrell Silvera
Special Effects: Vernon L. Walker
Costumes: Edward Stevenson
Assistant Director: Richard Wilson
Sound Recordists: Bailey Fesler and James G.
  Stewart
Executive Producer: George J. Schaefer
Associate Producer: Richard Barr

Cast

Charles Foster Kane	Orson Welles	Entertainer	Charles Bennett
Jedediah Leland	Joseph Cotten	Reporter	Milt Kibbee
Susan Alexander Kane	Dorothy Comingore	Teddy Roosevelt	Tom Curran
Kane's Mother	Agnes Moorehead	Dr. Corey	Irving Mitchell
Emily Norton Kane	Ruth Warrick	Nurse	Edith Evanson
James W. Gettys	Ray Collins	Orchestra Leader	Arthur Kay
Mr. Carter	Erskine Sanford	Chorus Master	Tudor Williams
Mr. Bernstein	Everett Sloane	City Editor	Herbert Corthell
Thompson	William Alland	Smather	Benny Rubin
Newsreel Narrator	William Alland	Reporter	Edmund Cobb
Raymond	Paul Stewart	Ethel	Frances Neal
Walter Parks Thatcher	George Coulouris	Photographer	Robert Dudley
Signor Matisti	Fortunio Bonanova	Miss Townsend	Ellen Lowe
Headwaiter	Gus Schilling	Waiter	Gino Corrado
Mr. Rawlston	Philip Van Zandt	Reporters	Alan Ladd, Joseph
Miss Anderson	Georgia Backus		Cotten, Louise
Kane's Father	Harry Shannon		Currie, Eddie Coke,
Kane's Son	Sonny Bupp		Walter Sande,
Kane, Age 8	Buddy Swan		Arthur O'Connell,
Hillman	Richard Barr		Katherine Trosper,
Georgia	Joan Blair		Richard Wilson, and
Mike	Al Eben		Erskine Sanford

A CORNER IN WHEAT

Produced by the Biograph Company, 1909
Directed by D. W. Griffith
Based on Frank Norris's *The Octopus* and "A Deal in Wheat"
Photography: G. W. Bitzer

Cast

The Wheat King	Frank Powell	Others	Blanche Sweet, Arthur
His Assistant	Henry B. Walthall		Johnson, Charles Hill
Young Farmer	James Kirkwood		Mailes, Frank Evans,
Farmer's Wife	Linda Arvidson		Grace Henderson, Billy
Older Farmer	W. Christie Miller		Quirk, Mack Sennett,
Woman at Bakery	Kate Bruce		Owen Moore, William
			Butler, and Eddie Dillon

8½

Produced by Angelo Rizzoli, 1963
Directed by Federico Fellini
Story by Federico Fellini and Ennio Flaiano
Screenplay by Federico Fellini, Tullio Pinelli,
    Ennio Flaiano, and Brunello Rondi
Director of Photography: Gianni di Venanzo
Cameraman: Pasquale de Santis
Scenery and Wardrobe: Piero Gherardi
Assistant Director: Guidarino Guidi
Editor: Leo Catozzo
Makeup: Otello Fava
Music: Nino Rota
Sound Effects: Mario Faraoni and Alberto
    Bartolomei

Production Manager: Clemente Fracassi
Artistic Collaboration: Brunello Rondi
Production Director: Nello Meniconi
Assistants to the Director: Giulio Paradisi,
    Francesco Aluigi, and
    Mirella Gamacchio (script girl)
Assistant Editor: Adriana Olasio
Assistant Director of Production: Alessandro
    Normann
Production Assistants: Angelo Jacono and
    Albino Morandin

Cast

Guido Anselmi	Marcello Mastroianni	Enrico	Mark Herron
Luisa Anselmi	Anouk Aimee	Two Girls	Eva Gioia and Dina de Santis
Carla	Sandra Milo		
Claudia	Claudia Cardinale	Cesarino, Production Supervisor	Cesarino Miceli Picardi
Rosella	Rosella Falk		
The Actress	Madeleine Lebeau		
The Fashionable Unknown Woman	Caterina Boratto	Bruno Agostini, Production Director	Bruno Agostini
Gloria Morin	Barbara Steele	Black Dancer	Hazel Rogers
Conocchia	Mario Conocchia	Edith, the Model	Hedy Vessel
Mario Mezzabotta	Mario Pisu	Production Accountant	John Stacy
Pace, the Producer	Guido Alberti	Carla in Screen Tests	Olimpia Cavalli
Fabrizio Carini (Daumier)	Jean Rougeul	La Saraghina in Some Screen Tests	Maria Antonietta Beluzzi
La Saraghina	Edra Gale		
Maurice, the Magician	Ian Dallas	Doctors	Roberto Nicolosi and Luciana Sanseverino
Guido's Father	Annibale Ninchi		
Guido's Mother	Giuditta Rissone	American Journalist	Eugene Walter
The Cardinal	Tito Masini	His Wife	Gilda Dahlberg
The Cardinal's Secretary	Frazier Rippy	The Producer's Girl Friend	Annie Gorassini
The Cardinal's Retinue	Comte Alfredo de la Feld and Sebastiano de Leandro	Maya	Mary Indovino
		Airline Hostess	Nadine Sanders
		Old Journalist	Matilde Calnan
Guido's Grandmother	Georgia Simmons	The Cardinal in the Screen Tests	Comtesse Elisabetta Cini
The Nurses	Maria Raimondi and Marisa Colomber		
An Old Peasant	Palma Mangini	Clown	Polidor (Ferdinand Guillaume)
A Little Girl	Roberta Valli		
Guido as a Little Boy	Riccardo Gugliemi	Agent	Neil Robinson
Guido as a Schoolboy	Marco Gemini	Claudia's Agent	Mino Doro
Jaqueline Bonbon	Yvonne Casadei	Claudia's Press Representative	Mario Tarchetti
Luisa's Sister	Elisabetta Catalano	School President	Maria Tedeschi
A Friend of Luisa's	Rosella Como		

Others   Giulio Paradisi,
          Valentina Lang,
          Annarosa Latuada,
          Agnese Bonfanti,
          Flaminia Torlonia,
          Anna Carimini,
          Maria Wertmüller,
          Francesco Raga-
          monti, Prince
          Vadim Wolkonsky,
          Grazia Frasnelli,
          Gideon Bachmann,
          Deena Boyer, and
          John Francis Lane

GREAT EXPECTATIONS

Produced by Ronald Neame for Cineguild, 1946
Directed by David Lean
Presented by J. Arthur Rank
Adapted for the Screen by David Lean, Ronald Neame, Anthony Havelock-Allan, Kay Walsh, and Cecil McGivern—from the Novel by Charles Dickens
Executive Producer: Anthony Havelock-Allan
Photographed by Guy Green
Production Designed by John Bryan
Film Editor: Jack Harris
Art Director: Wilfred Shingleton

Costumes Designed by Sophia Harris of Motley—Assisted by Margaret Furse
Assistant Director: George Pollock
Production Manager: Norman Spencer
Sound Recordists: Stanley Lambourne and Gordon K. McCallum
Sound Editor: Winston Ryder
Camera Operator: Nigel Huke
Continuity: Margaret Sibley
Dances Arranged by Suria Magite
Musical Score Composed and Conducted by Walter Goehr—with the National Symphony Orchestra

Cast

Pip	John Mills	The Pale Young Gentleman	John Forrest
Young Pip	Anthony Wager	Bentley Drummle	Torin Thatcher
Estella	Valerie Hobson	The Aged Parent	O. B. Clarence
Young Estella	Jean Simmons	Mr. Wopsle	John Burch
Joe Gargery	Bernard Miles	The Sergeant	Richard George
Mr. Jaggers	Francis L. Sullivan	Mrs. Wopsle	Grace Denbigh-Russell
Magwitch	Finlay Currie	Sarah Pocket	Everley Gregg
Miss Havisham	Martita Hunt	Relation	Anne Holland
Herbert Pocket	Alec Guinness	Mike	Frank Atkinson
Mr. Wemmick	Ivor Bernard	Night Porter	Gordon Begg
Mrs. Joe	Freda Jackson	Mrs. Whimple	Eddie Martin
Biddy	Eileen Erskine	The Dancing Master	Walford Hyden
Convict	George Hayes	Galley Steersman	Roy Arthur
Uncle Pumblechook	Hay Petrie		

THE GREAT TRAIN ROBBERY

Produced by the Edison Company, 1903
Directed by Edwin S. Porter
Scenario by Edwin S. Porter
Photographed by Edwin S. Porter

Cast

George Barnes, Max (Bronco Billy) Anderson,
A. C. Abadie, Frank Hunaway, Marie Murray,
Employees of the Edison Company, and Others

GREED

Produced by the Goldwyn Company, 1924
Directed by Erich von Stroheim
Released by Metro-Goldwyn-Mayer
Based on Frank Norris's Novel *McTeague*
Adapted by Erich von Stroheim
Abridged by June Mathis
Photography by Ben E. Reynolds, William H. Daniels,
    and Ernest Schoedsack

Cast

Trina	Zazu Pitts	Minister	William Barlow
McTeague	Gibson Gowland	Man from the lottery	
Marcus	Jean Hersholt	company	Lon Poff
Maria	Dale Fuller	Joe Frenna	S. S. Simon
Mother McTeague	Tempe Pigott	Sheriff of Placer County	Jack McDonald
Papa Sieppe	Chester Conklin	Cribbens	James Fulton
Mama Sieppe	Sylvia Ashton	Others	Frank Hayes
Selina	Joan Standing		Fanny Midgley
August Sieppe	Austin Jewell		Cesare Gravina
The Sieppe twins	Oscar Gottel and		Hughie Mack
	Otto Gottel		Tiny Jones
Dr. "Painless" Potter	Eric von Ritzau		J. Aldrich Libbey
Uncle Rudolph			Rita Revela
Oelbermann	Max Tryon		Edward Gaffney

THE INFORMER

Produced by John Ford for RKO Radio
    Pictures, 1935
Directed by John Ford
Associate Producer: Cliff Reid
Screenplay by Dudley Nichols—from the Novel
    by Liam O'Flaherty
Photography by Joseph H. August

Musical Score by Max Steiner
Art Director: Van Nest Polglase
Associate Art Director: Charles Kirk
Costumes by Walter Plunkett
Recorded by Hugh McDowell, Jr.
Edited by George Hively

Cast

Gypo Nolan	Victor McLaglen	Blind Man	D'Arcy Corrigan
Mary McPhillip	Heather Angel	Donahue	Leo McCabe
Dan Gallagher	Preston Foster	Daly	Gaylord Pendelton
Katie Madden	Margot Grahame	Flynn	Francis Ford
Frankie McPhillip	Wallace Ford	Aunt Betty	May Boley
Mrs. McPhillip	Una O'Connor	Lady	Grizelda Harvey
Terry	J. M. Kerrigan	Street Singer	Dennis O'Dea
Bartley Mulholland	Joseph Sawyer	Man at Wake	Jack Mulhall
Tommy Connor	Neil Fitzgerald	Young Soldier	Bob Parrish
Rat Mulligan	Donald Meek		

INTOLERANCE

Produced by the Wark Producing Corporation
(D. W. Griffith), 1916
Directed by D. W. Griffith
Scenario by Griffith
Settings Supervised by Griffith
Costume Designs Supervised by Griffith
Photographic Style and Technique Supervised
by Griffith
Research Supervised by Griffith
Research on "The Judean Story": Rabbi L. Myers
Architectural Conceptions of the City of
Babylon (Motifs Suggested by the Sun
Buildings and the Causeway of the Panama-
Pacific Exposition at San Francisco, 1915):
Griffith

Construction Supervisor and Chief Engineer on
the Babylonian Sets: Frank Wortman
Photography: G. W. Bitzer; Assistant Cameraman:
Karl Brown
Assistant Directors: George Siegmann, W. S.
Van Dyke, Joseph Henabery, Edward
Dillon, and Tod Browning
Chief Second Assistant Directors: Ted Duncan
and Mike Siebert
Editing: Griffith
Cutters: James and Rose Smith
Musical Score by Joseph Carl Briel and Griffith

The Principal Characters

OF ALL AGES

The Woman Who
Rocks the Cradle   Lillian Gish

OF THE MODERN STORY (A.D. 1914)

The Dear One   Mae Marsh
Her Father, a Mill
  Worker   Fred Turner
The Boy   Robert Harron
Jenkins, Mill Magnate   Sam de Grasse
Mary T. Jenkins,
  His Sister   Vera Lewis
Self-styled Uplifters
  and Professional
  Meddlers   Mary Alden
                            Eleanor Washington
                            Pearl Elmore
                            Lucile Brown
                            Mrs. Arther
                              Mackley
The Friendless One   Miriam Cooper
The Musketeer of the
  Slums   Walter Long
The Kindly Policeman   Tom Wilson
The Governor   Ralph Lewis
The Judge   Lloyd Ingraham
Father Farley, the
  Boy's Confessor   The Rev. A. W.
                            McClure
The Friendly
  Neighbor   Max Davidson
Strike Leader   Monte Blue
Debutante   Marguerite Marsh
A Crook   Tod Browning
Another Crook   Edward Dillon

OF THE JUDEAN STORY (A.D. 27)

The Nazarene   Howard Gaye
Mary, the Mother   Lillian Langdon
Mary Magdalene   Olga Grey
First Pharisee   Gunther von Ritzau
Bride of Cana   Bessie Love
The Bride's Father   William Brown
Bridegroom   George Walsh

OF THE MEDIEVAL FRENCH STORY (A.D. 1572)

Brown Eyes, Daughter
  of a Huguenot
  Family   Margery Wilson
Prosper Latour, Her
  Sweetheart   Eugene Pallette
Her Father   Spottiswoode Aitken
Her Mother   Ruth Handforth
The Mercenary (of
  the Swiss Soldiery)   A. D. Sears
Charles IX, King of
  France   Frank Bennett
Duc D'Anjou, Brother
  to the King and
  Heir to the Throne   Maxfield Stanley
Catherine de Médici   Josephine Crowell
Marguerite de Valois,
  Sister of Charles IX   Constance Talmadge
Henry of Navarre   W. E. Lawrence
Admiral Coligny   Joseph Henabery
A Page   Chandler House

OF THE BABYLONIAN STORY (539 B.C.)

The Mountain Girl   Constance Talmadge

		Old Woman of Babylon	Kate Bruce

The Rhapsode, Her Suitor and Secret Agent of the High Priest of Bel — Elmer Clifton

The Prince Belshazzar — Alfred Paget

The Princess Beloved — Seena Owen

The King Nabonidus — Carl Stockdale

The High Priest of Bel — Tully Marshall

Cyrus, Emperor and War Lord of the Persians — George Siegmann

The Mighty Man of Valour, Belshazzar's Bodyguard — Elmo Lincoln

Captain of the Great Gate of Imgur-Bel — Ted Duncan

The Runner, Messenger to the Princess Beloved — Guino Corrado (Lisserani)

Princess Beloved's Bodyguards — Ted Duncan / Felix Modjeska

Babylonian Judges — George Fawcett / Robert Lawlor

Old Woman of Babylon — Kate Bruce

Slave Girls, Dancers, Hand-Maidens from Ishtar's Temple of Laughter and Love; Virgins of the Sacred Fires of Life; Entertainers at Belshazzar's Feast, etc. — Alma Rubens / Carmel Myers / Mildred Harris Chaplin (Mrs. Charles Chaplin) / Eve Southern / Winifred Westover / Jewel Carmen / Colleen Moore / Natalie Talmadge / Carol Dempster / Ethel Terry / Daisy Robinson / Anna Mae Walthall

Also playing Bit Parts or Extra Roles: Douglas Fairbanks, Sir Herbert Beerbohm Tree, De Wolf Hopper, Frank Campeau, Donald Crisp, Nigel de Brullier, Wilfred Lucas, Owen Moore, Andre Beranger, Tammany Young, and Francis Carpenter

LAST YEAR AT MARIENBAD

Produced by Pierre Courau (Precitel) and
    Raymond Froment (Terrafilm), 1961
Directed by Alain Resnais
Screen Play by Alain Robbe-Grillet
Assistant Director: Jean Leon
Director of Photography: Sacha Vierny
Cameraman: Phillippe Brun
Stage Settings by Jacques Saulnier
Sound Effects by Guy Villette

Film Editors: Henri Colpi and Jasmine Chasney
Music: Francis Seyrig
Settings: Environs and natural settings in
    Munich (chateaux of Nymphenburg,
    Schleissheim, etc.); interiors:
    Studios Photosonor, Paris
Gowns for Mlle Seyrig: Chanel
Costumes: Bernard Evein

Cast

A	Delphine Seyrig
X	Giorgio Albertazzi
M	Sacha Pitoeff
Others	Francoise Bertin, Luce Garcia-Ville, Helena Kornel, Francoise Spira, Karin Toeche-Mittler, Pierre Barbaud, Wilhelm von Deek, Jean Lanier, Gerard Lorin, Davide Montemuri, Giles Queant, and Gabriel Werner

THE LONEDALE OPERATOR

Produced by the Biograph Company, 1911
Directed by D. W. Griffith
Photography: G. W. Bitzer

Cast

The Telegraph Operator	Blanche Sweet
The Engineer	Frank Grandin
The Fireman	Wilfred Lucas
The Other Telegraph Operator	Eddie Dillon
Others	W. Christie Miller, George Nicholls, Verner Clarges, and Charles West

THE LONELY VILLA

Produced by the Biograph Company, 1909
Directed by D. W. Griffith
Photography: G. W. Bitzer

Cast

The Father	Frank Powell
The Mother	Marion Leonard
The Daughters	Mary Pickford, Adele de Garde, and Gladys Egan
Others	Mack Sennett, Robert Harron, and Owen Moore

LOUISIANA STORY

Produced by Robert Flaherty for Robert Flaherty Productions, 1948
Directed by Robert Flaherty
Story by Frances and Robert Flaherty
Associate Producers: Richard Leacock and Helen van Dongen
Photography: Richard Leacock
Editing: Helen van Dongen

Musical Score by Virgil Thomson—performed by members of the Philadelphia Orchestra, under the direction of Eugene Ormandy
Sound: Benjamin Doniger
Sound Assistant: Leonard Stark
Editorial Assistant: Ralph Rosenblum
Technical Assistant for Music: Henry Brant
Music Recording: Bob Fine
Re-recording: Dick Vorisek

Cast

The Boy	Joseph Boudreaux
His Father	Lionel le Blanc
His Mother	Mrs. E. Bienvenu
The Driller	Frank Hardy
The Boilerman	C. P. Guedry

NANOOK OF THE NORTH

Produced by Robert Flaherty for Revillon Frères, 1922
Directed and Photographed by Robert Flaherty

Cast

Nanook and other Eskimos

THE NEW YORK HAT

Produced by the Biograph Company, 1912
Directed by D. W. Griffith
Based on a story by Anita Loos
Photography: G. W. Bitzer

Cast

Mary	Mary Pickford
The Minister	Lionel Barrymore
Mary's Father	Charles Hill Mailes
Others	Dorothy Gish, Lillian Gish, Jack Pickford, Robert Harron, Mae Marsh, Josephine Crowell, and Mack Sennett

NIGHT MAIL

Produced by John Grierson for the General Post Office Film Unit, 1936
Direction and Scenario by Basil Wright and Harry Watt
Camera Work by H. E. Fowle and Jonah Jones
Sound by Alberto Cavalcanti
Music by Benjamin Britten
Edited by R. Q. MacNaughton
Commentary in Verse by W. H. Auden

Cast

Workers of the Traveling Post Office and the
L. M. S. Railway

QUARTET

Produced by Antony Darnborough for
   Gainsborough Pictures, 1948
Presented by J. Arthur Rank
Released through General Film Distributors, Ltd.
In Charge of Production: Sydney Box
Screen Play by R. C. Sherriff
Adapted from Four Short Stories by Somerset
   Maugham
Music Composed by John Greenwood and
   Played by the Philharmonic Orchestra
   of London
Music Director: Muir Mathieson
Schubert Impromptu Played by Eileen Joyce
Production Controller: Arthur Alcott

Directors of Photoplay: Ray Elton and Alec Wyer
Supervising Editor: A. Charles Knott
Editor: Jean Barker
Supervising Art Director: George Provis
Art Director: Cedric Dawe
Production Manager: Billy Boyle
Camera Operator: Bernard Lewis
Assistant Director: Bob Attwooll
Special Effects: P. Guiddbaldi
Makeup: W. T. Partelton
Dress Designer: Julie Harris
Director of Sound: Brian C. Sewell
Recording: L. Hammond and W. S. Salter

"The Facts of Life"

Directed by Ralph Smart

Cast

Henry Garnet	Basil Radford	Professor Branksome	James Robertson-Justice
Leslie	Naunton Wayne		
Jeanne	Mai Zetterling	Nicky	Jack Watling
Mrs. Garnet	Angela Baddeley	Thomas	Jack Raine
John	Nigel Buchanan	Ralph	Ian Flyming
		Cabaret Artist	Jean Cavall

"The Alien Corn"

Directed by Harold French

Cast

George Bland	Dirk Bogarde	Aunt Maud	Mary Hinton
Lea Makart	Francoise Rosay	Coroner	Maurice Denham
Lady Bland	Irene Browne	Foreman of Jury	James Hayter
Sir Frederick	Raymond Lovell	Butler	Henry Morrell
Uncle John	George Thorpe	Frenchman	Marcel Poncin
Paula	Honor Blackman		

"The Kite"

Directed by Arthur Crabtree

Cast

Samuel Sunbury	Mervyn Johns	Prison Governor	Frederick Leister
Mrs. Sunbury	Hermione Baddeley	Prison Officer	George Merritt
Betty Baker	Susan Shaw	Man from *Advertiser*	Cyril Chamberlain
Herbert Sunbury	George Cole	Ned Preston	Bernard Lee
Herbert Sunbury, as a Boy	David Cole		

"The Colonel's Lady"

Directed by Kenn Annakin

Cast

Railway Passenger	Cyril Raymond	George Peregrine	Cecil Parker
Henry Dashwood	Ernest Thesiger	Evie Peregrine	Nora Swinburne
Henry Blane	Clive Morton	Daphne	Linden Travers
Blane's Clerk	Ernest Butcher	Assistant in Bookshop	Bill Owen
Martin	Felix Aylmer	Bannock	Lyn Evans
Second Woman	Yvonne Owen	John Colman	John Salew
Third Woman	Margaret Thorburn		

Queen Elizabeth

Produced by the Histrionic Film Company, 1912
Directed by Louis Mercanton
Adapted from the Play by Emile Moreau
Dresses, Armor, and Furniture from the Sarah Bernhardt Theatre, Paris

Cast

Queen Elizabeth	Sarah Bernhardt
The Earl of Essex	Lou Tellegen
The Countess of	
Nottingham	Mlle Romain
The Earl of Nottingham	M. Maxudian

and Other Members of Sarah Bernhardt's
Company

The River

Produced by the U. S. Farm Security Administration, 1937
Written and Directed by Pare Lorentz
Photography by Stacy Woodward, Floyd Crosby, and Willard van Dyke
Film Editors: Leo Zochling and Lloyd Nosler
Research Editor: A. A. Mercy
Musical Score by Virgil Thomson—Played by Members of the New York
    Philharmonic Society
Commentary Narrated by Thomas Chalmers

The Taming of the Shrew

Produced by the Pickford Corporation and the Elton Corporation, 1929
A United Artists Picture
Directed by Sam Taylor
Adapted by Sam Taylor from Shakespeare's Play
Photography by Karl Struss
Settings by William Cameron Menzies and Laurence Irving
Edited by Allen McNeil
Production Staff: Earle Browne, Lucky Humberstone, and Walter Mayo

Cast

Katherine	Mary Pickford
Petruchio	Douglas Fairbanks
Baptista	Edwin Maxwell
Gremio	Joseph Cawthorn
Grumio	Clyde Cook
Hortensio	Geoffrey Wardwell
Bianca	Dorothy Jordan

A TRIP TO THE MOON

Produced by Georges Méliès, 1902
Directed by Georges Méliès
Scenario by Georges Méliès
Sets and Costumes by Georges Méliès
Photographed by Lucien Tainguy

Cast

President of the Scientific Congress	Georges Méliès	The Girl in the Crescent	Bluette Bernon
Members of the Scientific Congress	Victor André Delpierre Farjaux-Kelm- Brunnet and Others	The Girls in the Stars The Sélénites	Ballerinas of the Théâtre du Châtelet Acrobats of the Folies-Bergère

WILD STRAWBERRIES

Produced by Svensk Filmindustri, 1957
Directed by Ingmar Bergman
Screenplay by Ingmar Bergman
Assistant Director: Gösta Ekman
Director of Photography: Gunnar Fischer
Assistant Cameraman: Björn Thermenius
Music: Erik Nordgren

Music Directed by E. Eckert-Lundin
Sets: Gittan Gustafsson
Costumes: Millie Ström
Makeup: Nils Nittel
Sound: Aaby Wedin and Lennart Wallin
Editor: Oscar Rosander
Production Supervisor: Allan Ekelund

Cast

Professor Isak Borg	Victor Sjöström	Uncle Aron	Yngve Nordwald
Sara	Bibi Andersson	Sigfrid	Per Sjöstrand
Marianne	Ingrid Thulin	Sigbritt	Gio Petré
Evald	Gunnar Björnstrand	Charlotta	Gunnel Lindblom
Agda	Jullan Kindahl	Angelica	Maud Hansson
Anders	Folke Sundquist	Mrs. Akerman	Anne-Mari Wiman
Viktor	Bjorn Bjelvenstram	Anna	Eva Norée
Isak's Mother	Naima Wifstrand	The Twins	Lena Bergman and Monica Ehrling
Mrs. Alman	Gunnel Broström		
Isak's Wife	Gertrud Fridh	Hagbart	Per Skogsberg
Her Lover	Ake Fridell	Benjamin	Goran Lundquist
Aunt	Sif Ruud	Promoter	Professor Helge Wulff
Alman	Gunnar Sjöberg		
Akerman	Max von Sydow		

Glossary of Motion Picture Terms

Angle Shot: shot resulting from the camera's being placed at other than a right angle to its object; also, a shot made from a different angle than that of a preceding shot in the same scene.

Author's title: see *credit title.*

Back lighting: lighting effected by extra illumination behind the object photographed.

Back projection: incorporation, into a shot, of a scene or scenes previously photographed and thus made the subject of a second camera, as, for example, background seen through the window of a train to give the effect of a moving train; also called *process shot, rear projection,* and *back,* or *background projection.* In *background projection,* the images are thrown onto a translucent screen by a projector behind the screen.

Bridging title: continuity title.

Cast list: see *Credit title.*

Close shot: shot for which the camera is brought near an object to emphasize the object or a part of it.*

Close-up: shot including not more than an actor's head and shoulders, filling or almost filling the screen.*

Continuity title: printed matter projected on the screen—usually between sequences—to aid in the telling of the story; also called *bridging title.*

Crane shot: shot obtained by the camera moving on a crane, as, for example, in an overhead view.

Credit title: list—usually projected on the screen at the beginning of a film—which includes the title of the film, the names of the production staff, the cast, etc.; sometimes differentiated by *main title* (the title of the film), *director's title, author's title, cast list,* etc.

Creeping title: title that moves over the screen, usually from bottom to top.

Crosscut: cut back and forth between scenes to present simultaneous action in separate locales and, usually, to prolong suspense; also called *cutback, switchback,* and *intercut.*

Cut: instantaneous end of a shot or instantaneous transference from one shot to another. A *cut* indicates continuous or simultaneous action.

Cutback: crosscut.

Cut-in: still of an object—such as a poster, a letter, or a page of a newspaper—which interrupts continuity; also called *insert.*

Director's title: see *credit title.*

Dissolve: blurring of images as one shot appears to melt into another, the first shot becoming increasingly indistinct and the second increasingly distinct; also called *lap dissolve.*

Distance shot: shot in which the object is represented as at a great distance from the camera to show a wide sweep of action or immensity of background.*

Documentary: nonfiction film taking for its subject the real world but, unlike a newsreel or travelogue, having a theme and dramatic implication.

Dolly Shot: shot—from *dolly,* a small-wheeled truck—made as the camera moves up to, with,

---

*The terms *close shot, close-up, distance shot, long shot, medium-close shot,* and *medium shot* are relative.

253

or away from the actors or along an object—such as the side of a building; also called *follow shot*, *tracking shot*, and *trucking shot*.

Double exposure: superimposition of one shot on another.

Dream balloon: double exposure in which a shot representing the thoughts of a character occupies part of the screen.

Edit: to arrange shots. In a sound film, editing includes combining the shots with the sound track.

Establishing shot: long shot, usually of an exterior, to establish the setting of a scene or the relationship of details to be shown subsequently in a closer shot or shots.

Fade-in: gradual disclosure of a scene as the screen becomes light.

Fade-out: gradual disappearance of the scene as the screen becomes dark.

Fast motion: action appearing faster than normal as a result of the film's having been moved through the camera more slowly than normal.

Flashback: scene or scenes interrupting the story to show past action.

Follow shot: dolly shot.

Frame: single photographic impression on the film. In each foot of 35-mm. film there are 16 frames. This film passes through the motion-picture machine at the rate of 90 feet per minute, or 24 frames per second.

Full shot: shot in which the standing figure of an actor extends from top to bottom of the frame.

High-angle shot: shot in which the camera points downward.

Insert: cut-in.

Intercut: Crosscut

Interior monologue: separation of sound from image, a speaker seen and heard expressing his thoughts but his lips not moving.

Iris: mask. See also *Iris-in* and *Iris-out.*

Iris-in: gradual appearance of the scene through an expanding circle.

Iris-out: gradual disappearance of the scene through a contracting circle.

Jump cut: break in continuity of a shot to compress time.

Lap dissolve: dissolve.

Long shot: shot in which the camera is remote enough to take in, for example, fifteen or twenty people with room enough for them to move about and with space in the foreground.*

Low-angle shot: shot in which the camera points upward.

Main title: see *Credit title.*

Mask: shot framed by a mask shaped, for example, like a keyhole or the lenses of binoculars—made by a cutout placed in front of the camera lens; sometimes called *iris.*

Medium-close shot: shot in which an actor standing would be cut off at about the waist.*

Medium shot: shot in which the camera is nearer to objects than in a full shot—near enough, for example, so that an actor standing would be cut off at the knees or below; also called *full shot* and *middle shot.**

Middle shot: medium shot.

Montage: arrangement of shots to suggest a concept other than the sum of the images in these shots. In one sense, *montage* means editing of the film. The popular, or Hollywood, conception of the term implies montage effects, as, for example, the tearing off of calendar leaves, or a succession of shots of the same landscape in different seasons, to represent the passage of time, or shots of a train to represent a journey or a change of place.

Moving title: title that expands, contracts, or otherwise moves on the screen.

Out-of-focus shot: shot in which the outlines of objects are slightly indistinct.

Pan focus: focus which makes objects in both foreground and background appear in sharp relief.

Pan shot (from *panorama*): shot obtained by a horizontal turning of the camera on its axis—hence the verb *pan.*

Photoplay: almost exact transference of a play to the screen, the camera remaining stationary as though representing the position of a spectator in a center orchestra seat.

Process shot: back projection.

Pull-back: shot in which the camera is pulled back from a close-up, close shot, etc. to reveal a wider angle; a form of tracking.

Reaction shot: shot to show the effect, on one or more characters, of something seen, heard, or otherwise realized.

Rear projection: back projection.

Reel: spool on which film is wound; also, amount of film on the spool—formerly about 1000 feet, now usually 2000 feet.

Rushes: Prints made of a day's takes for viewing before the next day's shooting.

Scenario: plan for a film, including dialogue.

Scene: shot or series of shots unifying time and place.

Sequence: combination of shots or scenes to build up a particular effect.

Shot: episode or scene without a break in time or space, photographed without actual or apparent interruption.

Slow motion: action appearing slower than normal as a result of the film's having been moved through the camera faster than normal.

Soft focus: softening of the sharpness of line in varying degrees from a hardly perceptible difference to mistiness; an effect obtained by a gauze or a greased glass placed in front of the camera lens or by out-of-focus photography.

Spatial length: length of a shot in reference to the distance of the camera from the object photographed, as distinguished from *temporal length.*

Split screen: two or more separate pictures in the frame.

Split title: continuity title broken—usually within a sentence—by an intervening shot or shots.

Spoken title: subtitle.

Stereoscopic film: film giving a three-dimensional effect on the screen.

Still: photograph made from one frame; also, a series of similar frames casting a motionless picture onto the screen.

Strip title: printed matter superimposed on a shot, usually to translate dialogue into another language.

Subtitle: title in a silent film to print speech, to explain or narrate action, or to indicate locale. *Subtitle* is sometimes used to mean only speech, as distinct from *title,* which is more inclusive.

Superimposition: dissolve in which the light intensity of the overlapping scenes does not vary.

Switchback: crosscut.

Take: Recording of a shot. Several recordings may be made of the same shot.

Temporal length: length of a shot in reference to its duration on the screen, as distinguished from *spatial length.*

Tilting: perpendicular movement of the camera on its axis.

Title: printed matter projected on screen, apart from that in an insert or in a scene. See *Continuity title, Credit title, Moving title,* and *Subtitle.*

Tracking shot:dolly shot.

Trolley shot: shot in which the camera moves on a trolley.

Trucking shot: dolly shot.

Two-shot: close-up of two objects, as, for example, the faces of two actors.

Vignette: shot which does not occupy the whole screen but fades off around the edges.

Voice-over: The voice of a narrator heard while pictures and other sounds continue.

Wipe: shift from one scene to another whereby the first scene appears to peel off, or to be similarly removed along a visible line, to reveal the second.

Zoom shot: shot in which the camera moves, or seems to move, quickly up to an object.

Notes

CHAPTER 1

1. Athanasius Kircher is said to have invented the magic lantern in 1646 because he makes that claim in his book *Ars Magna Lucis et Umbrae,* first published in that year. Kenneth Macgowan, in *Behind the Screen,* p. 27, points out that Kircher mentions the magic lantern only in the second edition of his book, in 1671, contending that he had described and pictured it in the first edition.

2. Eadweard Muybridge, *Animals in Motion,* p. 13.

3. Ibid., p. 14.

4. Quoted by Gordon Hendricks, *The Edison Motion Picture Myth,* p. 170, from *Wilson's Photographic Magazine,* January 5, 1889. Hendricks, however, questions the 1/5000th second as seeming short.

5. Foreword to article by Antonia and William Kennedy Laurie Dickson, "Edison's Invention of the Kinetophonograph," *Century Magazine,* 48 (June, 1894):208.

6. Thomas Alva Edison, *The Diary and Sundry Observations of Thomas Alva Edison,* p. 71.

7. Hendricks contends (*Edison Motion Picture Myth,* p. 40) that although film historians credit the Eastman Company with the invention of celluloid-based film, the invention was Carbutt's, a year or two earlier, and that "Eastman's contribution was improvement of manufacturing methods and not inventive novelty."

8. Ibid., p. 92.

9. The price seems not to have been constant. According to Hendricks, kinetoscopes sold for $250 in the spring of 1894 and $127.50 a year later. Gordon Hendricks, *The Kinetoscope,* p. 13.

10. Hendricks, *Edison Motion Picture Myth,* pp. 169–70. Hendricks finds evidence, however, that the apparatus which Marey described to the French Academy of Sciences in 1888 contained such a loop—"a continuously moving feed roller *with a loop to avoid jerking."*

11. *New York Times,* April 26, 1896.

12. Quoted by Terry Ramsaye, *A Million and One Nights: A History of the Motion Pictures,* 2 vols., 1:134.

13. *New York Times,* April 26, 1896.

CHAPTER 2

1. Georges Sadoul quotes Méliès at length on the difference between stage and screen, in *Histoire générale du cinéma,* 3 vols., 2:156–61.

2. Ibid., p. 42.

3. As Georges Sadoul points out, there are errors of fact in Méliès's account. *A Trip to the Moon* was not the longest film up to that time, Pathé having already made longer ones and Méliès himself having produced a film of the Paris Exposition, totaling 1105 feet, in 1900. The catalogue of Star Film indicates that *A Trip to the Moon* was apparently nearer 260 than 280 meters in length.

4. *Ce Soir,* December 23, 1937.

5. Maurice Bessy and Lo Duca, *Georges Méliès, Mage, et "Mes Mémoires" par Méliès.* p. 79.

CHAPTER 3

1. Ramsaye, *A Million and One Nights,* 1:346.
2. Kenneth Macgowan, *Behind the Screen,* pp. 112–13.
3. John Howard Lawson, *Theory and Technique of Playwriting and Screenwriting,* p. 313.

CHAPTER 4

1. *Queen Elizabeth* was advertised by the distributor as a four-reel film but, according to Kenneth Macgowan (*Behind the Screen,* p. 155), it had been filmed in three reels.
2. May Agate, *Madame Sarah,* p. 52.
3. Ibid., p. 170.
4. Ibid., p. 189.

CHAPTER 5

1. Lewis Jacobs, *The Rise of the American Film: A Critical History,* p. 96.
2. Linda Arvidson [Mrs. D. W. Griffith] *When the Movies Were Young,* pp. 47–48.
3. Ibid., p. 66.
4. "Core of the Movie—The Chase," *New York Times Magazine,* October 29, 1950, p. 22.
5. Iris Barry, "A Short Survey of the Film in America," Museum of Modern Art Film Library.

CHAPTER 6

1. Lillian Gish, "The Birth of an Era," *Stage* 14 (January, 1937):100–101.
2. Seymour Stern, "The Birth of a Nation," Special Supplement to *Sight and Sound,* Index Series no. 4 (July, 1945), p. 12.
3. Thomas Dixon, *Moving Picture World,* March 13, 1915, p. 1587.
4. G. W. Bitzer, *Billy Bitzer,* p. 107.
5. Seymour Stern, "An Index to the Creative Work of David Wark Griffith," Special Supplement to *Sight and Sound,* Index Series no. 2 (April, 1944), p. 9.
6. Theodore Huff, from Huff's shot-by-shot description of *The Birth of a Nation,* Museum of Modern Art Film Library Archives.
7. Fred Silva, *Focus on "The Birth of a Nation,"* p. 14.
8. Stern, "The Birth of a Nation," p. 4.
9. Karl Brown, *Adventures with D. W. Griffith,* p. 92.
10. *New York Herald Tribune,* October 4, 1942.

11. Billy Bitzer, "D. W. Griffith: An Appreciation," *Sight and Sound* 17 (Autumn, 1948):109–10. Bitzer's estimate of "well over a hundred and fifty feet" seems an exaggeration.
12. Bernard Hanson, "D. W. Griffith: Some Sources," *Art Bulletin,* vol. 54, no. 4 (December, 1927), p. 508.
13. Seymour Stern, "An Index to the Creative Work of D. W. Griffith, Part 2," Special Supplement to *Sight and Sound,* Index Series no. 8, (September, 1946).
14. Arthur Lennig, *Intolerance,* an unpublished manuscript, p. 130.
15. René Clair, *Time,* August 2, 1948, p. 72.

CHAPTER 7

1. Siegfried Kracauer, *From Caligari to Hitler: A Psychological History of the German Film,* p. 67.
2. Ibid., p. 70.

CHAPTER 8

1. Arthur Lennig, *The Silent Voice.*
2. Peter Noble, "The Return of the Master," *Theatre,* no. 8 (Winter, 1947), p. 16.
3. J. M. Barrie, *The Plays of J. M. Barrie,* p. 249.
4. Mortimer Adler, *Art and Prudence: A Study in Practical Philosophy,* p. 511.
5. Ibid.
6. Erich von Stroheim, *Greed,* p. 177.
7. Ibid., p. 137.
8. Ibid., p. 7.

CHAPTER 9

1. Sergei Eisenstein, "Autobiographical Note," *International Literature,* no. 4 (Moscow, 1933).
2. Marie Seton, *Sergei M. Eisenstein: A Biography,* p. 59.
3. Sergei Eisenstein, *The Film Sense,* p. 47.
4. Sergei Eisenstein, *Film Form: Essays in Film Theory,* ed. and trans. Jay Leyda, p. 240.
5. Ibid.
6. Ibid., p. 241.
7. Ibid., p. 74.
8. Ibid.
9. Ibid., p. 75.
10. Ibid., p. 76.
11. Seton, *Eisenstein,* p. 75.
12. Ibid., p. 80.
13. Sergei Eisenstein, "The Twelve Apostles," *The Cinema 1952,* p. 169.

14. Seton, *Eisenstein,* p. 81.

15. Eisenstein, *Film Form,* p. 56.

16. Ibid., p. 132.

17. Arthur Kleiner, "The Re-creation of a Lost Masterpiece: Edmund Meisel's Score for *Potemkin,*" American Film Institute Report, no. 1, 1972.

18. Kurt London, *Film Music: A Summary of the Characteristic Features of Its History, Aesthetics, Technique, and Possible Developments,* p. 93.

CHAPTER 10

1. Brander Matthews, "Are the Movies a Menace to the Drama?" *North American Review* 205 (March, 1917):453.

2. I am indebted to Miles Kreuger concerning the contributions of Sponable and Owens to the coming of sound. *See* Miles Kreuger, "The Birth of the American Film Musical," *High Fidelity Magazine* 12 (July, 1972):42–45.

3. *New York Times,* August 7, 1926, p. 6.

4. Ibid., June 22, 1927, p. 33.

5. Ibid., July 9, 1928, p. 25.

6. Ibid., January 21, 1929, p. 18.

7. Ibid., February 18, 1929, p. 28.

8. Frank Capra, *The Name Above the Title,* p. 103.

9. Ibid.

10. *New York Times,* January 1, 1929.

11. Ralph Hancock and Letitia Fairbanks, *Douglas Fairbanks,* pp. 207, 212.

12. Adler, *Art and Prudence,* p. 511.

13. John Masefield, *William Shakespeare* (New York: Henry Holt and Co., 1911), p. 106.

14. After a few prints were made, "Additional dialogue by Sam Taylor," was revised to read "Adapted and directed by Sam Taylor."

CHAPTER 11

1. John Ford, *Current Biography,* p. 297.

2. Peter Bogdanovich, *John Ford,* p. 40.

3. Frank S. Nugent, "Hollywood's Favorite Rebel," *Saturday Evening Post,* July 23, 1949, p. 96.

4. Robert Parrish, *Growing Up in Hollywood,* p. 131.

5. Andrew Sinclair, *John Ford,* p. 51.

6. William Wooten, "An Index to the Films of John Ford," Special Supplement to *Sight and Sound,* Index Series no. 13 (February, 1948), p. 25.

7. George Bluestone, *Novels into Film,* p. 81.

CHAPTER 12

1. *New York Sun,* February 8, 1926.

2. Forsyth Hardy, ed., *Grierson on Documentary,* p. 11.

3. Robert Lewis Taylor, "Moviemaker," *New Yorker,* June 11, 1949, pp. 30–41; June 18, 1949, pp. 28–38; June 25, 1949, pp. 28–43.

4. Paul Rotha, *Documentary Film: The Use of the Film Medium to Interpret Creatively and in Social Terms the Life of the People as It Exists in Reality,* p. 82.

5. Karel Reisz, *The Technique of Film Editing,* pp. 166–68.

6. Ibid., pp. 168–69.

7. Richard Barsam, *Nonfiction Film,* p. 104.

8. Richard Griffith, *The World of Robert Flaherty,* p. 149.

9. Ibid., p. 150.

10. Ibid.

11. Ibid.

12. Reisz, *Technique of Film Editing,* p. 137.

13. Ibid., pp. 137–38.

14. Ibid., p. 141.

15. Ibid., p. 138.

16. Ibid., p. 151.

17. Ibid.

18. Helen van Dongen, "Robert J. Flaherty, 1884–1951," *Film Quarterly,* vol. 18, no. 4 (Summer, 1965), p. 11.

19. Griffith, *World of Robert Flaherty,* p. 152.

20. Ibid., pp. 152–53.

21. Virgil Thomson, *Virgil Thomson,* p. 394.

22. Ibid.

23. Frederich W. Sternfield, "*Louisiana Story,* a Review of Virgil Thomson's Score," *Film Music Notes,* vol. 7, no. 1 (September-October, 1948), p. 7.

24. Ibid., p. 8.

25. Thomson, *Virgil Thomson,* p. 393.

26. Sternfield, "*Louisiana Story,*" p. 9.

27. Griffith, *World of Robert Flaherty,* p. 151.

28. Helen van Dongen, "Three Hundred and Fifty Cans of Film," *The Cinema 1951,* p. 60.

29. Arthur Calder-Marshall, *The Innocent Eye: The Life of Robert J. Flaherty,* p. 226.

CHAPTER 13

1. Hans Richter, "Film as an Original Art Form," *Film Culture,* vol. 1, no. 1 (January, 1955), p. 21.

CHAPTER 14

1. Notes by Jack Harris in Reisz, *Technique of Film Editing,* pp. 237–38.
2. Ibid., p. 240.

CHAPTER 15

1. "Facts of Life" appears in *Quartet,* stories by W. Somerset Maugham and screenplays by R. C. Sherriff. The story is copyright © 1939 by W. Somerset Maugham, and the screenplay is copyright © 1948 by R. C. Sherriff. Excerpts reprinted by permission of the publishers, Doubleday and Co.

CHAPTER 16

1. Nugent, *Ford,* p. 96.
2. Sinclair, *John Ford* (New York: Dial Press, James Wade, 1979), p. 57.
3. John Gassner and Dudley Nichols, eds., "The Writer and the Film," *Twenty Best Film Plays* (New York: Crown Publishers, 1943), p. xxxvi.
4. *The Citizen Kane Book* (Boston: Little, Brown and Company, 1971).
5. *New York Times,* January 11, 1941.
6. "Raising Kane," *The Citizen Kane Book* (Boston: Little, Brown and Company, 1971), p. 41.
7. Lewis Jacobs, ed., "Orson Welles' *Citizen Kane,*" *Introduction to the Art of the Movies* (New York: Noonday Press, 1960), p. 249.
8. "Score for a Film," *New York Times,* May 25, 1941.
9. Ibid.
10. Ibid.
11. Edith J. R. Isaacs, "Citizen Kane and One-Man Pictures in General," *Theatre Arts,* vol. 25 (June, 1941), p. 428.

CHAPTER 17

1. Ingmar Bergman, *Wild Strawberries,* trans. Lars Malmstrom and David Kushner.

2. Ingmar Bergman, "Each Film Is My Last," trans. P. E. Burke and Lennart Swahn, Janus Films, n.d.
3. Ingmar Bergman with interviewers Stig Björkman, Torsten Manns, and Jonas Sima, *Bergman on Bergman,* trans. Paul Britten Austin, p. 146.
4. Kenneth Macgowan, *Behind the Screen: The History and Technique of the Motion Pictures,* p. 419.
5. Jörn Donner, *The Personal Vision of Ingmar Bergman,* trans. Holger Lundberg, p. 153.
6. August Strindberg, *Plays, First Series,* trans. Edwin Björkman, p. 24.
7. Ibid.
8. Bergman et al., *Bergman on Bergman,* p. 147.
9. Alain Robbe-Grillet, *Last Year at Marienbad,* trans. Richard Howard, p. 10.
10. Alain Robbe-Grillet, *For a New Novel: Essays on Fiction,* trans. Richard Howard, p. 153.
11. Ibid., p. 153.
12. Ibid., p. 139.
13. Ibid., p. 33.
14. Ibid., p. 149.
15. Roy Armes, *The Cinema of Alain Resnais,* p. 111.
16. Deena Boyer, *The Two Hundred Days of 8½,* p. 143.
17. Angelo Solmi, *Fellini,* trans. Elizabeth Greenwood, p. 62.
18. Boyer, *Two Hundred Days,* p. 4.
19. Solmi, *Fellini,* p. 171.
20. Ibid.
21. Boyer, *Two Hundred Days,* p. 205.
22. "Free," *New Yorker,* July 6, 1963, p. 20.
23. Ibid.
24. Boyer, *Two Hundred Days,* p. 57.
25. Ibid., p. 94.
26. Ibid., p. 96.
27. Albert E. Benderson, *Critical Approaches to Federico Fellini's 8½,* pp. 70–71.
28. *See* Rudolf Arnheim, *Film As Art,* pp. 13–14.
29. Joseph P. Brinton III, "Subjective Camera or Subjective Audience," *Hollywood Quarterly* 2 (July, 1947):359–66.

Bibliography

Books

Adler, Mortimer. *Art and Prudence: A Study in Practical Philosophy.* New York: Longman, Green & Co., 1937.

Agate, May. *Madame Sarah.* London: Home & Van Thal, 1945.

Armes, Roy. *The Cinema of Alain Resnais.* New York: A. S. Barnes & Co., 1968.

Arnheim, Rudolf. *Film As Art.* Berkeley and Los Angeles: University of California Press, 1974.

Arvidson, Linda [Mrs. D. W. Griffith]. *When the Movies Were Young.* New York: E. P. Dutton & Co., 1925.

Bardèche, Maurice, and Brasillach, Robert. *History of the Film.* Translated and edited by Iris Barry. London: Allen & Unwin, 1938.

Barna, Yon. *Eisenstein.* Bloomington: Indiana University Press, 1973.

Barsam, Richard Meran. *Nonfiction Film: A Critical History.* New York: E. P. Dutton & Co., 1973.

Benderson, Albert Edward. *Critical Approaches to Federico Fellini's 8½.* New York: Arno Press, 1974.

Bergman, Ingmar. *Wild Strawberries.* Translated by Lars Malmstrom and David Kusher. New York: Simon & Schuster, 1960.

Bessy, Maurice, and Duca, Lo. *Georges Méliès, Mage; et "Mes Mémoires" par Méliès.* Paris: Prisma, 1945.

Bitzer, G. W. *Billy Bitzer: His Story.* New York: Farrar, Straus & Giroux, 1973.

Björkman, Stig; Manna, Torsten; and Sima, Jonas. *Bergman on Bergman: Interviews with Ingmar Bergman.* Translated by Paul Britten Austin. New York: Simon & Schuster, 1973.

Bluestone, George. *Novels into Film.* Baltimore: Johns Hopkins Press, 1957.

Bogdanovich, Peter. *John Ford.* Berkeley and Los Angeles: University of California Press, 1968.

Boyer, Deena. *The Two Hundred Days of 8½.* Translated by Lam Markmann. New York: Macmillan Co., 1964.

Brown, Karl. *Adventures with D. W. Griffith.* New York: Farrar, Straus and Giroux, 1973.

Calder-Marshall, Arthur. *The Innocent Eye: The Life of Robert J. Flaherty.* New York: Harcourt, Brace & World, 1966.

Capra, Frank. *The Name Above the Title.* New York: Macmillan Co., 1971.

Dickson, W. K. L., and Dickson, Antonia. *The Life and Inventions of Thomas Alva Edison.* New York: T. Y. Crowell, 1894.

Donner, Jörn, *The Personal Vision of Ingmar Bergman.* Translated by Holger Lundbergh. Bloomington: Indiana University Press, 1964.

Edison, Thomas A. *The Diary and Sundry Observations of Thomas Alva Edison.* Edited by Dagobert D. Runes. New York: Philosophical Library, 1948.

Eisenstein, Sergei M. *Film Form: Essays in Film Theory.* Edited and translated by Jay Leyda. New York: Harcourt, Brace & Co., 1949.

———. *The Film Sense.* Edited and translated by Jay Leyda. New York: Harcourt, Brace & Co., 1942.

Ford, John. *Current Biography.* New York: H. W. Wilson Co., 1941.

261

Grierson, John. *Grierson on Documentary.* Edited and with an introduction by Forsyth Hardy. London: William Collins Sons & Co., 1946.

Griffith, Mrs. D. W. (Linda Arvidson). *When the Movies Were Young.* New York: E. P. Dutton & Co., 1925.

Griffith, Richard. *The World of Robert Flaherty.* New York: Duell, Sloan & Pearce, 1953.

Hancock, Ralph, and Fairbanks, Letitia. *Douglas Fairbanks: The Fourth Musketeer.* New York: Henry Holt & Co., 1953.

Hendricks, Gordon. *The Edison Motion Picture Myth.* Berkeley and Los Angeles: University of California Press, 1961.

———. *The Kinetoscope: America's First Commercially Successful Motion Picture Exhibitor.* Brooklyn: Theodore Gaus' Sons, 1966.

Irwin, William Henry. *The House that Shadows Built.* Garden City: Doubleday, Doran & Co., 1928.

Jacobs, Lewis, ed. *Introduction to the Art of the Movies.* New York: Noonday Press, 1960.

———. *The Rise of the American Film: A Critical History.* New York: Harcourt, Brace & Co., 1939.

Kael, Pauline. *The Citizen Kane Book.* Boston: Little, Brown & Co., 1971.

Kracauer, Sigfried. *From Caligari to Hitler: A Psychological History of the German Film.* Princeton: Princeton University Press, 1947.

Lawson, John Howard. *Theory and Technique of Playwriting and Screenwriting.* New York: G. P. Putnam's Sons, 1949.

Lennig, Arthur. *The Silent Voice: A Text.* Albany: Lane Press, 1969.

Lindgren, Ernest. *The Art of the Film: An Introduction to Film Appreciation.* London: George Allen & Unwin, 1948.

London, Kurt. *Film Music: A Summary of the Characteristic Features of Its History, Aesthetics, Technique and Possible Developments.* London: Faber & Faber, 1936.

Lorentz, Pare. *The River.* New York: Stackpole Sons, 1938.

Macgowan, Kenneth. *Behind the Screen: The History and Technique of the Motion Pictures.* New York: Dell Publishing Co., 1965.

Méliès, Georges. *Complete Catalogue of Genuine and Original "Star" Films (Moving Pictures).* Paris and New York, 1905.

Morrissette, Bruce. *Alain Robbe-Grillet.* Columbia Essays on Modern Writers, no. 11. New York: Columbia University Press, 1965.

Muybridge, Eadweard. *Animals in Motion.* Edited by Lewis S. Brown. New York: Dover Publications, 1957.

Noble, Peter. *Hollywood Scapegoat: The Biography of Erich von Stroheim.* London: Fortune Press, 1950.

Parrish, Robert. *Growing Up in Hollywood.* New York: Harcourt, Brace, Jovanovich, 1976.

Perry, Ted. *Filmguide to 8½.* Bloomington: Indiana University Press, 1975.

Pickford, Mary. *Sunshine and Shadow.* Garden City: Doubleday & Co., 1955.

Quigley, Martin, Jr. *Magic Shadows: The Story of the Origin of Motion Pictures.* Washington: Georgetown University Press, 1948.

Ramsaye, Terry. *A Million and One Nights: A History of the Motion Pictures.* 2 vols. New York: Simon & Schuster, 1926.

Reisz, Karel, *The Technique of Film Editing.* New York: Focal Press, 1955.

Robbe-Grillet, Alain. *For a New Novel: Essays on Fiction.* Translated by Richard Howard. New York: Grove Press, 1965.

———. *Last Year at Marienbad.* Translated by Richard Howard. New York: Grove Press, 1962.

Rotha, Paul. *Documentary Film.* New York: W. W. Norton & Co., 1939.

Sadoul, Georges. *Histoire générale du cinéma.* 3 vols. Paris: Donoël, 1948–52.

Seton, Marie. *Sergei M. Eisenstein: A Biography.* New York: A. A. Wyn, 1952.

Silva, Fred, ed. *Focus on the Birth of a Nation.* Englewood Cliffs: Prentice-Hall, 1971.

Sinclair, Andrew. *John Ford.* New York: Dial Press, James Wade, 1979.

Snyder, Robert L. *Pare Lorentz and the Documentary Film.* Norman: University of Oklahoma Press, 1968.

Solmi, Angelo. *Fellini.* Translated by Elizabeth Greenwood. London: Merlin Press, 1967.

Thomson, Virgil. *Virgil Thomson.* New York: Alfred A. Knopf, 1966.

Verneuil, Louis. *The Fabulous Life of Sarah Bernhardt.* Translated by Ernest Boyd. New York: Brentano's, 1942.

Von Stroheim, Erich. *Greed: A Film by Erich von Stroheim.* Edited by Joel W. Finler. New York: Simon & Schuster, 1972.

ARTICLES

Ackland, Rodney. "*Greed:* A Personal Note." In *Hollywood Scapegoat: The Biography of*

Erich von Stroheim, by Peter Noble. London: Fortune Press, 1950.

"L' anne derniére á Marienbad." In *Letter from France* (French Film Office), vol. 5, no. 26 (May-July, 1961).

Barry, Iris. "A Short Survey of the Film in America." Series 1, program 2, Museum of Modern Art Film Library. n.d.

Bergman, Ingmar. "Each Film Is My Last." Translated by P. E. Burke and Lennart Swahn. Janus Films. n.d.

Brinton, Joseph P., III. "Subjective Camera or Subjective Audience." *Hollywood Quarterly* 2 (July, 1947):359–66.

Brunius, Jacques. "Every Year at Marienbad." *Sight and Sound* 31 (Spring, 1962):122–27.

Dickson, W. K. L., and Dickson, Antonia. "Edison's Invention of the Kinetograph." *Century Magazine* 48 (June, 1894):206–14.

Eisenstein, Sergei. "Autobiographical Note." *International Literature,* no. 4 (1933).

———. "The Twelve Apostles." *The Cinema 1952,* pp. 158–73. Harmondsworth: Penguin Books, 1952.

Fellini, Federico. "Free." Interview in *New Yorker,* July 6, 1963, pp. 19–20.

Flaherty, Robert. "Robert Flaherty Talking." *The Cinema 1950,* pp. 11–29. Harmondsworth: Penguin Books, 1950.

Fulton, A. R. "It's Exactly Like the Play." *Theatre Arts* 37 (March, 1953):78–83.

———. "Stroheim's 'Greed,'" *Films in Review* 6 (June-July, 1955):263–68.

Gish, Lillian. "The Birth of an Era." *Stage* 14 (January, 1937):100–102.

———. "D. W. Griffith—A Great American." *Harper's Bazaar,* October, 1940, pp. 74–75, 106.

Gray, Hugh. "Robert Flaherty and the Naturalistic Documentary." *Hollywood Quarterly* 5 (Fall, 1950):41–44.

Guernsey, Otis L. "Interview with D. W. Griffith." *New York Herald Tribune,* October 4, 1942.

Hanson, Bernard. "D. W. Griffith: Some Sources." *Art Bulletin,* vol. 54, no. 4 (December, 1972), pp. 493–515.

Herrmann, Bernard. "Score for a Film." *New York Times,* May 25, 1941.

Hitchcock, Alfred. "The Core of the Movie—The Chase." *New York Times Magazine,* October 29, 1950, pp. 22, 44–46.

Huff, Theodore. "Sadoul and Film Research." *Hollywood Quarterly,* vol. 2, no. 2 (January, 1947), pp. 203–6.

Ingster, Boris. "Sergei Eisenstein." *Hollywood Quarterly* 5 (Summer, 1951):380–88.

Isaacs, Edith J. R. "Citizen Kane and One-Man Pictures in General." *Theatre Arts* 25 (June, 1941):427–32.

Johnson, Julian. "The Shadow Stage." *Photoplay,* December, 1916, pp. 77–81.

Kael, Pauline. "Raising Kane." *The Citizen Kane Book,* Boston: Little, Brown & Co., 1971.

Kleiner, Arthur. "The Re-creation of a Lost Masterpiece: Edmund Meisel's Score for *Potemkin."* American Film Institute Report, no. 1 (1972).

Kreuger, Miles. "The Birth of the American Film Musical." *High Fidelity Magazine* 22 (July, 1972):42–48.

Lean, David. "Brief Encounter." *Penguin Film Review,* no. 4. London: Penguin Books, 1947.

———. "David Lean Talks to Roger Manvell." *The Cinema 1952,* pp. 19–20. Harmondsworth: Penguin Books, 1952.

———. "Extract from the Post-Production Script of *Great Expectations:* Pip Steals the Food." *The Cinema 1952,* pp. 20–29. Harmondsworth: Penguin Books, 1952.

Manvell, Roger. "Britain's Self-Portraiture in Feature Films." *Geographical Magazine* 26 (August, 1953):222–34.

Matthews, Brander. "Are the Movies a Menace to the Drama?" *North American Review* 205 (March, 1917):447–54.

Morton, Lawrence. "Film Music of the Quarter." *Hollywood Quarterly* 5 (Fall, 1950):51–52.

Nichols, Dudley. "The Writer and the Film." *Twenty Best Film Plays.* Edited by John Gassner and Dudley Nichols. New York: Crown Publishers, 1943.

Noble, Peter. "The Return of the Master." *Theatre,* no. 8 (Winter, 1947), pp. 15–17.

Nugent, Frank S. "Hollywood's Favorite Rebel." *Saturday Evening Post,* July 23, 1949, pp. 25, 96–98.

Pommer, Erich. "The Origin of Dr. Caligari." *Art in Cinema:* A Symposium on the Avant-garde Film together with Program Notes and References for Series One of *Art in Cinema.* Edited by Frank Stauffacher. San Francisco, 1947.

Redford, Cedric, "Orson Welles' *Citizen Kane." Introduction to the Art of the Movies.* Edited by Lewis Jacobs. New York: Noonday Press, 1960.

Sadoul, Georges. "Early Film Production in England." *Hollywood Quarterly,* vol. 1, no. 3 (April, 1946), p. 256.

Sadoul, Georges. "Earley Film Production in England." *Hollywood Quarterly.* vol. 1, no. 3 (April, 1946), p. 256.

――――. "English Influences on the Work of Edwin S. Porter." *Hollywood Quarterly,* vol. 3, no. 1 (Fall, 1947), pp. 41–50.

Stern, Seymour. "The Birth of a Nation." Special Supplement to *Sight and Sound,* Index Series no. 4 (July, 1945).

――――. "D. W. Griffith: An Appreciation." *Sight and Sound* 17 (Autumn, 1948):109–10.

――――. "An Index to the Creative Work of David Wark Griffith, Part 1: The Birth of an Art, 1908–1915." Special Supplement to *Sight and Sound,* Index Series no. 2 (April, 1944).

――――. "An Index to the Creative Work of D. W. Griffith, Part 2." Special Supplement to *Sight and Sound,* Index Series no. 8 (September, 1946).

Sternfield, Frederick W. "Louisiana Story, a Review of Virgil Thomson's Score." *Film Music Notes,* vol. 7, no. 1 (September-October, 1948), pp. 5–14.

Taylor, Robert Lewis. "Moviemaker." *New Yorker,* June 11, 1949, pp. 30–41; June 18, 1949, pp. 28–38; June 25, 1949, pp. 28–43.

Van Dongen, Helen. "Robert J. Flaherty 1884–1951." *Film Quarterly,* vol. 18, no. 4 (Summer, 1965), pp. 2–14.

――――. "Three Hundred and Fifty Cans of Film." *The Cinema 1951,* pp. 57–78. Harmondsworth: Penguin Books, 1951.

Weinberg, Herman G. "An Index to the Creative Work of Erich von Stroheim." Special Supplement to *Sight and Sound,* Index Series no. 1 (June, 1943).

White, W. L. "Pare Lorentz." *Scribner's,* January, 1939, pp. 7–11, 42.

Wooten, William Patrick. "An Index to the Films of John Ford." Special Supplement to *Sight and Sound,* Index Series no. 13 (February, 1948).

Index